Queering India

Queering India

Same-Sex Love and Eroticism in Indian Culture and Society

edited by

Ruth Vanita

ROUTLEDGE
New York and London

Published in 2002 by
Routledge
29 West 35th Street
New York, NY 10001

Published in Great Britain by
Routledge
11 New Fetter Lane
London EC4P 4EE

Routledge is an imprint of the Taylor & Francis Group.

Copyright © 2002 by Routledge

Printed in the United States of America on acid-free paper.
Design and typography: Jack Donner

Photo of Bal Gandharva and Petkar acting in a Marathi Drama is courtesy of Archives of the national Centre for the Performing Arts, Mumbai.
Photo of Master Nainuram is courtesy of Pratibha Agrawal, Director, Natya Shodh Sandsthan.
Photo of Jayshankar Sundari from *Jayshankar Sundari and Abhinayakala* by B.B. Panchotia is courtesy of Sri B. B. Panchotia and the Bharatiya Vidya Bhavan, Mumbai.

Library of Congress Cataloging-in-Publication Data

Queering India : same-sex love and eroticism in Indian culture and society / edited by Ruth Vanita.
p. cm.
Includes bibliographical references and index.
0–415–92949–0 — ISBN 0–415–92950–4 (pbk.)
1. Homosexuality—India. I. Vanita, Ruth.
HQ76.2.I4 Q84 2001
306.76'6'0954—dc 21
2001019111

For Sujata, Kirti, Shohini, Sanju, and Saleem

अत्रा॒ सखा॑यः स॒ख्यानि॑ जानते
भ॒द्रैषां॑ ल॒क्ष्मीर्निहि॒ताधि॒ वा॒चि ।

There friends have known their friendships,
and an auspicious Lakshmi resides in their speech.
—*Rig Veda* X: 71, 1–2

Contents

Acknowledgments

I would like to thank Saleem Kidwai for suggesting that I put together this anthology, all the contributors for their cooperation and flexibility, and Ilene Kalish, my editor at Routledge, for her helpfulness. I am grateful to the University of Montana for granting me a course reduction; my colleagues in liberal studies, women's studies, and English for their support; the Institute for Research on Women and Gender at the University of Michigan for giving me a visiting scholar position during my semester in Ann Arbor; Arindam Chakrabarti and Madhav Deshpande for help with the dedicatory epigraph. My partner Mona's patience, good humor, and love have been invaluable in sustaining me through the ups and downs of this project.

Introduction

Ruth Vanita

At a critical moment in Deepa Mehta's film *Fire*, Sita remarks to her lover Radha, "There is no word in our language to describe what we are or how we feel for each other." To which language does she refer—Punjabi, some variant of Hindi, Urdu, or, more likely, some combination of all three? We do not know because on screen the characters speak English. In this metonymic moment, two things happen: English is disowned as "our language" (even though Indians have been speaking English for two hundred years) and "our language" is framed as a catch-all unnamed Indian language that lacks any word for same-sex identities or relationships.

Sita's (Mehta's) comment reflects an idea dominant in academia today—that prior to late-nineteenth-century European sexologists' and psychologists' invention of labeled identity categories such as *invert, homosexual, lesbian,* and *heterosexual,* inchoate sexualities and sexual behaviors existed but were not perceived or named as defining individuals, groups, or relationships. For those who accept this formula, it follows that in parts of the world where these categories are not yet widely known, people do not perceive even long-term same-sex relations as significant markers of identity or personality.[1] Hence the tendency of queer theorists to avoid using terms like *homosexual* to refer to persons or relationships in earlier periods of Euro-American history or in places other than the first world today.

This formula has been challenged by several historians of Europe who have pointed to the use of terms like *Ganymede, tribade, Sapphist,* and even *lesbian* as early as (in one case) the tenth century, and certainly from the Renaissance onward, to mark individuals habitually given to same-sex sexual relations.[2] In the context of South Asia, Michael Sweet and Leonard Zwilling have demonstrated the formulation of sexual categories in Hindu and Jain texts as early as the sixth century B.C.E., it is evident that the *Kama Sutra* (fourth century C.E.), while mentioning casual sexual relations between "men," also classifies men who prefer men as "the third nature"; and scholars of the medieval Islamicate have written both on male-male love and on the representation of female-female love by male writers.[3]

However, since these essays have not been widely read beyond particular disciplines, such as South Asian studies, their implications for conceptualizing same-sex love have not become apparent to most theorists in lesbian and gay studies. The present volume seeks to make those implications evident, and also to foreground debate around them, by showcasing the cutting-edge work of scholars from a variety of disciplinary perspectives—history, media studies, literary studies, and anthropology.

Lesbian and gay studies in the Euro-American academy by and large take the view that same-sex desire has historically been unrepresented in South Asian languages, and that its representation appears only in the work of recent Indian writers in English, many of them diasporic. For instance, in *The International Lesbian and Gay Literary Heritage*, edited by Claude Summers,[4] all Indian literature in other Indian languages is dismissed in less than a page, while Indian writing in English occupies more than two pages. Summers connects this absenting not to the queer theory position outlined above that sexuality as we know it was a late invention, but to a particular feminist view of Indian "tradition," especially religious tradition, as repressive of desire, pleasure, and freedom. Sita's comment regarding the absence of discourses on same-sex love is in keeping with *Fire*'s one-sided representation of Hindu tradition and practice as almost entirely repressive of individual desire and pleasure and also of women's freedom.

In our recent book, Saleem Kidwai and I began the enterprise of tracing and interpreting a range of discourses on same-sex love, often within religious traditions, through South Asian history. We found many texts that represent same-sex relations and also many that constitute a continuity of discourse, by speaking to one another across time within particular linguistic and literary-critical traditions. An example of such continuing intertextual discourse is the way the fourteenth-century Bengali epic poem the *Krittivasa Ramayana*, when describing a child born of the sexual intercourse of two women, refers to the second-century medical text *Sushruta Samhita*, which states that such a child will be born as a boneless lump of flesh. The later text also rewrites the earlier one by envisioning the conferring of bones on the child through a sage's blessing.[5] Other examples of intertextual discourse on same-sex desire within particular literary genres are to be found in the recurrent use of particular tropes to figure male-male desire in the Perso-Urdu *ghazal* (love poem) and *masnavi* (narrative poem).

Apart from the question of whether there are words in Indian languages for sexual identity categories, let us return to the second part of Sita's comment, with its emphasis on relationship and emotion. Are there words for "what we feel for each other" in Indian texts prior to the nineteenth century? I found one such naming in the eleventh-century Sanskrit story cycle *Kathasaritsagara*, where a young woman, reflecting on the instantaneous attraction between herself and a married woman, refers to their relation as one between "*swayamvara sakhis*," and notes that there are many earlier examples of such relations.[6] This phrase is a coinage from the term *swayamvara* (literally, "self-chosen"), usually used to refer to the ceremony in which a woman chooses her bridegroom from assembled suitors, and the term *sakhi* (female friend). In her essay in this volume, Carla Petievich documents the occurrence in some Urdu dictionaries of the terms *dogana* and *zanakhi* to denote a woman's self-chosen primary female friend. In some very explicitly sexual Urdu poems in the *rekhti* genre, which Kidwai and I translated, *dogana* occurs as a term of address used by a woman to her female lover, and *chapti* (rubbing/clinging) occurs as a term for female-to-female sexual relations.[7] Given that very little research has been done on the histories of friendship and love in South Asia, I am convinced, on the basis of conversations I have had with people from widely varying backgrounds in India, that these and other such terms found by scholars represent the tip of the iceberg, and that further research in these and other languages will uncover many more such terms.

Such terms do not denote exclusive, sealed-off sexual categories. In India, most people have been, and many continue to be, married off at a very young age. Hence, exclusive same-sex relationships are necessarily rare. However, ongoing same-sex relationships, for both men and women, often coexist with the obligations and privileges of marriage, and may function as primary erotic and emotional relationships.

What, then, happened in history to make such terms and conventions unavailable to Sita and Radha? Perhaps the answer is to be found in another of Sita's comments, made when she and Radha discuss the performance of wifely duty: "Somebody just has to press my button, this button marked 'tradition,' and I start responding like a trained monkey." This suggests that there is only one tradition and one button to be pressed. Are there other traditional buttons that could be pressed to trigger a performance of same-sex desire? Consider the literary conventions of the ghazal, wherein, until recently, lover and beloved, for a variety of historical reasons, were always gendered male, so that even a poet writing about cross-sex love in the ghazal form felt compelled, by the pressing of the traditional button, not only to gender verbs for both lover and beloved male but also to use tropes that figure the ideal love as one between males.

The present volume focuses on colonial and independent India, specifically on the way colonialists and nationalists attempt to rewrite multivocal traditions into a univocal, uniform tradition, and the way these rewritings are contested. Kidwai and I pointed to the nineteenth century as the crucial period of transition when a minor strand of precolonial homophobia became the dominant voice in colonial and postcolonial mainstream discourse.[8] The rhetoric of modern Indian homophobia (with concepts and terms like *unnatural* and *sinful*) draws directly on a Victorian version of Judeo-Christian discourse; this borrowing is indicated in *Fire* when Radha's husband Ashok, having seen his wife and Sita in bed together, says, "What I saw is a sin in the eyes of God and man." This is a direct quote from the Bible (the words of the prodigal son to his father, in Christ's parable of sin and repentance, in the Book of Luke). This instance begins to explain why Mehta found it so hard to translate such phrases into Hindi, and decided to make the film in English; it would be almost impossible to literally translate Ashok's sentence into Hindi and have it sound convincing.[9]

Focusing on rewritings in the colonial period does not, of course, imply that other transitions had not occurred before, or that rewriting did not take place before; that it did is indicated by the example of the *Krittivasa Ramayana* cited above, and also by Indrani Chatterjee's discussion of medieval erotic treatises' rewritings of the *Kama Sutra*. Notwithstanding some scholars' discomfort with ascribing to colonialism the modern erasure of earlier homoeroticisms (and other eroticisms), evidence so far available indicates overwhelmingly that a major transition did indeed occur at that historical moment. Kidwai and I pointed to the heterosexualization of the ghazal, the suppression of Rekhti, and the introduction of the antisodomy law as three markers of this transition.

The present volume begins to flesh out the transition by documenting how colonialists and nationalists rewrote traditions by suppressing and misreading texts. However, these essays also demonstrate that trying to construct a univocal "tradition" is a doomed enterprise: the multivocal returns immediately and flourishes in different forms, not only in the persistent continuities of some traditions and their surprising resurfacing in unexpected places (for example, the ghazal in Hindi movies, queer eroticisms found in popular cinema, and queer readings of apparently homophobic fictions).

To return, then, to an adaptation of Sita's question: What words should we use to describe same-sex love and desire in "our language[s]," when writing about the past? Should we avoid all present-day terms and employ, as David Halperin suggests, only the terms used in a particular past to write about that past? Since neither the producer/author's intentions nor the "original" audience's reception can ever be definitively recovered, is it meaningful for us as readers to try to read texts not from our own perspective but from that of some imagined past reader? Important as is the search for terms used in the past in "our language[s]," should this search preclude the use of now-current terms when we describe the past in languages that are now our own?

When discussing same-sex relations in the past, many theorists and historians today are terrified of using terms like *homosexual*; pioneering historian John Boswell has been much criticized for using the word *gay* to describe persons in late antiquity and early medieval Europe.[10] Many of us carefully use terms such as *homoerotically inclined, queer,* or *alternative sexualities* to talk about the past. But, surely, these terms were not used in the past either—certainly not with their present connotations—and it is only a convenient fiction that leads us to find them more acceptable.

As scholarly discussions have established, the exact meaning of terms from the past, such as *amradparast, tritiya prakriti,* or *dogana,* is highly debatable and cannot finally be fixed. When we deploy them today we suggest what we understand them to have meant, which is probably an approximation but not an exact equivalent of what they "actually" may have meant, presuming they ever had one meaning, which itself is an inaccurate presumption.

Furthermore, the same historians who are horrified by the "ahistorical" use of such terms or concepts as *homosexual* or even *same-sex* seem to be relatively untroubled about using a host of terms and concepts such as *family, marriage, slave, master, law, woman,* or *man* when discussing past societies (say, in South Asia) where the other-language approximates of these English words are well known to have had widely different meanings from those they have today. Historians rightly consider it sufficient to point out as many of the differences as possible and then proceed to use the term presently in use.

If one were serious about using the languages of the past to describe the past, the only honest strategy would be to write about historical texts entirely in their own language—to write only in Persian about Persian texts and only in Sanskrit about Sanskrit texts. While a scholar writing in the Persian language today cannot write any of the variations of Persian of seventeenth-century Delhi, at least she would presumably come closer to the categories and terms of that past than when writing in English or Hindi.

Theorists who think only terms from a particular past time should be used when discussing that time also think that only terms "indigenous" to a particular place should be used in that place; therefore terms like *gay* should not be used in India. The impulse to make connections between vastly differing and yet in some ways critically similar human experiences has led many people living and organizing in India over the last two decades to adopt and even translate words like *gay* and *lesbian*.[11] It is significant that it is usually those who have already obtained most of their basic civil rights and liberties in first-world environments who object to the use of these terms in third-world contexts. Witness some U.K.-based anti-AIDS activists' insistence that terms like *men who have sex with men* or region-specific and often profession-specific "in-group" slang terms like *kothi* be used in India in preference to *gay* or *homosexual*, because the latter are not indigenous words and their use is therefore "elitist," "neocolonial," and "globalized."[12]

It is important to note that the choice of terms has crucial consequences for lesbian and gay movements in urban India. Activist Ashok Row Kavi, founder in 1990 of the Bombay-based gay magazine *Bombay Dost*, emphasizes the importance of not alienating those he terms "self-identified homosexuals" from groups who identify as *kothis*, because the former are crucial as activists reaching out to populations at risk for HIV.[13] Furthermore, the Indian press and media have overall represented gay organizations and their demands for human rights in a supportive way, thus making terms like *gay* and *lesbian* accessible to urban bilingual populations whose opinions are crucial in determining who gets civil rights and who does not. For those demanding, say, the repeal of the antisodomy law or more government funding for AIDS work, the political viability of a term like *gay* is likely to be much greater than a term like *men who have sex with men*; also, far fewer men are likely to identify themselves as belonging to the latter category than to the former.

It is also worth noting that antigay groups have no compunctions about using familiar terms. While intellectuals squabble about politically or historically correct language, Evangelical missionaries from the United States are actively campaigning against *gay* and *homosexual* people in India. As part of his six-continent tour, Peter Lane of Exodus International spoke at several forums in Bangalore in September 2000. The September–October 2000 issue of *Relief* (an acronym for Respect Every Life in Every Family), the newsletter of Respect for Life India, a Christian antiabortion mission based in Bangalore, reported that Lane encountered vociferous opposition from students of the law college who contested his use of words like *unnatural* to describe homosexuality; the reporter Maya Philip ruefully remarked, "Gay

Rights Activists had succeeded in their propaganda in making homosexuality acceptable to these young people."[14] These "gay rights activists" are those bilingual urban Indians who have been running organizations, newsletters, magazines, and help lines, usually without any funding, that are now being dubbed "elitist" by U.K.-based activists who project themselves as more "anti-colonial" when competing for grants and recognition by government and foreign funding agencies.

These questions about terminology become doubly fraught when the past under discussion is a non-Western past. While feminism has now made respectable the enterprise of bringing to light suppressed and undervalued texts by and about women in the past, entrenched heterosexism makes a similar search for suppressed or bowdlerized texts about same-sex attachments more vulnerable to interrogation. I would argue that if, notwithstanding the vast differences between middle-class women in Delhi today and women writing mystical poetry in sixteenth-century Gujarat, there is enough commonalty between them to justify including their writings in one collection,[15] there is similarly enough commonalty between people engaged in same-sex relationships in Bombay today and those engaged in very differently structured same-sex relationships in eighteenth-century Lucknow to justify including writings about them in one collection. To quote Martin Duberman, "gay people [in this case, gay Indians] have a desperate *need* to know" that they are "bearers of a diverse, rich, unique heritage."[16]

Caught in this impasse created by policing the boundaries of periods, identities, categories, and terms, perhaps we can take a cue from Suniti Namjoshi's resolution of her persona Suniti's predicament in her novel *The Conversations of Cow* (1985). Frightened by the many metamorphoses of her own changing self as well as those of others' selves, she is unable to name any of these selves until she adopts the strategy deployed by Hindu texts and practices (a strategy also found in many other religious traditions) that call on gods and goddesses by thousands of different and often apparently mutually contradictory names. This strategy serves to enable instead of paralyze. It also acknowledges that all names, terms, signs, and concepts, like all material realities, are constantly in flux and are only approximations necessitated by and necessary to human communication.

The essays in this volume adopt a range of naming strategies to enable a discussion of same-sex love, desire, and sexual relations, especially as these have been reformulated in the colonial and postcolonial periods. In part 1, Suparna Bhaskaran's essay provides the historical context for the most dramatic shift from the precolonial—the uniform criminalization of all sexual relations deemed "unnatural." Her survey of the case law indicates that the antisodomy statute is honored more in the breach than in the observance, given the small number of actual convictions—especially for consensual sex. But the effects of the intervention that the law signifies are far more wide-ranging, as demonstrated by Scott Kugle, Indrani Chatterjee, and Carla Petievich. Through his engaging translations of precolonial Perso-Urdu poetic texts, Kugle shows how once widely celebrated tropes of male-male love were erased or rewritten by Urdu litterateurs in the period immediately following the British suppression of the 1857 revolt, as well as by later nationalists. In a related enterprise, Petievich examines how, in the same period, a whole genre of Urdu poetry was labeled obscene and excised from the canon, with the result that today only a small portion of it is extant and much of even that is hard to access. Chatterjee argues that the colonial labeling of all male-male relations as inappropriate, even "unnatural" and "criminal," displaced pre-colonial readings of such relations as appropriate or inappropriate based on social status (free/slave; agent/object) rather than gender, and that this displacement continues to be dominant even today. Michael Sweet looks at readings and misreadings of the *Kama Sutra* in nineteenth- and twentieth-century India.

Parts 2 and 3 examine the way contesting discourses of same-sex love are deployed in two broadly defined sets of texts—printed literature and audiovisual media—from the late nineteenth century to the present. Leela Gandhi shows how homosexual anticolonial utopianism, developed by British radical Edward Carpenter and rewritten by novelists Aubrey Menen and Vikram Seth, attempts, in a Wittigian fashion, to deconstruct the binaries of straight/gay, Hindu/Muslim, and even human/nonhuman. Anannya Dasgupta finds similar boundary-crossing impulses at work in Suniti Namjoshi's fables and poetry.

Modern Indian heterosexism continues to be manifested in the politics of reception, canon formation, and misreading.[17] Writers, however gifted, who are openly gay or lesbian, often suffer critical neglect—this has been the fate of both Menen and Namjoshi in the canon of Indian writers in English. Rosemary George points out how critics, especially Indian feminist critics, have consistently ignored or misread the same-sex content of acclaimed writer Kamala Das's work. My essay considers the always-fractured nature of reception, as exemplified in the public controversy around novelist Pandey Bechan Sharma Ugra's short-story collection *Chocolate* (1927), which he claimed was written to denounce homosexuality, but which many readers, both gay and antigay, read as a positive representation of male-male relations. I then proceed to contrast the largely homophobic representation of same-sex desire in twentieth-century Indian fiction with homoerotic images in commercials over the last couple of decades; I speculate as to how difference of genre may affect representation. Lawrence Cohen, revisiting Uttar Pradesh, the heartland of the ghazal, finds lively circulations of male-male desire in sites less elevated, such as dorm rooms, political scandals, roadside pornography, and real and fictional muscle men.

Part 3 opens with Kathryn Hansen's exploration of the pleasures of performance and spectatorship released by female impersonation in the late nineteenth and early twentieth centuries. She argues that these pleasures were not substitutive (with men acting women's roles because women were not available) but aleatory (with men acting women's roles even when women too were acting). In an argument comparable to those of recent theorists in Euro-America regarding how drag queens fashion the performance of femininity for women, and butch women or drag kings the performance of masculinity for men, she demonstrates how Indian female impersonators set in motion stylistic and behavioral trends that influenced both cinema actresses' and "real" women's performance of femininity.

The remaining essays in this section deal with the postindependence period. Muraleedharan T., in his examination of male bonding in three popular Malayalam films, argues provocatively that films "ostensibly addressed to straight audiences have greater potential for encouraging a wide range of queer responses than films clearly addressed to gay and lesbian audiences." Further light is shed on this claim by Tom Waugh's finding that homoeroticism, though determinedly suppressed in new-wave and left-wing films, nevertheless disrupts their apparently innocent homosocial configurations.

Shohini Ghosh finds female-female eroticism, marginalized in earlier cinema, appearing more centrally in the films, and especially television, of the 1990s. Finally, in parallel essays, Geeta Patel and Monica Bachmann examine the anxieties at play in, respectively, the right-wing and liberal responses to Mehta's *Fire*.

The essays in this volume demonstrate the richness of the relatively new corpus of work on same-sex love in India, with its immense potential for dialog and debate. Many of these essays speak to one another, contextual differences notwithstanding. Despite the many differences between constructions of male-male and female-female bonding pointed out by Ghosh and Muraleedharan T., both take the view that the queer is to be found in the apparently straight, in terms both of construction and of reception. They even notice a common trope in Hindi and Malayalam popular cinema—that of the cavorting same-sex couple fully covered by a sheet during a song! Muraleedharan T. and Rosemary George also comment on a trope common to different types of love trysts, this time in Malayalam cinema and literature, respectively—that of outdoor bathing.

Violence and nonviolence, dominance and submission, as they imbricate same-sex relations and cross-sex relations, appear in many of the essays. Petievich, Chatterjee, and Gandhi all address these issues in widely varying precolonial and colonial contexts. Bhaskaran, Patel, Bachmann, Waugh, Cohen, and I scrutinize the new incarnations of violently stratified relations in the postcolonial nation-state, and how they impact the construction and imagination of same-sex attachments—whether in the dorm, the home, the cinema, the bureaucracy, the polity, the park, the street, or the courtroom.

Central to many essays is the structuring of homophobia by masculinities that become normative in colonial and postcolonial nationalisms. Following Ashis Nandy's classic account, several scholars have analyzed how anxieties around masculinity involve fear of the "feminine" in women and in men.[18] In the *Fire* debates that Patel and Bachmann document, the fear emerges that female-female desire may undermine both masculinity and female homosociality. These gender-based anxieties are deeply intertwined with anxieties around religious, community, and national identities.

Inevitably, therefore, almost all the essays in this volume are haunted by the complexly desiring anxieties of Hindu-Muslim relations. The simultaneous and contradictory myths that Muslims introduced homosexuality into India or repressed its expression are widely prevalent in South Asia today, and any formulation regarding same-sex desire cannot help but take note of them. In perhaps the only essay that looks at Pakistan, Scott Kugle briefly engages the conflicting myths that hover around the overdetermined image of Sultan Mahmud. These myths are also centrally constitutive of *Chocolate*, the 1927 text I examine, and they shape the production of most texts, whether ghazals, movies, or novels, throughout the nineteenth and twentieth centuries. Kugle utopically puts forward the figure of Mahmud the lover as a possible site for reclaiming synthesis. In a very different context that nevertheless has some similar features, Dasgupta and Gandhi point, in Dasgupta's words, to the "homoerotic in . . . a consciously heterosexist world and the East in a consciously West-centric world." Many of these essays find the Muslim in consciously Hindu worlds and the Hindu in consciously Muslim worlds; in this continuing presence there may be cause for hope.

Already visible too are the faultlines of fruitful disagreement among scholars approaching the same or related materials. The clearest evidence of debate is found in the interpretation of precolonial and early colonial Persian and Urdu poetry. Thus Petievich, agreeing with the standard view that the gender and identity of the beloved in the ghazal are ambiguous, argues that this ambiguity serves to protect the ghazal's male homoerotic content from colonial critiques. On the other hand, Kugle, like Kidwai, argues that the beloved in the ghazal is not always ambiguously gendered but is often clearly identified as male—precisely the identification that was attacked by colonialists and nationalists. Petievich also sees little explicit female homoeroticism in Rekhti, a point on which she is in disagreement with Kidwai and me.

Similarly, Kidwai and Kugle find representation, often even celebration, of male-male love and desire in both the ghazal and the masnavi.[19] While this representation is couched in the literary conventions appropriate to these genres, it sometimes refers to documented historical personages, if only to fictionalize them, and it works to evoke passionate and romantic emotion. Also, while some of the personae are in relations of dominance and subordination to one another, many others are not, nor can the erotic relationship simply be reduced to a relation of one-way power and agency. Conversely, Chatterjee—following some scholars of classical Rome and Greece—argues that apparent expressions of love and desire in this poetry are in fact appropriately conventional and public idealization of slaves by free men in the context of Sufi mysticism, where such desire is conventionally expressed to demonstrate the poet's heroism in overcoming it. They therefore tell us more about power relations between free agents and slaves deprived of agency than about same-sex relationships.

These debates lead back to questions of production and reception addressed by Ghosh, Patel, Bachmann, Waugh, Gandhi, and Muraleedharan T., among others. Neither producers nor readers of texts in various pasts and presents have ever spoken in one voice. Even when particular individuals identify as masters, slaves, colonizers, nationalists, Sufi mystics, poets in a particular tradition, men, women, feminists, conservatives, progressives, heterosexuals, or homosexuals, and even when they write within generic conventions, the texts they generate do not always speak in entirely predictable ways. They often assume unexpected ideological or amorous positions or make surprising connections between different conventions, and we need to be responsive to these ever-shifting configurations. In their alert openness to the nuances of texts and their receptions, the essays in this volume work within the best traditions of scholarship that illuminates what it touches.

Notes

1. This idea was formulated by Michel Foucault in *The History of Sexuality* vol. 1, trans. Robert Hurley (New York: Random House, 1978); and reworked by his followers, notably David M. Halperin, *One Hundred Years of Homosexuality and Other Essays on Greek Love* (New York: Routledge, 1990). In his well-taken critique, Lee Siegel ("The Gay Science," *New Republic*, November 1998), argues that Foucault's followers like Halperin and Eve Kosofsky Sedgwick have misapplied his theories.

2. See John Boswell, *Christianity, Social Tolerance, and Homosexuality* (Chicago: University of Chicago Press, 1980) for *Ganymede* and *sodomite*; Bernadette J. Brooten, *Love between Women: Early Christian Responses to Female Homoeroticism* (Chicago: University of Chicago Press, 1996) for a tenth-century use of *lesbian* with same-sex sexual connotation; and Emma Donoghue, *Passions between Women: British Lesbian Culture 1668–1801* for *tribade, lesbian,* and other such terms.

3. Michael J. Sweet and Leonard Zwilling, " 'Like a City Ablaze': The Third Sex and the Creation of Sexuality in Jain Religious Literature," *Journal of the History of Sexuality* 6, no. 3 (1996): 359–84; "The First Medicalization: The Taxonomy and Etiology of Queers in Classical Indian Medicine," *Journal of the History of Sexuality* 3, no. 4 (1993): 590–607. For the *Kama Sutra*, see my essay in Ruth Vanita and Saleem Kidwai, eds., *Same-Sex Love in India: Readings from Literature and History* (New York: St. Martin's Press, 2000), 46–54; for the Islamicate, see Saleem Kidwai, "Introduction to Medieval Materials in the Perso-Urdu Tradition," ibid., 107–25, and the bibliographies in the essays by Petievich and Kugle in the present volume. Giti Thadani, *Sakhiyani: Lesbian Desire in Ancient and Modern India* (New York: Cassell, 1996) briefly surveys female homoeroticism in some ancient and modern Indian texts. The medieval period (and thus the Islamicate) is entirely absent from her history.

4. Claude Summers, ed., *The International Lesbian and Gay Literary Heritage* (New York: Henry Holt & Co., 1995).

5. Vanita and Kidwai, *Same-Sex Love in India*, 100–2, 58–62.

6. Ibid., 67–68, 85–89.

7. Ibid., 220–28, 191–94.

8. Ibid., 191–217.

9. See Mehta's remarks on pages 11–12 of Ginu Kamani, "Burning Bright: A Conversation with Deepa Mehta about *Fire*," *Trikone*, October 1997, 11–13.

10. See Boswell's eloquent defense of his choice of terms in "Revolutions, Universals, and Sexual Categories," in *Hidden from History: Reclaiming the Gay and Lesbian Past*, ed. Martin Duberman, Martha Vicinus, and George Chauncey (New York: Meridian, 1989), 17–36.

11. Among the more prominent organizations are Humsafar Trust (gay and lesbian; anti-AIDS), *Bombay Dost* magazine, and Stree Sangam (lesbian) in Bombay; Humrahi (gay men's group and help line), Sangini (lesbian group and help line), ABVA (AIDS Bhedbhav Virodhi Andolan, or AIDS Antidiscrimination Movement), and NAZ Foundation India Trust (both anti-AIDS) in Delhi; Good As You in Bangalore; Counsel Club in Calcutta; Friends India in Lucknow. Friends of Siddhartha Gautam, Delhi, organizes an annual film festival to commemorate AIDS activist Gautam. See the ABVA Report, *Less Than Gay* (1991), and the updated resource guide, *Humjinsi*, edited by Bina Fernandez, and published by the India Center for Human Rights (Mumbai) in 1999.

12. Shivananda Khan of the NAZ Foundation, London, outlines the taxonomy in "Males Who Have Sex with Males in South Asia," *Pukaar* (October 2000); for more elaboration, see Jeremy Seabrook, *Love in a Different Climate: Men Who Have Sex with Men in India* (London: Verso, 1999). In her preface to Seabrook's book, Anjali Gopalan, who heads the Delhi chapter of the NAZ Foundation, endorses the taxonomy.

13. Ashok Row Kavi, "MSM Terminology," unpublished paper, 2000.

14. Maya Philip, "Thoughts on Homosexuality," *Relief,* September–October 2000, 5. I am thankful to Suresh M.S. for bringing this to my attention.
15. For example, Susie Tharu and Lalitha K., eds., *Women Writing in India 600 B.C. to the Present* (Delhi: Oxford University Press, 1993).
16. Martin Duberman, "'Writhing Bedfellows' in Antebellum South Carolina: Historical Interpretation and the Politics of Evidence," in Duberman, Vicinius, and Chauncey, eds., *Hidden from History,* 167.
17. For a brief account of how this has often worked in the Indian academy in recent years, see Ruth Vanita, "The Straight Path to Postcolonial Salvation: Heterosexism and the Teaching of English in India Today," in *Lesbian and Gay Studies and the Teaching of English: Positions, Pedagogies, and Cultural Politics,* ed. William J. Spurlin (Urbana, Illinois: NCTE, 2000), 272–87.
18. Ashis Nandy, *The Intimate Enemy: Loss and Recovery of Self under Colonialism* (New Delhi: Oxford University Press, 1983).
19. Saleem Kidwai, "Introduction: Medieval materials in the Perso-Urdu Tradition," in Vanita and Kidwai, eds., *Same-Sex Love in India,* 107–25.

Part 1

Colonial Transitions

1

The Politics of Penetration

Section 377 of the Indian Penal Code

Suparna Bhaskaran

The Indian Law Commission, presided over by Lord Macaulay, introduced the colonial antisodomy statute, Section 377, into the Indian Penal Code on October 6, 1860, in British India. The section reads:

> Whoever voluntarily has carnal intercourse against the order of nature with any man, woman or animal, shall be punished with imprisonment for life, or with imprisonment of either description for a term which may extend to ten years, and shall also be liable to fine.
>
> Explanation. Penetration is sufficient to constitute the carnal intercourse necessary to the offence described in this section.
>
> Comment. This section is intended to punish the offense of sodomy, buggery and bestiality. The offense consists in a carnal knowledge committed against the order of nature by a person with a man, or in the same unnatural manner with a woman, or by a man or woman in any manner with an animal.[1]

In 1994 the discovery and rise of AIDS/HIV in India's largest prison, Tihar Jail in Delhi, led to a survey coordinated by Indian Medical Association president Dr. K. K. Aggarwal, which concluded that two-thirds of Tihar prisoners had participated in "homosexual activity."[2] This finding resulted in some doctors and activists demanding distribution of condoms to all prisoners as part of an HIV prevention policy. Agents of the state, including high-profile policewoman Kiran Bedi, then head of Tihar Jail, resisted condom distribution on the grounds that it would amount to legalizing homosexual activity. Subsequently, Janak Raj Jai, lawyer and president of the Family Conciliation Service Center, filed a petition supporting the official position. Jai, a Gandhian socialist who was jailed during Indira Gandhi's "emergency," claimed that decriminalizing homosexuality would have upset Mahatma Gandhi. He stated that in Mahatma Gandhi's lifetime AIDS was unknown and "male white fluid" was not wasted. Like many postcolonial nationalists responding to nonnormative sexuality, Jai defended a colonial sexual code as "Indian tradition" and posited advocacy for the civil rights of prisoners, gay men, and sexual minorities as elitist mimicry of the West. This official response and Jai's petition catalyzed debates around India's colonial antisodomy statute.

On April 14, 1994, the ABVA (AIDS Bhedbhav Virodhi Andolan, or AIDS Antidiscrimination Movement), a nongovernmental organization (NGO) working on issues related to the human rights of people with HIV/AIDS, filed a petition in the High Court of Delhi, engaging the following as defendants: the Union of India, the Delhi Administration, the inspector general of prisons, the National AIDS Control Organization, and the superintendent of the Tihar Jail. Among ABVA's requests were that Section 377 be deemed unconstitutional, illegal, and void, and be repealed; that steps be taken to prevent the segregation and isolation of prisoners identified as homosexual and/or suffering from AIDS/HIV or "suspected to have participated in consensual anal intercourse"; that condoms be made available free of cost to Tihar prisoners at their dispensary without the threat or fear of persecution for requesting condoms; that disposable syringes be used at the Tihar dispensary; and, finally, that jail officials regularly consult with the National AIDS Commission. This case is still pending, as cases in Indian courts often remain pending for decades. Subsequently, several other Indian and diasporic civil rights organizations as well as gay, lesbian, and queer organizations have bolstered ABVA's efforts.

The Colonial Context

[M]etropole and colony have to be seen in a unitary field of analysis.
—B. S. Cohn, *Colonialism and Its Forms of Knowledge: The British in India*

Section 377 must be understood within the context of the consolidation of empire in India via increasing militarization by the British Imperial Army. Ronald Hyam, in *Empire and Sexuality*, suggests that expansion of the British Empire dictated state policies of sexual and political restraint and relaxation, which framed modes of relation and interaction between the rulers and the ruled. He argues that sexual politics at the home base, Britain, were driven by "fanatical Purity Campaigns" that were intrinsically linked to those located at bases set up in the colonies. Under the policies of integration in the late eighteenth century, the keeping of Indian mistresses by British men had been a well-established practice, justified as a means of increasing their knowledge of "native affairs." Native mistresses included both Indian and Anglo-Indian women and "a deliberate policy of intermarriage was encouraged by the company, in the interests of building up the army."[3] Around the 1890s, however, these policies were reversed. The reversal was influenced by factors that included the 1857 Indian Revolt and shifts in British attitudes toward native governance. This shift led the British to develop an isolationist and indifferent bureaucratic imperial state wherein it was imperative that the rulers maintain their sexual, social, and racial "purity."

Special economic and social measures were taken to prevent miscegenation by army men. Increase in venereal diseases was seen as a major threat to the well-being of the Imperial Army. While some white British women were exported to India to serve the project of racial and sexual purity, this was not a viable solution for the whole army, as marriage quarters and allowances would prove too expensive. There were concerns that not having wives would encourage the Imperial Army to become "replicas of Sodom and Gomorrah,"[4] or, as Viceroy Elgin put it, to pick up "special Oriental vices."[5] The fiscal solution was to turn unofficial, unregulated brothels into officially regulated ones for the army. The mid-1850s saw the establishment of state-regulated brothels where native women had to register and undergo regular medical exams. These regulated brothels or *lal bazaars* (red markets) were primarily for white use, although "Indians could use them while whites were on morning parade."[6]

In 1894, Viceroy Elgin claimed that having no prostitutes would lead to "even more deplorable evils . . . there is already an increase in unnatural crimes" such as homosexual activity.[7] A popular cure for men (both Indian and British, civilians and soldiers) who might deviate from normative sexuality or "pukka-ness," was sending them to female prostitutes. For example, in October 1893 an advice column in *Sanjibani*, a Bengali weekly edited by Keshab Chandra Sen and Krishna Kumar Mitra, suggests that Indian schoolboys engaging in "unnatural and immoral habits" be cured by visits to prostitutes.[8]

In the second half of the nineteenth century, debates around sexual behavior in Britain traveled to India. Christian and feminist "purity campaigns" in the metropole targeted many forms of nonprocreative sexual activity. Their opposition to brothels, primarily frequented by married men, led to the Contagious Diseases Act of the 1860s that ended state-regulated brothels in England.[9] In the 1880s, lal bazaars began facing criticism and were officially suspended in 1888. These campaigns exported categories of manliness and womanliness wherein the *pukka sahib* and *memsahib* and their projected brown counterparts were to maintain a fiscal imperial polity and economy free of common vices such as prostitution and "special Oriental vices" such as homosexual activity.

Antisodomy Statutes in the Metropole

The first civil injunction against sodomy in British history, passed in 1533 by Henry VIII and the British Parliament, had made the "detestable and abominable vice of buggery committed with mankind or beast" a felony. According to Ed Cohen, the "transformation of sodomy from an ecclesiastical to a secular crime must be seen as a part of a large scale renegotiation in the boundaries between the Catholic Church and the British State."[10] The Buggery Act was piloted through Parliament with the help of Thomas Cromwell in an effort to support Henry VIII's plan to reduce the legal authority of the ecclesiastical courts and to seize Catholic Church properties.[11] The new Buggery Act allowed the monarch to issue death sentences against those convicted and to appropriate their property.

The statute against sodomy involved a shift from the canonical laws of the Catholic Church to the secular laws of the British state, monarchy, church, and legal imaginary. Sodomy shifted from being a sin against God to also being a crime against the state. The statute was deployed against Catholics whom reformers often accused of indulging in sodomy in monasteries. The connection between criminalizing sodomy and challenging papal authority can be seen in the history of the

Buggery Act during the sixteenth century under monarchs of different persuasions. Under Henry VIII it was reenacted in 1536, 1539, and 1541. Under Edward VI it was repealed, but reenacted in 1548 with amendments so that the felon's property was no longer forfeited to the crown. Under the Catholic Queen Mary the act was repealed in 1553, and under her sister, Queen Elizabeth I, who wanted to establish her claim as true heir to her father Henry VIII, it was reenacted with the same severity as in 1533.

Within three centuries after the 1533 Buggery Act was passed, jurist Edward Coke, in his legal treatise *Third Part of the Institutes of the Laws of England* (1797), which systematized the English Penal Code, defined buggery as "a detestable and abominable sin among Christians not to be named, committed by carnal knowledge against the ordinance of the creator and order of nature by mankind with mankind, or with brute beast, or by womankind with beast."[12] Here the civil and legal, and the ecclesiastical and canonical, are intertwined. According to Coke, carnal knowledge was acquired or inflicted only if the body "bore the marks of penetration."

In 1826 the Offenses Against the Person Act recriminalized sodomy as a capital offense and dropped the need for two simultaneous proofs for conviction; only proof of penetration was required. The earlier emphasis on procreation was rearticulated into a moral standard for individual behavior. This was in line with the creation of the new British middle-class masculinity of the nineteenth century. The movement to raise the age of sexual consent for girls from thirteen to sixteen coexisted with, defined, and reinforced the political discourse on "gross indecency." Thus, the Labouchere Amendment of 1885, which outlawed "gross indecency" between men (a category wide enough to cover any type of sexual activity), was passed as part of the debate around the age of consent for girls. This legal provision, under which Oscar Wilde was convicted, was not duplicated in India. Buggery remained a capital offense in England until 1861, and from then until 1967 it became a conviction punishable with imprisonment for a period that could extend to life.

Colonial Homogenizing of Indian Law

British commercial interests were consolidated in India with the creation of the British East India Company in 1600. Armed with a charter from Queen Elizabeth I that gave the company full trading rights in Asia and Africa, the Company, comprised of merchants from London, politicians, and British royalty, acquired judicial powers to form its own constitution, to regulate its affairs, and to set up factories in India. Between 1612 and 1690 factories were set up in the towns of Surat, Madras, Bombay, and Calcutta by acquiring land rights, or *zamindari*,[13] from the Mughal emperor, from Muslim and Hindu kings, and from earlier European traders such as the Portuguese.

In 1668 the Company changed from a trading association into a territorial sovereign, when it was authorized to declare war and make peace for the crown. In 1726 overall control over presidency towns was given to an appointed governor.[14] In a charter issued by George I in 1726, a uniform judicial system was created for the three presidency towns of Madras, Bombay, and Calcutta. Each presidency had a mayor's court, and the rules and regulations in these towns were formulated and enforced by Englishmen (following the principles of English law) on both Indians and Europeans. Mofussil courts in areas adjoining the presidency towns primarily followed Muslim criminal law although English criminal law was introduced for selected issues (such as delineating punishment for different crimes, declaring witchcraft a capital offense, and removing the exemption of Brahmans from capital punishment) in 1790 by Cornwallis.[15]

The Company increased its political authority by 1757, after winning more power through the Battles of Plassey and Buxar and the Divani rights of Bengal, Bihar, and Orissa.[16] In 1772 the Company claimed bankruptcy and asked the British Parliament for loans. This resulted in the Regulatory Act of 1773 whereby Parliament gained significantly more control over company affairs. In 1774 the first supreme court with a chief justice was set up in Calcutta, followed by supreme courts in Madras and Bombay. Beginning with the first governor-general, Warren Hastings, the First Plan of Reform, intended to unify, standardize, and translate Anglo-Indian law, was initiated. Although some Indian judges were allowed in the lower ranks of the judicial system, they could handle only civil cases (such as matters of inheritance or succession among Muslims or Hindus) that the British labeled "personal law." The British decided that native Muslims and Hindus had separate "personal laws" that applied principally to marriage, inheritance, succession, and "other religious matters."[17]

One of the earliest English translations and codifications of Hindu law was conducted under Warren Hastings's governorship. Pundits, selected by Hastings and his collector, translated works from Sanskrit to Persian (since there were no Europeans in Calcutta who knew Sanskrit) and Persian-to-English translation was done by British civil servant H. B. Halhed.

Heterogeneous Islamic communities also underwent colonial homogenization as "Muhammedans" (the British term for Muslims). Until 1860, many criminal courts (excluding presidency courts) selectively followed Muslim law, after which many more courts (mofussil courts) were incorporated into British criminal law. Also, by 1864 court maulvis (Muslim scholars) and the Persian language were replaced altogether in the criminal courts by jurors trained in English law and the English language. This change reflected the shift in power from the Muslim rulers to the British. These shifts were significant for same-sex practices. Saleem Kidwai has pointed out that, despite Emperor Akbar's (1556–1605) disapproval of homosexuality, men engaging in same-sex sexual behavior did not face legal prosecution in pre-British India.[18]

A charter of 1833 instituted a series of law commissions that met from 1833 onward to codify a uniform criminal and civil law for the whole of India. Although the British intended to "carefully" consult scriptures and/or scriptural experts like pundits/Brahmans, maulvis, and qazis while establishing the "personal laws" of Hindus and Muslims, British law was the basis for codification. The Law Commission was chaired by Lord Macaulay, governor-general of British India.

In 1857 Indians rose against British rule in what the British termed the "Sepoy Mutiny" and Indian nationalists the first major war of independence. In 1858, after this revolt was crushed and the last Mughal emperor imprisoned and exiled to Burma, Queen Victoria assumed direct control and administration of India and proclaimed herself empress of India. This resulted in the dual role of the crown overseeing economic expansion and state making. In 1860 the Indian Penal Code was passed and in 1861 the Code of Criminal Procedure was passed. In describing the task of codifying all law (criminal and civil) for the whole of British India, Macaulay claimed, "I believe that no country ever stood so much in need of a code of law as India and I believe also that there never was a country in which the want might be so easily supplied. Our principle is simply this—uniformity when you can have it; diversity when you must have it; but, in all cases, certainty."[19]

Those who prepared the Indian Penal Code (IPC) drew on English law, Hindu law, Muslim law, Livingston's Louisiana Code, and the Code Napoleon.[20] Disregarding the numerous complex variations of customary law and practice prevailing among Hindus and Muslims in different parts of the country, Macaulay decided that all Muslims were governed by the Quran and all Hindus by the *Manusmriti*. The Indian Penal Code, passed after revisions in October 1860, dealt with substantive law,[21] and the Code of Criminal Procedure, passed in 1861, dealt with "adjective law."[22]

The colonial enterprise, whether it advocated policies of coercive integration (under Warren Hastings) or policies of coercive isolationism (under Lord Cornwallis) with the native populations, rearticulated, dismantled, destroyed, collaborated with, and froze existing modes of sociopolitical-economic relations in India. The Indian Penal Code may have fulfilled William Jones's prophetic analogy of the "British as Romans." Jones liked to compare himself to Tribonian, the compiler of the Justinian Codes, but "in a scientific mode," and, by association, Governor-General Cornwallis would be like "the Justinian of India."[23] Hastings's and Jones's quest for the "Ancient Indian Constitution" was rearticulated as "English law as the law of India."[24]

Section 377: Penetration and its Permutations

The earliest case mentioned in the commentaries as related to Section 377 is dated 1832.[25] Since Section 377 was codified in 1860, this case appears to relate either to heterosexual rape or to a British antisodomy case. The judgment in this case is not available, but the brief interpretation of the case in the IPC commentaries raises two issues. First, it occurred almost thirty years before the antisodomy statute was promulgated in India. Second, the judge commenting on the 1832 case cites it to discuss the nature of "penetration." What counted as penetration continued to be an ongoing, arbitrary, and unsystematic discussion in several future judgments and commentaries. Section 377 states that "penetration is sufficient to constitute the carnal intercourse necessary to the offence described in this section." The commentary in the 1832 case suggests that the presence or absence of "seminal emission" (sometimes referred to as "spermatozoa" or "ejaculation" in the IPC commentaries) is not necessary for a conviction. However, judges maintain that its presence can certainly offer important evidence.

Later judgments also make distinctions regarding what it is that is penetrated. For instance, in *Brother John Anthony v the Madras High Court* (1992), the judge identifies two types of penetration as grounds for prosecution under Section 377. Brother John Anthony was a subwarden of a boarding home attached to St. Mary's

Higher Secondary School in Tuticorin and the petition claims that since 1987 "an impression was gaining momentum" in the school of his "perverted sexual assaults" on the inmates of the home. M. Thiagarajan, a minor and an inmate of the home, filed a report with the Tuticorin police stating that the school administration had taken no action despite reports lodged with them. Thiagarajan claimed that the administration threatened with expulsion students who complained. Brother Anthony's counsel filed a petition rejecting the public prosecutor's case that several violations under Section 377 had occurred. The judge points out that the case law for Section 377 is slim but that "sexual perversion takes shope [*sic*] in manifold forms" going by different names such as "sodomy," "buggery," "bestiality," "tribadism," "sadism," "masochism," "fetishism," and "exhibitionism." He then goes on to define and describe each form of sexual perversion. The next question the judge ponders is whether or not all of these forms come within the purview of Section 377. In order to answer that question he explores how penetration should be understood in relation to prior cases filed under Section 377 and to definitions of "intercourse, carnal knowledge and coitus." The judge concludes by stating that in fact two kinds of penetration had occurred in this case. He points out that both kinds were against nature and carnal because they were not intended for "coitus." Both entailed a process where a "visiting organism is enveloped at least partially by the visited organism."[26] The first kind involved the "insertion of the penis of the petitioner into the mouth of the victim boy and doing the act of incarnal [*sic*] intercourse up to the point of semen into mouth."

The judge supports this definition of penetration by referring to the case of *Lohana, Vasanthlal, Devchand v The State* (1968).[27] This case involved the rape of a boy, Babulal Vithaldas, by three adult men (Lohana, Vasanthlal, and Devchand). Two of the men anally raped Babulal Vithaldas and the third man raped him orally because "the boy complained of acute pain" and the accused "did the act in question by putting the male organ in the mouth of the boy and there was also seminal discharge and the boy had to vomit it out."[28] The contention presented by the appeal was that the third act was not an offense under Section 377. The judge in the case consults other Section 377 cases and also consults "the learned author Mr. Havelock Ellis, in his book 'Psychology of Sex.'" The judge quotes Ellis, noting "Cunnilinctus (often incorrectly termed cunnilingus) and fellatio cannot be regarded as unnatural for they have their prototype forms among animals, and they are found among various savage races. As forms of eretrectation [*sic*] and aids to tumescence they are thus natural and are sometimes regarded by both sexes as quintessential forms of sexual pleasure though they may not be considered aesthetic. They become deviations, however, and thus liable to be termed 'perversion,' when they replace desire of coitus" (AIR 1968, 1277).

The judge concludes that the third man committed an imitative unnatural carnal act where "there was the enveloping of a visiting member by the visited organism. There was thus reciprocity; intercourse connotes reciprocity" (AIR 1968, 1281). It is interesting that the judge is complicit with Ellis's social Darwinist understanding of the savage races' propensity for primitive and degenerate sexuality. Ellis associated acceptance of homosexual practices with backward classes and races:

On the whole, the evidence shows that among lower races homosexual practices are regarded with considerable indifference, and the real invert, if he exists among them, as doubtless he does exist, generally passes unperceived or joins some sacred caste which sanctifies his exclusively homosexual inclinations.

Even in Europe today a considerable lack of repugnance to homosexual practices many be found among the lower classes. In this matter, as folklore shows in so many other matters, the uncultured man of civilization is linked to the savage.[29]

All three men (Lohana, Vasanthlal, and Devchand) were convicted and their petition was dismissed.[30]

Getting back to Brother Anthony, the second kind of penetration identified by the judge was the "manipulation and movement of penis whilst being held by the victim" to "create orifice like thing" and to allow for "insertions and withdrawals" and ultimately an ejaculation. Thus the judge defines manual sex as penetration, a definition that differs from a commonsense definition. The judge supports his interpretation by referring to a 1969 case in which the penis was defined as a "visiting organism" that was "enveloped" between thighs ("the visited organism") and thus made a "connection" that counted as carnal intercourse. [31] In that case the accused (K. Govindan and Kannan Nair) were convicted both for heterosexual rape (under Section 376, IPC) and unnatural offenses (Section 377) against a fourteen-year-old "*dhobi* girl," Narayani. The sessions judge had rejected Narayani and her mother's first petition and the conviction was the result of their successful appeal. The enveloping of the "male organ" between Narayani's thighs was understood as unnatural sexual intercourse. The judge in the Brother Anthony case also concluded, without adducing any reasons, that of the sexual perversions he had originally listed, only sodomy, buggery, and bestiality would "fall into the sweep" of Section 377. One reason could be that key words such as *penetration* and *intercourse* were missing from the judge's definition of the other sexual perversions.

Consent Irrelevant?

Contradictory and overlapping definitions of "sodomy," "buggery," "the sin of Gomorrah" and "the sin of Sodom" coexist alongside the discourse on penetration. The "sin of Sodom" and "sodomy" almost always seem to refer to anal penetration (*per anum*), whereas "buggery" and "the sin of Gomorrah" include oral penetration and "bestiality" (*per os*).

Arrests, convictions, and successful appeals can be broadly categorized into five major themes. They involve (1) adult male(s) and a child, (2) adult male and a nonhuman creature, (3) adult male and adult male, (4) adult male and female; and (5) adult "habitual sodomites."

The first category is by far the most prevalent, and most convictions occur in this category. In general it involves an adult male accused of raping (or attempting to rape) an unconsenting child (referred to as *lad, boy,* or *girl*) between seven and thirteen years of age, and an adult relative, parent, or coworker reporting the alleged incident to the police. Rape gets entirely conflated with sodomy in these cases.[32]

In some judgments involving an adult man and a child (usually a boy) the judge considers the possibility of a revenge motive inciting a false accusation. For instance, in *Mirro v Emperor* (1946), the judge attempts to discern if there was any "communal feeling" between "Musalmans" and "Hindus" or between the *"chamars"* (caste group) and *"non-chamars"* that may have led to accusations and counteraccusations. Mirro,[33] a "Musalman" and a "notorious bully," was charged with sodomizing Ram Dayal (a young *chamar* boy). In the lower sessions court Mirro was sentenced to seven years' rigorous imprisonment. The judge who presides over Mirro's appeal in the Allahabad High Court overturns the sentence due to lack of evidence. He is convinced that there was no revenge plot since a "Musalman" police officer, Imdad Husain, had turned in Mirro and all the Hindu assessors in court (Mehendra Singh, Narain Singh, and Chhattarpal) did not find Mirro guilty. Furthermore, despite the fact that semen stains were found on Mirro's dhoti the overall medical evidence went in favor of Mirro: "There is no question of any communal feeling. Sakoor the principle prosecuting witness is a Musalman. All of the assessors who found the accused not guilty are Hindus."[34]

The second category involves human penile penetration of animals such as a bullock and a "domestic fowl."[35] It is defined as buggery or bestiality and always involves a short conviction. In the case of *Khandu v Emperor* (1933), Khandu was a convict undergoing a jail sentence. A fellow convict, Allah Yar, caught Khandu with his penis up the nostril of a bullock that was tied to a tree. The judge denies Khandu's appeal to reduce his sentence (five years of rigorous imprisonment) and states that "he [Khandu] showed a highly depraved nature and set a degrading example of sexual immorality." Although no cases are cited, a commentary by judge Dr. Hari Singh Gour states that women, too, should be convicted if they use inanimate objects to penetrate animals.[36]

In the third category, where the parties involved are two adult men, the issue of "consent" continues to be unproblematized in the judgments, and the word *rape* is not used in any of them.[37] Three variations emerge—forcible sex, consenting sex, and sex with "habitual sodomites." In the first, Charanjit Singh, a truck driver and employee of an engineering company, is convicted when his male coworker, Ramesh Chand, files a charge of "forcible sex." The judge is impressed by Ramesh Chand's braving of "social stigma" to "expose the culprit." This case was corroborated by medical evidence and testimony that forced sex had taken place.

In the second variant, two consenting men, both under twenty-one, are involved. The incident took place on March 5, 1978, but the circumstances as detailed in the 1988 appeal judgment are vague. Abdul Nur was fifteen-and-a-half years old, and Ratan Mia was estimated to be around twenty when the incident took place. They were sentenced in 1981 for a length of time that is not clear in the 1988 judgment. Their first appeal, on the grounds that they were "first time offenders," was rejected by the sessions judge who remarked that this argument should have been introduced in the initial hearing. In 1988, when they had completed six years of their sentence they appealed again, this time more successfully, since the judge first gave them six months and then changed it to seven days of rigorous imprisonment. Not once in this judgment is the fact that both men were consenting parties raised as an issue.[38]

If the "victim" of allegedly unwanted unnatural acts is suspected of being a "habitual sodomite" the charges are usually dropped and the victim is viewed as equally liable. This is similar to the tendency of judges not to uphold rape charges when a female victim is proved to be sexually promiscuous. Thus, in *Ratan Mia v State of Assam*, two witnesses, Solomon and Gulabdin, lodged a complaint with the local police to "protect" an eighteen-year-old "lad," Ratansi, the employee of their neighbor, Nowshirwani Irani, a restaurant keeper. In this case the judge is unconvinced by the witnesses' conflicting and inconsistent accounts and also by their claim that Ratansi is a victim. The judge describes Ratansi as a "hefty young man" who "appears to be a despicable specimen of humanity." The judge decides that Ratansi is a voluntary "catamite." The judge's description of Ratansi's hefty body seems to illustrate Mrinalini Sinha's point about the colonial imagination's contradictory tendency to assign hypervirile masculinity and thus degenerate sexuality to some colonized males (often associated with the nonintellectual class) and hypereffeminacy (often paradoxically associated with the colonized elite who were the intellectual nonlaboring class) to others.[39] According to the judge, since Ratansi "on his own admission is addicted to the vice of a catamite," and since the medical examiner's report suggests no recent penetration, the charges should be dropped. It is interesting that despite medical evidence, and despite the nature of "penetration" being in doubt (since witnesses' accounts varied), Ratansi's vices remain a strong component of the judge's ruling. Although consent is immaterial under Section 377 and the commentaries assert that if the so-called victim of penetration is consenting he is equally liable, the judge does not pursue Ratansi's liability or punish him in this case.

The judge describes the two witnesses, Solomon and Gulabdin, as "equally queer" due to several factors. First, as witnesses claiming to protect an unconsenting Ratansi, they quietly watched through a peephole the unnatural act of Ratansi sitting on Irani's lap while Irani ejaculated; second, the revenge motive appears again, since the judge finds that Solomon and Irani bear grudges against one another because Solomon does not pay regularly or fully for refreshments at Irani's shop; and third, initially Solomon conceals the fact that he is a policeman.

Three of the earliest cases, *Khairati v Emperor* (1844), *Ghasita v Emperor* (1844), and *Esop v Emperor* (1836), are mentioned in commentaries, but judgments are not available. Since Section 377 was not codified in 1844 I am speculating that the courts employed British antisodomy law. Both Khairati and Ghasita and their "victims" were suspected to be "habitual sodomites" (or "confirmed sodomites") who also habitually cross-dressed. Khairati is described as a man who habitually wore women's clothes and exhibited physical signs of having committed the offense. The judges state that such factors should not be used to convict him since corroboration and medical evidence are required for a conviction. Therefore, charges made by the "victims" were dropped. In another contradictory commentary a judge describes "hijras" as those "who form a class by themselves and who dress in women's clothes and dance and sing and ape the manners and vices of nautch girls" but who, like young boys, cows, mares, fowl, and buffalo, are especially targets of adult male penetration.[40]

Esop v Emperor suggests a "consensual" situation in which Esop, who was on board one of the East India Company's ships, was accused by his superiors of sodomy.[41] Esop's defense was that he was a native of Baghdad and his act was not considered an offense there. Esop's defense was rejected and he was convicted. Arthur N. Gilbert has suggested that British Navy ships often used certain guidelines to arbitrarily convict servants or officers (British and non-British) and the rates of convictions varied depending upon whether or not active wars were being fought by the British Navy. He describes the navy as a "total institution" (as used by sociologist Erving Goffman) where buggery was viewed as rampant and inevitable yet was publicly punished (often more so than murders on ship).[42] Esop's case demonstrates one of the British Navy's extraspecial concerns on board.

The fifth category is that of heterosexual married couples, and there are very few cases in this category. Grace Jayamani petitioned for divorce from her husband, E. P. Peter, on the grounds of sodomy.[43] Jayamani and Peter are identified in the records as Protestant Christians married in 1971 by proper religious rites. Grace Jayamani's primary ground for the petition is sodomy, but she and her father also introduce other factors such as cruelty. Jayamani states: "At the time of having sexual intercourse, the respondent used to put his male organ into my mouth or he used to put it into my anus. He was not prepared to have sexual intercourse in the usual way nor was he prepared to have sexual intercourse at my desire in the usual way. He used to conduct with me in a very cruel way at the time of having intercourse." (AIR 1982, 48). Grace Jayamani's main witness, her father, corroborated: "My son-in-law was troubling my daughter like anything. He was biting her breasts. He was beating her. My son-in-law i.e., the respondent was forcing my daughter for sexual intercourse during menstrual period. He was coercing her when she was ill. My daughter used to fall unconscious because of over indulgence on the part of respdt. in sexual intercourse. My daughter developed fear foebia [sic] on account of cruel attitude of the respt. towards her. . . . My son-in-law was behaving like a beast" (AIR 1982, 48).

The district judge spends an unusual amount of time discussing how sodomy should be defined in this case of a heterosexual married couple since he believes that the early colonial legislators "in keeping with delicacy of the earlier writers on English Common Law were reluctant to set out in detail the elements of sodomy because of its loathsome nature" (AIR 1982, 48). After consulting sources such as the *Shorter Oxford English Dictionary*, *Jowitt's Dictionary of English Law*, *American Jurisprudence, II Edition Volume 70*, and some earlier cases such as *Jellyman 8 C & P 604* in 1838 (a case involving a heterosexual married couple where the judge found the wife not guilty as she did not consent to anal penetration by her husband), the judge states that sodomy is "noncoital, carnal copulation with a member of the same or opposite sex, e.g. per anus or per os. Thus a man may indulge in sodomy with his wife" (AIR 1982, 48). In other words, the judge decided that a husband could be "guilty of sodomy on his wife if she was not a consenting party." Grace Jayamani's lack of consent led to a decree for dissolution of the marriage. This was the only Section 377 case involving two adults in which the issue of consent was actually articulated. It is significant that a wife's lack of consent serves to release her from a marriage but an adult male's consent lands him in prison.

Of the total of twenty-seven cases pertaining to Section 377 that I have examined, judgments are available in nineteen while the other eight are discussed in commentaries. In fifteen of the nineteen judgments convictions are handed down, and in three of the eight cases discussed in commentaries convictions occur. Section 377 states that punishment can be imprisonment for life or up to ten years.

The severest punishment was handed to Ratan Mia and Abdul Nur, who had already completed six years in prison, and appealed three times. This was one of the few cases where both parties were consenting men. Their third appeal (discussed above) reduced their sentence to seven days of rigorous imprisonment. It is unclear what the length of their sentence was in their original 1981 trial. This case is significant since it appears that the sex here was consensual. Much of the legal activism around Section 377 has been aimed at legalizing consensual sex and identifying nonvaginal, forced sex as "rape" (sometimes problematically referred to as "homosexual rape"). The mildest punishment was two months' imprisonment, inflicted on Chitaranjan Das. This judgment was extremely brief and did not indicate whether the circumstances involved unconsenting or consenting parties. Chitaranjan Das was described by the judge as a "highly educated and cultured person suffering from mental aberration" who "will suffer loss of service and serious consequences for his career."[44] Although the judge makes no reference to Havelock Ellis in this case, the circumstances seem to echo Ellis's claim that true sexual inversion (often coupled with "neurotic and degenerate" tendencies) exists among two groups—"men of exceptional abilities" and criminals.

The Ladies (or Lesbians) Are Lucky

Within the limited legalistic discourse of Section 377, the issue that remains unaddressed by activists is the unconscious and conscious privileging of the phallus even in the denaturing of compulsory heterosexuality. The question of penetration by any object other than a phallus does not seem to have been raised in the case law or commentaries so far. Some gay activists maintain that sex segregation, seclusion of women, and invisibility of lesbians in the private sphere makes life less difficult for lesbians. Furthermore, they suggest that "the ladies are lucky. Section 377 doesn't really affect lesbians."[45] Despite the structural and cultural relegation of women to the private sphere (where maintaining honor and purity, preventing shame, and reproducing national culture is valued), and despite the conceptual invisibility of female sexual autonomy in the overt legalisms of Section 377, this law has been sought to be used against some women who have wished to live as long-term lovers or friends and create new forms of kinship.

Although no women have been convicted so far, the statute is used to intimidate women. Women who have tried to apply for marriage licenses in civil court have been threatened with Section 377 by their fathers or by civil servants at marriage registries. Newspaper reports of such cases suggest that many of these women are from working-class or lower-middle-class, semi-urban, non-English-speaking families. In a piece entitled "Gender Jam: Case of a Curious Marriage," *India Today* reported that Tarunlata, age thirty-three, underwent a sex-change in 1987 to become a man—Tarunkumar—in order to marry Lila Chavda, age twenty-three, in December of 1989. Muljibhai, Lila's father, filed a case in the Gujarat High Court, stating that since "it is a lesbian relationship," action should be taken on grounds of Section 377 to annul the marriage. His petition states, "Tarunkumar possesses neither the male organ nor any natural mechanism of cohabitation, sexual intercourse and procreation of children. Adoption of any unnatural mechanism does not create manhood and as such Tarunkumar is not a male." Muljibhai's lawyer claimed that "even an impotent Hindu male can marry because impotency is no bar to his marriage. In this case Tarunkumar was not a Hindu male at the time of birth." Tarunkumar and Lila declared that even if their marriage was found null and void by the Gujarat High Court, they would "continue to live together because we are emotionally attached to one another." Muljibhai won the case and the marriage was found to be void and annulled. The couple now live in Tarunkumar's parents' home and they assert that the real reason Muljibhai objects to their marriage is that he will not get a dowry from the groom, which is common in their community.[46]

Conclusion

The case filed in 1994 against Section 377 is still in litigation. Heteropatriarchal ideologies of shame and duty, coupled with cultural and structural violence, continue to be powerfully articulated by post- and neocolonial forms of homophobia. But this exists in tension with mushrooming queer, national, and diasporic activism, writing, and research. Over the last decade, a number of organizations have appeared in urban areas, with newsletters, helplines, and more recently Internet listservs and websites (for a list see notes 11 and 12 of Ruth Vanita's introduction). They have organized protests, conferences, and petitions to the Indian government and the United Nations. These tensions carry the promise of further re-visionings of tradition, rights, kinship, and transnational community.

Notes

1. Ratanlal Ranchhoddas and Dhirajlal Keshavlal Thakoree, *The Indian Penal Code*, 27th ed. (Nagpur: Wadhwa, 1992).
2. Conversation with Anuja Gupta, 1994; and her report to the United Nations International Human Rights Tribunal, New York, 1996.
3. Ronald Hyam, *Empire and Sexuality: The British Experience* (London: Manchester University Press, 1990), 116.
4. Hyam, *Empire*, 123.
5. Ibid.
6. Kenneth Ballhatchet, *Race, Sex, and Class under the Raj: Imperial Attitudes and Policies and Their Critics* (London: Weidenfeld and Nicholson, 1980), 91.
7. Ibid., 101.
8. Report on Native Newspapers, *India Gazette File*, 1893. I am grateful to D. Dasgupta for pointing this out to me.
9. The Contagious Diseases Act was promoted to curtail middle-class men's access to women (especially working-class women) outside of marriage. Intended to curtail prostitution, it was directed toward the "protection of women and girls."
10. Ed Cohen, *Talk on the Wilde Side: Towards a Genealogy of a Discourse on Male Sexualities* (New York: Routledge, 1993), 174. For the history of British law on homosexuality, see also Stephen Jeffrey-Poulter, *Peers, Queers, and Commons* (London: Routledge, 1991).
11. Thomas Cromwell (1485–1540) was the king's chief advisor and minister. He presided over Henry VIII's divorce from Catherine of Aragon in 1533. Henry's break with the Roman Catholic Church, assumption of headship of the Church of England, and a series of administrative measures strengthened the power of the crown.
12. Cohen, *Talk on the Wilde Side*, 175.

13. Zamindari rights were conferred on landowners by the Mughal administration; they included collecting revenues and maintaining civil and criminal law and order.

14. Areas of India remapped by the British into zones of political control were referred to as presidencies.

15. S. K. Puri, *Indian Legal and Constitutional History* (Allahabad: Allahabad Law Agency, 1992), 160.

16. A divan was a fiscal or revenue officer under the Mughal administration. Rights of revenue collection were acquired by the company from local rulers and were often rearranged to suit Company needs.

17. Puri, *Indian Legal and Constitutional History*, 91.

18. Ruth Vanita and Saleem Kidwai, eds., *Same-Sex Love in India: Readings from Literature and History* (New York: St. Martin's Press, 2000), 113.

19. *Life and Works of Lord Macaulay* vol. 9 (London: Longmans Green, 1897), 56.

20. From conversations with ex–chief justice Padma Khastagir, in Calcutta, 1994.

21. Substantive law creates, defines, and regulates the rights and duties of parties.

22. Adjective law prescribes practice, procedure, or legal machinery by which substantive law is enforced. V. D. Kulshreshta, *Landmarks in Indian Legal and Constitutional History* (Lucknow: Eastern Book Company, 1992), 52.

23. William Jones, quoted in B. S. Cohn, "The Command of Language and the Language of Command," in *Subaltern Studies 4: Writings on South Asian History and Society*, ed. Ranajit Guha (Delhi: Oxford University Press, 1995), 295. The analogy of the British conquerors in India to the classical Romans, conquerors of the Greeks, notes Cohn, was also expressed via "visual reminders" in the Victoria Memorial, Calcutta, where there are statues of Jones and Hastings in the garb of Roman senators.

24. Cohn, "The Command of Language," 295.

25. Robert Reekspear, 1832, in Ratanlal and Dhiraljal, *The Indian Penal Code*, 431.

26. *Criminal Law Journal*, 1992: 1357.

27. A prior Section 377 case. AIR 1968 Gujarat 252: (1968 Cri LJ 1277) (*Lohana, Vasanthlal, Devchand, and The State of Gujarat*. Hereafter cited parenthetically as AIR 1968.)

28. *All India Reporter*, 1968: 1277.

29. Havelock Ellis, *Studies in the Psychology of Sex* vol. 2: *Sexual Inversion* [1897]; 3rd ed., 1915), 210.

30. A similar case involving a Section 377 conviction and oral rape of a child is *Khanu v Emperor*, 26 Cri LJ, 1925.

31. 1969 Cri LJ 818 (*State of Kerala v K. Govindan*).

32. *Ganpat v Emperor*, AIR 1918 Lahore 322 (2); *Sardar Ahmed v Emperor*, AIR 1914 Lahore 565; *Devi Das v Emperor*, 1928 Cri LJ 31; *Sain Dass v Emperor*, 1926 Cri LJ 27; *Mahomed Yousif v Emperor*, 1932 Cri. LJ 34; *Kaku Mashghul v Emperor*, 45 Cri. LJ 1944; *Fazal Rab Choudhary v State of Bihar*, 1983 Cri. LJ 632; *Bal Mukundo Singh v Emperor*, 1937 Cri. LJ 38; *Mirro v Emperor*, 1947 Cri. LJ 48; *Khanu v Emperor*, 26 Cri. LJ 1925; *Brother John Anthony v The State*, 1992 Cri. LJ 1352; *K. Govindan v State of Kerala*, 1969 Cr. LJ 75; and *Lohana, Vasanthlal, Devchand v The State*, 1968 Cri. LJ 74.

33. The British introduced surnames when making land settlements in India (in fact, surnames first appear in England, too, in an earlier period, in the course of land settlements). Many Indians, especially in rural areas and among the urban poor, still do not use surnames. It is only when they come in contact with government or other bureaucracies that surnames have to be invented for them (usually community, village, or father's first name is turned into a surname). Film stars often assume a screen name that does not have a surname attached to it.

34. *Mirro v Emperor*, AIR 1947 All. 79. 48 Cri. LJ 376.

35. *Brown* (1899) 24 QBD 357 and *Khandu v Emperor* AIR 1934 Lah 261: (1934) 35 Cri. LJ 1096 (Lah).

36. *The Penal Law of India* vol. 4 (Allahabad: Law Publishers, 1990), 3261.

37. *Esop v Emperor* (1836) 7 C7P 456; *Charanjit Singh* 1986 Cri LJ 173 (HP); *Ratan Mia v State of Assam*, 1988 Cri. LJ 980.

38. *Ratan Mia v State of Assam*, 1988 Cr LJ 98D (981) (Gau): (1988)1 Crimes 404.

39. Mrinalini Sinha, *Colonial Masculinity: The "Manly Englishman" and the "Effeminate Bengali" in the Late Nineteenth Century* (London: Manchester University Press, 1995), 19.

40. *The Penal Law of India* vol. 4 (Allahabad: Law Publishers, 1990), 3260.

41. *Esop v Emperor* (1832) 7 C & P 456.

42. Arthur N. Gilbert, "Buggery and the British Navy, 1700–1861," *Journal of Social History*, 1992, 72–158.

43. *Grace Jayamani, Petitioner, v E. P. Peter, Respondent*, AIR 1982 Karnataka 46. Hereafter cited parenthetically as AIR 1982.

44. *Chitaranjan Dass v State of Uttar Pradesh*, 1975 Cri. LJ 30.

45. Conversation with gay activist, Manohar, in Calcutta, 1994.

46. *India Today*, April 15, 1990.

2

Sultan Mahmud's Makeover

Colonial Homophobia
and the Persian-Urdu Literary Tradition

Scott Kugle

In Lahore, the cultural capital of modern Pakistan, one cannot help running into conflicting images of Sultan Mahmud of Ghazna. In the late medieval and early modern periods, Mahmud was a subject of immense literary appeal, due to his lifelong romance with his cupbearer, servant, and lover, named Ayaz. This homoerotic romance, the subject of epic as well as lyrical poems, first in Persian and later in Urdu (sometimes called Hindustani, the linguistic forerunner to modern Hindi), was suppressed during British colonial occupation of South Asia. However, made-over images of Mahmud of Ghazna continued to play a key role in British colonial ideology, as well as in later anticolonial religious/nationalist ideologies among both Muslims and Hindus. This study attempts to recapture the repressed image of Mahmud as a romantic hero by translating passages of Persian poetry that have been ignored both by Westerners and by South Asians.

Mahmud the Lover in Persian Poetry

Mahmud became Sultan of Ghazna (in modern Afghanistan) at the age of twenty-three, at the turn of the eleventh century C.E. He was the grandson of a Turkic slave-soldier, and his father had risen to the position of supreme military ruler of eastern Iran and Afghanistan. Sultan Mahmud combined Turkic military prowess with Persian administration to forge an empire that bridged West, Central, and South Asia. He spent his thirty-two-year reign in military campaigns, against rival Turkic sultans to the west in Iran and rival Hindu rajas to the east in the Indo-Gangetic Basin. He was the first Muslim leader to make military alliances with Hindu kings and also to make deep incursions into continental South Asia. He annexed the Punjab into his Islamic realm and set up Lahore as a regional capital with a Muslim garrison, thus initiating the Islamic period of this city's history.

Muslim authors lifted the story of Mahmud out of a historical framework and gave him a more vivid life as an archetypal lover. Although he married and had sons (as any dynastic ruler would), literary texts celebrated not so much his conquests as his lifelong relationship with Ayaz. Ayaz was purchased as a non-Muslim slave from eastern Afghanistan, on the border of Kashmir.[1] Slavery in Islamic courts and armies was a different institution from European or American slavery, and Ayaz was trained as a courtier. He was also known in historical chronicles by the name Abu al-Najm Ahmad. Although Ayaz helped Mahmud's son and heir Mas`ud to oust his brother and ascend the throne, Masud slighted Ayaz, calling him "my father's sneeze" and passing him over while assigning governorships. However, Ayaz continued to play an important role in the court at Ghazna while trying to solve the bitter succession quarrel between Mas`ud's two sons. In the midst of this conflict, both Ayaz and the rival he supported, Majdud, were assassinated, ostensibly by the second son, Mawdud, who took the throne in 1042 C.E. Persian historical chronicles remember Ayaz as a man not conventionally beautiful, but "adept in the art of pleasing."[2]

In Persianate lands (including India, Iran, Afghanistan, and Central Asia) Mahmud and Ayaz were always mentioned as a pair, on par with heterosexual romantic partners like Laila and Majnun, or Heer and Ranjha. This erotic Mahmud was the subject of a whole body of poems, some epic and some lyrical.

The best example of an epic poem, is the *Masnavi* of Zulali, an Iranian poet who died 1615 C.E.[3] In his vivid account of their love, romance overshadows empire building. Mahmud goes to invade Kashmir, and takes a morning snooze. In his dream he sees a beautiful young slave pouring wine at a banquet. Mahmud goes to seize him and the youth winks and smiles, striking love into Mahmud's heart.

When the cupbearer of the tavern pours out beauty and sorrow
Understanding's heart surges beyond the bounds of moderation

May no glasslike heart remain unshattered
May no wine-filled goblet be without a rapt drinker

That night, Mahmud himself became wine, burgundy as spilled blood
He was the glass in the cupbearer's hand like a trained royal falcon

The cupbearer came in, circling with amorous flirtation
The sting of his playful glance cut the vein of Mahmud's glass

With what teasing the cupbearer poured pure red wine
Rubbing tart salt into the wounds of such sweet dreams

Pure wine he poured from the glass lip of his soul
Its potency saturated everyone who looked upon him[4]

His lashes like an executioner, blade balanced on his shoulder
His sidelong glance like a sword, ready to flash out at vulnerable necks

His hair twists with a kind of ensnaring
That could capture a hundred sleepless eyes

From whichever angle you glance at his form
You are left devastated by his elegant inattention

In the assembly came players with drums and flutes
In one breath, music roused a flood of brimming wine cups

Crying and moaning, Mahmud danced from longing for his love
As if his skin were being shed from his body

Serving handsome companions dressed in sheer muslin with gold cups
Droplets of sweat from the cupbearer's brow rolled along his ear

The wine jug circled around, bringing the two into intimacy
Mahmud's ecstasy boiled over in his delicious dream vision

The Sultan of Ghazna approached as if to capture him
When with a wink of abandon, Ayaz slew him on the spot

The best of the verdant youthful beauty of Kashmir
The delicacy of his lip would make him the royal cupbearer

His lip, like a bud breaking into bloom, pouring forth smiles
The way his mouth curls in laughter stills all pain

If one could taste the breath of that lip, like a sugared pistachio
From the sweetness of his lip one would break into endless laughter

To speak of that slender tender mouth
Would bring Mahmud's very soul to his lips

In the softness of the hair that frames it
The way to his mouth could be easily lost

When Ayaz approached him, glass in hand
Mahmud contemplated him from the depth of his breast

Splendor the color of blood, a rending and lifting of veils
Ayaz captured Mahmud's heart and left his chest intact

Such a youth, who carried off Mahmud's heart
With one word to him became Mahmud's own breast.[5]

Mahmud awakens, agonized by longing for the youth he saw in his dream. He learns that the young man is a slave for sale in the markets of Badakhshan, the mountainous region between Afghanistan and Kashmir. His planned invasion of Kashmir is called off; instead, he goes to find Ayaz:

In that market in Badakhshan, trade in young men thrives
But Mahmud was searching for a rose of a different hue

His gaze fell upon the face of his Ayaz, in a flash
He knew they must be together, he must buy him as a master

The gaze of the lover lingered over the one he loved
And struck his heart like the sting of a wasp

When the two found each others' eyes
Their breathing transformed into sighs

As Mahmud imbibed the fresh beauty of Ayaz
If just seeing that lip made him drunk, a kiss would floor him

What beauty, like a roseate glass of wine
That kindles a flame, searing the souls of lovers

His slender waist easing into his hips and thighs
Like a deer captured, but unbroken by its bonds

If his face shone like the moon, his dark tresses were a sigh
Of Mahmud when cool shade flickers over his nape.[6]

Mahmud purchases Ayaz as a slave, and takes him back to Ghazna. Mahmud tries to overcome their separation as master and slave, and beseeches Ayaz to become his cupbearer and constant companion not out of coercion but out of love. In the following scene, pouring wine becomes a metaphor both for kissing and for love's intoxication. The redness of wine blends suggestively into the redness of lips and the redness of blood shed from a longing heart:

Mahmud set a cup beside him and a decanter before him
Full of burgundy wine, as if distilled from his own heart

He filled the cup with wine like his love's ruby lips
Entangled in the curls of Ayaz, Mahmud began to lose control

He filled the cup with wine from the clouds of forgetfulness
The glow of Ayaz set the glass aflame with scintillating colors

He lifted the cup to Ayaz and bade him drink
His heart melted as he held the cup to his lips

Mahmud urged him to drink wine from his own hand
Yet a complaint showed in the eyes of Ayaz, a fear of intoxication

But as a servant, Ayaz drank from the cup
As a ruby droplet rolled from his lip to his shirt

His words lay in jumbles as the drop rolled to his foot
And the wine sent him spinning in drunkenness

Hard of breath, Mahmud said, "In this intimacy one can pursue desire
But I can only utter sighs while watching you delicately drink!

Tonight, I'm in the mood to finally reach you
How long has my only wish from God been delayed

Your lips have become ruby red, as intense as the wine
Such a ruby spells the death of better discretion

Your mouth is a wine bottle overflowing
Since the color of wine flows over your lips

Those are not black curls nestled against your cheeks
Since your glance is aflame they must be wisps of smoke

Gazing at you, they seem not like musk-scented curls
For where there is burning desire there must be smoke

Come to me now, bare all, that I may kiss your lips
Those very rose petals that make a beard tender and soft

Your lip is a single drop of wine distilled
My heart's desire is only to taste it unconstrained

Against the black lashes, how bright are your eyes
Am I fated to glimpse them only from a distance?

You never look at me directly in the eye
Though with one glance you will rob me of my heart

This is the last breath I will release from my soul
Without your beauty open before me, I will surely die

If you let me embrace your full form
From my grave stately box-trees will grow tall like you

That idol of Kashmir, like a rose blooming in a graceful cypress
From head to toe your elegant form has set me boiling!"

Ayaz's sweet mouth drawing close, closer
His smile fully prepared, his lip set for the charge

Then from his smile, sweetness boiled over
He took the wine-cup from the Sultan's hand

From that moment, Ayaz was the cupbearer of Mahmud
Whose whole world became drunk with his playful grace.[7]

In this epic poem, the two lovers endure a series of misunderstandings, separations, and interference by outsiders. Ayaz is tripped up by jealous courtiers, seduced by a young woman, and eventually kidnapped by the king of Kashmir. Yet they are reunited and their love triumphs. The poet's emphasis on universal love through the very particular relationship between the two men leads him to rewrite many of the facts of Mahmud's adventures. Mahmud invades India and destroys Hindu temples in order to rescue the hostage Ayaz. Love is the lens through which his military exercises are to be understood—not plunder or piety. Love is the key symbol in his story, in accord with the worldview of Sufism that exalts love as the highest human value, and ultimately the sole cause for the creation of the world.[8]

Mahmud and Ayaz also appear in more clearly devotional Sufi poetry in less overtly sensual ways. In Rumi's writings Ayaz becomes an allegory for the perfect man's loyalty and sincerity, while in Sa'di's poetry he is the exemplar of true love. Since students of Persian traditionally and even today begin with Sa'di's *Bustan*, they cannot avoid encountering Mahmud as lover. Apart from valorizing this love as one that overcomes the hierarchical difference between master and slave, some poets also emphasize that it is based more on inner than outer beauty. Sa'di writes: "A petty fellow once slandered the king of Ghazna, saying, 'How strange that Ayaz is not beautiful at all! A rose with no beautiful hue has no fine fragrance, so how bizarre that a nightingale should go mad with love for such a rose!' When this story reached the ears of Mahmud, he became rapt in thought, saying, 'I love him for the way he behaves, not for his stature and appearance.'"[9]

Given the later colonial and postcolonial denunciatory stereotyping of all male-male love in medieval Islamic contexts as "pederastic," it is important to note that there is little evidence in the poetry itself to fix the age of a masculine beloved. There are few concrete linguistic or imagistic clues to determine whether "boy," "youth," or "young man" would be most accurate in translation. Poets were fond of praising a man whose beard had grown in, just as they would praise a youth whose face was still smooth. The case of Mahmud and Ayaz is significant in this ongoing debate over the nature of premodern male-male love. It demonstrates that the ideal love between males was not necessarily "boy love" at all.[10] Mahmud and Ayaz are the archetype of perfect male lovers, but both are adult men and some poets dwell on Ayaz's facial hair as a sign of his desirability.

Lyric love poetry also participated in the celebration of the emotional and sensual relationship between Mahmud and Ayaz. Mahmud Lahori (d. 1574) was a native South Asian who wrote in the high cultural language of Persian in his home city of Lahore.[11] His collection of short, intense *ghazals*, entitled *Chronicle of Mahmud*, is not so much about the historical person as about his archetypal role as a lover yearning for his distant beloved. In the final couplet of each poem, the two lovers are identified as "Mahmud" and "Ayaz":

> By your beguiling black mole, this charred heart has flared up again, tulip-red
> One sly glance from your dear eye makes even white gazelles hide in shame
>
> From the effect of your ruby lip the tulip in the garden
> Sways drunken, with never a sip from any other scarlet cup
>
> Faint whiskers emerge from the soft edge of your cheeks like wisps of perfume
> Who could think that the luminous halo that circles the moon mars its beauty?
>
> Ayaz has vexed the heart of Mahmud and left him in troubled agitation
> Mahmud gazed upon him—if only he'd pondered this poem instead![12]

The poet makes clever use of the convention whereby in the last couplet of a ghazal the poet addresses himself by his own name, as if speaking to a third person. In this case, the poet's name, Mahmud, allows him to identify with the historical Mahmud. One is left to wonder who the poet's Ayaz is, to whom the whole collection is addressed:

Cast the veil from the moon of your countenance
So the sun won't be able to claim a beam of beauty

You try to stop me from drinking this roseate wine!
Here, take my heart and soul and roast them over the fire

I come to kiss your foot with my head on the ground
Crying like a woman, I come with ever-new agitation

I recall sitting in your company and heave a sigh
As if from grief each breath becomes a lute string

Ayaz has looted the heart of Mahmud and carried off
Patience, joy, repose, the power to eat, the possibility of sleep.[13]

The purpose of the ghazal is not to tell a story but rather to evoke the various, evanescent moods of love. However, the constant references to Mahmud and Ayaz anchor the archetypal images of wine and the cupbearer. Some ghazal writers leave the gender of the beloved ambiguous, or alternate between masculine and feminine objects of desire in order to mask the beloved's identity. In contrast, Lahori consistently identifies the beloved as male, through the trope of Mahmud's passionate longing for Ayaz.

The cupbearer fills the glass now from the right now from the left
With a wine of ancient vintage now from the right now from the left

Advisors warn me against wine, but to what effect!
The cupbearer takes care of me now from the right now from the left

If the rose would brag before his beauty, I invoke the breeze
To blow it down in shame now from the right now from the left

On both sides of your path, pure lovers wait in passion just for you
Revealing their hidden beauties like tulips now from the right now from the left

The pure radiance of your face impassions old men and youths alike
Who circle you, a nimbus around the moon, now from the right now from the left

What pure splendor the cupbearer lends to Mahmud's cheeks
When his dark, musky ringlets brush now from the right now from the left.[14]

.   .   .   .

That impertinent lover pays no attention to my state of heart
I've never met another so well trained in the laws of flirtation

Experienced men cry at his merciless inattentiveness
Have they ever met a young man so whimsically bold!

His blossoming garden throws every lane into ruin
No one is more malicious in mischievous love

Many people have petitioned God for more beauty
Yet even the spirits of heaven can't match his capriciousness

What a delightful surprise when such a mischievous flirt comes
To his tear-stained lover with his mischief seemingly concealed

Mahmud lies ruined by his love since the moment
His Ayaz first turned his glance meaningfully away.[15]

The copies of Lahori's poems found in the library of Punjab University in Lahore were thick with dust and had not been checked out since the library adopted stamped cards. This body of poetry is now completely marginalized in the consciousness of South Asian Muslim men. In addition, the implicit acknowledgement of homoerotic activity that it represents is also abjected as a sign of "Western influence and decadence."[16] If there is ever a discussion of homosexuality, it is framed as a Western import of sexual liberation, cable television, and Internet pornography. How did such a massive repression take place across South Asia?

The Suppression of Homoerotic Texts under Colonialism

British colonial ascendancy in South Asia incited an assault on these images of Sultan Mahmud as a homoerotic lover. Under British influence, Urdu poets and critics, drawing on what had been less-than-dominant homophobic elements in Islamic tradition, excised the homoerotic Mahmud from their literary tradition. The massive violence of the British conquest of Delhi in 1857, which extinguished the last vestiges of the weak but symbolically vivid Mughal regime, shocked the Muslim educated class into a major restructuring exercise. Intellectuals and authors were forced to remake their cultural orientation in order to survive, find employment, and create meaningful lives in the new colonial regime. Their cultural inheritance was subject to a brutal critique by colonial administrators who set the new standards of "civilization and cultivation." In particular their poetic tradition was attacked for its perceived homoerotic "vulgarity."

The British not only policed the corridors of literary imagery but also framed homoerotic love as "criminal activity." Thomas Babington Macaulay, who designed the colonial education system that would teach South Asians "civilization" on British Victorian models, also helped frame the legislation that labeled sodomy and other acts of love between men "unnatural" and made them criminal offenses. The law was part of the new colonial criminal code, and remains in the penal codes of India and Pakistan today.[17]

British historiography defined Muslims as one of the "martial castes," and the figure of the homoerotic male lover was discarded as a cultural "abject" along with previously abjected figures such as the gender-transgressive Qalandars.[18] Hijras faced similar criminalization under British rule, as did female concubines, musicians, and dancers, who were labeled "prostitutes."[19] All can be seen as "sexual minorities" who nonetheless had a somewhat respected (or at least grudgingly accepted) role in precolonial society.

The legal enactment was not directly effective; there have been very few prose-cutions based on "sex acts against the order of nature" (see Suparna Bhaskaran's essay in this volume). However, it had more insidious effects as a threat and a goad to reform. The Mughal court and, to a lesser extent, regional courts that were based on the Mughal pattern and owed nominal allegiance to the Mughal ruler in Delhi, had acted as the main patrons for literary production. After 1857 these lay in ruins and their role was deliberately monopolized by the education wing of the British administration. This administration allowed an older generation of authors who had been loyal to Mughal rule to fall into poverty. The poet Asadullah Khan Ghalib's memoirs, written in this period, bear eloquently tragic testimony to this process as he repeatedly and unsuccessfully petitioned the Queen of England (now Empress of India) to continue the poet's stipend he had received under Mughal patronage.[20] The administration raised up a new generation of "reformist" Urdu literati who were educators in colleges. Their salaries were paid by the colonial administration and they were commissioned to write "new poetry" that discred-ited older styles of writing.

What followed was a complex revision of the literary tradition of Urdu and Persian poetics as Muslim poets, literati, and historians purged their literature of most erotic themes and especially of homoerotic themes. This purge was partly motivated by fear of colonial laws and partly by ambition to gain salaried positions in the colonial administration. Viewed more sympathetically, this revisionism can be seen as the result of an acute moral bewilderment after the dramatic destruction of the Mughal ruling dynasty in Delhi. The two main architects of these cultural readjustments were the poets Altaf Husayan Hali and Muhammad Husayn Azad. Hali saw the poetic tradition he had inherited as a rudely built hall of mirrors that reflected only the moral defects of its creators: "[W]ith inexpert hands they have fashioned a house of mirrors for the nation, which they may enter to study their features and realize who they were and what they have become."[21] Hali and Azad transformed the violence they experienced and the terror they internalized into a self-generated critique, as if their culture "deserved" the harsh treatment it received from the British due to its own prior decadence and fall from Islamic norms. It is largely due to their efforts that the love of Mahmud and Ayaz nearly disappeared from the Muslim male imagination.

Altaf Husayn Hali (1837–1914) grew up in a traditional Muslim atmosphere where *knowledge* meant knowledge of Arabic scripture and Persian poetry. At the age of seventeen he ran away from home and a marriage arranged by his family to seek further education in Delhi. He found refuge at an Islamic college, and con-tinued his studies of Arabic language and literature. He submitted his poetry to the renowned poet Ghalib for correction and refinement. Under family pressure, he took a job in the British Deputy Collector's office. He was twenty when north-ern India was enflamed by rebellion against the British the British eventually sacked Delhi and the city was transformed, in Ghalib's words, into "a sea of blood."[22] Although he personally escaped harm, his family was burdened with supporting refugees. Hali was one of many Muslims who—about fifteen years after the sack of Delhi, the execution of the Mughal royal family, and the persecution of all who were suspected of supporting them—began to recover from the shock of these events and to seek employment in the new administration. In 1870 he emigrated to Lahore and found work in the government book depot, checking translations of English books into Urdu.

These years saw a concatenation of events that signaled the formation of a rising class of Muslims who were willing to participate in the colonial system in hopes of replacing the former aristocratic class devastated by the British. The year 1875 witnessed the opening of the Anglo-Oriental College at Aligarh, the first educational institution run by Muslims to impart English-oriented education. The poet and scholar Muhammad Husayn Azad (1834–1910) organized a new poetry competition in Lahore in 1874 to replace the old-style poetry recitals that had flourished under Mughal patronage. Azad and Hali became friends at the Punjab Society organized by Colonel Holroyd, the British director of public instruction in Lahore, to sponsor the association of "educated natives" with British administrators and to foster a revival of "oriental learning" under British guidance. Azad, a major ideologue in this Anglo-Oriental learned society and an employee of Colonel Holroyd, aimed to elicit a new body of Urdu poetry on "moral" and "natural" themes, thus cleansing poetry of "obscene" and homoerotic imagery. Along with Azad, Hali participated in the society's poetry competitions that sparked his own literary career.[23]

Hali found the scapegoat he needed in "Persian" culture. He pictured Persian poets as effete, slothful, and corrupt, although he admitted that their poetic creations may also have been refined, graceful, and expressive. He tried to reject "Persianate" models in order to revert to an imagined earlier, "purer" Arabic poetry that had the manly virtues of vigor, fortitude, directness, and "naturalness." This shift in models explains the force of his long didactic poem *Madd o Jarr-i Islam* (The Flow and Ebb of Islam, better known as his *Musaddas*). In both form and content, this poem praises the original Islam "of the Arabs" over the medieval Islam of the Persians and Persian-speaking Turks. He deliberately eschewed the poetic forms of the ghazal and the *masnavis*, which were preeminently vehicles for love poetry and were the dominant poetic forms up until Hali's time (as demonstrated by the translations above). Rather, he adopted a six-lined stanza form, the *Musaddas*, to launch his devastating critique of past poetic traditions and to announce his aim of returning to the more "manly" poetic and pious ideals that he claimed were enshrined in Arab culture and literature.

> The filthy archives of poetry and odes
>> more foul than a cesspool in its putridity
>
> By which the earth is convulsed as if by an earthquake
>> and makes the angels blush in heaven
>
> Such is the place of our literature among other branches of learning,
>> by which learning and faith are quite devastated.[24]

The key to understanding the full impact of this rhetoric is the image of "the earth convulsed as if by an earthquake," an image that resonates with the saying commonly attributed to the Prophet Muhammad that when a man sexually mounts another man the earth beseeches God to allow it to convulse and swallow them up to conceal their act. Through such images Hali draws on older sources of homophobia that had not acquired social dominance in precolonial South Asia, and gives them new authority for modern South Asian Muslims. In precolonial times, even conservative religious scholars equivocated before attributing this supposed saying to the Prophet, and indeed some of the most learned outright rejected its authenticity.[25]

Hali also brought into vogue the idea that while Arabs were not given to homoeroticism either in poetry or in social practice, Persians and Turks were homoerotically inclined and bequeathed this legacy to South Asian Muslims.[26] Hali's "Introduction to Poetry and Poetics" was a history of Urdu literature that continues to influence the field until today.[27] In it he worked out his moral condemnation of the supposed vulgarities and obscenities enshrined in Persian and Urdu poetry. Primary among these was homoerotic desire. In his view, "all the poets of Iran laid the foundation of lyric love poetry only on the love of young men and beardless boys," which made the ghazal vile and immoral. In his critique, Hali left certain words transliterated from English. Their moral force would have been lost had they been detached from the English language and thus from the colonial regime. Such terms include the polarities of "natural/unnatural," "moral/immoral," "civilization/despotic government," and even "poetry/literature."[28] Hali deemed these terms, central to the new British morality, to have no linguistic equivalent in Persian and Urdu. The argument that homoerotic desire is against "human nature" reveals his translation of British morality into Urdu prose: "For a man to fall madly in love with a man, and seek union and enjoyment with him, is something that human nature entirely rejects."[29] Only in the twentieth century have new Urdu terms been coined to approximate the inflections of the English word *unnatural*.[30]

Hali advocated a radical "ethical cleansing" of the Urdu and Persian ghazal. He claimed that love lyrics should express love in a pure and simple form, devoid of any sensuality. He called this "spiritual love." Above all, he felt, the poet should never specify the gender of the beloved, especially in ways that imply the male gender. Frances W. Pritchett cites Hali as even listing those words that should be suppressed in poetry, precisely because they might indicate that a male poet is addressing a masculine love object. If these terms were not suppressed, argued Hali, "we will be adjudged guilty according to the [British obscenity] law."[31]

It was Hali who adopted what later became a popular strategy of dismissing earlier poetic expressions of homoerotic love as simply literary conventions that did not reflect sexual or social practices. Even some recent literary critics who are sympathetic to the earlier Urdu poetic tradition have valorized his line of apology. Pritchett, though normally as skeptical of Hali's pronouncements as she is insightful about them, buys this line of apology wholeheartedly: "Particularly classical poetry did not legitimize the physical expression of pederastic desires . . . but the people of the old [precolonial] culture felt able to invoke attraction to beautiful boys as a powerful, multivalent poetic image."[32] However, as the recurrent poetic trope of the historical figures of Mahmud and Ayaz suggests, imagery was not always totally divorced from social "reality" of some sort.

Critics who follow Hali more closely uphold his harsh condemnation of homoerotic desire in the Persian-Urdu poetic tradition without dabbling in the subtleties of whether or not the erotic images reflected sexual practice. Ram Babu Saksena trumpets that in Urdu poetry "the boy is regarded as a mistress and his curls, his tresses, the down on his cheeks, his budding moustaches, the moles on his face, are celebrated with gusto in a sensual manner revolting to the mind."[33] This train of thought is taken up again by Muhammad Sadiq, who writes that lyric poetry "is ultimately traceable to homosexual love which had taken deep roots among the Persians and Persianized Arabs."[34] This barrage of condemnation and apology derives from Hali's original acts of self-censorship, which are repeated with more vitriol and less sympathy than exists in the original.

In Hali's own time Urdu prose works embodied British moral rhetoric more directly than did poetry. A prime example is the 1874 Urdu novel *The Repentance of Nasuh*, by Nazir Ahmad, who was a college classmate of Hali's and also an educational administrator in the British government. In the novel, a father discovers his son's hidden library of Urdu and Persian poetry. Overcoming his own nostalgic sentiments for this literature, he decides to burn the whole corpus as a nest of "irreligion and idolatry, discourtesy and shamelessness, obscenity, slander and lies."[35]

As the figure of Sultan Mahmud was emptied of homoerotic imagery (or for that matter *any* romantic imagery), he was preserved as a figure of political importance in British colonial historiography. Colonialist discourse discredited deposed Muslim rulers as fanatics and framed Hindus as passive masses, thus valorizing the British as the only race moderate, temperate, and rational enough to rule a multiethnic, polyglot, religiously confusing region like South Asia. Paul Hardy has documented how historians writing from within the colonial enterprise positioned Sultan Mahmud as the justification for their racialized notion that morality is the basis of civilization and different types of morality are inherent in distinct races.[36] British historians presented all of South Asian history before colonial rule as a clash of races defined primarily by religion. In this framework, Mahmud became the stereotyped Muslim Turk whose personal qualities characterized his "race." His incursions into "Hindu India" were the site wherein both Hindus and Muslims were judged inferior for opposite reasons—Hindus for their supposed lassitude, servility, and contemplative effeminacy, and Muslims for their supposed intemperate warlike nature and tyrannical indolence. Thus the erasure of homoerotic elements in Sultan Mahmud's personality worked hand in glove with the need of colonial historians to present a racialized history of Muslim rule in South Asia that would justify their own political domination.

Nationalist and Postindependence Versions of Mahmud

It seems that in every age Mahmud and Ayaz are emptied of one meaning and assigned another. South Asian political movements that opposed British rule did not dispose of the British historical framework that placed Mahmud at the original point of a communal and civilizational drama of domination; rather, they simply shifted the fragments of the image around within that framework in order to reflect their own political, material, and moral needs.

The modern moralism expressed in Hali's campaigns intensified as Muslims began to resist British colonialism. Nationalist poet, philosopher, and lawyer Muhammad Iqbal cited Mahmud and Ayaz as cultural icons, but did so in a way that disengaged them from homoeroticism:

Mahmud and Ayaz stand in the same row to pray
Neither of them was a slave and neither a master.[37]

Here Mahmud and Ayaz are models for modern Muslim men not because of their love for one another but because they represent slavery and masterhood transformed by Islamic piety into brotherly equality. Iqbal imagines a literal deflation of their erotic energies in a famous ghazal:

> No more enflaming in that passion, no more enticement in that beauty
> Not in the Ghaznavi's outrageous desire nor in the curls of Ayaz's locks.[38]

In this couplet Iqbal notes without remorse that the beauty Mahmud saw in Ayaz and the passion Ayaz invoked in Mahmud are no longer possible. The generation of Hali and Azad strove to deny them, but Iqbal's generation could simply pronounce them gone. This pronouncement performed an important function in Iqbal's ideology of modernity that tried to wrest Islam from the framework of love and refashion it into a metaphor for existential struggle and political activism. The couplet above follows these earlier couplets in the same ghazal:

> Finally, oh long expected essence, let me see you clothed in metaphor
> For a thousand prostrations pulse in this subservient forehead of mine

> When I lowered my head in prostration, the ground began to speak
> "If your heart is still aware of idols, what do you expect of prayer?"

> Uncontrollably you hoard and save, but in reality your mirror is that mirror
> That once broken is only more valuable in the eyes of the mirror-maker.[39]

The rhetoric of "essence" and "metaphor" once referred mainly to love—essential love being that directed by creator to creature, and metaphoric love that of one human for another. The broken mirror that in Sufi rhetoric represented the heart shattered in passionate love now refers to the ego made subservient to pious prayer that unites a community of patriotic believers.

In the postindependence period marred by partition and the escalating violence of nation-states and communal ideologies, Mahmud continues to be a pivotal figure. Among communalist Hindus and Muslims, the person of Mahmud is the touchstone for the triumph of one community over the other. Revivalist Hindus revile him as the first Muslim invader. In their view, his symbolic action of desecrating idols represents their emasculation and the loss of Hindu political power. Although Mahmud never settled on Indian soil, they argue, he introduced desecration, pillage, and rape, opening the way for waves of invasion by Muslim rulers from the Khyber Pass to the northwest. Their current retribution for this action of almost a thousand years ago is to revile Muslims as a community and attempt to drive them out of India. Through constant citations of Sultan Mahmud, organizations like the Shiv Sena and the Bajrang Dal, whose stated ideological purpose is the militant reassertion of "Hindu masculinity," target Muslims for attack and persecution.

In an inverse but parallel dynamic, communal-minded Muslims revere Mahmud as the prototype of Muslim military triumph on the subcontinent. They trumpet his iconoclasm as the desirable moral response of Muslims to a Hindu civilization that is both subservient to it and threatens to absorb it. Muslim revivalist movements, especially those that advocated the creation of Pakistan as a separate state for Muslims, propagated a religious chauvinism that, in their perception, Mahmud himself initiated. They envision him as the prototype of Islamic piety, whose incursions into continental South Asia were primarily to extinguish Isma'ili heresy among the Muslims of Sindh rather than to conquer Hindus. And if he stripped Hindu temples of treasure, it was to "distribute all the money to the poor" in a display of Islamic virtue rather than to enrich his coffers or pay his soldiers' wages.[40] This ideology still rests upon contested notions of male sexuality and dominance, as can be seen in this account of Mahmud "desecrating" the temple of Somnath as narrated by a Pakistani lecturer at Lahore's Government Training College who writes, "The Sultan walked straight into the temple [after the city of Somnath surrendered to his forces]. . . . In the middle of the hall stood the nine-foot high *Ling Mahadev* [a phallic pillar representing the God Shiva] hewn from solid rock. The sight of the ugly *Ling* filled the victor with contempt. With one thrust of his spear, he chopped off its nose. He dealt such a blow with his mace that the *Ling Mahadev* broke into pieces."[41] The imagery here conveys not just desecration, but a symbolic circumcision, nose cutting (which, in Hindu narratives, represents dishonor), and castration. Communalist narratives do not simply suppress the homoerotic content of Mahmud's image; they convert its sexual energy into the violence of domination and castration.

These two opposing ideologies dominate the landscape of South Asia today, one reviling Mahmud as the ultimate villain, the other venerating him as the ultimate hero. In both formulations, an image of Mahmud acts as the "quilting point" for an ideology that equates an aggressive, militant, and violent manhood with communal virility based on emasculation of the rival "other."[42] Political statesmen and military strategists on either side of the newly created Pakistan-India border took up these ideologies to incite war against the "neighboring enemy." In 1947 V. P. Menon warned his Indian government that the newly created state of Pakistan was comparable to Turkic "raiders" who had conquered India in the past: "The raiders are a grave threat to the integrity of India. Ever since the time of Mahmud of Ghazni [*sic*]. . . ." Similarly, former Pakistani prime minister Zulfiqar Bhutto labeled his secret military plan for an attack that would cut Delhi off from Bombay the "Somnath offensive," echoing the famous military adventure in which Mahmud plundered the wealthy Hindu temple at Somnath in Gujarat.[43]

Even less communal versions of Mahmud's fractured image suppress its homoeroticism. Left-leaning Muslim intellectuals and literati in South Asia see Mahmud's rule as the origin of the composite culture of Hindustan, which developed through the Persian language and court life that brought Muslims, Hindus, and Sikhs into a common cultural milieu. They cite Mahmud as the royal patron of a Persian revival in literature and language that set the stage for medieval Hindustani cultural life, including the later development of Urdu and of Indo-Muslim architecture. They also credit him with the creation of a multiethnic, polycommunal standing army. They date the inception of this composite culture to the activities of Mahmud's court in Ghazna, his expansion into India and his annexation of the Punjab: "Mahmud was the first of the great Turko-Persian Emperors. The inspiring motive of his life and the lives of his contemporaries was not Islam but the spirit of the Persian Renaissance. . . . [Mahmud was] a man of refinement and culture with an instinctive admiration for everything beautiful in literature and art."[44] In their view, this was a composite culture that defined masculinity in terms of cultivation and skill in martial fields (such as archery, riding, hunting, and war) as well as literary fields (such as poetry, rhetoric, satire, and administration).

When these various ideologies—each "quilted" around a fractured image of Mahmud—are placed side by side, one fact becomes clear. The British appropriation of political power and civilizational legitimacy forced each of these groups to grope backwards into history to find an original point for their various responses. Whether the response to the British was Hindu-Muslim rivalry or Hindu-Muslim cooperation, Mahmud was the figure around whom the ideologies revolved.

Given how quickly and thoroughly the image of Sultan Mahmud has been transformed, perhaps the emerging gay movement in South Asia can give Mahmud a face-lift and bring Ayaz out of the closet where Victorian morality ruthlessly shoved him. To acknowledge the homoerotic past of Mahmud and Ayaz would give the movement a well-known historical prototype and also show how recently the communalist portraits of Mahmud were invented, and how far they are from capturing an "authentic" historical reality. As Julia Kristeva argues, "The abject is edged with the sublime."[45] Reviving the abjected image of Sultan Mahmud as lover of Ayaz could make him a symbol for rejecting the communalist constructions of culture that carefully control sexuality and gender as well as announce that this abjected image is the site for an uncapturable joy.

Notes

1. Mohammad Habib, *Sultan Mahmud of Ghaznin*, 2nd ed. (Delhi: S. Chand, 1951), 89 and 104.
2. Tarikh-i Bayhaqi, as cited in *Encyclopedia of Islam*, 2nd ed., s.v. "Ayaz."
3. Zulali Khwansari, *Mathnawi-yi Zulali* (Lucknow: Nawal Kishore, 1872). All citations are from this lithographic print, although manuscript copies of this epic are numerous. The text has also been published as *Divan-i Hakim-i Zulali-yi Masnawi fi Ahval-i Sultan Mahmud Ghaznawi o Ayaz* (Tehran: n.p., 1903). Zulali begins his account of Mahmud and Ayaz on page 62, after praising God, blessing the Prophet Muhammad and Imam Ali, flattering his patrons, and waxing eloquent about love. All translations of poems in this chapter are mine unless otherwise stated.
4. Ibid., 75.
5. Ibid., 78–79.
6. Ibid., 130.
7. Ibid., 150.
8. Shantanu Phukan, "None Mad as a Hindu Woman: Contesting Communal Readings of Padmavat," *Comparative Studies of South Asia, Africa, and the Middle East*, 16, no. 1 (1996): 41–54 puts forward this thesis about medieval renditions of the Padmavati narrative that reframed a chronicle of military conquest (between the Sultans of Delhi and the Rajputs at Chittaur) as a story of romantic love. Political chronicles were often retold through the lens of love informed by Sufi vocabulary.
9. Muslih al-Din Sadi Shirazi, *Kuliyat-i Sadi,* ed. Muhammad Ali Furughi (Tehran: Qaqnus, 1374 Hijri [1954–55 C.E.]), 304.
10. See Tariq Rahman, "Boy-Love in the Urdu Ghazal," *Annual of Urdu Studies* 7 (1990): 1–20; C. M. Naim, "The Theme of Homosexual (Pederastic) Love in Pre-Modern Urdu Poetry," in *Studies in the Urdu Ghazal and Prose Fiction*, ed. Muhammad Umar Memon (Madison: South Asian Studies, University of Wisconsin, 1979), 120–42; and Saleem

Kidwai, "Introduction to the Medieval Materials in the Perso-Urdu tradition," in *Same-Sex Love in India: Readings from Literature and History*, ed. Ruth Vanita and Saleem Kidwai (New York: St Martin's Press, 2000), 107–25.

11. Mahmud Lahori, *Mahmud Nama*, alternatively titled *Ishq Nama* (Lahore: Matba Muhammad Husayn, 1263 Hijri [1846–44 C.E.]. A modern work that might be compared to Lahori is Ahmad Suhavli, *Mahmud o Ayaz* (Tehran: n.p., 1999).

12. Lahori, *Mahmud Nama*, first ghazal rhyming in alif.

13. Ibid., second ghazal rhyming in ba'.

14. Ibid., third ghazal rhyming in pa'.

15. Ibid., Lahori, ninth ghazal rhyming in kha'.

16. I use *abject* as Judith Butler does when discussing how abject objects are created in the process of defining empowered subjects. See Butler, *Bodies That Matter: The Discursive Limits of "Sex"* (New York: Routledge, 1993).

17. Section 377 of the Pakistan Penal Code. Section 377 of the Indian Penal Code preserves the same statute, although the recommended punishment varies slightly. On the Pakistan Penal Code from the viewpoint of gender and sexuality, see *Women, Law, and Society: An Action Manual*, ed. Cassandra Balchin (Lahore: Shirkat Gah Women's Resource Center, 1996).

18. Katherine Pratt Ewing, *Arguing Sainthood: Modernity, Psychoanalysis, and Islam* (Durham: Duke University Press, 1997), 217. On the Qalandars, see Ahmet Karamustafa, *God's Unruly Friends: Derwish Groups in the Islamic Later Middle Period, 1200–1550* (Salt Lake City: University of Utah Press, 1994) and Khwaja Shamsuddin Azeemi, *Qalander Conscious*, trans. Maqsood al-Hasan Azeemi (Karachi: al-Kitab Publications, 1992), 7.

19. Sumanta Banerjee, *Dangerous Outcast: The Prostitute in Nineteenth Century Bengal* (Calcutta: Seagull Books, 1998).

20. Altaf Husayn Hali, *Musaddas* (1879), introduction to first edition, cited in Christopher Shackle and Javed Majeed, *Hali's Musaddas: The Ebb and Flow of Islam* (Delhi: Oxford University Press, 1997), 95.

21. Ibid.

22. Quoted in Frances W. Pritchett, *Nets of Awareness: Urdu Poetry and Its Critics* (Karachi: Oxford University Press Pakistan, 1995), 21.

23. These short biographies of Hali and Azad are drawn mainly from Pritchett's *Nets of Awareness*.

24. Hali, *Musaddas*, stanza 249, cited in Shackle and Majeed, *Hali's Musaddas*, 193.

25. One of the most renowned hadith scholars of South Asia, Muhammad ibn Tahir Patani, had denounced this saying as fraudulently attributed to the Prophet in his famous study of inauthentic hadith reports, *Tazkirat al-Mawduat* (Bombay: al-Maktaba al-Qayyima, 1343 Hijri [1924–25 C.E.), 107. He also declared inauthentic many other supposed sayings of the Prophet that were in circulation among Muslim populations, such as "No young man is more shameless than one who allows himself [to be penetrated] from behind" and "The one who perpetrates anal penetration and dies without repenting will be transformed in his grave by Allah into a pig."

26. This idea of questionable accuracy has a long pedigree in South Asia and is traceable to the literary history of Ali Azad Bilgrami, *Subhat al-Marjan fithar Hindustan*, as well as to Abd al-Qadir Badayuni, *Nijat al-Rashid*. Its social function changed totally when backed by British law.

27. Hali, *Muqaddima-yi Sher o Shairi (Introduction to Poetry and Poetics)*, ed. Wajid Qurayshi (Lahore: Maktaba-yi Jadid, 1953). Hali's introduction was first published in 1893.

28. Pritchett, *Nets of Awareness*, 146.

29. Hali, *Hayat-i Sadi (The Life of Sadi)*, ed. Muhammad Ismail Panipati (1886; Lahore: Majlis Taraqqi-yi Adab, 1968), 237–38.

30. Zuhur Shahdad Azhar, *Urdu Ghazal mein Shahid Bazi* (Srinagar: Gulshan, 1995) adopts the term *be fitri* as an ungracefully literal translation of "unnatural."

31. Pritchett, *Nets of Awareness*, 181 and 175.

32. Ibid., 175. The term *pederastic* is Pritchett's own, borrowed from the tradition of condemnatory criticism.

33. Ram Babu Saksena, *A History of Urdu Literature* (1927; Delhi: Asian Educational Services, 1990), 25.

34. Muhammad Sadiq, introduction to *A History of Urdu Literature* (1964; reprt. Delhi: Oxford University Press, 1984).

35. English as translated in Pritchett, *Nets of Awareness*, 186. The novel cited by Pritchett was reprinted in Urdu as Nazir Ahmad, *Taubatunnasuh* (Lucknow: Nawal Kishore, 1922).

36. Paul Hardy, *Mahmud of Ghazna and the Historians* (Lahore: Panjab University, Historical Research Institute, 1963), 6–15. See Scott Kugle, "In a State of Confusion: Rewriting Islamic Law in Colonial South Asia," *Modern Asian Studies*, forthcoming 2001, for an analysis of this dynamic in the field of legal reasoning.

37. Muhammad Iqbal, *Shikwa wa Jawab-i Shikwa* (Delhi: Oxford University Press, 1981); the translation is mine. Many thanks to Owais Khan for pointing out this couplet to me.

38. Muhammad Iqbal, *Bang-I Dara* (Lahore: Javid Iqbal, 1945). Thanks to Shantanu Phukan for sharing this ghazal with me.

39. Muhammad Iqbal, *Bang-I Dara*.

40. Interview with Rana Behzal Iqbal, student at Punjab University, September 7, 1999.

41. Fazl Ahmad, *Mahmood of Ghazni* (Lahore: Shaykh Muhammad Ashraf, 1958; reprinted, 1963), 89–90.

42. Slavoj Žižek, *The Sublime Object of Ideology* (London: Verso, 1989), chapter 3, coins the theoretical term "quilting point" to identify the ungraspable and absent center of ideological formations.

43. Stanley Wolpert, *Zulfi Bhutto of Pakistan: His Life and Times* (New York: Oxford University Press, 1993), 186.

44. Habib, *Sultan Mahmud of Ghazni*, 63 and 70. A professor at Aligarh University, Habib wrote from an explicitly Marxist perspective and dedicated his history to the memory of Mao Zedong. In his view, the depiction of Mahmud as a "religious hero" was possible only when "Islamic ideals were suppressed in order to manufacture Islam into a governing class creed."

45. Julia Kristeva, *Powers of Horror: An Essay in Abjection*, trans. Leon Roudiez (New York: Columbia University Press, 1982), 11.

3

Doganas and Zanakhis

The Invention and Subsequent Erasure of Urdu Poetry's "Lesbian" Voice

Carla Petievich

Teri faryad karun kis se zanakhi tu ne
Yih meri jan jalayi kih Ilahi taubah
To whom can I complain of you, my dear?
God, but hasn't your harshness
scorched my soul!

—Insha'llah Khan Insha

Tis pairu men uthi hui miri jan gayi
mat sita mujh ko dogana, tire qurban gayi
This throb below has nearly killed me
Dear One, don't tease me, you've already done me in!

—Sa'adat Yar Khan Rangin

For nearly three hundred years the Urdu *ghazal* has figured among the most popular art forms of South Asia. Deriving from the Perso-Arabic literary tradition, the ghazal's highly conventionalized aesthetics can tend toward the complex, metaphysical, and philosophical while also satisfying less arcane romantic impulses. As a result, this poetic genre both enjoys great prestige and is also highly popular, being claimed and consumed by diverse audiences. While Urdu as a language has become increasingly associated with Muslim culture in recent decades, the ghazal's popularity and prestige extend well beyond the language community of South Asian Muslims and the territorial bounds of "Hindustan," Urdu's historic heartland, an area roughly comprised of present-day Uttar Pradesh and the area around Delhi. The ubiquitous and extraordinarily popular Hindi film song, for example, is clearly inspired by the ghazal, and many of the most successful songwriters in the Bombay film industry have been Urdu poets.

During the course of its three-hundred-year tradition in northern India (Hindustan), Urdu has been patronized richly by the nobility, a class that has also produced great numbers of poets. Higher value is placed on poetry in both Indic and Islamicate cultures than most other art forms,[1] and historical moments of lavish patronage have given rise to experimentation and innovation as well as to great volumes of literary output. Moments of less patronage have tended, conversely, to see a shrinking and regrouping in the literary canon. During one long moment of high activity, a remarkable genre called *rekhti* was developed; during the hard times of this past century, it has been all but lost to the Urdu audience. This essay discusses rekhti poetry, its rise, and its subsequent suppression. Because of the ways in which it was innovative, its story is best told in the context of normative, canonical Urdu poetry, which was commonly referred to as rekhta during the nineteenth century.[2]

Rekhti (the grammatical feminine counterpart of the word *rekhta*) is considered not at all normative—though it observes a number of classical conventions—and *rekhti* is the name by which all premodern Urdu poetry narrated in the feminine voice has come to be called in Urdu literary scholarship.[3] It is associated with the domestic sphere of socially elite, secluded women during the late eighteenth and early nineteenth centuries, and is alleged by literary critics to speak in the particular idiom of their milieu. Its reputed creator was one Sa'adat Yar Khan "Rangin" ("the Colorful"; 1756–1834),[4] a famous poet associated with Lucknow. Other distinguished authors of rekhti (called *rekhti-go*s, or "rekhti speakers") include Insha 'Allah Khan "Insha" ("God Willing"; d. 1817), Qalandar Bakhsh "Jur'at" (the "Audacious"; d. 1810), and Mir Yar 'Ali Khan "Jan Sahib" ("My Life"; d. 1897).

While literary histories routinely refer to this poetic innovation, they usually dismiss its literary value, and they never reproduce any samples of it—which runs contrary to the conventions of Urdu critical writing. It is important to remember that (1) Rangin is said to have adapted rekhti from the idiom of women of ill repute with whom he consorted in his youth; and (2) the rekhti-go Jan Sahib is said to have dressed himself "like women and recited verses in the accent and gestures peculiar to them, much to the amusement of his audience."[5] This sort of "biographical" information has done much to determine rekhti's place in Urdu literature.

Lucknow Culture and Rekhti's Early Reception

To Rangin and his contemporaries rekhti doubtless represented an exciting innovation in a talent-glutted cultural marketplace. By the end of the eighteenth century the city of Lucknow had established itself firmly as a major cultural center.[6] It was second in status only to Delhi, the Mughal capital. Delhi had seen hard times through much of the eighteenth century due to a series of invasions by Persians, Afghans, Marathas, and Europeans. As the seat of Avadh, the largest spinoff state from a decentralizing Mughal empire, Lucknow was home to legions of refugee nobility and artists from Delhi and environs, even including Mirza Suleiman Shikoh, the Mughal heir apparent. The Mughal prince and the ruling Navabs of Avadh offered lavish patronage to scores of poets and artists. Featured prominently in Lucknow's cultural life were such literary luminaries as Khan-i "Arzu" (d. 1756), Mirza Muhammad Rafi "Sauda" (d. 1781), Mir Taqi "Mir" (d. 1810), and Shaikh Ghulam Hamdani "Mushafi" (d. 1824), in addition to the rekhti poets already mentioned. Great monuments were being built, schools and centers of Islamic learning were thriving, and literature was in ferment. Some of Delhi's erstwhile elite were actively engaged in the process of "perfecting" Urdu in Lucknow as an indigenous literary language to rival Persian.[7] The standard literary genres of Perso-Arabic tradition were flourishing under Urdu masters, and the sense of rivalry among them for patronage drove cultural production to new heights.

It was into this milieu that rekhti was introduced by Sa'adat Yar Khan "Rangin," the son of a Persian nobleman, who had migrated to Lucknow around the turn of the nineteenth century. By way of introduction to his literary innovation, Rangin explains that, in the course of a wild and misspent youth, he consorted extensively with the famous courtesans of the day.[8] In their company he developed familiarity with and appreciation of their particular idiom. The pithiness of their expressions and their wit so impressed him that he decided to compose poetry in this "Ladies' Language" (*begumati zaban*) and to call his collected poems "rekhti." The combination of its feminine narrator and its idiom made rekhti a distinct genre. Indications are that this immediately popular style of poetry was accepted quite unproblematically into Lucknow's thriving milieu. Anecdotal sources indicate that Rangin recited his rekhti for the general delight and delectation of the Lakhnavi elite.[9] No less a literary master than Rangin's bosom buddy, Insha 'Allah Khan "Insha," composed a collection of such poems;[10] and the poet Jan Sahib composed at least two full collections of rekhti, on which his literary reputation largely rests.[11] The few extant scholarly sources offer numerous other names identified as versifiers in rekhti,[12] though few of them are still known today. The very fact that so many names can be found, and so little poetic output can be connected with them, speaks volumes about how attitudes toward this poetry have changed. Before discussing it any further, let us have a taste of rekhti. Here is an example from Rangin that takes the form of a *sarapa* (literally "head-to-foot"), in which the beloved's beauty is enumerated by the lover/narrator, the term for whom is *ashiq*:

> All decked out, my other half is something special:
> Her complexion's golden, her figure splendid to match!
>
> That forehead gem's a killer! the braided coif a wonder:
> Her perfumed hair and fragrant forelock choice.
>
> In speech she's like no other, from toenails to hair-plait unique:
> Those powdered-black teeth complete the picture!
>
> How lovely on her body lies her lace chemise! Her head-scarf's really super—
> Those tight pajamas and bodice torment me!
>
> Even her blandishments enchant me; her side-glances cast calamity
> The winks are cruel, her coolness private torture.
>
> How could the heart not be ensnared! Dear One, have mercy!
> Your discourse casts a spell, your waist is gorgeous, our intimacy exquisite.
>
> Those foot slippers are gilded a rare, brilliant red;
> Tall and willowy is her build but deliciously curvy her thighs!
>
> She's unlike all others in all things, her speech strange and marvelous!
> Her costume distinct from all others, her adornments exquisite.
>
> How might I ever convey her to you, Rangin!
> From hand to foot she's formidable, hued in henna![13]

Rekhti's Reception by Modern Critics

In contrast to the apparently unproblematic early reception of rekhti, twentieth-century critical writing on the subject has been characterized by moralistic judgments and a great deal of evasion.[14] It has received very little scholarly attention in a literary culture nearly obsessed with its own past and present; the genre's name is known to aficionados, but none of them demonstrates familiarity with the poetic texts. Rekhti does not appear on the syllabi for university-level degree programs;[15] and with one exception (an expurgated anthology), it cannot be purchased nowadays in published form.[16] Although references can be found to several critical works published between 1930 and 1989, successive visits over the past few years to Urdu bazaars and institutions dedicated to the promotion of Urdu have yielded almost nothing.[17] Institutions dedicated to republishing out-of-print collected works of classical poets omit the rekhti as well as other genres determined by publishers to be inappropriate for common consumption, thus leaving "unfinished" the advertised "complete works" of a number of canonical poets.

The Majlis-i Taraqqi-i Adab (Society for the Promotion of Literature/Culture) in Lahore is a particular offender. The organization is to be lauded for the beautiful editions it has produced, during the past years, of the works of eighteenth- and nineteenth-century poets; but its director has told me that there are no plans to complete the final volumes of complete works of poets like Insha, who was highly reputed as a rekhta-go although he also wrote rekhti. The *Kulliyat-i Jur'at* (*Collected Works*), including his two infamous *Chapti Namas* (*Tribade Testimonials*), had to be published in Italy and is still not available in South Asia. Indian or Pakistani scholars of Urdu must travel to Europe or North America, at great expense and hardship, to avail themselves of the meager scholarly resources in existence.

The one copy of Rangin's rekhti collection (called *Divan-i Angekhta*) obtained during the course of research into this genre is held not in India or Pakistan, but in the British Library in London. Doubtless there are copies here and there in private collections—and excavations are ongoing by this researcher—but rekhti is a body of poetry that is clearly not available to the general public; whereas rekhta, Urdu poetry in general, especially in ghazal form, is just about ubiquitous.

Secondary materials are somewhat more available than primary, and consist mostly of comments in literary histories of Urdu. The following is a fair representation of Urdu criticism's more benign conventional wisdom on the subject: "Rekhti is a *badnam* (disreputable) genre of Urdu poetry which is thought to serve especially for the expression of women's particular emotions and generic concerns in women's idiom."[18] A slightly less benign, yet also representative, pronouncement comes from Ali Jawad Zaidi, who writes, "Rekhti is mostly a woman speaking to another about her delusions and anxieties, the infidelity of husbands or the daring of her companions who ventured into social taboos. . . . Rekhti never attained respectability and often sunk [*sic*] into vulgarity, catering for those who sought decadent pleasure. It is, however, useful for a study of the miserable life the womenfolk led under the feudal order, and the resultant discontent and the evil it bred. Linguistically, it provides a convenient collection of the idioms of the women of the time."[19]

The discrepancy between early enthusiasm and later distaste for rekhti may seem at first glance to be anomalous. But a judicious probe into the cultural constructions of gender resolves much of that anomaly, especially shedding light on the logic of its rejection by Urdu literature's modern custodians.

Critics who dismiss rekhti as decadent might be alluding to its generally informal/immodest speech, or to content such as flirtations with servant boys, or to fantasies about males from outside the household espied across the rooftops—all of which do find a place in the texts uncovered thus far. More than its casual tone and heterosexual naughtiness, however, the problem with rekhti probably lies in the open secret (among pitifully few cognoscenti) that a certain amount of its content is not only erotic but female to female. The previously quoted "decadent pleasure" of "venturing into social taboos" must surely allude to the erotic relationship between rekhti's feminine 'ashiq and "her" beloved, manifest in the sarapa presented above.

My reading is that the critics draw no meaningful distinction between "lesbianism" and the "particular emotions of women"; to them, these emotions constitute "decadent pleasure" and are necessarily socially taboo, rendering rekhti illegitimate poetry. Thus, by deductive reasoning, polite discourse and legitimate poetry are rendered the domain of men. So it should come as no surprise that in our time rekhti has become a thoroughly marginalized body of literature. One of the great ironies in all this is that, though narrated by one "woman" who usually addresses another in intimate terms, our only existing records indicate that rekhti was recited by male poets (sometimes in female dress) to a male audience.[20] Women were, as one writer has observed, quite incidental to this "women's" poetry.[21] Not only that, but none of the scholars to have mentioned, let alone analyzed, rekhti in Urdu critical literature has been a woman. This would not have been particularly remarkable during the late eighteenth and nineteenth centuries, since formal Urdu has been, and remains, a male arena. What does seem remarkable is that two centuries ago, during an expansive period in Urdu culture, men were open to exploring the notion of a distinct female experience, despite whatever necessary limitations their own gender placed on the exploration; but during the past century, that openness has been replaced by an anxiety so deep as to lead Urdu's (still male) elite to condemn any poetic expression—real or imagined—of women's experience in the feminine voice as delusional, decadent, even evil.

Does the existence of rekhti as a literary phenomenon mean that, within the milieu that produced it, lesbian desire was accepted as an inevitable product of life lived in seclusion? Can this expression be seen as a site of resistance, as at least one scholar has suggested, based on interviews with courtesans of Lucknow in the 1970s?[22] Despite the obsessions with honor and respectability that govern the seclusion of women, how do the expressive idiom and "concerns" of courtesans and socially elite women come to be conflated in rekhti, especially when it is a basic assumption of gender segregation that respectable women and courtesans are essentially different kinds of women with very different concerns, and that the "protection" offered veiled women is that they will not be mistaken for women of questionable repute? One is obliged to conclude that those who have developed these critical categories for understanding rekhti have reflected very little, if at all, on the concerns of living women in any given social category, and have certainly failed to incorporate into their formulations the reality that there are many different kinds of lived experience among any given society's women.[23]

The "Lesbianism" of Rekhti

> Don't try to talk me into 'it': scram! get outta here!
> What are you calling "love"?
> What kind of affection is this?
>
> This affection and love are bride and groom, Insha:
> One's ill-fated, the other hell-bent!
> —Insha

Erudite Urdu readers have asserted that rekhti's scholarly value lies in the catalogue it constitutes of names of female dress, adornments, household furnishings, or particular idiomatic expressions of an emergent dialect—that of secluded women; yet Rangin is said to have learned the idiom not from respectably secluded women, but from courtesans! No other critic seems to have observed this irony, or to have seen fit to comment on it. One is tempted to deduce that these readers and commentators reduce rekhti to catalog value partly out of reluctance to take on the subtext of its (lesbian) reputation, as is indicated in the following statement by Dr. Sabir Ali Khan, in a book on rekhti's alleged "inventor," Rangin: "According to [Urdu poets] what is meant by rekhti is poetry in which, in women's idiom, are versified the depravity, affairs and emotions of women who are sinful or have gone astray."[24]

In fact, contra the claim that this poetry is "useful for a study of the miserable life the womenfolk led under the feudal order," rekhti does not paint a "miserable" picture at all of women's secluded life. While racy, charming and idiomatic, and clearly set in the women's quarters, much of it is hardly obscene. Almost none of it, moreover, is explicitly sexual, let alone explicitly lesbian. Take, for example, the following:

> Noble Lady, just go to the tomb of Ali Kiblain
> and fill up the tank there with milk, Noble Lady.
>
> Today's the new moon—go bring from the market
> all the ingredients to make an offering to Fatima, Noble Lady.
>
> Beat me if, when you bring them back, I've budged:
> Sit face to face and have me cook, Noble Lady.
>
> When everything's cooked go call the married women
> See to it that they are fed, Noble Lady.
>
> When they've finished eating decorate their hands with henna—
> then ask them to pray for this:
>
> that whoever has tormented this poor servant unduly
> shall each get what they've got coming, Noble Lady![25]

Here the content is not at all suggestive of sexuality, but does indicate "women's culture" in the rituals described, the terms of address employed, and the idiomatic expressions. In fairness to the critics, it could be said that ultimately the expressed concerns of the narrator are frivolous, since they amount to revenge.

In other poems there is some suggestiveness, and more of the subculture reflected in the "Noble Lady" poem:

When did my *Zanakhi* last come to my house!
Poor me, when's the last time I had a bath!

That girl's been angry for a long time:
When have we ever cleared up matters between us!

When I sent the nurse round to her place
The wretch wasn't at home.

Truth is never scorched by fire:
When will this great truth be emblazoned!

When did she last apply henna, Rangin,
kneading my hands and feet![26]

Zanakhi and Dogana

The relationship depicted above (though currently on the outs) is clearly one of intimacy, perhaps—but not explicitly—sexual. Its "lesbianism" is marked by the term *zanakhi*, employed in the first verse to indicate the absent friend who is longed for. This and *dogana* are terms particular to rekhti and indicate a relationship of intimacy that extends to eroticism. While there is little explicit lesbian content in rekhti,[27] erotic relationships between the narrator and her beloved "other" are overwhelmingly alluded to by employing these terms. They are generally not found in dictionaries—especially not in contemporary reference works[28]—and are nearly untranslatable. Here is how Rangin is said to have explained the terms, in the glossary he provided by way of introducing his rekhti collection (*Divan-i Angekhta*):

Dogana—Having ordered almonds from the bazaar, they (feminine plural) shell them. Those almonds from which twin, or double, nuts are extracted, usually are formed in such a way one is implanted within the other. This implanted nut is called "masculine" (*nar*) and the one in which it is embedded is called "feminine" (*madah*). Then an unknown person (*shakhs*) is summoned and, giving him the two almond fruits, one of them tells him, "Give me one of the fruits and give to her the other." The one in whose hand he places the *nar* fruit then thinks of herself as the "man" (*mard*) and the one in whose hand the "feminine" fruit is placed becomes the "feminine"and they call each other "*dogana*" or "twin."

Zanakhi—After slaughtering a chicken and having it cooked, they (feminine plural) sit down to eat together. In this chicken's breast is a bifurcated bone (the wishbone) which they refer to as the "*zanakh.*" Simultaneously each of them takes one branch of the bone and pulls it toward herself. The one whose end snaps is the feminine and the one whose end remains whole is called the masculine, and if the wishbone snaps in the middle, then they order another chicken to be slaughtered and repeat the exercise *so that it may be fully determined who is masculine and who feminine.*"[29]

As a point of interest, the *Farhang-i Asafiyyah* mentions the exercise with a pigeon's or chicken's wishbone, citing an outside authority, referred to as "Faisal," to explain it as a ritual whereby a relationship of "girlfriendliness" (*saheli*) or sisterhood (*bahnape ka rishta*) is bonded. This citation omits the gender-role assignment based on its outcome. The woman in whose hand the larger bone ends up becomes the "big sister" and her counterpart the "little sister" (*badi* and *chhoti bahn*).[30] The *Farhang* itself says, "In the parlance of debauched women they say this of a woman who breaks a wishbone with another woman and thereby becomes her companion and confidante (*hamrah-o hamraz*)" but again quotes Faisal as saying, "This custom is not practiced by debauched women, but rather by women of the harem (*begumat-i qila'*) and that's why the editor of the *Lughatun Nisa* (*Dictionary of Women's Speech*) writes, 'It was a custom of sequestered women that, having established a relationship in this fashion one would address the other in such a way as sisters do not speak, eg. one calling the other [by such terms of endearment as] '*dil jan*' (heart's life-breath) or '*jan-i man*' (my life) or '*dushman*' (enemy) or '*zanakhi*.' The *zanakhi* relationship was counted stronger and more significant than other relationships. When they would decide to make a *zanakhi* relationship with someone, then they would come together and break the wishbone of a pigeon or chicken, as if to say, 'In this way true friendship (*pakki yari*) is established.' "[31]

Only the earliest commentator, Rangin (courtesy of Sabir Ali Khan, who reproduced his definitions), discusses the gendered nature of these designations, thereby adding a level of explicitness to them that later lexicographers leave to the reader's imagination. Rangin's definition confirms stereotyped views about how men view lesbian acts insofar as its voyeurism concerns itself with how to assign gender distinctions to the two intimates. It does not seem to occur to Rangin—or, by implication, to his intended audience—that sexual acts are not inherently gender marked. How else to understand the explained principle behind the definitions above, "to fully determine who is masculine and who feminine," when the terms *dogana* and *zanakhi* themselves are not gender-marked?

Perhaps of greater interest than why we need to know who does what to whom, and what that means in terms of gender roles, is that the Urdu critics' dismissive explanations of "lesbian" eroticism as a "depraved" by-product of "the feudal order" deflect the reader's attention away from the critique of patriarchy crying out to be made here.[32] One might also note that blaming "lesbianism" on feudalism, though quite consistent with the analytical terms of the Progressive Writers Association, is profoundly homophobic. It seems to this reader that rekhti is better explained as a by-product of patriarchy's cultural constructions than as a by-product of feudalism's gender oppression. After all, the gender oppression of patriarchy is alive and well in postfeudal South Asia and the rest of the world, and continues to be amply documented and witnessed. To undertake a critique of patriarchy we need to return to a discussion of standard ghazal convention.

Rekhti, 'Ishq, and Ambiguity

Perhaps ultimately the crucial problem posed by rekhti is this: When a "woman" addresses an unambiguously feminine beloved, "she" challenges the central axiom of Urdu love poetry; namely, that the beloved be of ambiguous identity, both in terms of gender and in human versus divine terms (in other words, the beloved might, theoretically, be human or divine). This ambiguity, while ostensibly gender neutral, proves to be less than benign. Conventionally and in material fact Urdu poetry has been the provenance of men and its domain masculine: the poets are men, the narrator-lover/hero ('ashiq) is male, and the beloved is referred to in the masculine gender. Even when physical attributes are described and strongly suggest a female person, the beloved is referred to as "he."[33] Here are two examples of ambiguous desire commonly expressed in *rekhta,* one more abstract and one less so (Both were written by the great Mirza Ghalib [1797–1869]):

> *Yih na thi hamari qismat kih visal-i yar hota*
> *Agar aur jite rahte yahi intizar hota*
> It was not my destiny to unite with the Beloved, yet
> Had I gone on living, I would still have kept on waiting.

> *Nind us ki hai dimagh us ka hai raten us ki hain*
> *Teri zulfen jis ke bazu par pareshan ho ga'in*
> Sleep is [his], peace of mind is [his], the very nights are [his]
> Upon whose shoulder lie strewn your scattered tresses.[34]

In neither of these verses do we see compromised the ambiguity of gender, nor— in the first verse—the ambiguity of the beloved's human versus divine identity. Anyone can claim them and identify with the desire they both express,[35] be the lover male or female.

The standard explanation for this masculine gender exclusivity is that Urdu adapted the ghazal genre from Persian, in which personal pronouns and verbal conjugations are not gender marked. Thus the masculine gender of the Urdu ghazal actually serves as neuter, allowing the Urdu ghazal to conform more closely with its Persian counterpart and predecessor. Another common explanation for why an often obviously implied female beloved is referred to as "he" is that it protects her from exposure in a society obsessed with female honor and chastity.

These explanations simply do not wash. In a highly conventionalized genre there is already built-in anonymity for both lover and beloved. After all, both are personae! We must look elsewhere for a plausible explanation of this convention. And while it must be speculative at best, we can conclusively observe that when masculine humans go in search of the divine (probably conceived of as genderless but referred to in the masculine) there is little place left for female humans, or even for the feminine principle. Rekhta has served for centuries as a central icon of cultural identity and self-esteem among South Asian Muslims. Its elevated value hinges on the aesthetic of love (*'ishq*) as the most noble of human endeavors, and this aesthetic was developed over centuries in the context of a rich mystical tradition, that of Sufism. Perfecting oneself as a lover is seen as the only true path toward unity with the divine; and the presumption that the ultimate beloved is the divine has been Urdu love poetry's best defense against the conservative forces of religious authority that might otherwise have tried to squelch it, along with other arts manifesting extravagant passion. Such a defense has been augmented by conventions that insist that the physical aspects of passion remain sublimated. Claiming the human-divine divide as its ultimate subject,[36] rekhta is a poetry of love in exquisite separation, and acknowledgment of human reality as gendered does not enter into it.

Not so with rekhti. Neither sublimated passion nor love in separation—let alone gender ambiguity—are its forte. The emotions expressed are understood as resulting from the social reality of women being thrown together, which is exactly the opposite of the separation on which "true love" is predicated. Rarely is melancholy achieved, though these lines may attract the ghazal enthusiast:

> How shall I break this intimate bond?
> How can I turn my face away from love?
>
> There's no respite from wiping away the tears:
> The cuffs of my sleeves need to be wrung out—but how?
>
> Rangin, having shattered my fragile heart
> now asks, "how shall I piece it back together?[37]

Even so, we must be careful in our analysis before rushing to celebrate rekhti as the corrective to rekhta's conceptual exclusions. It may be tempting for the feminist reader of rekhti to see in it a private world where women, obliged to live in seclusion, resist gender oppression by discovering rich emotional and erotic possibilities with one another. And if the authors of this poetry were indeed secluded women commenting on their own experiences, such an interpretation of rekhti would be far more persuasive. Alas, this is just not the case. We cannot look to rekhti for insight into what it means for women, living together, to develop a literature of same-sex eroticism. Intellectual honesty requires that we look there instead for insight into what it means for men, who keep women secluded and socialize with other men, to invent a parody of their own idealized love literature, and to perform it for other men while impersonating women. This critique of patriarchy need not presuppose malice on the part of the male poets and their audience because the way patriarchy is working here is structural rather than strategically deployed.

Yet while rekhti may have been undertaken in some sympathy for charting the particularities of female experience, it remains a medium of expression in which humans gendered male purport to represent the experience of humans gendered female, and their insight is limited to what they know about women without having lived as women. The same cannot be said for the position from which a poet expresses 'ishq in rekhta. Once rekhti was created and an allegedly female poetic space carved out therein, the exclusion I have been discussing was rendered complete.

Ironically, some of the raciest rekhti was written not by its "inventor," Sa'adat Yar Khan "Rangin," but by two other poets of Lucknow, Insha 'Allah Khan "Insha" and Qalandar Bakhsh "Jur'at."

The Suppression of Rekhti

As mentioned earlier, employment of the terms *dogana* and *zanakhi* constitute overwhelmingly the "lesbian" content of those rekhti verses that are extant today. Use of even these largely unglossed terms of address seems to have been enough to "spook" the Urdu literati. Examples of rekhti in historical surveys of Urdu litera-ture are all but absent. Furthermore, biographical and other potentially illuminat-ing information from rekhti poets and their contemporaries have been preserved not in Urdu but in Persian, with one partial exception.[38] While Persian was indeed the language of literary criticism used for Urdu until the end of the nineteenth cen-tury, it is not nearly so widely taught today, and the decision to keep primary infor-mation in Persian further excludes potential readers, mediating between them and the text, much as racy excerpts from Sanskrit literature such as the Atharva Veda were rendered into Greek or Latin by Orientalist scholars ostensibly translating the texts into English to afford wider dissemination.

Rangin's playful sarapa (presented earlier) may not strike us as particularly lofty or noble, but it hardly seems depraved. Its appeal lies in the entertainment value of a lusty description through the gaze of the admirer, as in any sarapa; but it must be acknowledged that the sarapa itself, even as a genre of rekhta, is marginalized. The reason, again, is that its concreteness of imagery in describing the beloved mil-itates against the ghazal's cherished ambiguity. Its elaborate description encour-ages us to visualize the beloved as female. Not only would that visualization be inconsistent with normative Islam's understanding of the divine, it echoes rather uncomfortably with the idolatry of Hinduism.[39]

Much reformist literature during the past century has focused on the feminiza-tion of Urdu/Indo-Muslim culture as a problem to be eradicated.[40] In the widely popular *Bihishti Zewar,* a handbook first produced about a century ago but still given to young Indo-Muslim women as part of their dowry, the author particularly skewers customs practiced by Muslim women that are associated more with indige-nous folk culture than with normative Islam.[41] There is little doubt that rekhti's suppression resulted from anxieties about the feminine in general as much as from a prudish aversion to lesbian expression. The explicitness of the feminine was seen to weaken Indo-Muslim culture.

Ironically, male homoeroticism, though controversial, also has a well-docu-mented history in ghazal literature. In a way, then, the beloved being protected by the ghazal's gender conventions is likelier to be male than female; such con-ventionalized anonymity reinforces male privilege more than it protects the repu-tation(s) of women! C. M. Naim claims that some later Lakhnavi rekhti reflects a "genuine concern for women's lives in domestic confinement"; but that has not been demonstrated sufficiently to save the genre from the hatchet man's block. Critical embarrassment surrounding male homoeroticism in the ghazal coincides with the suppression both of rekhti and of other aspects of Indo-Muslim culture deemed vulnerable by reformists to the accusation of effeminacy emanating from British colonial discourse.[42] Getting rid of the explicitly feminine and determin-ing that the masculine is ambiguous protects Indo-Muslim culture from hostile colonial critiques without precluding an expressive space for male homoeroticism. In better times, at the zenith of Indo-Muslim culture's prestige, there was room for extending the creative realm into private spaces, including those domestic and those exclusive of the masculine. Rangin, Insha, Jur'at, and Jan Sahib lived in such times. Twentieth-century writers and critics have not, and rekhti, a signifier of such space—whether "authentic" or not—can apparently be afforded no longer.

In closing, for an illustration of how powerful the calumny attached to lesbian expression has been, it is instructive to look at the experience of one of the twentieth century's most esteemed Urdu writers, Ismat Chughtai. "Lihaf" ("The Quilt") is perhaps her best-known short story, though one could well argue that it is not her best.[43] It is about a lesbian relationship enacted in the *zenana* of a noble household and witnessed by a young girl. The British colonial government charged the story with obscenity in 1942, and alleged that Chughtai had offended the sensibilities of a particular community.

The lawsuit was ultimately unsuccessful, but the case dogged Chughtai for the rest of her life. In a late interview, questioned about "Lihaf," Ismat claimed that she had been completely naive as to what lesbianism was when she wrote the story. She went on to denounce lesbianism, even going so far as to say that had she understood what she was writing about she would not have written the story! Apparently, she also mentioned that she met the Begum—the story's protagonist—some years later and was happy to see that the Begum was happily remarried, with a child in her arms.[44]

Disingenuous as such disclaimers surely are, they speak volumes about how constrained the creative environment has become since the time when Rangin first "invented" rekhti.

Notes

1. In a different but related context, Shoaib Hashmi suggests that drama has been neglected by Muslim patrons not so much because of Islamic injunctions against idolatry as because "Muslim civilization was not interested in the drama, one way or another, and the *dramatic conflict was worked out instead in poetry.*" See "Women in Drama," in *Women: Myth and Realities*, ed. Kishwar Naheed (Lahore: Sang-e Meel, 1994), 299–314, emphasis added.

2. *Rekhta* means "that which is scattered"; "unscattered" poetry was that written in Persian, the prestige language for Indo-Islamicate poetry for several centuries. For Urdu's naming history, see S. R. Faruqi, "Unprivileged Power: The Strange Case of Persian (and Urdu) in Nineteenth Century India," *Annual of Urdu Studies* 13 (1998): 3–30.

3. Cf. *Firozul Lughat (Urdu Jadid)* (Lahore: Ferozsons, n.d.), 388: "that verse which is spoken in women's idiom"; John T. Platts, *A Dictionary of Urdu, Classical Hindi, and English* (Oxford: Oxford University Press, 1893), 611: "Hindustani verse written in the language of women, and expressing the sentiments, etc. peculiar to them."

4. Andalib Shadani discusses the rival claims for Insha'Allah Khan Insha as the creator of rekhti; see "Rekhti ka Mujid," in *Tahqiq ki Roshni Men* (Lahore: Shaikh Ghulam Ali and Sons, 1963), 91–104. Ironically, Shadani quotes Insha's treatise on poetics, *Darya-i Latafat* (1807), which seems to support Rangin as the inventor of rekhti.

5. M. Sadiq, *A History of Urdu Literature*, 2nd ed. (London: Oxford University Press, 1984), 197.

6. For Lucknow's milieu, see Carla Petievich, *Assembly of Rivals: Delhi, Lucknow and the Urdu Ghazal* (New Delhi: Manohar, 1992), and C. M. Naim and Carla Petievich, "Urdu in Lucknow, Lucknow in Urdu," in *Lucknow: Memories of a City*, ed., Violette Graff (New Delhi: Oxford University Press, 1997).

7. For this aspect of Lucknow's history see Abdul Halim Sharar, *Guzishtah Lakhna'o*, translated by E. S. Harcourt and Husain Fakhr as *Lucknow: The Last Phase of an Oriental Culture* (Boulder: Westview Press, 1976). See also Insha Allah Khan "Insha's" *Darya-i Latafat* (1807), purportedly the first linguistic and literary treatise on Urdu.

8. While the histories associate courtesan culture especially with Lucknow, it flourished all over India. Rangin speaks of himself as a poet of Shahjahanabad (Delhi), though later

histories associate him with Lucknow. See his *Majalis-i Rangin* (Lucknow: Naval Kishore, 1929).

9. Sabir Ali Khan, *Sa'adat Yar Khan Rangin* (Karachi: Anjuman-i Taraqqi-i Urdu, 1956), 95.

10. See his *Divan-i Rekhti* in the *Kulliyat-i Insha* (Lucknow: Naval Kishore, 1876), 185–219.

11. Dr. Mubin Naqvi, *Tarikh-i Rekhti ma'a Divan-i Jan Sahib* (Allahabad: Matba Anwar Ahmadi, n.d.).

12. See especially Irfan Abbasi, *Tazkirah-i Sho'ara-i Rekhti* (Lucknow: Nasim Book Depot, 1989); Mubin Naqvi, *Tarilch-i Relehti*; Sibt-i Muhammad Naqvi, *Intikhab-i Rekhti* (Lucknow: Urdu Akademi, 1983); and Khalil Ahmed Siddiqi, *Rekhti ka Tanqidi Mutala'ah* (Lucknow: Nasim Book Depot, 1974).

13. Divan Rangin-o Insha (Bedayun: Nizami Press, 1924), 48–49.

14. This is evident in standard literary histories as well as lesser-known works. See T. Graham Bailey, *A History of Urdu Literature* (Calcutta: Associated Press, 1927); Ralph Russell, "The Pursuit of the Urdu Ghazal," *Journal of Asian Studies* 29, no. 1: 107–24; Sadiq, *A History*; Ram Babu Saksena, *A History of Urdu Literature* (Allahabad, n.p., 1940); Annemarie Schimmel, *Classical Urdu Literature from the Beginning to Iqbal* (Wiesbaden: Otto Harrassowitz, 1975); and Ali Jawad Zaidi, *A History of Urdu Literature* (New Delhi: Sahitya Akademi, 1993).

15. Rekhti is omitted from current M.A. syllabi at both Delhi University and Punjab University, Lahore.

16. Tamkeen Kazmi, *Tazkirah-i Rekhti* (Hyderabad: n.p., 1930) and Irfan Abbasi, *Tazkirah-i Sho'ara-i Rekhti*. Neither was to be found in any bookshop or Urdu library in Delhi or Lahore during sustained efforts by this writer between November 1997 and August 1999. The one exception is Sibt-i Muhammad Naqvi's *Intikhab-i Rekhti* (Lucknow: Uttar Pradesh Urdu Akademi, 1983), a selected anthology.

17. During a July 1999 interview with the director of one such major institution where I was not granted access to the archive, he apologized that there would be nothing in his custody of use to me, and referred me to a gentleman known to have a large collection of pornography! The director is himself a distinguished man of Urdu letters.

18. Hafeez Qateel, "Dakan Men Rekhti ka Irtiqa'," *Majalla-i Usmaniya,* Dakani Adab (1964): 139.

19. Ali Jawad Zaidi, *A History*, 137.

20. Perhaps the best-known example occurs in Farhatullah Beg's depiction of a poetic assembly in *Dilli ki Akhiri Shama'*, translated by Akhter Qamber as *The Last Musha'irah of Delhi* (Delhi: Orient Longman, 1979).

21. Adrienne Copithorne, "Poet in Drag: The Phenomenon of Rekhti," unpublished paper, 1998.

22. Veena Talwar Oldenburg, "Lifestyles of Resistance: the Courtesans of Lucknow," in Graffe ed., *Lucknow: Memories of a City*, 136–54.

23. See Indrani Chatterjee, *Gender, Law, and Slavery in Colonial India* (Delhi: Oxford University Press, 1999) for a welcome corrective.

24. Sabir Ali Khan, *Sa'adat Yar Khan Rangin*, 406.

25. *Divan Rangin-o Insha* (Badayun: Nizami Press, 1924), 58–59.

26. *Divan Rangin-o Insha*, 26–27.

27. The one clear exception is in Jur'at's *Chapti-Namas (Tribad Testimonials)*, translated recently in Ruth Vanita and Saleem Kidwai, eds., *Same-Sex Love in India: Readings from Literature and History* (New York: St. Martin's Press 2000), 222–25.

28. One exception is the *Farhang-i Asafiyyah*, compiled Sayyid Ahmed Dahlavi (New Delhi: Government of India, n.d.) vol. 5, 219 for *dogana*; and 241 for *zanakhi*. The only other published source for these definitions of which I am aware is that of Sabir Ali Khan, *Sa'adat Yar Khan Rangin*, who seems to have worked from the introduction to Rangin's *Divan-i Angekhta*, the fourth and final section of his *Nau-Ratan-i Rangin,* in the British

Museum's India Office Library during the 1940s. I have found no published edition of this work, nor seen one referenced in the critical literature.

29. Cited in Sabir Ali Khan, *Sa'adat Yar Khan Rangin*, 215–16; emphasis added.

30. Here the *Farhang-i Asafiyyah* is quoting the author of the *Farhang-i Asar*.

31. *Muhazzub ul-Lughat* vol. 6 (Lucknow: Matbu' ah-i Sarfaraz laumi Press, 1969), 241.

32. In addition to Zaidi's remarks in *A History*, see Krishan Chander's analysis of Ismat Chughtai's "lesbian" short story "Lihaf" ("The Quilt") in the introduction to Chughtai's short-story collection *Choten* (*Wounds*) 2nd ed. (Delhi: Saqi Book Depot, 1942).

33. This problematic is discussed in some detail in Petievich "The Feminine Voice in the Urdu Ghazal," *Indian Horizons* 39, nos. 1–2 (1990): 25–41. See also a more recent discussion by Nuzhat Abbas, "Conversing to/with Shame: Translation and Gender in the Urdu Ghazal," *Annual of Urdu Studies* 14 (1999): 135–49.

34. *Divan-i Ghalib*, ed. Ali Sardar Jafri (New Delhi: Jiya Prakashan, 1969), 85.

35. This was also somewhat the case in the *Hamd* above, though references to female figures and knowledge that the poem is considered rekhti might incline the reader to assume that the narrator is female.

36. '*Ishq* expressed toward the divine beloved is known as "true love" ('*ishq-i haqiqi*); while love for a human, being only an approximation of divine love, is called "metaphorical love" ('*ishq-i majazi*).

37. *Divan Rangin-o Insha*, verses 1, 2, and 5.

38. Sabir Ali Khan occasionally presents parallel translation from Persian into Urdu.

39. Adorning the deity (*sringar*) is a common Hindu ritual; and the head-to-toe description of the beloved seems to echo such poetic motifs from Sanskrit as *keshadipadavarnana*, or *nakh-shikh* in Hindi, in which a beautiful woman (or a deity) is described in elaborate detail, fashioning a sort of verbal sculpture.

40. See especially my discussions of the alleged "effeminacy" of Lucknow's culture in *Assembly of Rivals*.

41. For a fuller discussion of this text see Barbara Daly Metcalf, *Perfecting Women: Maulana Ashraf 'Ali Thanawi's Bihishti Zewar: A Partial Translation with Commentary* (Berkeley and Los Angeles: University of California Press, 1992).

42. I have written widely on the issue of colonial discourse and canon formation; see Carla Petievich, "The Feminine Voice in the Urdu Ghazal," 25–41; "Dakani's Radha-Krishna Imagery and Canon Formation in Urdu," in *The Banyan Tree: Essays on Early Literature in New Indo-Aryan Languages*, ed. Mariola Offredi (New Delhi: Manohar, 2000); and "Making Manly Poetry: The Construction of a 'Golden Age' in Urdu," in *Rethinking Early Modern India*, ed. Richard B. Barnett" (New Delhi: Manohar, forthcoming). See also recent discussions of this phenomenon in S. R. Faruqi, "Unprivileged Power: The Strange Case," 3–32; and Frances W. Pritchett, *Nets of Awareness* (Berkeley and Los Angeles: University of California Press, 1993).

43. See Petievich, "Representations of Female Sexuality in Modern Urdu Fiction," *B.C. Asian Review* nos. 3–4 (1991): 323–38.

44. I am indebted to Ruth Vanita for the report on the subsequent meeting of the two women (personal communication, June 2000).

4

Alienation, Intimacy, and Gender

Problems for a History of Love in South Asia

Indrani Chatterjee

Notwithstanding the debate around the presence and meanings of "homosexuality" in ancient Roman and Greek societies, there is one theme on which most of those who disagree can concur—the stratified nature of such societies, containing slaves, helots, and citizens.[1] This historical bedrock makes it possible to conduct the kind of debate that has emerged within that particular field of historical studies. For precolonial India, a history that puts slavery not at the margins of society but at its center is still to be written. The ubiquity of slaves, beginning their lives as social and natal isolates, through many epochs in the recorded Indian past, warrants such a study. Slavery in precolonial India would need to be carefully separated from the institution identified with eighteenth- and nineteenth-century plantation economies so that it would not be conflated with issues of *violence* but with a dialectic of *alienation and intimacy* originating in peaceful sales and commerce characteristic of the South Asian evidence. Reading sexual relations in the Indian past through the lens of slavery adds important dimensions to our understanding of it.

This paper highlights just a few of these dimensions: (1) the trope of slavery used in Perso-Urdu poetry written by free/adult males where the speaker/lover poses as the "slave" of the beloved boy betrays a contradiction, because the speaker is always a free adult male while the beautiful boy is usually an "idealized" slave; (2) this language of desire, when used in a way that literary and social conventions deemed appropriate—that is, in a way that maintains the paradox—becomes normative to the extent that other relations, even when they may not fit the paradigm, are expressed in this language; (3) when this desire seems to threaten a reversal of real power relations (the slave controlling the "slave of love," his master), however, it is denounced by contemporaries; and (4) when the colonizers read these languages, they add to it their own lens of all such male-male relations as "unnatural" in terms of gender-appropriate behavior. Gradually the latter lens (gender) displaces the former (slavery) in the language of the colonized.

Problems of Language

As David Halperin has argued in the context of Greek love, and Amy Richlin in
that of ancient Rome, it is necessary to think in terms of the language that the
ancients themselves used for specific behaviors and identities.[2] Yet this is precisely
what is absent from studies of same-sex love in the Indian past. C. M. Naim's comparison of homosexual love as outlined in Victorian Uranian poetry with the homosexual love outlined in the Urdu *ghazal* is a good example of such oversight.[3] The
Indian poets whose verses to "boys" Naim examines are Abru (d. 1733) and Mir (d.
1810). In eighteenth-century Hindustan, slave trading and slave keeping was common in gentry households that patronized and produced poetry. Nowhere in Naim's
elucidation of Urdu poetry of this period is it even remotely hinted that some male
love objects could have been slaves. This is possibly part of South Asianists' intellectual, moral, and psychic resistance—a resistance built upon engagements with
liberalism and egalitarianism—to associating the emotion named "love" with mas-
ter-slave relations. The term *slavery* in English has become so associated with plan-
tation-type servitude that it is hard to conceive of its coexisting with love. Therefore
one pole or the other—authority or intimacy—is reductively read as "false consciousness" or "exploitation." Alternatively, both "authority" and "intimacy" in
these particular male-male relationships may be dismissed as "criminal" since the
present Indian legal system, based on the colonial legal code, makes slavery "illegal," and similarly imprints all sexual behaviors between men and boys as "sodomy."

The failure to put slavery onto the Indian map has involved several slips in the
interrogation of linguistic usages over time. Many early translations of Persian and
Sanskrit texts were undertaken by British colonial scholar/officials, or under their
aegis, from the late eighteenth century onward. Terms used in these translations
often pass into scholarship today without adequate interrogation. A notable instance
is the word *boy,* which eighteenth-century British men and women regularly used
to denote the legal status of a male slave who was often a young man.[4] To late-nine-
teenth- and twentieth-century readers, the word "boy" connotes merely chronological age. Historians like Tariq Rahman, whose term "ephebophilia" indicates an
awareness of dissonance between chronological age and age-in-language, and Saleem
Kidwai, who discusses other meanings of "boy" while contesting the claim that all
relationships were represented in these texts as age stratified, do not trace its roots to
slavery.[5] Yet since Naim, Rahman, and Kidwai all discuss eighteenth- and
nineteenth-century Urdu literary production, it is necessary to point out that terms
in the poetry they translate are decidedly polyvalent. The word *launda* in the poems
of Mir and Abru (along with *ladka*) could very well have denoted a male slave rather
than the "boy" they interpret it to mean.

This can be illustrated by the way these terms are used by a contemporary of the
poets, called Mir Amman, who was employed by John Gilchrist of Fort William
College at Calcutta in 1801 to prepare a prose primer for the education of young
English officers of the East India Company. Amman was strictly instructed to use
colloquial, not Persianate Urdu in his primer, *Bagh O Bahar.*[6] Amman used the
words *launda, ladka,* and *ghulam* (slave) as synonyms of each other when indicating
males, and *laundi* (which today means "girl"), *bandi,* and *kaniz* (female slave) when
representing specific female characters. In no instance was age a significant aspect

of the usage. In the story of the first *darvesh*, for instance, the male and female slaves conduct business, acquire skills, and engage in sexual intercourse. The characteristics of slaves were almost inevitably discussed in terms of male beauty, female skill, and the eunuch or *khwajasera's* moral stature.

Twentieth-century commentators simply translate *launda* and *chela* as "boy" and "disciple," respectively.[7] These prevent us from thinking historically of the discursive realm of sexualities. When a particular motif—particularly that of the male slave as an appropriate love object, such as Ayaz was for Sultan Mahmud—is culturally sanctioned, all other relationships may indeed be represented as approximating this idyllic one.[8] What appears therefore as almost the *only* form of homosexual love in much Persian and Urdu literature—that between an adult free male and a male bought with money—may constitute a dominant trope for the representation of other relationships as well.

In his elucidation of Hanafi (Sunni) doctrine, Baber Johansen shows that while a free male, regardless of age, was considered an adult, for the purpose of stepping into a public space or role, a slave male, regardless of his age, office, or function, might not be considered to have "legal personality" as an adult.[9] In the imagination he might thus be aligned with the "beardless"—that is, the free women and children.

In addition, the discursive *suhbat* ("public") realm was a composite of the mosque, the court, the market, and the poetic assembly (*mushaira*), where words and actions were required to be elaborately and strictly regulated. The discursive "public" was inhabited both by free and slave males, but the free were the agents who spoke for and represented the "others," both in this discursive public and in the nondiscursive (*khalwat*) realms.

It was appropriate for a free man to always speak as an adult and for a slave, regardless of age, to be spoken of as a boy, because slaves, like free women and children, were imagined to be in need of guidance and control, simultaneously weak (*zaif*) and threatening. The threat was expressed in sexual terms. Carnal love itself emerged as a form of slavery, which could reduce the free moral agent of the "public" realm. Hence it was discursively excluded from the discursive-public and the free adult worlds. Any speaking of passionate carnal love between free and adult men, or between free men and women, would be construed as a sign of the dissolution of the moral universe and of the hierarchies of the social and political universe. An instance of such "appropriate" discourse is found in the writings of Mutribi, a Central Asian traveler at the court of the Mughal emperor Jahangir in the early seventeenth century whose panegyrics to two "youths" were about two male slaves at the court.[10]

Can the Slave Speak of Love?

Historians like myself prefer to explain the presence of beautiful young slave "boys" in personal proximity to the free man not as expressive of individual sexual choices but, like slave girls, as socially acknowledged and living symbols of the free nobleman's rank. Thus the Mughal emperor Aurangzeb, considered an orthoprax, did not object to some of his officials being surrounded by beautiful young "boys." One such official was Muhtasham Khan, who "developed a special attraction for beardless youths whom he patronized openly. The pleasure-loving and smooth-faced lads, with moustaches just beginning to show up and who had shaved their eyebrows, were dressed and adorned with great pains."[11] Free adult males would not require, nor would their honor accord with being "dressed and adorned" by another, except as formal acknowledgments of dependence. Within the culture of the Mughal Empire as a whole, such acknowledgment was expressed when the emperor granted ceremonial robes to a subordinate official.

Like Mutribi, free men ennobled by the Mughal emperor readily avowed their "slavelike" fidelity to superiors (both God and emperor). They addressed poetry to "real" slaves in society, thus transforming slaves into idealized objects of contemplation. We certainly hear little of what the slaves might have thought upon their first sight of either Mutribi or any of the other later poets. It is important to remember that the poetic and narrative discourses do not register slaves' agency. No poet that I know of writes lyric verse from the idealized slave Ayaz's point of view. Slaves could hardly have referred to themselves either as "beloveds" or "lovers" of the free and the brave. This becomes particularly clear when one contrasts the description of an eighteenth-century Mughal official's household by a contemporary of his own status with the autobiography of a male slave reared in that very household. The official in question was Mir Mannu, of whom the Deccani noble Dargah Quli Khan remarked, "[He] is one of the nobles of the times who has perfected the art of seduction. Many other aristocrats learn these arts from him. He is the best suited to organize these gatherings of *ghilman*."[12] (*Ghilman* in Persian can be used both as the plural of *ghulam* (male slave) as well as refer to the beautiful boy promised in paradise to believers.)

Which translation of *ghilman* we choose is important only if we consider the Persian-language autobiography of a male ex-slave, Tahmas "Miskin," who had been brought up from childhood in the household of Mir Mannu after that nobleman was appointed governor of Multan and Lahore. Written many years after his emancipation and subsequent ennoblement, Miskin's memoir makes absolutely no allusion to sexual intimacy with his late master during the period spent in the noble's house.[13] Where sexual matters are explicitly written about at all, they are linked with "public" women, one of whom is named as his paramour during his youth. There is also a very faint allusion to the sexual attraction of a free mistress who is represented as initiating an attempted seduction. The self of the slave as sexual or desiring agent is so thoroughly erased from the relevant paragraph that even the Persian word for *I* (*man*) is erased, as are verb endings appropriate to the first person. Finally, Miskin gives a very reverential and completely asexual description of Mir Mannu, whom visitors like Dargah Quli Khan described as adept in male seduction.

Superficially this ex-slave's memoirs could be read as evidence of the absence of homoerotic attachments between the nobleman and himself. I think it far more useful to recognize that conventions of *adab* (norms of comportment, as well as literatures conveying those norms), of Islam, of freedom, and of noble heroism structured the discourses of the ex-slave as much as they did those of the free nobleman. For a male ex-slave to represent himself as having desired or been desired by his free adult mistress perhaps seemed much more dangerous and illicit than any other heterosexual or homosexual desire he may have experienced.

Also, since this memoir was crafted from a Sufi perspective, and in an older

Islamic historiographical tradition, it is possible that memories of love and physical intimacies with either male *pir* (spiritual guide) or ex-master might be bleached of particular actions specifically abrogated by the legal canon (such as *liwat,* or sodomy). There is, too, a haunting reference in the memoir to male slave peers in the same household having challenged Miskin's virility (*taqat-I bah*). From this we can infer that the author, writing as a free nobleman of his past as a slave, was aware of a preexisting discourse of shame and degradation around the sexual passivity (*ibna*) of a male.

This remembered taunt may offer us an explanation for his silence about sexual relationships, whether those between a slave and his free master, free mistress, or spiritual guide. In the memoir Miskin tries to establish his own persona as a heroic, now free noble. His exquisitely detailed memories of his own and his young sons' bravery in battle in various parts of Hindustan accorded perfectly with this persona. But the conventions of nobility, masculinity, and freedom simply could not accommodate the memory or representation of any kind of "shameful" sexual episode within this persona. We can only surmise that if there had been any sexual relations between his master and himself, norms of comportment demanded that it be omitted from public discourse.

Discourses of Condemnation

Some of the discourses responsible for silencing the ex-slave may be found in medieval historical writing. In sharp contrast to the literary glorification of the appropriate love between Sultan Mahmud and his male slave Ayaz, the fourteenth-century chronicler Ziauddin Barani denounces such relationships when the free lovers apparently reverse power relations with their enslaved beloveds. An example is Barani's account of Qutb al-din Khalji and his slave lover Hasan, a.k.a. Khusro Khan.

Writing in old age and poverty, and attempting to legitimize the reign of the Tughlaks who succeeded the Khaljis,[14] Barani's history was also structured by *adab*. Any good "Muslim" history was required to instruct the community of the faithful. Sodomy was condemned in the Quran and *hadith* (traditions of the Prophet) and there was also an old Arabic tradition of depicting love as lust that incites to evil. Energizing the motif of sodomy in the case of the Khalji rulers, Barani suggests that their *'aql* (intellect, which leads one to submit to God) had been overpowered by their obsessive and base attachments.[15]

More importantly, Barani depicts all sexual intercourse between ruler and slave (castrated or otherwise) in terms of the "doer" and "done." The king, no matter how weakened by his lust, is never depicted as passive, while Khusro Khan, however wily and vengeful, is never represented as the initiator, or the one "on top." Barani uses clear spatial metaphors: "This illegitimate traitor, while *being sodomized* by the Sultan, which is a strange state. . . . He, who was *used to lying under men. . . .*"[16] For writers like Barani, the pleasures and desires of slaves, male or female, were just as immaterial as they might have been for earlier historians of ancient Greek and Roman societies.[17] Barani's language also seems to indicate a discourse on sex defined around an asymmetrical gesture, that of the penetration of the body of one person by the body—or specifically, the phallus, or its symbolic substitute—of another. Sex appears as the enactment of social and political hierarchies: the dominant is construed as the insertive actor and the subordinate as the receptive one. Clearly, *particular kinds* of *sexual activity were imagined and represented in the past as markers of people's status*—an attitude that is certainly in circulation to this day.

Barani emphasizes that the kingdom can be lost when free adult men allow themselves to become "dependent" on slaves, thus subverting the appropriate domination of slave by master. This subliminal script of social and political order is also, I think, present in several later histories of the sixteenth-century Mughal emperor Akbar's objections to his nobles' relationships with some slaves.

Historians have represented Akbar's objections as an attempt to distance high imperial servants from homoeroticism and from Central Asian traditions of public relations between men.[18] I argue, however, that Akbar, like Barani, objected to an inappropriate appearance of reversal of power relations, and of the noble's appropriation of the property rights of the emperor. An example is the account of the *ashiqi* (amours) of a nobleman, Ali Quli Khan, Khan Zaman, with the beautiful, elegant, well-mannered Shaham Beg. According to one account, Shaham Beg, the son of a camel driver, was one of Akbar's bodyguards. Bodyguards were more often than not slaves. According to the account, Khan Zaman "had cast his eyes on him, he sent men secretly to him, and having allured him, summoned him. Shaham Beg fled from the sublime presence, and arrived near Khan Zaman. As the latter had habits of excessive drinking, he sometimes stood before that young man and addressed him as my *Badshah*! [my king!] my *Badshah*! and saluted him and behaved with him, in the wicked manner of Transoxiana. When an account of these evil practices was submitted to His Majesty, a *farman* was issued to Khan Zaman, that he should send Shaham at once to the court. . . . *Farmans* were also issued to the *amirs*, who had *jagirs* near his, to the effect that if he delayed in sending Shaham, they should attack him; and bring home to him the reward of his recusancy."[19]

The severity of the measures indicates the enormity of the offense. First, a "bodyguard" of the emperor had been lured away without the emperor's consent—a theft of imperial property. Second, the emperor was told that the nobleman was prostrating before the servant, even addressing him as his king, which was an act of metaphorical "sedition." This is precisely the charge levied by Abu'l-Fazl, Akbar's court historian, against Shaham Beg—the camel driver's son had caused a noble officer to be negligent and disloyal.[20] The emperor promised to pardon the nobleman if the bodyguard was returned to the imperial service, and the noble reaffirmed his loyalty to the emperor.

Contemporaries writing of this episode represent both Shaham Beg and Khan Zaman not as men with special homosexual predilections but as men controlled by their "lower" natures (*nafs*), and hence lustful. That is why they describe a female prostitute, Aram Jan, who had been given by Khan Zaman to Shaham Beg. In most accounts, Shaham Beg in turn "gave" the woman to another noble, Abdur Rahman Beg, and then demanded her back after a while. When Abdur Rahman Beg refused to return the "gift," Shaham Beg took the woman back by force, during which he was attacked and killed.[21]

What we can infer, then, is that neither bodyguard nor nobleman had an exclusive hetero- or homosexual orientation. It follows that Akbar, too, did not punish the nobleman's homosexual behavior or attachment; rather, he punished the noble's flouting of social and political hierarchies. Nonslave members of the empire were required to display slavelike devotion to the person of the emperor, while maintaining relationships of generosity, responsibility, and humaneness between themselves. It was not birth but the maintenance of a comportment of "noble manhood" that qualified men for ennoblement.[22] Part of this comportment was enacting control of the socially ignoble slave or "boy."

This is the emphasis in an eighteenth-century biographer's account of Akbar's attempt to deprive an official, Shah Quli Khan Mahram, of his "boy." The official had become enamored of a "boy," Qabul Khan, who was "versed in musical arts, and always kept him in his company. Emperor Akbar who considered such acts . . . highly disgusting, and did not approve of them at all, and *especially in the case of an amir*—in the third year of the reign ordered that the boy be taken away from Shah Quli Khan. The Khan . . . set fire to his house and home, and donned the dress of a *jogi* and went into retirement. Bairam Khan laboured hard to straighten up the matter, and got him back into the emperor's favour."[23]

Appropriate Sexual Behavior in Erotic Treatises

Even when a sexual act did not involve phallic penetration, the person who was represented as initiating the act, "being pleasured," was clearly regarded as the agent, and the one whose body parts were devoted to pleasuring was conceived of as the "passive" inferior. Thus, the Sanskrit-language corpus of erotic manuals of the seventeenth and eighteenth centuries represent certain sexual actions as forbidden between the male "actor" (*nayaka*) and "respectable women" (*kulastri*) who were presumably his wives. In a late-seventeenth-century or early-eighteenth-century tract written in southern India, where the minutae of oral sex (*auparistakam*) are gendered, and detailed, it is said, "The taking of the penis in the mouth (*samgara*) and swallowing the semen mentioned above / Should be done only by the woman who is dissolute, libertine, prostitute, slave and servant / And not resorted to by the respectable women / Nor by all women—so said Vatsyayana."[24] This attribution to Vatsyayana of a division in the economy of sexual pleasure illustrates the selectivity with which classical texts were read even in the precolonial period.

The verses on *auparistakam* in Vatsyayana were much more elaborate than the seventeenth-century versifier allows. In the chapter on *auparistakam*, the *Kama Sutra* situates all eight varieties of oral sex into two distinct categories—one descriptive, the other prescriptive. In the descriptive category, oral sex is represented as practised by all genders and status groups. In the prescriptive category, Vatsyayana reiterates an apparently older prohibition on oral sex with married women, but appears to allow it with "female attendants and serving maids" as well as with "male servants of some men."[25] An indirect argument about the low status of oral sex is made in the recommendation that such pleasuring be spurned by those of high status ("a learned brahman," a "minister that carries on the business of a state, or by a man of good reputation").

The seventeenth/eighteenth-century versifier, however, transforms Vatsyayana's indirect argument into an explicit defense of specialization. The low status of oral sex in later writing explains its absence from the medieval *Ratirahasya* attributed to Koka Pandit, and widely known as *Koka-Shastra*,[26] and from discussions of marital sex, like the manual written for husbands, the *Ananga Ranga*.

Reading Status Crime as Gender Crime: The Colonial Period

Within the discursive norms of Hindustan during the seventeenth and eighteenth centuries, every sexual act was represented in terms of status differentials. Contemporary European observers, insensitive to local slave/master norms, often misinterpreted incidents they reported. Later readers, blind to the nuances of slave/master language, accepted these misinterpretations. An example is seventeenth-century French traveler Jean-Baptiste Tavernier's account, in which he writes, "A Mimbachi who commanded a thousand foot [soldiers] disgraced a young boy who was in his service; . . . the boy overwhelmed with grief, chose his time to avenge himself, and being one day out hunting with his master, and removed from the other attendants by about a quarter of a league, he came behind him and cut off his head with a sword . . . although all the relatives of the defunct did all they could to procure his execution, the Governor did not dare to condemn him, as he feared the people, who protested that the young man had acted rightly."[27] In this early example of a trajectory that would ossify by the eighteenth century, Tavernier (or his editor) puts a Judeo-Christian spin on the story: "unnatural crime does not rest unpunished by the Muslims." He does not mention the social/legal status of the men involved. If the "young boy" had been a slave who had murdered his master, both the murder and the public opinion on his behalf would be open to a very different interpretation than Tavernier's.

By the eighteenth century, two traits of Tavernier's account—making the slave-free topos invisible and characterizing homosexual relations of any kind as criminal—are evident in European-language discussions of Indian same-sex relations. Since there has been a heated debate about the ruptures and continuities between precolonial and British colonial social and political forms, it is necessary for me to state at the 'outset that the very discourses that undergirded the representation of same-sex relations shifted with the onset of western European epistemologies. I illustrate this in what follows.

In Barani's narrative, as in later Sanskrit manuals, discourses of the active versus passive existed in exact correspondence with a free versus slave topos. English language discussions appropriated active/passive norms without necessarily indicating the free/slave valences of these tropes. Thus they turned the force of such discussions entirely into issues of "natural"/ "unnatural" and individual/collective propensities. This can be illustrated by the terms in which an English officer reported the behavior of a potentate of Awadh, an important kingdom in northern India. Describing Mirza Manir, the twenty-five-year-old son of Shuja al-Daula, the vazir of Awadh, the officer wrote that he was "abandoned to the most unnatural of Passions in the Gratification of which . . . he has indulged himself to such an Excess that now no longer *capable of performing an active part* in the most detestable *Crime*, his highest gratification consists in *becoming the passive* in it; he keeps men and boys for that."[28] This may have been garnered from a "native" informant (the English official report does not pretend to eyewitness claims),[29] but the slippages between the native informant's episteme and the colonial official's episteme need to be interrogated. While the "native"-language speaker would have indicated the (slave or free) social status of the "boys" or "men" who apparently act as "penetrators" of the nobleman's body and thus would have suggested (perhaps elliptically, or even ironically) a threat to social order posed by such behavior, the English report erases the polyvalence of such "native information," leaving in its place only an assessment of the individual's "criminality."

In the discourse of criminality, what appears is not so much a rupture as a consolidation of an earlier historical shift. Within the Sharia, there were obligations toward human beings and obligations toward God. Failure to fulfill either set of obligations was "criminal" behavior. In the realm of conduct toward human beings, strict limits were imposed on slander by making accusations of any sort punishable unless strict procedures of substantiating these accusations were fulfilled. Thus Islamic law required four adult male eyewitnesses to give evidence of both sodomy (*liwat*) and adultery (*zina*), thus protecting individuals against slanderous accusations of "criminality" in the public discursive realm. It appears that these standards of proof began to be eroded within the precolonial Mughal administration.[30] This erosion of procedural norms of the Sharia, in the context of heterodox populations in the subcontinent, was accentuated by the inquisitorial method of English information gathering, "reportage," and legal processes.[31] While both the Mughal and the early colonial states claimed to be maintaining the rubric of "Islamic" law (see the essay by Suparna Bhaskaran in this volume), procedural norms regarding prosecution of sexual behaviors had, in practice, changed.

A more significant rupture in the public and formal discourse that coincided with the onset of British legal and juridical restructuring in eighteenth-century India was the implication that homosexual behavior constituted an *alternative* to heterosexual behavior, as if the presence of one necessarily meant the absence of the other. An illustration of this is the defense offered by William Orby Hunter in a case presided over by an English judge at the Faujdari Adalat of Tirhut in 1796. Hunter, an indigo merchant, had been accused by his concubine of mutilating one of her three slave girls. Among the many charges levied by this woman was the charge that Hunter had "dishonored" her by raping three girls.[32] Against this rape accusation Hunter defended himself at first by making two different counterallegations, both of which were meant to show up the concubine's "indelicate" character. The first countercharge was that the slave girls were regularly sent in to him "naked" by their mistress for "making use of . . . if I chose it." The second was one that made him blush, even though in self-defense and justification, to mention before the court: "One particular day the Bibbee called me into her apartment to shew me how her slave servants passed the night—I then saw two women naked one upon the other with some fictitious instrument made of Cloth bound round with String doing as Fathers and Mothers do."[33]

In Hunter's discourse, one can begin to see the beginnings of two significant tropes that reformulated the norms of a discourse on sexuality. Both were meant to work in counterfactual ways to establish the absence or presence of *one* kind of sexual behavior. In the first round, the description of slave girls using dildos to pleasure themselves is offered as an example of their "inherent" licentiousness, which is meant to preclude any relationship with him at all. However, as other witnesses were examined in the course of the trial, and his coercive regime vis-à-vis the slave women became apparent to the court, Hunter entirely dropped the story of the women having sex with each other and replaced it with a narrative in which the girls themselves desired him and climbed into his bed, thus exculpating him of any need to rape them.[34] By later elaborating the picture of the slave women having desired him, simultaneously silencing the possibility that they continued to desire each other, Hunter's defense provides a classic example of the relatively new thinking on desire. Desire for men and desire for women were two alternatives from which the individual could "choose."

Where earlier discourses appear to have distinguished between social status within each gender group, in terms of legal personality, capacity, bodily types, regional variations, and temperaments, colonial officials and travelers appear to have used much broader categories and thus fashioned new stereotypes. Groups like "high-caste women" or "low-class men" came to be perceived in terms of given characteristics, sartorial styles, appropriate tasks, and specific sexual behaviors. When people transgressed those assumed codes, or combined a great many of the features of other categories, language use felt the strain. "Masculine women" and "feminine men" aroused anxieties of different groups of commentators and historians for different sets of reasons. The French general Claude Martin spoke in his will not just of slave women who were concubines, free boys, slave men, and eunuchs named Mahbub and Amber, but also of a more ambiguous figure: "There is a woman that has always be wearing mans Cloths and pass for eunuque under the name of Myan Jawar."[35] So confused was Martin himself in trying to characterize this person that his pronouns shifted from one sentence to another: He provided that she be given fifteen rupees a month, and also stipulated that a sum of fifty rupees per year be given to this figure "during his lifetime."

Such slipping between masculine and feminine pronouns may have been necessitated by the absence of a third or fourth gender in the English language. But other coinages, like "berdaches" and "Amazons," appeared to describe some servants who were both entertainers and dressed in warriors' clothes at some of the native courts. For instance, the female soldiers guarding the Begams of Awadh were described as "men-like women pacing up and down before the various entrances to the female apartments" who bore "the ordinary accoutrements of sepoys in India—a musket and bayonet, . . . quite familiar with marching and wheeling . . . had their own corporals and sergeants."[36] Similarly, Alexander Burnes describes "Amazons" in the court of the ruler of preannexation Punjab, Ranjit Singh, as "thirty to forty dancing girls, dressed uniformly in boys' clothes . . . small bow and quiver in the hand of each"; there were as well two of the ladies whom he called the "Commandants of this regiment."[37]

The crux of such linguistic usage was an attempt to segregate gender by sartorial, behavioral, and other codes. With this definitive segregation of genders, represented in language, came a changed format for the representation of sexual behaviors. Having conceptualized these women (who were in reality very young females sold and gifted to the court) dressed in military uniform as "Amazons," such language predisposed the reader (especially one trained in the European classics) to imagine a community of armed, independent, men-spurning women. While accounts by local scribes would locate the actions and gestures of such "girls" within the interpretive frame of dependence on free and noble males, English-language discussions relocated the girls within a conceptual framework bleached of power relations, where only tests of gender-appropriate norms remained. Such young women were considered worthy of comment because they were seen as having crossed into the "masculine" terrain of soldiering.

Perhaps one can read the pressure toward coherence and uniformity to be the criterion of colonialism's radical epistemological and social revolution in the subcontinent, a pressure turned as much on its own officers as on the colonized.[38] This pressure to choose one, forsaking all others, whether it came to roles, genders, or sexual partners, is represented very well in the story told by a traveling Brahman in the mid-nineteenth century. Reporting the information relayed to him by his cousin, one of whose ritual assistants had given his daughter as a second wife to the widowed and last male ruler of Jhansi, Gangadhar urf Babasaheb, he said of the latter,

> His conduct was this. In his apartments (*vada*), every two or four days, he would discard male dress and put on women's clothes. He would wear a *paithani*, take a *jari-katthi choli* (blouse); he had grown a very long tuft of hair at the crown and he would add false hair to it, scent it with oil, and make a braid. Sometimes he would put a jewel in the braid and sometimes he would make it into a bun. He would put on other ornaments. Then he would have a garland of *mohurs* and a *sari*, a ring in his nose and bangles on his arm, women's slippers on his feet and all the feminine ornaments. He would then speak and behave like a woman. *For this reason, even poor households said that rather than give a daughter to such a husband, they should drown her in water.* Many people say that there are eight kinds of neuter genders (*sharhat*) and this is one of them. In the Shastra, the eight kinds are mentioned with their signs (*lakshana*). One sort would be aroused by playing with another man's penis (*sisun*). This Raja must have been of that type. This is likely because his first wife had borne a son—and that woman was not immoral. She was simple and faithful, so everyone said. Therefore the Raja was definitely a *purush* [male]. . . .
>
> One day the Resident Saheb gently and politely asked, "For many days I have heard the same story and I have long wished to ask you about this matter. . . . Maharaj you are an important ruler among the states and you also have the Brahmandharma. It has come to my ears that you customarily wear women's dress. Each month you observe the period of impurity and you cover your arms with bangles. Is all this worthy of you?" Whereupon Babasaheb replied, "I am but a small feudatory. In front of the English (*Angrez Bahadur*), all the kings and princes, east to west, north to south, have put on bangles. There is no hero in front of you. There is no male on earth who is not wearing bangles. You have come from another continent and conquered us."[39]

Historians cannot confirm whether or not such a conversation occurred between the colonial official and an indigenous ruler, nor is it possible to prove conclusively that this particular king was given to particular sexual or cross-dressing behaviors. What can be confirmed is the increasing perception of cross-dressing as transgressive of *gender* norms, norms apparently being articulated within local populations also. Expressing submission in terms of a sartorial code (wearing bangles) reworked

older tropes established in the discourses of warrior groups. A Rajput bard represented the earth as a woman, and kings as her husbands.[40] The history of colonial
domination was the history of a woman, who, even while her husbands lived and
her bangles were unbroken, was taken into the house of the Englishman, presumably as an enslaved concubine.

Because of this preexisting discourse of freedom and virility in the public arena,
a free nobleman's donning of female dress should be reinterpreted as a "knowing"
political statement—the response of the vanquished rather than a statement of
individual predilections. It is remarkable that in the mid-nineteenth century, prior
to the mutiny of 1857, many Indian rulers seem to have simultaneously enacted
on their bodies the signs of their submission by the manipulation of sartorial codes.
The soon-to-be-deposed king of Awadh is one. Another perhaps even more audacious attempt to signal submission may have been that of the last Naib Nazim of
Dhaka, Ghazi al-din, who "often don[ned] the clothes of an Englishwoman."[41]

Conclusion

By the mid-nineteenth century, then it would appear that new force was attached
to some terms while older meanings were bleached from others. One can illustrate
this by the way insult-words worked in slave-owning societies. The old Islamicate
world, where shared virtues of honor, masculinity, agency, and adulthood were
denied to male slaves, ensured that a term like *gandu* ("one who has his anus
taken"—a popular insult in north India even today) could function as an insult in
a Hindu ruling household's conflicts as well as in the description of a nineteenth-
century monarch's personal companions.

Gandu is used as a term of abuse in an eighteenth-century document from the
Hindu kingdom of Orchha in central India.[42] One contender for the throne had
incorporated his slave-born children into the lineage. His rival's scribe used the
term *gandu* to describe all the free men within that lineage who had sat and eaten
with these slave-born children. In a clearly homological way of thinking of the body
and its orifices, polluting oneself through the mouth by eating with the slave-born
was equivalent to acting like a slave by offering one's anus for sexual penetration.
No free, honorable man, it was understood, should readily undertake either activity. The ridicule visited on a free man who was publicly thought to be the "recip-
ient" or the one "done to" (hence, like a slave) was thus incorporated into the local
languages in northern India.

In a catalog of behaviors listed for another local ruler (Naib Nazim of Dhaka),
it is said, "He was preoccupied with the conversation of the vulgar and the
debauched, and immersed in endless pleasure—like the dancing of women, of dancing boys [dressed as women], and those who had their anuses taken—, and in horse-
racing, cock-fighting, drinking, going to girls, commerce with whores, and so
on."[43] It is possible from the continuation of such meanings that sexual acts continued to be thought of as acts of power and status, and that such conventions might
have structured other hierarchical relationships, like that between upper-"caste"
(*jati*) and lower-"caste" persons. The almost normative requirement for men of ruling houses to take at least one bride of lower station indicates the uniformity of
such expectations. Instead of being outlawed, sex between social superior and sub-

ordinate might well have been mandated in order to underline the social distance between them. Richard F. Burton recalled an incident within a regiment from the Bombay presidency posted in Sind from 1843 to 1844, in which a young Brahman "had connection with a soldier comrade of low caste and this had continued till, in an unhappy hour, the Pariah patient ventured to become the agent. The latter, in Arab Al-fa'il = the doer, is not an object of contempt like al-maful = the done; and the high-caste sepoy, stung by remorse and revenge, loaded his musket and deliberately shot his paramour. He was hanged by court martial at Hyderabad."[44]

While current sociological investigations reveal the continuing vitality of older conceptual and epistemological worlds in the lives of the many men in India who continue to have sex with both men and women, and to represent sexual behavior in terms of passive and active,[45] historians have not yet investigated the social and political roots of these conceptual worlds. I have urged here that historical writing in English by South Asianists should not appropriate the terms of a relatively recent discourse nor collaborate with colonial translators' bleaching of terms such as *chela*, *launda*, or *gandu*. Historians wishing to distance themselves from the colonizers' tropes cannot be satisfied with switching the labels around; if we are dissatisfied by the colonial historians' praise of Emperor Akbar for having put down the "licentiousness" of a noble, we cannot today simply valorize the noble and revile the emperor as the homophobe. This is not only ahistorical but also tantamount to reading medieval literatures, as the colonizers did, on the assumption that precolonial chroniclers, scribes, and poets had no epistemological moorings other than those we as readers have.

This is particularly true of the way the literatures of the Islamicate have been mined for writing Indian history in the nineteenth and early twentieth centuries. Repeating discussions around the Indian past in the impoverished languages of individuality and sexual "choices" involves retaining the same tropes of reading and writing that constitute the epistemological deprivations imposed by colonialism. Instead, I have suggested that reinstating slavery, alienation, and subordination into our histories would offer us alternative points of entry into the discourses themselves and also make visible once more the figures deprived of their masculinity, agency, and adulthood in historical pasts.

Notes

I thank Muhammad Qasim Zaman Khan, Carla Petievich, Ruth Vanita, Donna Wulff, and Sumit Guha for many insightful discussions, suggestions for revision, and bibliographic aid. Any mistakes herein are mine alone, however.

1. See John Boswell, "Revolution, Universals, and Sexual Categories," and David Halperin, "Sex before Sexuality: Pederasty, Politics, and Power in Classical Athens," both in *Hidden from History: Reclaiming the Gay and Lesbian Past*, ed. Martin B. Duberman, Martha Vicinus, and George Chauncey (New York: New American Library Books, 1989), 17–53; Wayne R. Dynes and Stephen Donaldson, eds., *The History of Homosexuality in Europe and America* vol. 5 (New York: Garland, 1992); and Craig A. Williams, *Roman Homosexuality: Ideologies of Masculinity in Classical Antiquity* (New York: Oxford University Press, 1999).
2. See Halperin, "Sex before Sexuality," and Amy Richlin, "Not before Homosexuality: Materiality of the *Cinaedus* and the Roman Law against Love between Men," *Journal of the History of Sexuality* 3, no. 4 (1993): 523–73.

3. C. M. Naim, "The Theme of Homosexual (Pederastic) Love in Pre-Modern Urdu Poetry," in *Studies in the Urdu Ghazal and Prose Fiction*, ed. M. U. Memon (Madison: South Asian Studies, University of Wisconsin, 1979), 120–42.

4. For English-language wills probated in India during the eighteenth century, see Indrani Chatterjee, "Colouring Subalternity: Slaves, Concubines, and Social Orphans in Early Colonial India," in *Subaltern Studies 10: Writings on South Asian History and Society*, ed. Gautam Bhadra et al. (Delhi: Oxford University Press, 1999) 49–97.

5. Tariq Rahman, "Boy-Love in the Urdu Ghazal," *Annual of Urdu Studies* 7 (1990): 1–20, n. 3; Saleem Kidwai, "Medieval Materials in the Perso-Urdu Tradition," in *Same-Sex Love in India: Readings from Literature and History*, ed. Ruth Vanita and Saleem Kidwai (New York: St. Martin's Press, 2000), 107–25.

6. Rashid Hasan Khan, introduction to Mir Amman, *Bagh O Bahar*, ed. Rashid Hasan Khan (Delhi: Maktaba-I Jam'ia, 1995). This book has had many editions; for the reliability of this edition see Annemarie Schimmel, *Classical Urdu Literature from the Beginning to Iqbal* (Weisbaden: Otto Harrassowitz, 1975), 210–11. For the social and legal use of these terms in the late eighteenth and nineteenth centuries, see Indrani Chatterjee, *Gender, Slavery, and Law in Colonial India* (Delhi: Oxford University Press, 1999), 212–23; and Radhika Singha, *A Despotism of Law: Crime and Justice in Early Colonial India* (Delhi: Oxford University Press, 1998), 159.

7. For an example of such mistranslation see Stephen Murray, "The Will Not to Know," in *Islamic Homosexualities: Culture, History, and Literature*, ed. Stephen Murray and Will Roscoe (New York: New York University Press, 1997), 28, 30–31. For the Mughal emperor Akbar's order to rename the imperial slaves as disciples, see Irfan Habib, "Akbar's Social Views: A Study of Their Evolution," Papers of the Indian History Congress, 53rd Session, 1992–93, 223.

8. For the significance of such motifs, see Everett K. Rowson, "The Categorization of Gender and Sexual Irregularity in Medieval Arabic Vice Lists," in *Bodyguards: The Cultural Politics of Gender Ambiguity*, ed. Julia Epstein and Kristina Straub (New York and London: Routledge, 1991), 50–79, and Scott Kugle's essay in this volume.

9. Baber Johansen, *Contingency in a Sacred Law: Legal and Ethical Norms in the Muslim Fiqh* (Leiden: Brille, 1999), 192–94.

10. *Conversations with Emperor Jahangir by Mutribi al-Asamm Samarqandi*, trans. Richard C. Foltz (Costa Mesa, CA: Mazda Publications, 1998), 48–49.

11. *Maathir al-Umara*, 2nd. ed., H. Beveridge (Patna: Janaki Prakashan, 1979), vol. 2, part 1, 231.

12. "Dargah Quli Khan: Portrait of a City," in Ruth Vanita and Saleem Kidwai, eds., *Same-Sex Love*, 179; also see Muhammad Umar, *Muslim Society in Northern India during the Eighteenth Century* (Delhi: Munshiram Manoharlal, 1998), 444–46.

13. See Indrani Chatterjee, "A Slave's Quest for Selfhood in Eighteenth-Century Hindustan," *Indian Economic and Social History Review* 37, no. 1 (2000): 53–86.

14. See Kishori Saran Lal, *History of the Khaljis, A.D. 1290—1320* (New York: Asia Publishing House, 1967), and Peter Jackson, *The Delhi Sultanate: A Political and Military History* (Cambridge: Cambridge University Press, 1999).

15. Lois Anita Giffen, *Theory of Profane Love among the Arabs: The Development of the Genre* (New York: New York University Press/London: University of London Press, 1971), 117–34.

16. Ziauddin Barani, translated in Vanita and Kidwai, *Same-Sex Love*, 134, 135; emphasis added.

17. For a discussion of the versions of Barani's history, see Iqtidar Husain Siddiqui, *Perso-Arabic Sources of Information on the Life and Conditions in the Sultanate of Delhi* (Delhi: Munshiram Manoharlal, 1992), 151–66. Both versions agree on Barani's contempt for

those of lower status who were elevated to positions of trust. This attitude appears to have been shared by his contemporaries, for which see *The Travels of Ibn Battuta, A.D. 1325–1354* , trans. from Arabic text ed. C. Defremery and B. Sanguinetti, by H. A. R. Gibb (Cambridge: Hakluyt Society at the University Press, 1958), vol. 3, 646–50. On the slave antecendents of Khusro Khan, see Lal, *History of the Khaljis*, 309–22. For the particular tropes involved in Barani's depiction of "profligacy" in the empire, see Jackson, *The Delhi Sultanate*, 151 and passim.

18. Rosalind O'Hanlon, "Manliness and Imperial Service in Mughal North India," *Journal of Economic and Social History of the Orient* 42, no. 1 (1999): 47–93.

19. Khwajah Nizamuddin Ahmad, *The Tabaqat-I-Akbari* vol. 2, trans. Brajendra Nath De, rev. and ed. Baini Prashad (1936, reprt. Delhi: Low Price Publishers, 1992), 225–26.

20. Abu'l- Fazl, *The Akbar Nama* vol. 2, trans. H. Beveridge (reprt. New Delhi: Ess Ess Publications, 1973), 126.

21. Ibid,. 128–9, 227.

22. John F. Richards, *The Mughal Empire* (Cambridge: Cambridge University Press, 1993), 47–49, and his "Norms of Comportment among Imperial Mughal Officers," in *Moral Conduct and Authority: The Place of Adab in South Asian Islam*, ed. Barbara D. Metcalf (Berkeley and Los Angeles: University of California Press, 1984), 255–89.

23. Nawab Samsam al-Daula Shahnawaz Khan and Abdul Hayy, *Maathir al-Umara, Being Biographies of the Timurid Sovereigns of India from 1500 to about 1780* vol. 2 (2nd ed.), trans. H. Beveridge, rev. Baini Prashad (Patna: Janaki Prakashan, 1979), part 2, 774; emphasis added. Sixteenth-century historians of Akbar's reign were completely silent about this event in the official's career. This account was read as a story about "personalities" and inserted into the index of Beveridge's translation of Abu'l Fazl in the nineteenth century.

24. *Ratiratna Pradipika of Sri Devaraja Maharaja*, trans. Pt. K. Rangaswami Iyengar (Mysore: Royal Press, 1923), 42–43 (chapter 6, verses 37, 38).

25. *The Kama Sutra of Vatsyayana: A Complete and Unexpurgated Edition of This Celebrated Hindu Treatise on Love* (Paris: De la Fontaine D'Or, n.d.), 117–23.

26. *The Koka Shastra, Being the Ratirahasya of Kokkoka and Other Medieval Indian Writings on Love*, trans. Alex Comfort (London: George Allen and Unwin, 1964), 124, 148.

27. Jean-Baptiste Tavernier, *Travels in India* vol. 1, trans. from French edition of 1676 by V. Ball (London: n.p., 1889), 122–23.

28. "Observations on the Family of Shujaud Dowlah," British Library, Hastings Papers, Add. Mss 29, 202, vol. V, 1786–1816, ff. 110–19; emphasis added.

29. For details see C. A. Bayly, *Empire and Information: Intelligence Gathering and Social Communication in India, 1780–1870* (Cambridge: Cambridge University Press, 1996).

30. I refer to the incident of incest, which was "reported" to and investigated by Emperor Akbar; see Ahmad, *Tabaqat-I Akbari*, 436–38. Significantly, since the offending male was a Hindu wearing the sacred thread, he was given a lesser punishment than would have been merited by a Muslim male for the same offence.

31. See Radhika Singha, *A Despotism of Law* (1998) and C.A. Bayly, *Empire and Information* (1996).

32. Deposition of Mussamat Boogwaun Kowar, OIOC, Bengal Criminal Judicial Consultations, October 14, 1796, no. 20.

33. Deposition of William Orby Hunter, OIOC, Bengal Criminal Judicial Consultations, September 16, 1796, no. 22, enclosure no. 3.

34. Deposition of William Orby Hunter, OIOC, Bengal Criminal Judicial Consultations, September 19, 1796, no. 50.

35. Will of Claud Martin, Major-General in the Company's Service, OIOC, L/AG/34/29/12/1800, folio 130.

36. William Knighton, *The Private Life of an Eastern King,* ed. S. B. Smith (1855, reprt. Oxford University Press, 1921), 130–31.

37. Alexander Burnes, *Travels into Bokhara, Being the Account of a Journey from India to Cabool, Tartary, and Persia with a Narrative of A Voyage on the Indus from the Sea to Lahore* vol. 3 (1834, reprt. New Delhi: AES, 1992), 162.

38. Many early-nineteenth-century British eyewitness accounts of Indian soldiers and officials at local courts can be read for an obsession with "manliness"; see Mrinalini Sinha, *Colonial Masculinity: The "Manly Englishman" and the "Effeminate Bengali" in the Late Nineteenth Century* (New York: St. Martin's Press, 1995). For rare evidence regarding a particular English official's homosexual predilections, see the account of General John Jacob in Arthur Swinson, *North-West Frontier: People and Events, 1839–1947* (New York, Frederick Praeger, 1967).

39. *Mazha Pravas of Vishnubhat Godse,* ed. D. V. Potdar (4th ed. 1966, reprt. Pune: Bharat Itihasa Samshodak Mandala, 1990), 32–35; emphasis added. I thank Sumit Guha for providing me with an English translation of these pages.

40. Narottamdasa Swami, introduction to Bankidasa Asiya, *Bankidasa ri Khyat,* 2nd ed. ed. Narottamdasa Swami (Jodhpur: Rajasthan Oriental Research Institute, 1989), 3–4. I thank Sumit Guha for bringing this to my attention.

41. Rafiqul Islam, *Dhakar Katha, 1610–1910* (Dhaka: Ahmed Publishing House, 1982), 110.

42. Hiralal, "Sagar Ka Bundeli Shilalekh," *Nagaripracharini Patrika* 8 (1926): 395–400.

43. *Tarikh-i Nusratjangi* (Persian), ed. Harinath De, *Journal of the Asiatic Society of Bengal,* folio 141.

44. Richard F. Burton, *A Plain and Literal Translation of the Arabian Nights' Entertainments* vol. 10 (New York: Burton Club, 1886), 237–38. Criticism of Burton has established the need to be suspicious about his "facts." In his "Terminal Essay," one of the four sections of which is devoted to the "vice" of pederasty in the quaintly termed "Sotadic Zone," Burton cited the journal of the French traveler Victor Jacquemont as his source for the statement regarding Ranjit Singh's sexual relationship with Gulab Singh. But Jacquemont's journal, in *The Punjab a Hundred Years Ago as Described by V. Jacquemont and A. Soltykoff,* ed. and trans. H. L. O. Garrett (Reprint Lahore, Sang-e-Meel, 1997), 1–87, gives no names for any of Ranjit Singh's sexual partners, male or female.

45. Jeremy Seabrook, *Love in a Different Climate: Men Who Have Sex with Men in India* (London: Verso, 1999).

5

Eunuchs, Lesbians, and Other Mythical Beasts

Queering and Dequeering the *Kama Sutra*

Michael J. Sweet

From the vast literary output of classical India one work alone has attained nearly universal recognition: Vatsyayana's *Kama Sutra* (KS). Its fame, of course, rests on its treatment of sex in its more mechanical aspects, although that actually forms only a part of its subject matter. It is the only source for most people's knowledge of classical India; imagine if, conversely, modern Euro-American civilization were to be known in Asia only through *The Joy of Sex*. The insatiable thirst of the modern West for sex knowledge from the mystic and lubricious East has resulted in the publication of hundreds of versions of the KS including translations, recastings, expositions, and specially illustrated versions ranging from the coffee-table book with its glossy pictures of Indian erotic statuary to pornographic videos, not to speak of cards, lotions, massage oils of all flavors (who can forget the "Kama Sutra Love Oil" of the 1960s?), tapestries, and even bottle openers. While the reception and especially the commodification of the KS and other Indian exotica such as Tantra is a subject worthy of an extended inquiry, I confine myself here to an examination of one aspect in the West's encounter with Vatsyayana's classic—namely, its elements of "queerness" as denied, interpreted, and hallucinated by Orientalists, sexologists, and the proponents of a gay liberation ideology who have sometimes refashioned this text according to their own wishes.

The Perversity of the East

Edward Said and subsequent writers have clearly delineated how concepts of "Asia" in general and India in particular have been used as sites for the projection of Western fantasies of the erotic and mysterious.[1] To the brilliant adventurer and erotomaniac Sir Richard Burton, the KS was a heaven-sent opportunity to spit in the eye of late-Victorian sexual hypocrisy, and, in the quasi-respectable guise of Orientalist scholarship, to speak aloud of unabashed and polymorphous perverse sexuality. I recall that reading the chapter on oral sex (*auparistaka*) in

the early '60s in Burton and F. F. Arbuthnot's rendering was an electrifying revelation,[2] despite its use of fusty and occasionally baffling terms like "mouth congress" and "shampooer," and the awkwardness of finding my desires identified with
those of "eunuchs." This was, of course, a misunderstanding on the part of the translators yet one that had the status of a received opinion until recently. The translators relied on what they knew of the classical world and the examples provided by
Persian, Turkish, Arabic, and Byzantine civilizations and conflated the classical
Indian conception of a person of the third sex (tritiya prakriti) with the eunuch.[3] In
the Victorian imagination, the making of eunuchs was invariably associated with
the decadent East, but in reality they were rare, if not entirely nonexistent, in pre-
Muslim India. Should Burton and Arbuthnot have known better? Perhaps, since
both men would very likely have been familiar with the *cinaedus* of Latin literature,
a genitally intact but effeminate and sexually voracious male.[4] Nevertheless, their
choice of term may have rendered the description of oral sex more palatable to their
contemporaries; to have the receptive partner presented as an exotic eunuch, a type
of person not often met with in London or New York, rather than the all-too-visi-
ble fairy, or worse yet the more insidious because not readily identifiable butch
queer. In fact, the effeminate and masculine homosexual types may be homologized,
without too great a stretch, with the "feminine" and "masculine" third-sexers presented in the KS.

Another form of Orientalist distortion minimizes the existence of nonnormative
sexuality and gender in India, and thus approves of India from a heteronormative
perspective as "far healthier than most other ancient cultures."[5] This is a view
expressed often by contemporary Indians and other South Asians who have assimilated an earlier Western, sex-negative perspective and thus make the claim that
homosexuality is an exclusively foreign vice, imported by Muslims or Europeans.[6]
This opinion is found, for example, in the writing of the early-twentieth-century
Hindi translator and commentator on the KS, Pandit Madhavacharya, who had
apparently so thoroughly introjected Victorian sexual mores that he managed to
misinterpret this thoroughly pleasure-affirming text as a prescriptive warning
against all nonprocreative and nonmarital sexual activity, expressing special repugnance toward oral and anal sex.[7]

Foucault and Orientalism Redux

The case of Michel Foucault is altogether different. Anyone writing about the history of sexuality or cultural studies must acknowledge a debt to Foucault's brilliant
insights about the nature of discourse and power, including the very idea that sexuality and gender have had a history. However, like many great speculative thinkers
who have altered the way we see the world, Foucault could often be spectacularly
wrong. Such is the case concerning his famous contention that sexuality as we know
it today did not exist prior to the bureaucratization of society that accompanied
modern capitalism.[8] Textual research on areas as diverse as classical Rome,
Tokugawa Japan, Renaissance Italy, and various Native American cultures has
shown that this is simply not the case, and that conceptions of fixed identities based
at least partially on sexual orientation long predated the nineteenth century.[9] Even
Foucault's most vocal partisans, such as David Halperin, appear to have retreated

to the position that Foucault's views were mere heuristics, intended to stimulate novel thinking but not to be taken literally.[10]

Foucault's unreliability is even more pronounced when he ventures outside of the European tradition, and it is most surprising that this anticolonialist, transgressive French intellectual of the 1960s and '70s was prey to the same fantasies of Oriental licentiousness that afflicted his predecessors almost a century before. He evokes the delirious "East" of Eugène Delacroix and Jean-Léon Gérôme in his contention that all the extremely diverse cultures from Suez to the Sea of Japan, as well as those of the classical Mediterranean, propound a lush, reflexive sensuality in which "truth is drawn from pleasure itself, understood as a practice and accumulated as experience; pleasure is not considered in relation to an absolute law, nor by reference to a criterion of utility, but first and foremost in relation to itself."[11] Such societies, according to Foucault, possess an "*ars erotica*" of pragmatic sexual lore for the connoisseur, and while he does not mention the KS by name (in itself indicative of the lesser worth he ascribes to non-Western cultures), it is clearly the model for his notion of the Eastern erotic treatise, distinguished from the rationalistic and controlling modern Western *scientia sexualis*. This awesome display of willful ignorance surely must have arisen from a desire to shock plodding academics; how could Foucault, a highly educated man and the contemporary of many outstanding Francophone Indologists have been unfamiliar with the *Manusmriti*, the literature on *ayurveda*, and the Buddhist Vinaya (just to confine ourselves to India)? These texts make detailed and categorical distinctions on the basis of gender normativity, and the first and last of them prescribe precise penalties for transgressing socially normative practices. It is true that the KS is worldly and nonjudgmental in its tone, but it speaks for and to a tiny minority—that is, the urban, upper-class intelligentsia;[12] insofar as it advocates sexual permissiveness it is in the form of libertinism, the privilege of upper-caste wealthy males. The overwhelming mass of premodern Indians were hedged around with sexual taboos and gender constraints; India was not a Rousseauian paradise of sexual freedom by any stretch of the imagination.

Daniélou: Anachronistically Translating the Text

Burton and Arbuthnot's translation of the KS was a pioneering but flawed work that contains numerous mistranslations, and omissions, and is marked by a general confusion of Vatsyayana's own *sutras* with the Jayamangala, the classical and authoritative commentary on it written by Yashodhara many centuries later. A retranslation into English was thus long overdue, and it was forthcoming from a figure whose life rivaled that of Burton in its picaresque variety: Alain Daniélou, who at various points in his very long career (he died in 1996 at the age of ninety-two) was a painter, dancer, musician, translator, international endurance race car driver, and musicologist. Although without formal academic credentials, Daniélou wrote many books on Indological topics, and was an important pioneer in the field of Indian musicology. He was self-identified as a practicing Hindu, and he was also openly gay; his autobiography is immensely entertaining and full of amusing and scandalous stories.[13] His French translation of the KS into English, which he accomplished himself with some assistance, is in some respects a great advance over Burton and Arbuthnot, as can be seen by comparing their treatment of the first sutra of the chapter on oral sex:

There exist two kinds of eunuchs or hermaphrodites; those who choose the role of men, and those who disguise themselves as women. (Burton and Arbuthnot 116)

People of the third sex are of two kinds, according to whether their appearance is masculine or feminine. (Daniélou 183)

As we can see, in Daniélou's translation the eunuchs and hermaphrodites have disappeared, properly replaced by "people of the third sex," and the language is clear and accurately conveys the meaning of the original. However, Daniélou has other problems as a translator, which I believe stem from a presentist bias that imposes modern concepts on an ancient text, out of his commendable zeal for gay liberation, much as John Boswell has been critiqued for doing in his work on same-sex unions in premodern Europe.[14] This can be illustrated in Daniélou's version of another sutra from the chapter on oral sex, translated to read, "There are also citizens, sometimes greatly attached to each other and with complete faith in one another, who get married together" (191). This is an astonishing translation, one that locates gay marriage in ancient India! This would be a highly significant discovery, if it were true, but unfortunately, the text says only that "they mutually embrace one another (*kurvanti . . . parasparaparigraham*), and the commentary makes clear that the passage is speaking of mutually agreed-upon sex between two upper-class urban sophisticates (*nagarikas*) who doubtless conformed to all social expectations of (heterosexual) marriage and dalliance. This is still very interesting, showing that in certain circumstances same-sex behavior could be engaged in by normative males, apparently without incurring any stigma. Nevertheless, the passage is far from speaking of "gay marriage," and here Daniélou's advocacy has overcome his knowledge of Sanskrit and of classical Indian culture. Nor is this the only example of an anachronistic or inadequate reading of queer subject matter in his translation; for example, in another sutra (188) he states that "buccal coition" (a horridly learned euphemism almost as bad as "mouth congress") can be also be performed by "lesbians." How could the author of the KS have been talking about lesbians, a truly nineteenth-century European conception (Foucault being right in this case)? The answer is of course that he did not; the word that Daniélou translated as "lesbian," *svairini*, means instead a self-willed, sexually unrestrained woman. Daniélou actually addresses this question in his introduction (6), justifying his translation on the very debatable grounds that "dictionaries do not give the meaning of technical terms," but providing no basis for his own rendering. A similar instance is his translating the word *vita* as "gigolo." The *vita* is a cultivated sensualist and voluptuary and a stock character in Sanskrit drama, where he figures as the bosom companion of a dissolute prince, but he is certainly not one who is paid for his sexual services by women. In another burst of creative translation Daniélou goes so far as to render "oral sex" (*auparistaka*) as "homophile relations" (188). Clearly we are dealing with a case of wishful thinking that led an otherwise serious scholar to project his dreams and desires on the KS, as others had done before him. At times, it must be confessed, Daniélou's translation is so far-fetched as to lead one to the conclusion that his intellectual abilities were seriously impaired by the time he was working on the KS. For instance, a passage found in the chapter on oral sex, Daniélou translates, "If one wishes to, it is customary to pinch the gigolo's nipples" (188). "Gigolo" is entirely a fiction of Daniélou's; the Sanskrit "equivalent" for it is absent from the sutra, and "nipple" is a blunder resulting from reading *stanana* "erotic noises" as *stana* "nipple"; the sutra actually says that erotic noises can be made in the course of sex play between a "third sexer" and a man.[15] Thus, an accurate English translation of the KS that will do justice to the queer elements, not to speak of the rest of the text, without bowdlerization, anachronism, or other distortions, still remains a desideratum.

Queer Revisions: Gay Kama Sutras

Such is the prestige of the KS that its name has been claimed by writers seeking validation for gay sexuality, apparently through association with this venerable and canonical work. The most thorough and literal of these attempts was executed by Jeffrey Hopkins, an academic and professor of Buddhist studies who is primarily known for his translations and studies of Tibetan scholastic texts. Hopkins, who came out as a gay man very publicly some years ago,[16] had published a work on the KS; it was not the famous work of Vatsyayana, but a reworking of the same material based largely on later sources that was compiled by Gendün Chöphel, a highly influential and iconoclastic Tibetan scholar of the twentieth century.[17] Chöphel's text is resolutely heterosexual, with no reference to sex between men or between third sexers and normative males.[18] Hopkins seems to have found this lack troubling, and sought to remedy it with a recasting of this text in gay male terms, with the explicit aim of providing "care, support and encouragement" to the gay male community.[19] For the most part this resolutely odd work is nothing but his previous translation of Gendün Chöphel's text with male body parts substituted for female ones in the appropriate places, along with the addition of some contemporary touches such as advice on how to use a condom in anal intercourse (53), and soft-core erotic photos (of a black/East Asian male couple) that do not illustrate the text in any naturalistic fashion. Moreover, the Indo-Tibetan cultural references have not been changed, thus leaving phrases likely to be highly puzzling to the contemporary Western reader. For example: "There is no sense in urgently exhorting people to do what they wish—like asking nomads to eat pork, city-folk to drink melted butter, and so on" (5). And then there is the truly bizarre and grotesque chapter, "Males of Various Places." Here the belief that women from specific geographic regions of the subcontinent are associated with particular sexual practices is retained, though the gender has been changed to male. Homosexual men are described in terms of various types of sexual physiology and behavior without any basis in anything except perhaps the imagination of the author. For example: "In the city of Yama itching arises in the anus from time to time; hence he urges men to do it with him and also sometimes uses a wooden dildo" (65). It is difficult to conceive how this was meant to be understood.

In a separate section following the text itself, Hopkins presents an interesting series of "ruminations" on topics such as the alleged sex-positive nature of Tibetan Buddhism; homophobia; and the connection between tantric sex and sexual practice. He claims that in the experience of orgasm a person can attain at least a hint of the liberating experience of the nondual and pure consciousness of "clear light" that is the aim of many tantric practices. In this, Hopkins follows Gendün Chöphel, who makes a similar claim,[20] possibly as an *apologia pro vita sua* for having broken his monastic vows and engaged in a life of apparent libertinism. Connecting the KS with the Tantra is a modern innovation, and the classical Indian treatises on erotology, written as they were by Hindus, clearly distinguish the aim of pleasure (*kama*) from that of liberation (*moksha*). This synthesis has proliferated in the current spiritual marketplace, which finds New Age–type institutes offering courses in "Tantric sex" incorporating sexual positions taken from the KS.[21]

Hopkins's book aside, the name *Kama Sutra* has been appropriated by at least one other gay sex manual, *The Gay Kama Sutra* by Colin Spencer. This book includes perspectives and art from a number of ancient and modern cultures, and while taking Vatsyayana's KS as its starting point, Spencer sensibly recognizes that "at least two-thirds of it has little direct relevance to modern society, either gay or straight."[22] He puts the descriptions of sexual positions into modern language, illustrates them with explicit line drawings, and has a respectful but critical attitude toward ancient Indian sexology.[23] There are many other sex manuals that have only the most minimal relationship to the original, using the KS in their titles as a conventional sign for cultivated eroticism.[24]

Conclusion

In the nearly 120 years since the first publication of Burton and Arbuthnot's translation the KS's queer aspects have been both exaggerated and minimized, depending on the taste and agenda of the translator or commentator. The KS has served both to validate same-sex relations and to deny their existence; this aspect of the text's reception may be of more interest than the treatment of the subject in the KS itself, in which same-sex relations occupy a rather marginal position. One thing has been consistent: since the "eunuchs" of the old colonialists, followed by the guilt-free *ars amoris* of Foucault and his followers, to the lesbians, gay marriages, and other gay reinterpretations of Daniélou and others, people have seen in the KS what they have wished to, with little regard for the text itself or its historical and social context. That in itself is perhaps the queerest thing about this book and its interpreters after all.

Notes

The original stimulus for this article was my review of Alain Daniélou's translation; see Michael Sweet, "A New Translation of the *Kama Sutra*: Perceptions and Misperceptions of Ancient Indian Sexuality," Trikone 10, no. 1 (1995): 11–12. Upon more careful consideration, my opinion of this translation has become even more critical. The present chapter was greatly improved by the insights and keen editing of my partner and scholarly collaborator Leonard Zwilling. The Sanskrit text of the KS consulted here was Vatsyayana, *Kamasutram*, 2 vols., *with the* Jayamagala *commentary of Yashodhara and a Hindi translation, subcommentary and notes by Pandit Madhavacharya* (Kalyana-Bambai: "Laksmiveṅkatesvara" Stim Press, 1934).

1. Edward W. Said, *Orientalism* (New York: Vintage Books, 1979).
2. Richard Burton and F. F. Arbuthnot, *The Kama Sutra of Vatsyayana* (1883, reprt. New York: G. P. Putnum's Sons, 1963). Arbuthnot was a British Indian civil servant and amateur Sanskitist who did the actual translation, which was revised and edited by Burton.
3. A full discussion of the eunuch misconception is found in Michael J. Sweet and Leonard

Zwilling, "The First Medicalization: The Taxonomy and Etiology of Queerness in Classical Indian Medicine," *Journal of the History of Sexuality* vol. 3, no. 4 (1993): 595–96. Most recent writers on this subject have eliminated references to "eunuchs" in their discussion of the third sex and other nonnormative gender and sexuality in classical India; however, for a contrary opinion, see Albrecht Wezler, "Sanskrit *panda-/pandaka-*," *Zeitschrift der Deutschen Morgenländischen Gesellschaft* 148 (1998): 261–76.

4. On the *cinaedus* (*kinaidos* in Greek) see Amy Richlin, "Not before Homosexuality: The Materiality of the *Cinaedus* and the Roman Law against Love between Men," *Journal of the History of Sexuality* 3, no. 4 (1993): 523–73, as well as her *Garden of Priapus: Sexuality and Aggression in Ancient Rome*, rev. ed. (New York: Oxford University Press, 1992).

5. This was the opinion of the great Australian Indologist, A. L. Basham, expressed in his magisterial *The Wonder That Was India* (New York: Grove Press, 1959), 172.

6. For a review of this belief see Ruth Vanita's preface, in Ruth Vanita and Saleem Kidwai, eds., *Same-Sex Love in India: Readings from Literature and History* (New York: St. Martins Press, 2000), xxiii–xxiv.

7. See exposition and analysis of his commentary in Ruth Vanita, "The *Kamasutra* in the Twentieth Century," in Vanita and Kidwai, eds., *Same-Sex Love*, 236–40.

8. I have treated this subject extensively before, and thus will not belabor it here; see Leonard Zwilling and Michael Sweet, "'Like a City Ablaze': The Third Sex and the Creation of Sexuality in Jain Religious Literature," *Journal of the History of Sexuality*, 6, no. 3 (1996): 359–84. Other critiques of Foucault are found in Bernadette J. Brooten, *Love Between Women: Early Christian Responses to Female Homoeroticism* (Chicago: University of Chicago Press, 1996), 4–9, 21–26, 143–73; and most fully in Stephen O. Murray, *Homosexualities* (Chicago: University of Chicago Press, 2000); see especially 111–13, 159–60. The canonical statement of Foucault's view is found in Michel Foucault, *The History of Sexuality* vol. 1, *The History of Sexuality: An Introduction*, trans. Robert Hurley (New York: Random House, 1980), 42–43. Representative later restatements are in David M. Halperin, *One Hundred Years of Homosexuality* (New York: Routledge, 1990), 15–40, and John J. Winkler, *The Constraints of Desire* (New York: Routledge, 1990), 3–4.

9. See Richlin's research on the *cinaedus* in classical Rome ("Not before Homosexuality"), as well as Zwilling and Sweet, "'Like a City Ablaze,'" 5. On Tokugawa Japan see Paul Shalow's introduction to Ihara Saikaku, *The Great Mirror of Male Love*, trans. Paul Shalow (Stanford: Stanford University Press, 1990), 1–46. On medieval European categories based on sexuality see Jonathan Walters, "'No More than a Boy: The Shifting Construction of Masculinity from Ancient Greece to the Middle Ages," *Gender and History* 5, no. 1 (1993): 20–33; about the "sodomitical subculture" in Renaissance Florence and Venice see Giovanni Dall'Orto, "La Fenice di Sodoma: Essere omosessuale nell'Italia del Rinascimento," *Sodoma: Revista Omosessuale di Cultura* 4 (1988): 31–53; the homosexual subculture of eighteenth-century Netherlands is described in Theo van der Meer, *De wesentlijke sonde van sodomie en andere vuyligheeden: Sodomietenvervolgingen in Amsterdam, 1730–1811* (Amsterdam: 1984). On Native-American conceptions of gender/sexual difference see Walter Williams, *The Spirit and the Flesh: Sexual Diversity in American Indian Culture* (Boston: Beacon Press, 1987).

10. David M. Halperin, "Forgetting Foucault," *Representations* 63 (1998): 93–120.

11. Foucault, *The History of Sexuality*, 57. I have omitted references to the French original as Hurley's translation is complete and accurate.

12. As Alain Daniélou expressed in his introduction to *The Complete Kama Sutra* (Rochester, VT: Park Street Press, 1994), "The work is essentially addressed to the citizen . . . meaning a wealthy, bourgeois male who is an art-lover and either a merchant or civil servant

living in a large city" (7). Hereafter, page numbers from Daniélou's translation will be cited parenthetically in the text.

13. Alain Daniélou, *The Way to the Labyrinth: Memories of East and West*, trans. Marie-Claire Cournand (New York: New Directions, 1987).

14. John Boswell, *Same-Sex Unions in Pre-Modern Europe* (New York: Vintage, 1994). For a detailed critique see Brent D. Shaw, "A Groom of One's Own?" *New Republic*, July 18 and 24, 1994, 33–41.

15. This is accurately translated (*Ut cuiusque disiderium est, ita clamores et ictus adhibeantur*) in Richard Schmidt, *Das Kamasutram des Vatsyayana: Die Indische Ars Amatoria* (Stuttgart: Franz Decker Verlag, ca. 1915), 215; even Burton and Arbuthnot give a fairly accurate translation of this passage: "Striking, scratching, and other things may be done during this kind of congress" (117). Daniélou's translation of the comment on this sutra is similarly fanciful.

16. See Mark Epstein, "In the Realm of Relationship: Mark Epstein Interviews Jeffrey Hopkins," *Tricycle*, Summer 1996, 53–58. This interview, in which Hopkins explicitly speaks of gay sex from a spiritual perspective, incited several virulently homophobic letters from readers of this ostensibly liberal publication.

17. Jeffrey Hopkins, *Tibetan Arts of Love: Sex, Orgasm, and Spiritual Healing* (Ithaca, NY: Snow Lion, 1992); hereafter, page numbers will be cited parenthetically in the text. Gendün Chöphel's dates 1905–1951. For the best biography of this fascinating figure see Heather Stoddard, *Le Mendiant de L'Amdo*, (Paris: Société d'Ethnographie, 1985).

18. Hopkins, *Tibetan Arts of Love*, 91–92.

19. Jeffrey Hopkins, *Sex, Orgasm, and the Mind of Clear Light: The Sixty-four Acts of Gay Male Love* (Berkeley: North Atlantic Books, 1998), xii.

20. See ibid., 115–20.

21. For example, the tantra.com web site, which presents itself as a "resource for Tantric Sex, Sacred Sex, and the Kama Sutra," contains material such as the following extract from *The Kama Sutra and the Sixty-four Arts* by Nik Douglas and Penny Slinger: "The Sixty-Four Arts should be conceived as paths of creative energy. They are emanations of the goddess Saraswati, the "anima" of Jungian psychology. . . . Burning up all negativity, these flames of the creative attitude purify the psyche and bring about an inner transformation."

22. Colin Spencer, *The Gay Kama Sutra* (New York: St. Martin's Press, 1996), 10.

23. Ibid., 10–17, and throughout.

24. For example, a number of books of photographs illustrating sexual positions use KS in their title, including Bjorn Andersen, Ray Lightbown, and Simon Watney, *Kama Sutra of Gay Sex* (London: Prowler Press, 1995), the heterosexual *Illustrated Kama Sutra: An Intimate Photographic Guide to the Arts of Love*, ed. Zek Halu, Misha Halu, and Jane Graham-Maw (London: Thorsons, 1995), and a number of others of this ilk. A recent sex manual, with tiny chunks of the KS interspersed throughout as a kind of masala, is Johnina Wickoff and Deborah Romaine, *The Complete Idiot's Guide to the Kama Sutra* (Indianapolis: Alpha Books, 2000).

Part 2

The Visions of Fiction

6

Loving Well

Homosexuality and Utopian Thought in Post/Colonial India

Leela Gandhi

In the otherwise monumental *Gay and Lesbian Literary Heritage*, edited by Claude Summers, the weak constitution of a dangerously slim entry on South Asia is attributed to the ill effects of a puritanical tradition. The voluminous literature of ancient and medieval India, we are told, is consistently "silent on the subject of homosexuality," a reticence that "perhaps reflects the generally conservative mores of the people."[1]

Where, once, the redoubtable Katherine Mayo gleaned from India a catalog of sexual irregularities, severely in need of civilizational cleansing, Summers laments the reverse—a nation fraught with repression and piety, compelling its homosexual refugees to seek amnesty in other, more sexually enlightened cultures, "either the United States or Britain—countries that have well established gay and lesbian communities with a tradition of organized resistance—and therefore have greater sexual and artistic freedom."[2] To "come out," in other words, is to "go out"; a process that requires the emotionally hazardous barter of a cultural heritage for a sexual community. Is this necessary, or true?

According to Ruth Vanita and Saleem Kidwai, editors of the recent anthology *Same-Sex Love in India*, the politically careless imputation of a schism between homosexuality and Indian tradition only serves to nourish the hysterical and homophobic rhetoric of conservative lobbies at home, eager to perpetuate the "myth that same-sex love is a disease imported into India from the West."[3]

Defying both the scholarly and unscholarly consensus on this subject, Vanita and Kidwai insist that the rich vein of same-sex desire in South Asia, journeying from the ancient Sanskrit epics through medieval Puranic narratives and Urdu poetry, is eventually frozen not from within India but from without, through peculiarly English sexual anxieties and accompanying legislative proscriptions, introduced into India during the colonial encounter. Thus, foregrounding repression rather than license as the Western import into India, Vanita and Kidwai invite us to reconsider the British origins of the enduring antisodomy law introduced into India in 1861 as Section 377 of the Indian Penal Code (IPC).

Likewise, British (homo)sexual anxieties are amply reflected in the Purity campaigns of the 1880s and 1890s, which resulted in the growing public condemnation and legal curtailment of homosexuality at home and abroad, in the colonized world.[4]

This essay surveying same-sex desire in Indo-Anglian literature concurs with the historical assumptions that inform the work of scholars like Vanita and Kidwai. It argues that any coherent understanding of homoerotic articulation and disarticulation in such literature requires that we return, once again, to the scene of the colonial encounter. For it is there that we might begin to comprehend homosexual definition, with some semantic help from Eve Kosofsky Sedgwick, not only as an "issue of active importance for a distinct, relatively fixed homosexual minority" but equally "as an issue of continuing, determinative importance in the lives of people across a spectrum of sexualities."[5] In the main, my argument is this: If empire introduced a virulent strain of homosexual anxiety/homophobia at home and abroad in the colonies, it also generated, at its margins, a counteractive form of dissident or radical homo/bisexual *reasoning* that became the agent, on both sides of the colonial divide, of wide-ranging social, political, and epistemological transformations. What follows is a rough story line for the emergence of homosexual utopianism in the shadow of empire, from its early prophets to its tentative, residual strains within the boisterous world of Indo-Anglian literature.

The theoretical overture with which I would like to begin this narrative takes its cue from Monique Wittig's prematurely "outdated" thesis in *The Straight Mind*.[6]

Like many gay/lesbian theorists before and since, Wittig postulates heterosexuality as an institution—indeed, as the prevailing social contract—founded on the ineluctable categories of sex. The "category of sex," she writes, "is the political category that founds society as heterosexual. . . . For to live in society is to live in heterosexuality. In fact, in my mind, social contract and heterosexuality are superimposable notions. The social contract I am talking about is heterosexuality."[7] Framed in these terms, homosexual desire/identity is inescapably politicized in and as an existential obligation to break with the prevailing social contract by destroying the sociological reality of the sexes:[8] "If we as lesbians and gay men, continue to speak of ourselves, and to conceive of ourselves as women and as men, we are instrumental in maintaining heterosexuality."[9]

Two features of Wittig's thesis require closer attention. First, although she represents the categories of sex as a male/female dialectic, she is at one with the wider tradition of French feminist philosophy in conceiving of heteronormativity principally as a closed masculine economy wherein "femaleness" (or effeminacy?) is variously effaced, repressed, or banished from modes of production and signification.[10] We will return later in the discussion to this account of the continuity between masculinity and heterosexualization. Second, by imagining homosexuality as a third position outside the binary of sex—indeed, outside of the social contract itself—Wittig secures a powerfully utopian provenance for the activity of homosexual identification.[11] To withhold consent to the categories of sex, she insists, entails nothing less than the dream of reformulating a new social order through "voluntary associations" with a range of other "fugitives."[12] If, as Wittig suggests, the "straight mind" is susceptible to the wider inequities nourished by binary thinking— "Shouldn't we mention that the paradigm to which female, dark, bad and unrest belong has also been augmented by Slave, other, different?"—then the "bent mind" is, or ought to be, in some green Blakean world, constitutively exempt from, and innately critical of, these susceptibilities.[13]

In recent years Wittig's work has been subjected to a severe, if curiously tautological, critique that alleges that the better "no place," already implicit in the etymology of the "utopia" directly invoked in *The Straight Mind*, is not a real (political) place. In her eloquent but pessimistic verdict on Wittig, Annamarie Jagose insists that "the point is not that the revolution is a long time coming, but that it may not be coming at all," adding that, contrary to orthodox leftist "assumptions about the nature of transgression," the circumambience of power renders any "radically revolutionary gesture ultimately recuperable," so much so "that an apparently subversive gesture is complicit with normative regulatory practices."[14] While remaining alert to the realism of such admonishments we need also to apprehend utopianism—Wittig's or anyone else's—first as a politics of possibility whose content is aspirational rather than practical, and second as a politics of evasion that, knowing too well the treacherous web of power, its techniques of appropriation and recuperation, makes its escape precisely by situating itself beyond representation, beyond knowledge and co-optation, beyond order and prohibition. Furthermore, to borrow opportunistically some words from Judith Butler, and to bring this phase of my discussion to a close, it is precisely because the "totality" of Wittig's homosexual utopia "is permanently deferred, never fully what it is at any given juncture in time," that it also possesses the capacity for "open coalition . . . an open assemblage that permits of multiple convergences and divergences."[15]

In order to proceed with a search for the availability of a Wittig-type homosexual utopianism in post/colonial India, let me propose that both empire and its antagonist, the anticolonial nation, need to be recognized as profoundly heteronormative projects that founded their competing authorities on the categories of sex—that is, on a closed, masculine signifying economy. In recent years, as a range of scholars have turned their attention to the role played by gender in determining the relations between colonizer and colonized, it is generally understood that if late-Victorian culture increasingly came to privilege masculinity as the repository of colonial authority, it simultaneously insisted upon the contrasting "effeminacy" of colonized Indian men as an alibi for conquest and domination.[16] However, even though the "effeminate" East was often identified within colonial discourse as a homosexual or "sotadic zone,"[17] the imperial project itself, circumscribed as it was by the anxious prerogatives of masculinity, was not homoerotic (as Sara Suleri argues) so much as it was aggressively homophobic, for, while homophobia may well be construed as the manifestation of an ambivalent or guilty desire, it also folds rather more readily into the paranoid upkeep of heterosexual identity/culture. As Sedgwick explains, "male heterosexual identity and modern masculinist culture may require for their maintenance the scapegoating crystallization of a same-sex desire that is widespread and in the first place internal."[18] In these terms, then, the oft-cited anticolonial/nationalist endeavor to self-reform in the image of the aggressor, by recuperating a "lost" native masculinity, can be said to herald the onset of a postcolonial heteronormativity—tragically collaborationist and fraught by the pressures of a newly internalized homophobia, or fear, in other words, of effeminacy.[19] Thus, Swami Vivekananda's claim that the salvation of Hindus depended on the three B's, beef, biceps, and Bhagvad-Gita (in a sharp departure from the easy eclecticism and aspirational androgyny of his guru Sri Ramakrishna), and Nathuram Godse's assassination of Mahatma Gandhi in the name of a "remasculated" Hindu polity, each bespeak Indian nationalism's capitulation to the culture of colonial heteronormativity.

Among the countless examples—literary and otherwise—of the homophobia that has since permeated Indian society,[20] Salman Rushdie's evolving oeuvre offers, perhaps, the most revealing map of the contiguity between the psychic territories of post/colonial anxiety and homosexual panic.[21] In *The Satanic Verses* (1988), the protagonist Saladin Chamcha—Anglophile "toady" by name and nature—discovers, with a belated sense of historical déjà vu, that he has become the object of racist/English homophobic invective. Homo/sexually assaulted and humiliated by immigration officials in a police van,[22] he is negatively contrasted throughout the novel to Gibreel Farishta, the "unreconstructed" migrant whose credo of aggressive heterosexual masculinity is consistently rehearsed through a phantasmic sexual possession of a conversely feminized England.[23] Chamcha's character and fictional career implicitly postulate "emasculation" as just punishment for those who willingly submit to the indignity of cultural conquest. But while Chamcha is surprised to find himself negatively homosexualized, the antinationalist and empire-loving Aires da Gama, in *The Moor's Last Sigh* (1995), is, as though unavoidably, portrayed as an incurable and impotent homosexual. Much like the cultural nationalism to which Rushdie—despite his protestations to the contrary—owes his genealogy, his novels are troubled by a profoundly internalized colonial homophobia, suspicious of native effeminacy, and desperate to recuperate the cultural privileges of heterosexual masculinity. Such, too, are the anxieties that inform the making of Ormus Cama in *The Ground beneath Her Feet* (1999), a wishfully manly Indian migrant who discovers, like conservative lobbyists in contemporary India, that homosexuality is a peculiarly Western perversion. Surrounded, in England, by sexual "deviants"—his benefactor Mull Standish and sodomitical drug squad cops—he exacts his cultural/sexual revenge through a punitive relationship with the lesbian lover of Standish's amateur-orientalist ex-wife.[24]

There is sufficient evidence to make a case for the family resemblance between imperial and anticolonial heteronormativity. Accordingly, might we not hypothesize that a postcolonial culture of homosexual dissidence that withholds consent to the nationalist social contract may, if it exists, also be shown to emerge out of an earlier culture of colonial homosexual dissidence that withheld consent, in this instance, to the imperialist social contract? Let us consider, in such a hypothetical mode, the career of Edward Carpenter (1844–1929), the late-Victorian British socialist, author, and homosexual, whose writing consistently defended homosexuality as a utopian project equipped—pace Wittig—through its refusal of the rigid polarities of gender, to eschew a range of contingent and prevailing binaries and hierarchies. Carpenter developed these and other related ideas in a variety of texts, of which his *Love's Coming-of-Age* (1896) and *The Intermediate Sex* (1908) are the most representative.

Written in an atmosphere of fear following the 1895 trials of Oscar Wilde, *Love's Coming-of-Age* squarely blamed the late-Victorian cult of masculinity (sustained, he argues, through a dialectical relation to femininity) for a multitude of sins, including imperialism and race prejudice. Resisting the mainstream valorization of masculinity for its material and mechanical achievements, Carpenter detected in it the revealing symptoms of a defective or "ungrown" nature, constrained by an undeveloped heart and by a natural tendency to tyranny. The "men who have sway of the world today" were, in his reasoning, the architects of deformed societies, were men "to whom it seems quite natural that our marriage and social institutions should lumber over the bodies of women, as our commercial institutions grind over the bodies of the poor, and our 'imperial' enterprise over the bodies of barbarian races."[25] Modern civilization, in other words, was diseased with hypermasculinity and could only be cured, on Carpenter's strong recommendation, through the therapeutic intervention of "intermediate types" or homosexual physicians.

Drawing on and subverting the rhetoric of eugenics and evolutionism popular at the time,[26] Carpenter projected homosexuals as a possible species of the future who might improve upon the palpably inadequate temperaments produced by the prevailing categories of sex. As he argues in *The Intermediate Sex*, "We do *not* know, in fact, what possible evolutions are to come. . . . It may be that, as at some past period of evolution the worker-bee was without doubt differentiated from the two ordinary bee-sexes, so at the present time certain new types of human kind may be emerging, which will have an important part to play in societies of the future—even though for the moment their appearance is attended by a good deal of confusion and misapprehension. It may be so; or it may not. We do not know."[27]

Here, as elsewhere, Carpenter's tactical utopianism situates the homosexual beyond knowledge, and, so, beyond governing habits of judgment. But, equally, by withholding from homosexuality itself what Butler calls "the normative telos of definitional closure,"[28] he effectively reformulates the homosexual project as an "open coalition" capable of accommodating conjunctural solidarities and counterallegiances between disparate and shifting groups. "Eros," he writes, "is a great leveller. Perhaps the true Democracy rests, more firmly than anywhere else, on a sentiment which easily passes the bounds of class and caste, and unites in the closest affection the most estranged ranks of society."[29]

True to the political obligations of utopian thought, Carpenter's own sympathies were consistently expansive and inclusive. A prominent figure in the ranks of late-nineteenth-century British socialism, he endeavored—through a Whitmanic rhetoric of democratic comradeship—to draw the "worker" into the campaign against the "beefy satisfaction" of public school masculinity.[30] Likewise, convinced of a natural affinity between male homosexuals and women, he combined forces with the Woman's Freedom League, formed in 1908, to further the cause of the suffrage campaign. Active, along with Henry Salt, in the animal rights movement, Carpenter was also notable as a passionate antivivisectionist and advocate for the establishment of animal sanctuaries.[31]

Such, then, were the political susceptibilities that underscored, in the main, Carpenter's fierce anti-imperialism and contingent disavowal of Western civilization. Numerous passages in his early prose poem, *Towards Democracy* (1883), scorn "the blessings of empire," extracted as they are from "Ireland . . . / Rack-rented, drained, her wealth by absentees in London wasted . . . / India the same—her life blood sucked—but worse: / Perhaps in twenty years five hundred million sterling, from her famished myriads, / Taken to feed the luxury of Britain.[32] Carpenter's tentative exploration of Indian philosophy in this work culminated in his homo-sexual/spiritual odyssey to India and Ceylon in 1890. Recorded in *From Adam's Peak to Elephanta* (1892), this journey yields the joyful discovery of sympathetic "transitional types" in India, and brings confirmation of imperial bigotry, as it were, on the field.[33]

In her thoughtful article on Carpenter's Indian sojourn, Parminder Kaur Bakshi charges him, perhaps too readily, with "sexual colonialism," predicated, despite his apparent disaffection with English civilization, on the sexual/colonial opportunities of empire.[34] And yet, while the Carpenter case study does confirm, à la Said, the impossibility of ever securing full immunity from the contagious discursive/material networks of orientalism and its cousins, it also diversifies and complicates the logic of these networks, for it is precisely out of solidarity with the defiant "effeminacy" and affectivity of (some) Indian men that Carpenter developed his dissenting condemnation of conquest and colonialism, calling, in a scathing article published in 1900 in *The Humane Review*, for the "ruin . . . *the sooner the better*" of "these fatuous Empires."[35]

Carpenter's eclectic radicalism was by no means confined to his own personal politics; it equally helped to promote and nourish a unique style of collaborationism within the larger culture of late-Victorian dissidence. This, he maintained, was the homosexual's unique gift and obligation: to show society "the wealth and variety of affectional possibilities which it has within itself."[36] Evidence of his influence is found, for instance, in the pages of *Justice*, the journal produced by the Social Democratic Federation, to which Carpenter gave substantial financial and ideological support.[37] Edited by H. M. Hyndman, William Morris, and J. Taylor, *Justice* maintained a systematic attack on British imperialism, asserting full parity between the cause of workers at home and that of colonized "races" abroad. And, in an extraordinarily polemical article, "Shall We Fight for India?" published as early as 1885—well before Indian nationalism developed a coherent agenda—Hyndman called, categorically, for the cessation of the Indian empire, writing, "I do say here, however, unavailingly, that for the sake of England and of India, I would far rather that we were driven right out of the country than that we should continue the miserable rule which has disgraced us and injured the people for the last eight and twenty years; and I can only hope that not only Socialists but all working Englishmen will look carefully into the facts."[38]

Carpenter presided over a similar series of disparate affiliations in the activities of the Humanitarian League. Begun in 1891, with his support, to improve the treatment of animals, the league substantially expanded its constituency and concerns, drawing workers' movements into the cause of animal welfare and, simultaneously, asserting continuity between the struggles for animal rights and against imperialism. Writing in this vein to M. K. Gandhi in 1932, Henry Salt, the League's founder, reiterated his own abiding commitment to the freedom and welfare of India, while observing the lamentable symbiosis between racial/national hierarchies and those separating the human and nonhuman worlds: "I feel as strongly as ever that food-reform, like Socialism, has an essential part to play in the liberation of mankind. I cannot see how there can be any real and full recognition of Kinship, as long as men continue either to *cheat*, or to *eat*, their fellow-beings!"[39]

With characteristic cynicism, George Orwell once caricatured the "magnetic force" with which "Socialism and Communism draw toward them . . . every fruit-juice drinker, nudist, sandal-wearer, sex-maniac, Quaker, 'Nature cure' quack, pacifist, and feminist in England."[40] If ungenerous, this catalog does capture some sense of the promiscuous alliances that were threaded through the fragile and brave world of late-Victorian radicalism. More remarkable still is the fact that, for a brief while, and despite the terror consequent upon the Wilde trials, homosexuality had insinuated itself into the secret—the *developed*—heart of socialism. Indeed, the unsettling proximity of socialism and homosexuality was, if unfortunately, well foregrounded in a libelous attack on Carpenter in 1908, through a pamphlet entitled *Socialism and Infamy: The Homogenic or Comrade Love Exposed: An Open Letter in Plain Words for a Socialist Prophet to Edward Carpenter*.[41] By 1910 the attack had found its mark and Carpenter was purged, with apologies, from the local council.

Carpenter's influence had, in fact, begun to wane well before this direct attack. As early as 1894, Robert Blantchford, the editor of a socialist paper called *The Clarion*, was urging him to prioritize "industrial change" over the "sexual question."[42] Blantchford's reprimands, in turn, reflected a major shift in the ideological concerns of British socialism following the creation of the Independent Labour Party in 1883. Committed, from the outset, to getting labor candidates into parliament, the ILP firmly adopted the path of respectability and, shedding, thus, its "immature'" revolutionary origins, soon forgot both Carpenter and his utopianism. And with it, homosexuality, too, forgot the substance of its grand affair with socialism. What then of Carpenter's legacy in India? Or rather, can we find some version of his peculiar brand of radicalism among Indian materials?

In *The Intimate Enemy* Ashis Nandy famously finds examples of bisexual radicalism in Gandhi, and in the larger tradition of Gandhian politics. "It was colonial India," he writes, "still preserving something of its androgynous cosmology and style, which ultimately produced a transcultural protest against the hyper-masculine world view of colonialism in the form of Gandhi."[43] Combining a unique (but also recognizable) set of ingredients in anticolonialism, vegetarianism, and a formative antipathy to "modern civilization," Gandhian *ahimsa* or nonviolence is, indeed, predicated upon a rigorous refusal of heteronormative masculinity. In Gandhi's understanding, the *ahimsaic* agent or activist is obliged to feminize the activity of resistance by emulating the normative, albeit stereotypical, selflessness of motherhood, self-containment of the widow, and so on. His own "queering," as it were, of gender positions is frequently expressed in his aspiration to transcend gender relations, or the desire, as he puts it, to "mother" his companions and, in so doing, to become "God's eunuch."[44] Gandhi's religious hermaphroditism, however, does not signify the zone of a transgressive sexuality, but projects sexlessness—true *brahmacharya*—as the necessary effect of bringing femaleness to bear upon maleness. His aversion to sexuality itself is sharply crystallized in his delineation of the inherently violent or *himsaic* nature of marriage, and, thus, of the patriarchal family, whose filiative structure, he insists, necessitates and condones repetitive acts of violence on the naturally nonconsenting bodies of women. In his words, "Young men in India . . . are married early. . . . Nobody tells them to exercise restraint in married life. Parents are impatient to see grandchildren. The poor girl wives are expected by their surroundings to bear children as fast as they can."[45]

Nandy, in his study, quite appropriately endeavors to distill an indigenous provenance for Gandhi's politicotheoretical bisexuality. And without contesting, for a moment, Gandhi's complex blending of submerged traditions within Hinduism, Jainism, and Buddhism, I would also like to direct attention to his influential transcultural exchanges with late-Victorian radicalism and radicals. As is well acknowledged, Gandhi's early sojourn in England brought him in close contact with the very socialists, vegetarians, and theosophists whom we have been considering in the discussion so far.[46] While we cannot credit these groups for introducing Gandhi to ideas that were, quite simply, implicit in his inherited tradition, they certainly authenticated and revivified the practices and convictions to which he was merely habituated or accustomed. So, if Gandhi found Hinduism exhilaratingly universalized by the theosophists, his early exposure to Henry Salt's *Plea for Vegetarianism* gave "vital legitimacy," as Rajmohan Gandhi writes, to "his Indian inner voice."[47] So too, Gandhi's *Hind Swaraj* openly concedes Edward Carpenter's influence, among others, in shaping his own skepticism about modern/Western civilization. "Societies," he writes, "have been formed to cure the nation of the evils of civilization. A great English writer has written a work called 'Civilization: its Cause and Cure.' Therein he has called it a disease."[48] We have already encountered the theoretical progression of Carpenter's own negotiations with modernity, and it is worth mentioning, in this context, that it was Carpenter's *Civilization* that provoked Robert Blantchford into his nervous recommendation that socialism quickly abandon the issue of sexual organization. Later in his life, of course, Gandhi would find himself similarly berated for his eccentricities, and excluded from the mainstream, as the incipient Indian nation prepared to transform itself into a respectable postcolonial state. Acknowledging these complex shared circuits between Gandhi and Carpenter, Henry Salt wrote to the former on December 2, 1929, to inform him that "all good causes have suffered a loss this year by the death of Edward Carpenter."[49]

In turning now to the residual traces of these Gandhian mediations in Indo-Anglian literature, my account does not seek to be comprehensive so much as to supply a gestural and fragmentary map for reading. I focus on two writers, Aubrey Menen and Vikram Seth, selected for the reason that in their writing same-sex desire frequently projects a skeptical view of heteronormativity and, in so doing, supplies an idiom for expansive (and utopian) sympathies with heterodox/marginalized/subjugated beings, ideasm and knowledges.

Born in 1912 in London to an Indian father and Irish mother, Menen is author of an oeuvre that bristles with the compromises contingent upon being an outsider/insider in the pernicious shadow of empire. The anxieties of cultural alienation further combine, in his case, with those of sexual alienation to produce a scathing account of the seamlessness between British colonialism and masculinity. Withholding consent to both, through the alibis of his Indo-Irish blood and homosexual orientation, Menen's fiction deftly imagines a dissident alternative world populated by irreverent Wildean figures who find themselves in sympathetic counterallegiance with, among others, trees, "orientals," children, criminals, and "primitives." His first novel, *The Prevalence of Witches* (1947), discloses a homoerotic community of young Englishmen in an Indian outpost appropriately called Limbo, where, freed from obligatory polarities of being, they learn to comprehend the "etiquette" of the jungle and to believe—against the oppressive rationalism of the

British administration—in the prevalence of witches. The peculiar pretensions of London society (and European civility) are lampooned in *The Stumbling Stone* (1949), in which a saintly celebrity starts a fund-raising drive secretly to send a juvenile offender on a hedonistic holiday to Rome. And, in a similar vein, the hypocrisies of English heterosexualism are parodied in *The Abode of Love* (1956), which retells the "true" story of a promiscuous curate who defies Victorian respectability by founding a religion in which sexual freedom receives spiritual sanction and accommodation in a comfortable country house. The theme is reiterated in *The Fig Tree* (1957), wherein a puritanical scientist invents, by accident, a devastatingly aphrodisiacal oral contraceptive. Homosexuality itself is fully explicated in *Fonthill* (1975), a fictional biography of William Beckford, author of the orientalist tale *Vathek* (1786), and infamous creator of Fonthill Abbey, a gothic extravaganza. As Menen's story progresses, Fonthill is transformed into a utopian "closet" where, safe from the brutal homophobia of philistine Englishmen, Beckford itemizes the expansive beauty (and enlightened "homo-susceptibilities") of the Orient in the edifying company of his lover Franchi, an affectionate dwarf who hates the human race, and the India-loving Farquhar, a "monkey man" who extols the polite company of trees.

Writing nearly a generation after Menen, Vikram Seth's formal eclecticism is also underscored by a corresponding ethical range. Although homo-/bisexuality lurks everywhere beneath the surface of his accomplished texts, we need rigorously to resist the critical temptation simply to expose or "out" its content. Rather, as Christopher Lane urges in another context, it is more fitting to study the ways in which Seth deploys the medium of sexual ambiguity "to demonstrate what is precarious and lacking in heterosexual meaning" and contingent "national formations."[50] Thus, in Seth's epic novel *A Suitable Boy*, the central actor Maan is in possession of an easy bisexuality that is fitfully elaborated in the secret enclaves of the story. The novel hints at his love affair with Firoz, the aristocratic son of the Nawab of Baitar, and elsewhere Maan is tellingly gentle and amused when rejecting the sexual advances of yet another man, the Rajkumar (prince) of Marh. But perhaps the most important feature of Maan's bisexuality—for Seth and certainly for the narrative—is that it qualifies his almost unconscious resistance, and refusal, to give consent to the normative values of his world, which is tethered on the one hand to the bullying protocols of heterosexual masculinity and on the other to a linked culture of religious intolerance, brutally separating Hindus and Muslims in postindependence India. Trapped within this ethos, Maan opts out of the obligations of respectable masculinity enforced by his tyrannical father by failing first to earn a living and second to secure a wife. Instead, breaking with the surrounding communal proscriptions, he devotes his energies to bridging the Hindu-Muslim divide through a variety of unorthodox means: embarking on a love affair with Saeeda Bai, a Muslim prostitute; taking a long sabbatical to learn Urdu in the village of his Muslim tutor Rashid; and turning, heroically, against a crowd of Hindu rioters to save the life of his Muslim friend Firoz. Writing in a milieu where the masculinist spite of Hindu nationalism is directed inward, toward a vulnerable Muslim minority, Seth produces a hero whose alienated bisexualism sympathetically extends toward this persecuted minority as easily as Carpenter's once did toward the colonized "races." And, as though in confirmation of his sympathies, Maan finds within the literary culture of Islam a sustaining corpus of same-sex desire, rehearsing, for example, with Saeeda Bai the *ghazal*s of Mir Taqi Mir, "Urdu poetry [which] like much Persian and Arabic poetry before it, had been addressed by poets to young men."[51]

In his poetry Seth continues his negotiations with Islam, turning on more than one occasion to the *Baburnama*, the autobiography of Zahiruddin Muhammad, the first Mughal ruler of India, which includes an account of the emperor's distracting passion for a boy called Baburi.[52] It is in poetry, too, that Seth draws upon the discourse of sexual ambivalence to detail affinities between the human and nonhuman world.[53] In *Mappings* (1994) male lovers are frequently figured in animal form, and moths, fox cubs, and spiders intercede, variously, in the troubled world of same-sex desire. So too, in Seth's libretto, *Arion and the Dolphin* (1994), where dolphins are praised as the benign deities of homosexual love, once saving Enalus and his lover from their "too-fluid fate."[54] As the narrative evolves, the tragic love between the singer/poet Arion and a dolphin takes its place within a typology of inconceivable desire(s). Seth's *Beastly Tales* (1991) further enumerates a catalog of unlikely pairings, between, for example, a crocodile and monkey, a cat and cock, an elephant and tragopan. Concluding with a manifesto for nonviolent, interspecies cohabitation, this anthology bemoans the incurable rapacity of modern "man": "He sees the planet as his fief / Where every hair or drop or grain of sand / Is destined for his mouth or hand. / If he is thirsty, we must thirst—For of all creatures, man comes first. / If he needs room, then we must fly; /And if he hungers, we must die."[55] Pure Carpenter? Close enough.

Notes

1. Claude Summers, ed., *The Gay and Lesbian Literary Heritage: A Reader's Companion to the Writers and Their Works from Antiquity to the Present* (New York: Henry Holt, 1995), 664.
2. Ibid.
3. Ruth Vanita and Saleem Kidwai, eds., *Same Sex-Love in India: Readings from Literature and History* (New York: St Martin's Press, 2000), xxiv.
4. See Christopher Lane, *British Colonial Allegory and the Paradox of Homosexual Desire* (Durham, England: Durham University Press, 1995), 158, and Ronald Hyam, *Empire and Sexuality: The British Experience* (Manchester: Manchester University Press, 1990), 88. Hyam is especially insistent about the English origins of "third-world" homophobia: "More damaging by far has been the willingness of Third World governments to adopt the peculiar Purity laws and conventions of Britain in the 1880s as if they represented ultimate truths about human civilisation. They do not. All they represent, like most other sets of conventions, is a localised cultural perception (or some may think misperception) and, in particular, a puritanical code politically attuned to the supposed needs of ruling a world-wide empire with aloof if benevolent dignity" (215).
5. Eve Kosofsky Sedgwick, *Epistemology of the Closet* (Harmondsworth, England: Penguin, 1994), 1.
6. Monique Wittig, *The Straight Mind and Other Essays* (Boston: Beacon Press, 1992).
7. Ibid., 5, 40. Wittig's thesis has been notably "updated" by, among others, Judith Butler in *Gender Trouble: Feminism and the Subversion of Identity* (New York: Routledge, 1990): "The institution of a compulsory and naturalized heterosexuality requires and regulates gender as a binary relation in which the masculine term is differentiated from a feminine term, and this differentiation is accomplished through the practices of heterosexual desire. The act of differentiating the two oppositional moments of the binary results in the consolidation of each term, the respective internal coherence of sex, gender, and desire" (22–23).

8. In Wittig's words, "For the category of sex is a totalitarian one . . . we must destroy it and start thinking beyond it if we want to start thinking at all, as we must destroy the sexes as a sociological reality if we want to start to exist"; Wittig, *Straight Mind*, 8.
9. Ibid., 30.
10. Consider, for example, the following qualification: "The category of sex is the one that rules as 'natural' the relation that is at the base of (heterosexual) society and through which half of the population, women, are 'heterosexualized' . . . and submitted to a heterosexual economy"; ibid., 6. Butler objects strenuously to the allegations of "global phallogocentrism" that mark much Western feminist thought: "Feminist critique ought to explore the totalizing claims of a masculinist signifying economy, but also remain self-critical with respect to the totalizing gestures of feminism. The effort to identify the enemy as singular in form is a reverse-discourse that uncritically mimics the strategies of the oppressor instead of offering a different set of terms"; Butler, *Gender Trouble*, 13. While this critique is salutary, Butler posits an unnecessary homology between "men" and "masculinity." Indeed, in its inventive exploration of the asymmetrical relations of sex, gender, and desire, queer theory especially ought to allow for the possibility of a male eschewal of masculinity, or, in reverse, a masculinist repression not only of "women" but also of "womanliness"/"effeminacy" in men. The plurality of such oppositions eludes the pitfalls of mere reversal within the fixed identifying signs of a binary system.
11. See also Marjorie Garber's notion, in *Vested Interests: Cross-Dressing and Cultural Anxiety* (Harmondsworth, England: Penguin, 1993), of the third space of the transvestite, "which questions binary thinking and introduces crisis" (11). I am indebted to Brian Flanagan for drawing my attention to this example, as also for his provocative discussion of heteronormativity and radical drag in "Refashioning the 'Straight-Jacket': Queer Gender Performances in Heteropatriarchy's Sartorial Prison," *Lateral* (http://www.latrobe.edu.au/www/english/lateral.html).
12. ". . . breaking off the heterosexual social contract is a necessity for those who do not consent to it. For if there is something real in the ideas of Rousseau, it is that we can form 'voluntary associations' here and now, and here and now reformulate the social contract as a new one, although we are not princes or legislators. Is this mere utopia? Then I will stay with Socrates's view and also Glaucon's: If ultimately we are denied a new social order, which therefore can exist only in words, I will find it in myself; Wittig, *Straight Mind*, 45.
13. So often in Wittig's prose does homosexuality figure, quite simply, as shorthand for an opposition to binary reasoning that it emerges as a position implicitly enabled by sexual preference, but not limited by it.
14. Annamarie Jagose, *Lesbian Utopics* (New York: Routledge, 1994), 6–7, 5.
15. Butler, *Gender Trouble*, 16.
16. See Ashis Nandy, *The Intimate Enemy: Loss and Recovery of Self under Colonialism* (Delhi: Oxford University Press, 1983); Mrinalini Sinha, *Colonial Masculinity: The "Manly Englishman" and the "Effeminate Bengali" in the Late Nineteenth Century* (Manchester: Manchester University Press, 1995); Sara Suleri, *The Rhetoric of English India* (Chicago: University of Chicago Press, 1992); Revathi Krishnaswamy, *Effeminism: The Economy of Colonial Desire* (Ann Arbor: University of Michigan Press, 1998), and Kate Teltscher, " 'Maidenly and Well Nigh Effeminate': Constructions of Hindu Masculinity and Religion in Seventeenth-Century English Texts," *Postcolonial Studies* 3, no. 2 (2000): 159–70.
17. Krishnaswamy argues this point: "The metropolitan production of heterosexuality/homosexuality in nineteenth-century psychological/psychoanalytic, medical, and anthropological discourses interestingly intersects with the colonial elaboration of Indian effeminacy . . . homosexuality could be named more safely in an anthropological discourse about the colonized Other"; ibid., 31.
18. Sedgwick, *Epistemology*, 85.
19. Krishnaswamy is apposite, once again: "Hindu men felt forced to reform themselves and

their religion in the image of a muscular, monotheistic, heterosexual, masculine Protestantism"; *Effeminism*, 44.

20. For a comprehensive account of homophobia in postindependence India see Vanita and Kidwai, eds., *Same-Sex Love*, 191–217.

21. I discuss Rushdie's postcolonial homophobia more comprehensively in my "Ellowen Deeowen: Salman Rushdie and the Migrant's Desire," in *England through Colonial Eyes in Twentieth-Century Fiction*, ed. Ann Blake, Leela Gandhi, and Sue Thomas (Macmillan, 2001).

22. Salman Rushdie, *The Satanic Verses* (1988, reprt. Dover, England: The Consortium, 1992), 155–62.

23. See especially the Rosa Diamond episode, ibid., 129–56.

24. See Salman Rushdie, *The Ground beneath Her Feet* (London: Jonathan Cape, 1999), 288–89, 296.

25. Edward Carpenter, *Love's Coming-of-Age: A Series of Papers on the Relation of the Sexes* (1896, reprt. London: George Allen and Unwin, 1948), 56.

26. For further comment on Carpenter's complex appropriation of contemporary eugenics and evolutionism see Sheila Rowbotham and Jeffrey Weeks, *Socialism and the New Life: The Personal and Sexual Politics of Edward Carpenter and Havelock Ellis* (London: Pluto Press, 1977), 110–11. Although Carpenter favored the gentler Lamarckian model over the Darwinian, he is one among many late-Victorian radicals who co-opted evolutionism for distinctly radical ends. The appendix to *Love's Coming-of-Age* includes a curious excerpt from Charles Leyland's "The Alternate Sex," which claims that Darwin is an "intermediate type" by temperament: "Great geniuses, men like Goethe, Shakespeare, Shelley, Byron, Darwin, all had the feminine souls" (170).

27. Edward Carpenter, *The Intermediate Sex: A Study of Some Transitional Types of Men and Women* (1908, reprt.; London: George Allen and Unwin, 1952), 11.

28. Butler, *Gender Trouble*, 16.

29. Carpenter, *The Intermediate Sex*, 114–15.

30. Carpenter, *Love's Coming-of-Age*, 54.

31. Among the many paeans to the nonhuman world in Carpenter, *Towards Democracy* (1883, reprt. London: GMP, 1985), the following excerpt with its promise of loyalty, is especially eloquent: "I saw deep in the eyes of the animals the human soul look out upon me. I saw where it was born under feathers and fur, or condemned for awhile to roam fourfooted among the brambles. I caught the clinging mute glance of the prisoner, and swore that I would be faithfull'"(146).

32. Ibid., 373–74.

33. *From Adam's Peak to Elephanta: Sketches in Ceylon and India* (London: George Allen and Unwin, 1892).

34. Parminder Kaur Bakshi, "Homosexuality and Orientalism: Edward Carpenter's Journey to the East," in *Edward Carpenter and Late Victorian Radicalism*, ed. Tony Brown, *Prose Studies Special Issue* 13, no. 1 (1990): 151–77.

35. Edward Carpenter, "Empire in India and Elsewhere," *Humane Review* 1 (1900): 207; emphasis in the original.

36. Carpenter, *Love's Coming-of-Age*, 181.

37. Carpenter put up the initial three hundred pounds that launched *Justice* and, along with William Morris, met its running costs for much of the first year.

38. H. M. Hyndman, "Shall We Fight for India?" *Justice*, March 1885, 4.

39. Henry Salt to M. K. Gandhi, in George Hendrick and Willene Hendrick, eds., *The Savour of Salt: A Henry Salt Anthology* (Fontwell, Sussex, England: Centaur Press, 1989), 176. In 1904 Salt published a single satirical issue of the *Brutalitarian: A Journal of the Sane and Strong*, a paper that claimed to support imperialism, flogging, and blood sport. Much like Carpenter's, Salt's writing, too, holds middle-class Victorian masculinity responsible for a multitude of sins.

40. George Orwell, *The Road to Wigan Pier* (1937, reprt. Harmondsworth, England: Penguin,

1967), 152.

41. For more detail on this controversy see Rowbotham and Weeks, *Socialism and the New Life*, 89.

42. Blantchford, cited in Chushichi Tsuzuki, *Edward Carpenter, 1844–1929: Prophet of Human Fellowship* (Cambridge: Cambridge University Press, 1980), 122.

43. Nandy, *The Intimate Enemy*, 45.

44. M. K. Gandhi, cited in Ved Mehta, *Mahatma Gandhi and his Apostles* (London: Deutsch, 1977), 191, 192.

45. M. K. Gandhi, *Self-Restraint versus Self-Indulgence* (Ahmedabad: Navjivan, 1928), 105. This discussion of Gandhi draws on my earlier article, "Concerning Violence: The Limits and Circulations of Gandhian Ahimsa or Passive Resistance," *Cultural Critique* 35 (1997): 105–48.

46. See James Hunt, *Gandhi in London* (1978, reprt.; Delhi: Promilla, 1993), 18–34, and Stephen Hay, "The Making of a Late-Victorian Hindu: M. K. Gandhi in London, 1888–1891," *Victorian Studies* (Fall 1984): 76–98.

47. Rajmohan Gandhi, *The Good Boatman: A Portrait of Gandhi* (Delhi: Penguin Books India, 1995), 63.

48. M. K. Gandhi, *Hind Swaraj and Other Writings*, ed. Anthony J. Parel (Cambridge: Cambridge University Press, 1997), 34.

49. Henry Salt to M. K. Gandhi, December 2, 1929, in Hendrick and Hendrick, eds., *Savour of Salt*, 175.

50. Christopher Lane, *British Colonial Allegory and the Paradox of Homosexual Desire* (Durham, England: Durham University Press, 1995), 4.

51. Vikram Seth, *A Suitable Boy* (Delhi: Penguin Books India, 1993), 84.

52. See, for instance, Seth's poem "From the Babur-Nama," in *The Humble Administrator's Garden* (Delhi: Oxford University Press, 1987):

> A lad called Baburi lived in the camp-bazaar.
> Odd how our names matched. I became fond of him—
> "Nay, to speak the truth, distracted after him."
> I had never before this been in love
> Or witnessed words expressive of passion, but now
> I wrote some Persian verses: "Never was lover
> So wretched, so enamoured, so dishonoured
> As I"; and others of this type . . . (38)

53. For an account of Seth's negotiations with the nonhuman world see Ruth Vanita, *Sappho and the Virgin Mary: Same-Sex Love and the English Literary Imagination* (New York: Columbia University Press, 1996), 235–37.

54. Vikram Seth, *Arion and the Dolphin* (Delhi: Penguin Books India, 1994), 44.

55. Vikram Seth, *Beastly Tales from Here and There* (Delhi: Penguin Books India, 1991), 74.

7

"Do I Remove My Skin?"

Interrogating Identity in Suniti Namjoshi's Fables

Anannya Dasgupta

In one of her prefatory notes to the selections in *Because of India,* Suniti Namjoshi observes how a male-centered humanist universe consigns every other creature to the position of the "other." She converts this reductive exclusion to a positive alliance and accepts identification with "birds and beasts" and in effect with the rest of creation. However, the category of the beast, although less confining, lacks specificity: "All right, I was a beast, a creature. But what sort of beast was I?"[1]

Namjoshi's works engage extensively with problems of self-conception that arise when a decision to adopt a particular identity has to be carefully negotiated with a resistant and unwieldy universe. Her works respond to the exigency of individuation, explored through a series of situations where "otherness" and alienation are scrutinized and the possibility of radical regroupings examined. The basis of the group shifts from biology to a kinship of shared perception.

Namjoshi's experience of the diaspora as an Indian lesbian puts her through a threefold marginalization so that she develops what she calls the "Asian perspective," the "alien perspective," and, later, the "lesbian perspective"(22). These outsider perspectives become the filtering consciousness she uses to reevaluate the norms of a patriarchal, heterosexist society. As opposed to Northrop Frye's all-devouring Anagogic Man (whom Namjoshi mythologizes as Spindleshanks, the all-devouring cow, in *The Conversations of Cow*),[2] her central protagonist is a metaphoric "beast" who accepts her difference, and, unlike Spindleshanks, does not feel the need to devour the "other" in order to assimilate it. Namjoshi refrains from using the term *humanity,* either as normative or as an admiring epithet. Instead, she has a Blue Donkey, a One Eyed Monkey, and "Suniti," among many other creatures who explore their eccentric beings in relation to themselves and to each other.

I here examine Namjoshi's uses of the fable especially in relation to questions of identity and location. I scrutinize the strategies she uses to dislocate paradigms of gender and race in favor of newer ones. This process is exemplified in Spindleshanks's failed attempt to become substantial by stuffing her insides with

everything she sees outside. The attempt fails because a sense of nothingness cannot be assuaged by an indiscriminate absorption of extraneous givens. The alternative in this text is Bhadravati, the Cow of a Thousand Wishes, who transforms
herself and experiences her desires and fears turned inside out. The anxieties attendant on an individual's identity and location constitute a theme in most of
Namjoshi's works. I will connect this theme to the extratextual issue of Namjoshi's
location in the context of Indian writing in English.

No One from Nowhere

Most accounts of Indian writing in English or anthologies of critical essays on this
writing either omit Namjoshi or mention her perfunctorily.[3]

This omission is surprising given her relative popularity in India. Namjoshi
published her first book of poems in 1967, with the Writers' Workshop, Calcutta.
Since then she has written and published poetry and fables, at first with minor
women's presses and later with bigger publishing houses. In the 1980s Penguin
India compiled and reprinted her works; today some of them are familiar to the
average reader in India who reads Indian writing in English. Her writings' popularity is evidenced by their presence in the subaltern underbelly of the book business in Delhi, the Sunday book bazaar, a secondhand and remaindered book market
that flourishes on the pavements of Daryaganj in Old Delhi on Sundays. This market operates on the straightforward logic of demand and supply. Pirated copies of
any book with more than a moderate demand are available here. Namjoshi's *Blue
Donkey Fables* may be sighted among piles of Linda Goodman, Arundhati Roy, and
now the books of the Harry Potter series. The only consolation for the authors
robbed of royalties may be that their presence here is a backhanded compliment—
evidence of popularity.

Unexpected, often unacknowledged, allusions to Namjoshi's fables crop up in
discussions and representations of feminist issues. For instance, dancer Mallika
Sarabhai, in her solo production "Sita's Daughters," dramatized parts of *Feminist
Fables*. She combined classical dance with storytelling to represent snippets from
the women's movement in India. These proofs of popularity make it harder to
fathom the reasons for critics' neglect of Namjoshi.[4]

I suggest that one reason may be the sheer difficulty of classifying and contextual-
izing her works. As a poet and fabulist with a lesbian-feminist agenda, she does not
seem to stem from the kind of literary ancestry or milieu that can easily be identified
as shared by writers otherwise as stylistically distinct as R. K. Narayan, Shashi
Deshpande, Anita Desai, and Amitav Ghosh. Namjoshi also weaves poetry into the
structure and logic of the fable, which can be disconcerting even to those who have
known the literary effrontery of Kamala Das's verse. In her fictions Namjoshi employs
a combination of an ancient gnomic form and a fantastic mode, with uniquely genre-
defying results. Although her immediate literary context challenges the reader's
imagination, her literary ancestry is easily traceable to Indian, West Asian, and
European folklore, myth, fabulous stories, and fairy tales. Her narrative also reflects
some of the oral traditions of storytelling. Thus, in terms of technique she stands
quite apart from Indian novelists like Bharati Mukherjee, Rohinton Mistry, and
Vikram Seth, whose styles are reminiscent of the nineteenth-century realist novel.

Unlike Salman Rushdie, whose near-pyrotechnic style has inspired much stylistic virtuosity in writers since *Midnight's Children*, Namjoshi's style, although ingenious, did not dazzle the literary scene and has not collected a band of imitators. Namjoshi seems to occupy a solitary space, neither following from nor followed by recently canonized literary traditions.

A "Lesbian" from "India"

Both Indian and Western readers seem ambiguous about accepting Namjoshi's works as authentically Indian, partly due to her lesbian perspective, and partly owing to the absence of a tangible India in her works. Ironically though, it is precisely this politics of two identities, those of an "Indian" and a "lesbian," that constitutes the most important semantic cluster in her work. She repeatedly returns to the liberating as well as limiting effects of the uneasy conflation of these two identities. An encounter with racism in her initial visits to the United States and Canada lent keenness to her identity as an Indian, a racial other. At the same time her politicization in the 1970s among white American feminists provided her with a liberating gender discourse, but only fractionally accounted for her differing sexuality and did not accommodate her skin color at all. Repeatedly the question arises, as it does in *Because of India*: "[A]s a creature, a lesbian creature, how do I deal with all other creatures who have their own identity?" (84).

Instead of retreating into a distinctly Asian subculture that only duplicates the pattern of "othering," an option exercised by many subsequent South Asian diasporic writers, Namjoshi interrogates her own ideology and identity and articulates a desire to understand her location vis-à-vis "other creatures": "'I am a perfectly good donkey,' she said at last. 'What exactly is the matter with you?' 'Your Blueness troubles us,' wailed the citizens.'"[5] Namjoshi does not react with an anxious reinforcement of her difference or an equally anxious attempt to blend with the surroundings. She ironizes the convenience of these options for diasporic writers in "Poem for Grey Day": "And yet, the artificial bird in its natural rage / could ignite, if it chose, a candid page, / and stand there an exotic alien burning bright" (*BDFMM*, 68).

Having charted Namjoshi's relation to the West and its response to her, one finds that the dynamics of her relationship with India is far more complex. One can identify a Hindu-Brahman "Indianness" in the landscape of her work. Although she says that for her it is "as familiar as unconscious" (*BOI*, 28), it comes with a self-reflexive pinch of discomfort. This discomfort arises from her awareness that in India her Indianness is secure and even privileged because of her high caste, but it has required her to "BE DISCRETE" (*BOI*, 28)—a euphemism for dishonesty about her sexuality. A different level of unease stems from her use of the English language: "[H]ow to write about India in English? After all my Indian experience was as everyday and as familiar to me as anything could be; but in English, things Indian became exotic." (*BOI*, 42).

Namjoshi figures her Indianness and her lesbianism in ways that do not seem mutually exclusive to readers in India nor spectacular and exotic to readers in the West. To focus on the ordinariness of a creature who happens to be different, she uses the fable, a genre at once realistic and fantastic, exploratory and didactic.

Historically, the fable, because of its instructive value, came in handy to propagate dominant ideologies, whether to reinforce class and gender inequality or legitimize certain behaviors, sexual or otherwise. The much-celebrated resurrection of the genre in England during the Enlightenment coincided with its popularity in instruction books in schools. Some of the respectability attained by the genre was reflected onto its originator. Literary historians "rescued Aesop from his earlier depictions of the halting, misshapen churl and recast [him] as a genial peasant, advisor to the mighty and Western father of wisdom literature."[6]

In *Blue Donkey Fables* as well as *Feminist Fables* a lesbian feminist consciousness intersects with a genre traditionally pressed into the service of the dominant patriarchal culture. In Namjoshi's hands the fable regains some of its vitality, for it is made to perform the function of understanding human behavior rather than prescribing it.

Idiosyncratic "Truths" and Intertwined "Patterns"

The two defining features of the fable are a mandatory moral at the end of the story and nonhuman protagonists enacting the plot that illustrates that moral. Mary Ellen Snodgrass finds the defining characteristic of the fable in its "implicit or pictorial representation of truth."[7]

The fable is closely linked to the proverb, another repository of truth that claims universal application. It is essential for these genres to deal with types, not individuals. Namjoshi makes it clear at the outset that her ideology and perspectives are shaped by her specific situation—that of an Indian lesbian in an alien culture. Namjoshi systematically examines how the traditional fable, being a product of patriarchy, is written from a position shaped by an implicit ideology and is therefore neither entirely universal nor entirely true. She thus sets herself up against the "truths" of a given order. However, instead of appearing to invent a contesting "truth" (for an appearance of invention would weaken its claim against the "truth" that claims established universality) she adopts a stance of discovering it. She also creates interesting new creatures to go with the traditional beasts that people the fables of Aesop, Jean La Fontaine, and the *Panchatantra*.

Unlike traditional fables, which apply generalizations to individuals, Namjoshi's fables address idiosyncratic individuals and reveal the general appeal of idiosyncrasies. In her handling, "truth"—and by extension the semantic enterprise of keeping words and things connected—is discovered as provisional, highly variable, and open to a multitude of interpretations. Thus her fables offer a kind of truth validated by the fabulist's conscious feminism. If truth seems temporary, this reflects not so much the nature of truth itself but the nature of the subject proclaiming it.

The etymology of the word *fable* suggests that it should have had little to do with truth at all. The Latin root word *fabula* means a made-up story; this links the fable to the idea of falsehood. Namjoshi's tongue-in-cheek retelling of some canonical fables may suggest how they were faithful to their original sense, after all.

In 1981 Suniti Namjoshi published *Feminist Fables*, her first set of fables. In *Because of India* she attributes the writing of *Feminist Fables* to her politicization through her introduction to feminist theory and issues: "For me they were a way of exploring Feminist ideas and their implications for the patterns I had inherited through the mainstream literary tradition" (79). The "pattern" is a recurrent leit-motiv in Namjoshi's comments on her art. She uses the word *pattern* to suggest a visual representation of the organizing principle of logic in any work of art. When acknowledging her debt to Lewis Carroll, she posits that mathematics "makes beautiful patterns within self-contained systems." In her reading, Carroll's great facility with the fantastic stems from his ability to "combine patterns of logic which are sometimes only patterns of convention" (*BOI*, 104).

For Namjoshi an obvious advantage of using the fable is that with each fable she can move between different worlds, where each world is a self-contained system with a specific logic and pattern of assumptions. For instance, in a patriarchal heterosexist world the pattern of logic is such that oppression is disguised in a rhetoric of privilege, as the feminist daughter unsuccessfully tries to explain to her mother in "The Mother's Daughter."[8] In this fable, daughter and mother inhabit different worlds so the pattern of each is nonsensical for the other. Namjoshi consistently employs this technique of juxtaposing mismatched worlds in order to interrogate the values of each system without allowing it the comfort of its familiar rhetoric.

The Lesbian in the World

Most "self-contained systems" are sustained by a myth validating the principles that hold the system together. Thus the creation stories and originary myths of patriarchal heterosexist systems imagine the earth to have been the outcome of a cosmic heterosexual act. Namjoshi's fables are similarly involved in myth-making for a self-contained lesbian system. Two fables attempt to account for the world's beginning. One ironically corroborates the heterosexist myth while the other chronicles the parthenogenetic origin of the earth. The first, "Exegesis," briefly describes creation, and then debates the gender of the sun. The violent, impregnating qualities attributed to the sun discount the possibility of its being the earth's sister; the fissures on the earth's body are read as evidence of the sun's violent masculinity: "The sun must be male. The earth must be woman. These are principles. Look at the gashed and fissured earth. Look at the harsh light giving sun" (*FF*, 57). However, the moral of the fable lies not so much in the obvious imagery of rape and violence associated with masculinity but in the playful substitution of the word *woman* for *female*. The word *woman* carries all the associations of social construction, unlike the biological connotations of the word *female*. The punch line reinforces the premise that in order to be human it is important to be male: "there are no human women" (57).

The second creation story, "The Saurian Chronicles" (*FF*, 112), uses the logic of simple inversion when a wise old female lizard recounts "the world's beginnings." The beginning is paradisal—only the First Mothers roamed the earth. However, the story of the beginning is also the story of fall and punishment brought about by a female request for a male companion. The young male lizard listening to the story feels the weight of his ancestor's fault but is unable to question the validity of "ancient wisdom."

Another theme in the fables is the attempt to define a lesbian in relation to her world. "Troglodyte" tells the story of an ancient female cave dweller who loved another cave woman and drew sketches of her. However, the evidence is lost in time, and the absence of documentation is taken as proof of her nonexistence. She is not allowed to exist even as a hypothesis or a myth. The moral of the fable points to the societal denial of lesbian existence.

"The Badge-Wearing Dyke and Her Two Maiden Aunts" distinguishes between sexual behavior and the identity that may or may not follow from it. *Behavior* is about homosexuality as sexual orientation, while *identity* is about making that orientation a political position as well. The dyke in the story is a young mouse who wears gay liberation badges and visits her two spinster aunts who have loved one another and lived together for twenty-five years in the labyrinths of the city of mice. They decline their niece's offer of badges. The moral perhaps is that if women love women, they will continue to do so even if the formal recognition of their love as valid is slow in coming.

However, not all the fables end on such a happy note. In "The Example," a lesbian wren is victimized because of her sexuality in spite of the fact that, unlike the badge-wearing dyke mouse, she does not proclaim it. Her protest that it is a private matter is countered by the homophobic sparrows who appropriate the feminist slogan "the personal is political." In another fable, "A Moral Tale," the lesbian becomes completely "private" and withdraws from the "public" realm altogether. In this retelling of "The Beauty and the Beast," the lesbian chooses to identify with the beast, who "was a woman. That's why its love for Beauty was so monstrous. . . 'I know what it is,' she said one day, '. . . I am not human.' The only story that fits me at all is about the Beast. The Beast doesn't change from a Beast to a human because of its love. It is just the reverse . . . it lives alone and dies alone. And that's what she did" (*FF*, 23).

Rewriting Romance Paradigms

The presence of witches, ladies, dragons, quests, and occasional knights in Namjoshi's fables alerts us to her use of the structures and rhetoric of the quest narrative of medieval romance. This is a strategic appropriation because the rituals of heterosexual courtship and love today still hark back to those courtly romances. Namjoshi parodies these rituals and subverts them by changing the traditional alliances. The lady and the dragon are both oppressed by man in "The Dragon Slayers," and they change this power equation in "Perseus and Andromeda," where Namjoshi writes, "And as usual the prince, the princess and the dragon: the function of the Prince is to fight the dragon, the function of the princess is to serve as bait, and the function of the dragon is to take the blame. But suppose the princess has ambitions of her own" (*FF*, 50). The princess has the prince tied to the stake and goes off with the dragon.

The rituals of courtship are further transformed as all the moves and responses are examined and some of their assumptions replaced. A highly reshuffled subtext of the Spenserian quest romance and narrative of unrequited courtly love can be identified in Namjoshi's fables. For Edmund Spenser, as well as several other Renaissance poets, unrequited love occasions poetry used to woo the beloved: "Leaves, lines, and rymes, seek to please her alone."[9] The lover's art is posited as incapable of competing with the beloved, who is seen as a superior work of art by nature herself. The high point of courtship is of course consummation, beyond which both works of art, beloved and poem, are subsumed in domesticity. What remains of the beloved is the exaggerated image of her beauty, kept alive in verse: "but you shall live by fame: / my verse your vertues rare shall eternize."[10]

Namjoshi deals with the relationship of love and art in "The Disinterested Lover" (*FF*, 108) where Narcissus, looking for the beautiful woman's image in the water, gazes at his own reflection, which he mistakes for hers. The woman senses his ardor and offers herself to him, but he rejects her in favor of the image he thinks is hers but is actually his own. Jeanette Winterson, following Sigmund Freud, notes that the myth of Narcissus "warn[s] us of the dangers of recognizing no reality but our own."[11]

Namjoshi adds a twist to this reading because she sees Narcissus as the artist/lover who loves representations and images, whether his own or somebody else's. Thus, in a very Paterean/Wildean sense,[12] art comes to symbolize the pulsating moments of unique experience not subject to the diminishing pleasure that would follow consummation. Namjoshi's Narcissus does not confuse the real with the representation. The representation becomes its own objective. This is the kind of art that Winterson describes as art that "can only be itself, it can never substitute for anything else. Nor can anything else substitute for it."[13] Thus, the definition, the need for, and the practice of art and poetry undergo a change when placed outside dominant ideas of heterosexual sex and love.

While avoiding a crudely reductive reading of art as directly reflective of sexuality,[14] one can still look at the ways in which homoeroticism may transform the idea of art. In Namjoshi's poem "The Lion Skin" (*BDFMM*, 35), unrequited love, following mainstream conventions, occasions poetry: "And yet there is poetry of penury / that far outdoes the paeans of plenitude." The poem, which the poet calls the "dream," is informed by a very physical craving for the beloved's body, yet it is "made of such stuff / that to dream is best and the dream enough." Unlike Spenser's *Amoretti*, where the sonnets are ostensibly for the beloved's perusal, Namjoshi's lover keeps the dream to herself: "I shall be content, for the dream that absorbs / me can have no other end." What she parts with instead is the lion's skin, chopped up like leather balls, resembling "the lopped / heads of poets crammed with passion and despair"; this provides "mirth and holiday" to the beloved. In *Blue Donkey Fables* lions and tigers are recurrent representatives of conventions legitimized by the dominant order, as in the poem "Among Tigers" (70) or in the fables "Serious Danger" (83) and "The Disciple" (28). Thus, the lion's skin that the poet/lover dons is metaphoric of received conventions. This explains the resemblance of its chopped pieces to the stuffed heads of Petrarchan sonneteers. The lover sheds the conventions and retains the core of her dream and art, in a manner reminiscent of Narcissus, content with the beloved's supposed image.

The Fabulous Use of The Fantastic

The mythical, metaphorical, and real beasts in Namjoshi's works serve as allegories of human foibles. In *Blue Donkey Fables* animals function to allow an easier intersection of human identities based on gender, species, cultural location, and sexual orientation. Namjoshi's beasts constitute yet another "self-contained system" into which she finds a rare entry point: "I had done / nothing to find myself there. . . /

any moment now the fabric would tear; / someone would say I have no business there" (*BDFMM*, 80). She satirizes rude human intrusion, colonization, and patronizing of the beasts' world in "The Playboy" (62), "Mute Swan" (15), and "The Purposeless Pandas" (90–91), respectively.

Following their original othering by the humanist universe, the beasts in *Blue Donkey Fables* and *Feminist Fables* inhabit what Christopher Nash has classified as "other worlds" stories.[15] Their realm also bears a strong resemblance to J. R. R. Tolkien's "faerie realm"[16] although he excludes the beast fable from his classification. In their function Namjoshi's fables are close to Tolkien's fairy stories, which Tolkien describes in "Tree and Leaf," writing, "The magic of the faerie is not an end in itself, its virtue is in its operations: among these are certain primordial human desires. One of these desires is to survey the depths of space and time. Another is . . . to hold communion with other living beings."[17]

For C. S. Lewis the function of these "other worlds" stories lies in their ability to produce in the reader "profoundly wholesome new sensation, not merely the adventurer's 'excitement' . . . but the experience of *otherness for its own sake.*"[18] The value of this otherness lies in its broadening of our conception of experience. Besides, otherness is not, as Nash reminds us, exterior to us but is latent *in us*, and is materialized in us by fictions evocative of it.[19] Thus, the blueness of the Blue Donkey serves to emphasize her otherness (metaphoric of race or sexual preference),[20] which triggers in her both a desire for individuation and an anxiety of separation. It sets her off as a faery beast with whose difference readers must cope to the best of their ability. In "A Tale of Triumph" the Blue Donkey dreams of a contentious critic who attempts to prove to her that she is nonexistent: "Don't you see? You are a product of the imagination. You are a fabulous beast" (*BDFMM*, 41). The Blue Donkey is simultaneously a fable and a fabulous fabulist. Her blueness propels her through many roles, quests, and travels, and she forms and re-forms her identity as an individual who is in "communion with other living beings."

Namjoshi's concern with the individual's identity in relation to itself and the community is probed further in *The Conversations of Cow* (1985) and *The Mothers of Maya Diip* (1985). *Conversations* addresses the issue of attributed identity by literalizing the possibility of transformation. Bhadravati, a lesbian Brahmini cow, a sensuous goddess, plays on the Hindu concept of the *Kamadhenu* or wish-fulfilling divine cow. Ruth Vanita has demonstrated how the "lesbian cow" combines Eastern and Western representations and mythologies.[21]

The Sanskrit root *Kama* connotes both "desire/wish" and "sexual passion," a double meaning evoked in Bhadravati. *Conversations* is a work about possibilities, in a tractable conversational genre. The fantastic mode allows the narrative to operate outside the fixities of realistic etiologies. Bhadravati's many transformations undermine the solid boundaries of self and other. The central dilemma of the text is generated by this option of freewheeling identities. Suniti has the choice to change, but she doesn't know what she would like to be. She tries being a class B heterosexual companion (wife) to Baddy (Bhadravati's white male persona), and finds it the easiest way to be ordinary and acceptable, but at a price she is unwilling to pay. Suniti's alienation and self-absorption is made literal in her chaotic split self, S2. She finally realizes that alienation from one's self gets projected onto various "others," thus making them seem alien. The text's playfulness is disturbed by a strain of alienation, nothingness, and terror. In a nightmare shared with S2, Suniti sees the world stripped to nothingness and witnesses her own dismantling till she is reduced to nothing. It is only when Suniti learns to come to terms with her anxieties that S2 merges back into her, the cow reappears, and things return to a transfigured "normal."

Individual and Community

The idea of the "normal" is a central concern in *The Mothers of Maya Diip*. A take-off on *Gulliver's Travels*, it combines utopia and science fiction, fable and travelogue, and weaves poetry and myth to critique the idea of a separatist female community. Such communities are formed to realize social relations free of oppression. Maya Diip is a lesbian utopia, with "[n]o individual isolated and each woman bound to the others by ties of kinship, accepted loyalties and professional affiliation" (*BDFMM*,128). Motherhood is made a privilege, to be gained after much training and bureaucratic procedure. However, Maya Diip turns out to be an inverted patriarchy. The apparently radical norms are merely inversions of patriarchal rituals. The Therapists' Guild replaces the police in its role of suppressing excesses and behavioral oddity such as "[m]aladjusted mothers, unsisterly sisters, rivalries and jealousies of diverse sorts, non-conformity with Mayan customs, and of course the problem of the lovers" (128). Even violence and aggression, which Mayans believe to have been weeded out of their society by the systematic elimination of males, survives as a well-hidden secret in the form of atomic weapons stockpiled on the island. Although the crisis of succession is resolved within the text, Ashagarh, the all-male utopia headed by a woman, with its new-found knowledge of rape and war, becomes a time bomb for the Mayans. What begins as a lesbian feminist utopia soon takes the shape of a dystopian nightmare.

Both utopia and dystopia are conceptually related to the real through allegorical associations and represent possibilities to be accepted or avoided. However, in rejecting the idea of a separatist community, Namjoshi moves toward the "nonconceptual," a movement described by Rosemary Jackson as the opening up of "a space without/outside the cultural order."[22]

Namjoshi's use of the beast fable also incorporates elements of the "marvellous." The topography of her fables encompasses recognizable geography only to a limited extent; for the rest, it transports the reader to an alternative world, what Tolkien calls a "secondary world."[23] Jackson describes it as "a duplicated cosmos . . . relatively autonomous, relating to the 'real' only through metaphorical reflection, and never or rarely intruding into it."[24] We glimpse it in Namjoshi's poem "It's Not That the Landscape . . . ," in which she writes, "Oh neither you nor I could enter there. / We'd tread on the grass, we'd switch on the sun / and baffle the landscape with our mere / humanity" (*BDFMM*, 64).

It is interesting to consider the political implications of Namjoshi's choice of a genre and a mode critiqued for transcendental escapism by Karl Marx when Marx urges the importance of situating art firmly within the historical and cultural framework, as realist texts do. Jackson and others have counterargued that the fantastic is a literature of protest or of desire for that which is lost or absent. The fantastic (or the fabulous, in Namjoshi's case) "traces the unsaid and the unseen of culture: that which has been silenced, made invisible, covered over and made absent,"[25] like the Troglodyte's cave drawings of her beloved.

By retelling traditional tales, Namjoshi traces the homoerotic in the cultural unconscious of a consciously heterosexist world and the East in a consciously West-centric world. Her realm of real and imagined beasts allows more options for dealing with difference than the ones provided by separatist politics. Although her works are part of a lesbian counterculture, they never resort to cultural separatism. In this her position is akin to that taken by Winterson when she protests against the foregrounding of the writer's sexuality above all questions of literary worth: "We learn early how to live in our two worlds. Our own and that of the dominant model, why not learn to live in multiple worlds? The strange prismatic worlds that art offers?"[26] Namjoshi finds ways to blend her Indian and lesbian identities and heritages in the fables, which become "prismatic worlds" where the individual is allowed its uniqueness in a community that does not demand homogenization.

Notes

1. Suniti Namjoshi, *Because of India* (London: Onlywomen Press Ltd., 1989), 29. All quotations are from this edition; hereafter cited parenthetically as *BOI*.
2. "Frye's Anagogic man includes rather than excludes. But surely the demonic version of this is that he eats up everything instead of letting things be?" *Because of India*, 28.
3. See R. K Dhawan, *Indian Women Novelists* (New Delhi: Prestige Books, in Association with Indian Society for Commonwealth Studies, 1991); Chandra Chaterjee, *The World Within: A Study of Novels in English by Indian Women, 1950–1980* (New Delhi: Radha, 1996); R. S. Pathak, ed., *Recent Indian Fiction*. (New Delhi: Prestige Books, 1994); O. P. Saxena, *Glimpses of Indo-English Fiction*, 3 vols. (New Delhi: Jain Brothers, 1985); Aditya Behl and David Nicholls, eds., *The Penguin New Writing in India* (Delhi: Penguin, 1992).
4. Diane McGrifford, "Suniti Namjoshi (1941–)," in *Writers of the Indian Diaspora: A Bio-Bibliographical Critical Source Book*, ed. Emmanuel S. Nelson (Westport, CT: Greenwood Press, 1993), 291–97, notes that the only critical attention Namjoshi has received is in the form of reviews. She lists a handful of critical essays, mainly in Canadian journals.
5. Suniti Namjoshi, *Blue Donkey Fables, The Mothers of Mayadiip* (New Delhi: Penguin Books India, 1991). All quotes from these texts refer to this reprint, hereafter cited parenthetically as *BDFMM*.
6. Mary Ellen Snodgrass, *Encyclopedia of Fable* (California: ABC-CLIO, 1998), 99.
7. Ibid., 109.
8. Suniti Namjoshi, *Feminist Fables, Saint Suniti and the Dragon.* (Delhi: Penguin Books, 1995), 96. All quotations from these texts are from this reprint, hereafter cited parenthetically as *FF*.
9. "Amoretti," sonnet 1, in *The Poetical Works of Edmund Spenser*, ed. J. C. Smith and E. de Selincourt (London: Oxford University Press, 1960).
10. Spenser, "Amoretti," sonnet 75.
11. Jeanette Winterson, "Writer, Reader, Words," in *Art Objects: Essays on Ecstasy and Effrontery* (New York: Vintage International, 1995), 26. All references to Winterson's essays are to this collection.
12. See Walter Pater, *The Renaissance: Studies in Art and Poetry* (1873, reprt. Berkeley and Los Angeles: University of California Press, 1980). In the preface Pater argues that works of art are "powers or forces producing pleasurable sensations, each of a more or less peculiar or unique kind" (xx).
13. Winterson, "Writer, Reader, Words," 35.

14. Winterson's warning in the essay "The Semiotics of Sex": "The queer world has colluded in the misreading of art as sexuality. Art is difference but not necessarily sexual difference" (104).

15. Christopher Nash, *World Games: The Tradition of The Anti-Realist Revolt* (London and New York: Methuen, 1987), 104–5.

16. In his essay "Tree and Leaf" Tolkien describes the faerie realm: "Faerie is a perilous land . . . I have been hardly more than a wandering explorer in the land full of wonder but not information"; *The Tolkien Reader* (New York: Ballantine Books, 1966), 33.

17. Ibid., 41.

18. C. S. Lewis, quoted in Nash, *World Games* 104.

19. Nash, *World Games*, 104.

20. Ruth Vanita points out how Namjoshi's homoerotic vision employs beasts as a "multi-fariously suggestive trope for same sex love"; Vanita, *Sappho and the Virgin Mary: Same Sex Love and the English Literary Imagination* (New York: Columbia University Press, 1996), 215.

21. Vanita notes, "Namjoshi's lesbian cow yokes together two apparent irreconcilables—wittily focussing on the invisibility and the impossibility of the Indian lesbian both in Indian and Western contexts" (*Sappho*, 233). See also Vanita, "'I'm an Excellent Animal': Cows, Motherhood, and Love between Women," in *A Sea of Stories: The Shaping Power of Narrative in the Lives of Gay Men and Lesbians*, ed. Sonya Jones (New York: Haworth Press, 2000), 143–63.

22. Rosemary Jackson, *Fantasy, the Literature of Subversion* (London: Methuen, 1981), 43.

23. Tolkien, "Tree and Leaf," 60.

24. Jackson, *Fantasy*, 42.

25. Ibid., 3.

26. Winterson, "The Semiotics of Sex," 110.

8

"Queernesses All Mine"

Same-Sex Desire in Kamala Das's Fiction and Poetry

Rosemary Marangoly George

I am a freak. It's only
To save my face, I flaunt, at
Times, a grand, flamboyant lust.
                    —Kamala Das, "The Freaks"

I am Indian, very brown, born in
Malabar, I speak three languages, write in
Two, dream in one. Don't write in English, they said,
English is not your mother-tongue. Why not leave
Me alone, critics, friends, visiting cousins,
Every one of you? Why not let me speak in
Any language I like? The language I speak
Becomes mine, its distortions, its queernesses
All mine, mine alone.
                    —Kamala Das, "An Introduction"

I

Kamala Das requires no introduction to most readers of this anthology. Her reputation as a formidable literary presence in two languages (English and Malayalam) is now well established. Born in 1934 into an aristocratic Nair (Hindu) family in Kerala, Das is the author of many autobiographical works and novels in both languages, and of several highly regarded collections of poetry in English.[1] Her work has been widely anthologized in the Indian subcontinent and globally. Das's use of details from her own life to serve as examples of the oppression, sexual and otherwise, that women suffer under patriarchy has caught the attention of academic and lay readers alike. The centrality of sexuality in Kamala Das's writing is so commonly accepted that even brief mentions of her work include some comment on her representation of male-female relationships.

Yet, while sexuality and Kamala Das are almost manacled to each other in the literary criticism that her work has engendered, there is no discussion of Das's treatment of same-sex desire in this scholarly discourse. In this essay, I will demonstrate that the recent publication of "The Sandal Trees," the English translation of Kamala Das's short novella written in Malayalam and first published as "Chandana Marangal" (1988), calls for a radical rethinking of the heterosexist terms in which critical arguments about sexuality in this author's work have been made.[2] This is not because this lovingly narrated story of a forty-year romantic attachment between two women introduces a new topic into Das's work. Rather, "The Sandal Trees" simply brings to the fore a same-sex dynamic that has always been woven into Das's writing. In an attempt to contribute to, if not initiate, a new critical discussion—one that acknowledges the presence of same-sex desire as a recurring presence in Das's work—this paper examines this aspect of sexuality in some of the fiction and poetry written by Das from the 1960s onward and concludes with a reading of "The Sandal Trees."

In a recent article that examines this silence on same-sex relationships in critical responses to Das's 1976 autobiography, *My Story*, I have argued that Das's feminist readers have *straightened out* all the nonheteronormative protests and pleasures in this text in the process of making Das metonymic of a larger feminist project.[3] For instance, when Iqbal Kaur, author and editor of several feminist studies on Das, lists the important themes in this writer's work, the items correspond almost exactly to another list that Kaur draws up—a list of important foci of 1970s feminism in India.[4]

Mainstream, urban Indian feminism, like much mainstream middle-class feminism around the world from the 1960s to the 1980s, saw no connection between striving for feminist goals and efforts to legitimate same-sex relationships. From the 1970s to the present, English-language literary feminism in India has had a highly developed sense of patriarchal oppression but felt (and feels) little compulsion to work through the links between heterosexism and the oppressive weight of patriarchal systems. As many of the essays in this collection and the other projects of scholars included in this collection testify, articulations of and experiences of same-sex desire have always been in circulation in these discursive and material locations.

Literary feminism that produces and champions Indian women's writing in English operates within and against the parameters of a heterosexist middle-class notion of women's worth. Das emerges from this criticism as the quintessential victim whose feminist credentials are earned through her protest against male oppression in a patriarchal society. But while Das has repeatedly narrativized her gendered oppression, she has never consistently embodied this image of herself as an oppressed woman. Thus, Das's insistence on charting same-sex desire in her work is read as one facet of her occasional adoption of "unfeminist," contradictory stances in her self-presentation and in her writing. Part of Das's iconoclastic nonconformity is her refusal to consistently abide by the persona that her written work and interviews have constructed—the persona of the once sexually innocent child bride, then the sensuous woman artist married to a much older, unimaginative, and often cruel older man who was the embodiment of patriarchal oppression. Most recently, her widely publicized December 1999 announcement that she is going to convert to Islam, change her name to Suriya, and take to *parda*, has led to widespread speculation about her motives.

Indian literary feminists, especially when faced with aspects of Das's writing in which the antipatriarchal protest is blurred, have been exasperated by her "unreliability."[5] From the 1970s to the present, feminist critics writing on Das have celebrated and seconded her critique of the institution of marriage, of marital rape, and of the wifely obligations to fidelity even in an unhappy marriage, but not her critique of heterosexuality itself. Almost all critics (feminist and otherwise) writing on Das agree that the search for meaningful answers to life's mysteries *routed through a search for sexual satisfaction* is the all-consuming passion in her work.

I argue that Das has always considered homosexuality a very viable option available to those women and men who are in search of sexual fulfillment. Same-sex desire in fiction such as "The Sandal Trees" (1988, trans. 1995) and "Iqbal" (1974), and even in the much-anthologized poems "An Introduction" (1965) and "Composition" (1967), serves as one of the means by which Das moves beyond the bourgeois feminism practiced in her time and place. Not surprisingly, however, Das does not quite conform to a lesbian/gay politics or aesthetic. In her interviews and essays she has often spoken disparagingly of homosexuality but has also repeatedly spoken in favor of pursuing avenues for love and happiness that lie outside social sanction. In a 1993 interview with P. P. Raveendran, she notes, "I do not think I am lesbian. I tried to find out if I were a lesbian, if I could respond to a woman. I failed."[6]

Despite the autobiographical overtones of all her writings, and the usual classification of her style as "confessional" literature, I am not claiming that Kamala Das is a closeted lesbian waiting to be "outed" or resisting outing. She is not representative of the international phenomenon to which Dennis Altman and others have drawn our attention: namely, the internationalization of a certain form of social and cultural *identity* based on sexual orientation (homosexuality in particular) that is one of the signs of rapid globalization of culture.[7] Nor is she at the forefront, or even on the sidelines, of increasingly vocal gay and lesbian rights movements on the subcontinent.[8] Same-sex desire in Das's work does not usually operate along a hetero/homo divide; rather same-sex and opposite-sex relationships are intertwined in the sexual/spiritual journeys that form the core of so many of Das's narratives.

Das consistently encodes the homoerotic into her work and then just as consistently devalues its purchase. Homoerotic situations are depicted only to be repeatedly put aside, in *My Story* as well as in her fiction. Why does Das repeatedly go through the pleasures of such disciplining? And how long can this strategy—which some may see ultimately as homophobic—be maintained? In beautifully layered texts such as "The Sandal Trees" and a poem called "The Doubt," this backtracking and crisscrossing into same-sex relationships and back to heterosexuality with the possibility of return left open is greatly intensified. Along the route, however, Das presents in same-sex desire a pleasurable alternative to socially sanctioned heterosexuality.

II

I begin this reading of same-sex desire in Das's work by examining the telling reception of her story "Iqbal" by Indian critics who have interpreted this story in ways that reveal their failure to perceive connections between feminist resistance to patriarchal oppression and homosexual subversion of the institution of heterosexual marriage.[9] First published in 1974 in *Debonair* (a popular magazine for men), "Iqbal" concerns a love triangle between a husband, his wife, and his male lover. The story is told from the woman's point of view as she narrates her discovery of the real nature of her husband's relationship with this young man—a relationship that began before their wedding and has continued since. When Iqbal, the young lover, is hospitalized after an unsuccessful suicide attempt, the wife visits him in the hospital and apparently restores social order by flaunting her obvious pregnancy before him. Most critics have noted the homo-/heterosexual triangle that the story explores and have remarked that the "wife wins" because she is able to have her husband's child. The story does indeed end with the wife triumphantly revealing the "convexity of her middle" to Iqbal and taunting him with her ability to bear his lover's/her husband's child.

Even before Iqbal's suicide attempt we sense the grief that racks both men. The story contains several poignant and understated passages about the torment that this illicit relationship causes the two men; for example, when the wife discovers that she is pregnant: "We shall name him Iqbal, she said, we shall please your friend that way. Her husband buried his head in her lap and for a minute she felt that he was sobbing" (59). There is no further clarification of whether or not the husband was reduced to sobs, but his sorrow is delicately hinted at throughout the narrative. Yet, most critics who comment on this story classify it as a rare example of Das's comic writing. K. Radha writes, "The humour of the conclusion is indeed delicious,"[10] while Devindra Kohli notes, "'Iqbal' is refreshingly humorous in a writer who is habitually tense."[11] G. S. Balarama Gupta sees homosexuality as one of the "social problems" that Das deals with; he writes, "If 'Iqbal' has homosexuality for its theme, 'Sanatan Choudhari's Wife' tackles the problem of a wife's infidelity, and 'Leukemia' that of an aristocratic mother who has no time to take care of her ailing child."[12] In "Feminist Trends in the Short Stories of Kamala Das," Lalitha Ramamurthi argues that the final confrontation between the wife and the husband's lover ends in a "feminist" victory,[13] noting, "The encounter between the woman and the man in her life is a bold presentation. We do not have the traditional wife fussing over the situation nor even a practical wife trying to reason out but a feminist fully in control of the situation. . . . She does have the last laugh in the corridor!"[14] In the very next paragraph, Ramamurthi explains that of the many definitions of feminism, the one that is "most relevant in the Indian context is the one relating to the 'freedom from dependence syndrome.'"[15] The heroine of "Iqbal," according to Ramamurthi, is, like other Das heroines, one of the many "average Indian women," "not rebellious or radical by nature"; yet "[w]hen they are face to face with indignities or pushed against the wall we see the feminist in them responding to the situation."[16] Like Ramamurthi, Kohli also commends Das for the direction that the story is seen as taking: "Kamala Das, whose work is imbued with assured femininity, instead of exploring this homosexual attachment, focuses with a lightness of touch on the woman's pregnancy as a token of her individualism."[17] That Das is commended for the wisdom of choosing to follow up on "femininity" rather than homosexuality clearly reveals the focus of these feminist projects.[18]

Perhaps most illustrative of this lack of a theory of heteropatriarchy is the plot summary and analysis of "Iqbal" proffered by A. N. Dwivedi, who writes, in a 1995 essay, "As the story opens, Iqbal is confined to a hospital for consuming poison. Iqbal's room-mate of his YMCA days and his young beautiful wife are there to take care of him in the hospital. Iqbal's verses have convinced the young woman that he is deeply in love with a girl, but she does not know who this girl is. Her husband is always evasive on this point. Once or twice Iqbal comes to the young couple, on invitation of course to take his Sunday lunches, but later he stops visiting them on one or the other pretext. *In reality, Iqbal is a lover of this pretty, vivacious woman, and she too guesses it correctly. She says to Iqbal thus: 'You are jealous of me.'"*[19] Dwivedi completely misses or ignores the blatant homosexual content of this three-page short story. This stems, I believe, from the inability to see any sex but heterosex. But it also rests on the firm conviction that, in this story, as elsewhere in Das's writing, the husband's evasiveness and anger at being questioned about the object of Iqbal's love is symptomatic of his necessarily proprietary attitude toward his attractive young wife.

Homosexuality in Das's writing is always caught in the snare of heteropatriarchal relationships—it is not outside, foreign, Western, or alien, but borne alongside opposite-sex relations. In Das's work, constant sexual (re)orientations do not provide identities as much as they provide roles that intersect each other—often in philosophically profound ways and, at other times, in a trite fashion. A passage from an often anthologized poem, "Composition," demonstrates how closely Das weaves hetero- and homosexuality:

> . . . . When I got married
> my husband said,
> you may have freedom,
> as much as you want
> My soul balked at this diet of ash.
> Freedom became my dancing shoe,
> how well I danced,
> and danced without rest,
> until the shoes turned grimy on my feet
> and I began to have doubts.
> I asked my husband,
> am I hetero
> am I lesbian
> or am I just plain frigid?
> He only laughed.
> For such questions
> probably there are no answers
> or else
> the answers must emerge
> from within.
> I have lost my best friend
> to a middle-aged queer,
> The lesbians hiss their love at me.
> Love
> I no longer need,
> with tenderness I am most content.[20]

The irony is that her "freedom" is gifted to the speaker by her husband. Since this freedom is not self-generated it cannot generate much self-discovery—a disability that the poem mirrors in its use of short, staccato lines that leap from query to complaint. The speaker cannot pose the terms that will liberate her of her many questions, nor can she formulate answers. Here, as elsewhere in her work, meaningful answers to her "doubts" are tied up in discussions of love, tenderness, and lust. However, the protagonist, though enveloped in a heterosexual marriage, is at a crossroads where tenderness, love, betrayal, solitude, and solidarity can come packaged in both hetero and homosexual desires.

Das's doubts in "Composition" are elaborated in another poem evocatively entitled "The Doubt." In this poem, reproduced in its entirety below, Das ruminates at length about the very gendering of individuals into the categories of male and female:

The Doubt

When a man is dead, or a woman,
We call the corpse not he
Or she but it. Does it
Not mean that we believe
That only the souls have sex and that
Sex is invisible!
Then the question is, who
Is the man, who the girl,
All sex-accessories being no
Indication. Is she
A male who with frail hands
Clasps me to her breast, while
The silences in her sickroom, turning
Eloquent, accuse
Me of ingratitude!
And, is he female who
After love, smoothes out the bed sheets with
finicky hands and plucks
From pillows strands of hair!
. . . How well I can see him
After a murder, conscientiously
Tidy up the scene, wash
The bloodstains under
Faucet, bury the knife . . .
And, what am I in sex who shuttle
Obsessively from his
Stabs to recovery
In her small silent room![21]

In this poem, the protagonist, who could plausibly be either male or female, holds "gender" and "sex-accessories" apart to ponder what defines masculinity and femininity. The intricacy of the poem arises from Das's ability to juxtapose sex and the performance of gender so effectively that all conclusions about the self and *its* doubts have to be attentive to multiple considerations. More importantly, there are no normative identities since "all sex-accessories" are "no indication." The last turn that this poem takes, "And, what am I in sex who shuttles," brilliantly captures the refusal to present desire as divided into sexual dichotomies and the concomitant refusal to present protagonists for whom identity is equal to sexual orientation. While the "I" of this monologue is left moving "obsessively" from "his stabs" to "recovery" in "her small silent room," this cannot ultimately be read as indicative of the triumph of either hetero- or homosexuality, because we are still uncertain of the gender of the speaker. Furthermore, the usual correspondence between the biological sex and the socializing of gender attributes has been ripped apart in the course of the poem. Hence, available explanatory terms such as *bisexuality* offer only a facile and unsatisfactory account of the sexual dynamics in this poem. Similarly, the short story "The Sandal Trees" compels a rethinking of Das's literary treatment of sexuality as well as a revision of the parameters by which we comprehend the attachments we make over a lifetime.

III

"The Sandal Trees" is a complex love story about two women who conduct a life-long affair even as they fall in and out of love with their husbands. "Chandana Marangal" was written by Das in Malayalam in 1988 and was translated into English under the title "The Sandal Trees" in 1995 by V. C. Harris and C. K. Mohamed Ummer. Short fiction in Malayalam, the poet and editor K. Satchidanandan tells us, has a strong tradition of women's writing from the late 1800s to the present.[22] Satchidanandan names a long list of women writers before and after Das who have "written some powerful stories that expose the hypocrisy of most human relationships and observe society from a subaltern point of view, or probe the solitary world of the woman with her suppressed dreams and longings for freedom."[23]

In his introduction to a 1997 anthology of modern Malayalam short stories, Satchidanandan makes the following remarkable assessment of Kamala Das's work: "Madhavikkutty (Kamala Das) explores the innermost recesses of the female psyche in her uninhibited portrayals of man-woman and woman-woman relationships." What is remarkable about this one-phrase inclusion of "woman-woman" erotics (besides the fact that it is, despite its brevity, the only serious mention in literary criticism of same-sex dynamics in Das's work that I have seen) is that Satchidanandan puts it right alongside "man-woman" relationships. Literature in Malayalam is, and has been, amenable to discussions of sexuality, even "alternative" sexualities.[24] For example, well-known writer Vaikom Muhammad Basheer (1908–1994) wrote a powerful novelette, "Voices" ("Sabdangal," 1947), in which a young man recounts his fascination for an alluring streetwalker who reveals herself as a man in drag. The affair continues even after this revelation of the beloved's biological sex.[25] Another prominent writer, V. T. Nandakumar (1925–1999), wrote a popular novel entitled *Two Girls* (*Rantu Penkuttikal*, 1974), about two college students, Girija and Kokila, who become lovers even while several men compete for their affections. The novel ends with both women being recruited into heterosexuality, but not before lesbian desire is given sustained and sympathetic attention.[26] Some of the best-known short stories in Malayalam, written by Lalithambika Antherjanam (1909–1987) and K. Saraswati Amma (1919–1975), concern the double standards of sexuality and other gendered issues entrenched in the social mores of upper-caste Malayalis. Lalithambika's short story "Admission of Guilt" ("Kuttassammatham" 1940), in which a Namboodiri (priestly, highest-caste) widow argues that she and only she is responsible for her pregnancy, is an established masterpiece.[27]

"The Sandal Trees" charts a relationship between two women that spans five decades. The plot is vintage Das. A young Nair girl, Sheela, from a wealthy family, is seduced by and falls in love with another young Nair girl, Kalyanikkutty, from an impoverished family. When the degree and nature of their attachment to each other is discovered, Sheela is given in marriage to a family friend who is twenty-one years her senior. Subsequently, Kalyanikkutty marries a young man who adores her. Both women become doctors, and while Sheela's marriage survives many rocky years, Kalyanikkutty soon divorces her husband. The two women remain deeply attached to each other, for, as Kalyanikkutty tells Sheela, "I became your man and girl at the same time" (9). Frustrated by Sheela's refusal to leave her husband, Kalyanikkutty emigrates to Australia; she returns twenty-six years later the rich widow of a white Australian. The narrative time frame for this story is in the present when both women are in their fifties and Kalyanikkutty's return forces a reassessment of their lives, of time spent together and apart. Kalyanikkutty is still in love with Sheela, but realizes that the latter is not likely to leave her husband. Kalyanikkutty then decides to seduce her own ex-husband; despite his willingness to leave his current wife for her, Kalyanikkutty returns to Australia alone. At the close of the story, Sheela has acknowledged her as the one true love of her life—a fact that her husband tells her he has known and lived with for the three decades of their marriage. In the course of Kalyanikkutty's visit to Kerala, Sheela also realizes what Kalyanikkutty had suspected all along, that Kalyanikkutty is Sheela's prosperous father's illegitimate child and the two are half sisters.

Looking back at the critical reception of Das's work, it is clear that the fiction and poetry that best correspond with Das's autobiographical texts (autobiographies in both languages, and interviews) have always commanded the most critical attention. Because of the similarities between the details of "The Sandal Trees" and some of the events in *My Story*, it is impossible to dismiss same-sex desire in this short story as no more than just another "literary theme."[28] In turn, "The Sandal Trees" forces a more serious consideration of the relationship between the young Kamala and her "girlfriend" in *My Story*. I have argued elsewhere that the affair with the college student was suppressed in criticism of Das's autobiography because Das's feminist readers have a very strict notion of why she indulges in socially unsanctioned sexual relationships—she is *driven to it* by a cruel husband's numerous infidelities.[29] The affair with the college girl is given scant critical attention since it takes place prior to Das's marriage and also because it is not accepted as a sexual relationship. In the autobiography, once Das is married off to her much older relative, there is no further mention of her girlfriend. In "The Sandal Trees," even though Sheela's marriage is similarly arranged with a relative twenty-one years her senior, it is impossible to mistake the same-sex relationship for an insignificant attachment. While both these same-sex relationships start out alike and produce some of the same crises, "The Sandal Trees" traces the relationship between Sheela and Kalyanikutty through the vicissitudes of a lifetime.

In the literary criticism on Das and often in her work itself, homoeroticism is differently played out according to gender. When men are portrayed as engaged in same-sex relationships, this is interpreted as part of the sexual license available to men in patriarchal societies. A husband's indulgence in same-sex activities is presented as one more sign of his voracious sexual appetite. When women indulge in same-sex pleasures, it does not always register as sex—which is why in *My Story* the protagonist can engage in a seemingly satisfying physical relationship with a girlfriend and still claim to have no experience of sexual pleasure prior to sex with her husband. It is almost as if, in *My Story* and in the literary criticism on Das, what registers as sex for women must involve men. In *My Story*, when Das falls in love with her doctor, she writes, "I kept telling my husband that I was in love with the doctor and he said, it is all right, she is a woman, she will not exploit you."[30] In other words, this relationship is so "safe" in terms of patriarchal exploitation that it doesn't warrant serious consideration. Hence perhaps the critics' silence about this infatuation.

In "The Sandal Trees," however, it impossible to read homosexuality as insignificant or as an adolescent phase. This is precisely how same-sex desire is commonly explained in mainstream cultural discourses (both in Indian and other societies) and substantiated by established Indian psychologists like Sudhir Kakar.[31] Not surprisingly then, this is the logic applied on those rare occasions when same-sex desire in Das's work is mentioned (only to be immediately dismissed) by critics.[32] In "The Sandal Trees," however, marital sex is a disappointment to Sheela after her pleasurable initiation into sexual activity by her first lover Kalyanikkutty. While the narrator in *My Story* is reticent about comparing the two sexual experiences, in "The Sandal Trees" Sheela minutely compares Kalyanikkutty and her husband in their capacities as lovers and as soul mates. On her honeymoon, Sheela, the first-person narrator, muses, "I kept comparing the two. When I compared his mouth that smelt of beer, cigarette and onion with hers that had the sweet smell of *durva* grass, he failed. However hard I tried, I could not forget the way she caressed me, pressed her fingers hard into me and satisfied me with her lips, all with the intention of giving me pleasure" (5). "The Sandal Trees" carries other echoes of the relationship between Das and her college girlfriend in the autobiography. In *My Story*, when the two women meet for the last time before Kamala's wedding, they contemplate running away together, but realize that without adequate job skills they would find it impossible to survive outside the shelter of their families. In "The Sandal Trees," we are told,

> On the wedding eve, Kalyanikutty held me close to her and said:
> "Sheela. Let's get away from this place. I'll take up some job and protect you."
> "What job can you have? Your education is not over. We will starve to death on the street," I said.
> "Will you love this relative of yours?" Kalyanikutty asked. "You who love me—will you be able to satisfy him?"(4)

In *My Story*, Das ends the account of her last meeting with the girlfriend with this matter-of-fact conclusion, "When I put her out of my mind I put aside my self-pity too. It would not do to dream of a different kind of life. My life had been planned and its course charted by my parents and relatives" (96). In essence, this is also how Sheela comes to terms with marriage, but in "The Sandal Trees" the relationship between the two women does not end; instead it continues and over-whelms their relationship with their respective husbands. Thirty years later Kalyanikkutty still continues to try to persuade Sheela to leave her husband for her.

After their respective weddings, when Kalyanikkutty discovers that she is pregnant she visits Sheela at her clinic and demands an abortion:

> "I am not prepared to carry in my body for ten months the child of an ordinary man like him. I'll never give birth to his child."
> "Then whose child would you like to give birth to?" I asked.
> Suddenly she sat up and kissed me on my lips. The peculiar smell of her skin conquered me—a sweet smell that reminded me of fresh rain.
> "I wish to give birth only to your child," she said choking.
> "That's impossible," I muttered. (6)

Sheela refuses to perform the abortion so Kalyanikkutty goes to a local midwife who performs illegal abortions. When the botched abortion results in Kalyanikkutty nearly bleeding to death, Sheela takes her to her own house and nurses her back to health. Had Kalyanikkutty died, Sheela's husband angrily tells her, it would have become a police case and she would have been held responsible for the death. The narrative makes clear that such considerations are not important to Sheela.

In "The Sandal Trees," when same-sex desire floods the page, it is not because heterosexual options are closed. Das repeatedly takes the woman outside the marital home and into hotel rooms, as well as the homes and workplaces of lovers of both sexes. These same-sex seductions take place on trains, in rural bathing ponds, in bathrooms, in backyards, in classrooms, doctor's offices, and in marital beds—that is, with the same sense of adventure and excitement as the much-discussed opposite-sex affairs. In "The Sandal Trees," Das employs her substantial literary talents to describe Sheela and Kalyanikkutty's lovemaking. The turn from *seduced* to *active* participant is wonderfully elaborated in the description of the first of their sexual encounters at the bathing pond, where Das writes, "Using all her strength, she pushed me down on the floor of the pond-house daubed with cow dung. Then sending a deep thrill down my spine, she covered every inch of my body with kisses that really hurt. I shut my eyes in shame and humiliation. I don't remember how long I lay there like a living corpse under her assault. For ages I was a slave to her throbbing hands and legs. After that I became her beloved. The moistness and taste of her mouth became mine. The roughnesses and tendernesses of her body became all mine" (4). In a sociocultural and literary context in which all descriptions of pre- and extramarital female sexual pleasure are disruptive, Das's careful development of this scene—from initial surprise, shame, and humiliation to enjoyment—employs a recurrent turn that is scripted into *sympathetic* literary descriptions of female sexual pleasure. We should not assume that the same-sex content of the scene causes the initial unwillingness. For example, in Antherjanam's narration of the pivotal scene of seduction that ends "Admission of Guilt," the widow describes her encounter on the banks of the bathing pond with the man who impregnates her:

> A cry arose from the depths of my being, but it was smothered by a gentle kiss. A futile writhing, and I had perforce to yield to a strong embrace. In the surge of sensations my resistance ebbed away. Feelings of pleasure that I had never known or experienced before came alive.
>
> Or had I become weak, was I going to faint? It seemed to me that this was no dream, nor indeed was it sleep. Like everyone else, I too had to admit defeat in the struggle against my natural instincts. If that is a sin, I will sell my soul for it. . . . Do not ask whether that encounter ever recurred. Nor try to find out who that god was. I am guilty. You can punish me. No one else shares my guilt. (42)

I introduce this example from Antherjanam to substantiate the argument that Das's treatment of Sheela and Kalyanikkutty's lovemaking in "The Sandal Trees" is a reverently presented account of female sexual desire as "natural" and "authentic." This lovemaking passage, more than any other in Das's work, forces a revision of the hitherto automatic reading of any sex in Das's work as necessarily heterosexual. It also multiplies the punch carried by Das's devastating verdicts on marriage that are interspersed in this narrative. Early in the story, Sheela compares the young, lean, and sensuous Kalyanikkutty to sandalwood (2). Much later, when Sheela describes her dissatisfaction with marriage, the use of the sandal tree metaphor radically diverts the generic complaint about an inattentive husband. As Das writes, "If he had shown any interest in my daily routine ever, I wouldn't have become an unfeeling marble statue today. I wouldn't have practised silence. In fact I cultivated silence. It grew and stood between me and my husband like a sandal tree, giving me much happiness" (13). Here, the silence the wife cultivates evokes the real object of her desire, her silent source of happiness. Negative assessments of marriage are routinely woven into Das's poems, interviews, and autobiographical writings. But in "The Sandal Trees" a bleak and unrelenting account of marriage is implicitly contrasted with the highly satisfying relationship between the two women. Das writes, "For civilised people, a marriage that lasts for years, greying and rotting, is certainly impossible to bear. To lie close to each other in the same bed and exchange the foul smell of sweat; to witness the excrement of your spouse who has forgotten to flush the toilet after use at sunrise; to feign sleep while slyly watching him masturbate, with his pretty fingers that seem to have been made for blessing others, and at the same time follow its peculiar rhythm—no, no, I don't want this much praised *grihasthashram*" (12–13).

While feminist and other critics have always noticed Das's critique of marriage and *grihasthashram* (the householder stage in the Hindu life cycle), there has been no recognition of how closely this critique is linked to a critique of heterosexuality. A few pages later in the story, Das writes,

> Men who are past their youth will become shameless, if their wives' complaints are to be believed. Women of that age, on the contrary, will feel an increasing sense of shame. Once the inelegances of their body start multiplying, women hesitate to show off their physical features. But it is common for old men to display, as if by mistake, their private parts which hang loose and look unsewn. They don't know how much women hate such ugly scenes. Often I felt nauseated when my husband took off his underwear and slowly paced my room, letting the mark of his manliness, now the figure of a rotten bitter-gourd, swing like a pendulum. And one day he asked me:
>
> "Dr. Sheela, why do you vomit? Can women in menopause become pregnant?" (15)

The husband, unnamed in the story, takes to calling his wife "Dr. Sheela" since his retirement, using this show of mock deference to underline the fact that he no longer brings money into the household. In a somewhat similar fashion, he constantly "showcases" his loss of virility if only to win her sympathy. When Sheela describes Kalyanikkutty's appearance in her fifties, the terms are very different, to say the least: "A perfectly healthy, middle-aged woman dressed impeccably in a sophisticated manner. A beauty who still retained, though slightly artificially, the glow of youth in her face and in her hair"(10). Despite her constant, silent, cataloging of the ways her husband disgusts her (his rotting diabetic breath and sweat, his varicose veins that are "swollen and tangled like the roots of a jackfruit tree"), Sheela continues to play the wife. When the local rotary club asks them to participate in an "ideal couple" contest, Sheela says: "Why not? Our marriage has lasted so long. I haven't betrayed you, and you haven't betrayed me. We have not slept apart for a single night. We can certainly win this contest" (17).

Here, Das ruthlessly demonstrates that the markers by which success in marriage is usually gauged are profoundly inadequate to the task of measuring such relationships. It is not simply that Sheela and her husband are mismatched; rather, he cannot offer her the pleasures Kalyanikkutty can. Despite Sheela's occasional envy of women with younger husbands, it becomes clear that love as much as guilt ties her to Kalyanikkutty. For example, in "The Sandal Trees" (as in *My Story*) the aging husband encourages his young wife to have affairs with other men. Sheela tells us, "I did make some attempts at cheating him, at renouncing my chastity. But I saw my husband in every man who came close to me. And seeing him there I would back out. And with a shock slip back into my chastity. I continued to perform my wifely duties in the manner of eating leftovers, of eating leftovers over and over again. Sitting down to eat with him and lying down on the same bed with him became extremely distressing. As we spoke, the words, I felt, were like corpses that slid out of their shelves in the morgue. Silence was much better" (16). Silence in this story becomes a motif that conjures up the two women's relationship. Hence, when the preference for silence becomes a constant refrain in Sheela's narrative, we need to infer more than just her reluctance to openly express her dissatisfaction with her aged husband.

After a bitterly disappointed Kalyanikkutty leaves for Australia, once again unsuccessful in convincing Sheela to leave with her, Sheela describes her feelings, saying, "At last, when I could no longer see her, I stepped out of the airport with a sense of loss. I felt my legs weakening out of sheer exhaustion. I was reluctant to go back to that all-too-familiar world of mine that comprised my house, the lovely objects on display there, my aged husband, my patients, everything. But there is no other place for me to live, I told myself, and no one else to love me, is there?" (24). It is not accidental that Sheela lists her house and objets d'art before and alongside her husband and patients—the personal and material aspects of her domestic and professional life are inseparably yoked together. The day after Kalyanikkutty leaves, Sheela is driving home with her husband when he states, "'In my life I've had to contend with only one enemy—Dr. Kalyanikkutty. I understood very early that it was only she who could drive you off from me. Even during our honeymoon, her shadow had fallen between us. I realised that you were comparing every display of love on my part with hers. I was somebody who had reached you after her. I was a mere drizzle arriving hesitantly, timidly, after a full storm'" (26). Sheela responds with her customary silence, but in the narration she continues:

> After this I felt ashamed to look at his face. That moment I thought my reflection in the mirror was the face of a stranger. Was it I, that woman with the glowing cheeks, hair clearly displaying its silver strands and the yet-to-be effaced vermilion spot on the forehead! Never. I was transformed into a young lass who embraced her girlfriend and sought the blissful rapture of her kiss. A girl who found heavenly pleasures in the bodily touch of her beloved—her beloved who, having swum and bathed in the pond for hours together, smelt and tasted of weeds and mosses, water lilies and medicinal herbs. "Oh, my love, how can I live now!" I whispered to the darkness that slowly spread in the car.
> "Er, did you say something, Dr. Sheela!" he asked.
> "No," I said, shaking my head. "I didn't say anything to you." (26)

By closing the story thus, Das establishes the primacy of the women's relationship. Everything else dissolves to background. The story ends thus: "As we crossed the bridge and drove towards Fort Cochin, the wind bore the smell of fish. From the dark water rose Kalyanikkutty's girlish laughter" (26).

In Conclusion

In reading Kamala Das's work from "An Introduction" to "The Sandal Trees" through the lens of her consideration of same-sex desire, I try to disrupt the scholarly equation of all sexuality in her work with heterosexuality. Lines from a well-known poem by Das should give us reason to think outside a heterosexist frame as she writes, "Woman, is this happiness, this lying buried / Beneath a man? It's time again to come alive, / The world extends a lot beyond his six foot frame."[33]

On coming across the odd Das poem in literary journals or popular magazines from the sixties onward, such as the one reproduced in its entirety below, it is no longer possible to unthinkingly assume that the references are necessarily or exclusively heterosexual:

The Ferry

Will your slim body ferry me to that noiseless shore
Where I can lie, featureless,
As a planet blanched by the day?
My blood is salty with the tears of prophets, but
Tomorrow must erupt from between a barren woman's
Thighs. . . .[34]

Is this one more of Das's many poems about death? Or is that silent shore a metaphoric reference to a place beyond sex, or perhaps beyond exclusively heterosexual practices? Whose "slim body" will ferry this speaker (unidentified by gender) to this other place? What if we were to read "barren" outside its normative reproduction-based connotations? What kind of tomorrow might then erupt from "between a barren woman's thighs"?

Das's theorizing of sexual pleasure in which same-sex encounters play a significant part was (and is) a radical stance in the Indian feminist context, where women's sexuality has been viewed as one of the basic "problems" confronting feminists and where discussions of female sexual pleasure even in heterosexual contexts are rare. In the coming years, as queer activists in India get increasingly vocal, they could turn to the work of Kamala Das, who, for the past four decades, has been making literature out of her "queernesses" while insisting (in "Composition"), "What I narrate are the ordinary / events of an / ordinary life"[35]

Notes

1. For a complete list of Das's published works in English and Malayalam, see Iqbal Kaur, *Feminist Revolution and Kamala Das' My Story* (Patiala: Century Twentyone Publishing, 1992.): vi–viii. Das has also contributed editorials, regular columns, and "agony aunt" responses to readers' letters for several Indian newspapers and popular magazines.
2. See Kamala Das, "The Sandal Trees," in *The Sandal Trees and Other Stories*, trans. V. C. Harris and C. K. Mohamed Ummer (Hyderabad: Disha/Orient Longman, 1995), 1–27. Hereafter page numbers will be cited parenthetically in the text.
3. See my "Calling Kamala Das Queer: Rereading *My Story*," *Feminist Studies* 26, no. 3 (Fall 2000): 731–63.
4. See Kaur, *Feminist Revolution*, 4–5, for the list of topics that Kaur sees as central to Das's work, and page 22 for Kaur's summary of 1970s feminism.
5. See, for example, Vrinda Nabar, *The Endless Female Hungers: A Study of Kamala Das* (New Delhi: Sterling, 1994), vi. Also see Ranjana Dwivedi, "Autobiography: A Metaphor for the Self," *Between Spaces of Silence: Women Creative Writers*, ed. Kamini Dinesh (New Delhi: Sterling, 1994), 115–25.
6. See P. P. Raveendran, "Of Masks and Memories: An Interview with Kamala Das," *Indian Literature* 155 (May–June 1993): 145–61.
7. See Dennis Altman, "Rupture or Continuity? The Internationalization of Gay Identities," *Social Text* 48, no. 14.3 (1996): 77–94, and anthologies like Stephan Likosky, ed., *Coming Out: An Anthology of International Gay and Lesbian Writings* (New York: Pantheon, 1992). For thoughtful reassessments of different aspects of this internationalization, see Martin Manalansan, "In the Shadow of Stonewall: Examining Gay Transnational Politics and the Diasporic Dilemma," *GLQ* 2 (1995): 425–38; and Gayatri Gopinath, "Homo-Economics: Queer Sexualities in a Transnational Frame," in *Burning Down the House:*

Recycling Domesticity, ed. Rosemary Marangoly George (Boulder: Perseus Books/Westview, 1998), 102–24.

8. See Bina Fernandez, ed., *Humjinsi: A Resource Book for Lesbian, Gay, and Bisexual Rights in India* (New Delhi: India Centre for Human Rights and Law, 1999).

9. "Iqbal," reprinted in Kamala Das, *Padmavati the Harlot and Other Stories*, (New Delhi: Sterling Paperbacks, 1992), 57–60; hereafter, page numbers will be cited parenthetically in the text.

10. See K. Radha, "The Short Stories of Kamala Das in English," in *Perspectives on Kamala Das' Prose*, ed. Iqbal Kaur (New Delhi: Intellectual Publishing House, 1995), 68.

11. See Devindra Kohli, *Kamala Das* (New Delhi: Arnold Heinemann, 1975), 16.

12. See G. S. Balarama Gupta, "The Short Story Writers: Self, Society, and Emancipation," in Dinesh, ed., *Between Spaces of Silence*, 154.

13. See Lalitha Ramamurthi, "Feminist Trends in the Short Stories of Kamala Das," in Kaur, ed., *Perspectives*, 112–17.

14. Ibid., 114.

15. Ibid.

16. Ibid.

17. Kohli, *Kamala Das*, 17.

18. This sentiment was recently espoused by *some* Indian feminist groups who publicly and deliberately distanced their own project from that of Indian lesbians in the discussions and protests following the December 1998 vandalism organized by the Shiv Sena against the screening of Deepa Mehta's film *Fire*.

19. See A. N. Dwivedi, "The Other Harmony: Kamala Das' Prose," in Kaur, ed., *Perspectives*, 1–25, 20–21; emphasis added. For a full explication of the ways in which heterosexism works in collaboration with patriarchy, see Jackie Alexander, "Erotic Autonomy as a Politics of Decolonization: An Anatomy of State Practice in the Bahamas Tourist Economy," in *Feminist Genealogies, Colonial Legacies, Democratic Futures*, ed. Jacqui Alexander and Chandra Talpade Mohanty. (New York: Routledge, 1997), 63–100.

20. Kamala Das, "Composition," in *The Descendants*, (Calcutta: Writers Workshop, 1967), 46.

21. Kamala Das, "The Doubt," in *The Descendants*, 36–37.

22. See K. Satchidanandan, "Introduction: Transcending the Body," in *Only the Soul Knows How to Sing: Selections from Kamala Das* (Kerala: DC Books, 1996), 9–18, 11. For a concise yet nuanced history of the short story in Malayalam, see K. Satchidanandan, "Introduction: A Century of Malayalam Short Story," in *Under the Wild Skies: An Anthology of Modern Malayalam Short Stories*, ed. K. Satchidanandan (New Delhi: National Book Trust, 1997), 1–13. For an English-language literary history of Malayalam literature see Krishna Chaitanya, *A History of Malayalam Literature*. (Poona: Orient Longman, 1971).

23. See Satchidanandan, "Introduction," 12. Notable among Das's female predecessors in Malayalam literature are J. Bhagavati Amma, T. C. Kalyani Amma, M. Saraswatibai, Lalitambika Antherjanam, K. Saraswati Amma, Rajalakshmi, and others. More recent writers include Sarah Joseph, Gracy, P. Vatsala, Sarah Thomas, Manasi, Shobha Variyar.

24. Satchidanandan, "Introduction: A Century of Malayalam Short Story," 1–13. While my Malayalam reading skills are too recently acquired to allow me to read literary criticism in the language, I base my assertions on extensive reading of work written in and translated into English, and on consultation with scholars working in the literature. I would especially like to thank Muraleedharan T. and Vanamala Viswanathan for generously sharing information on this issue with me.

25. See Vaikom Muhammad Basheer, "Voices," trans. V. C. Harris, in *Vaikom Muhammad Basheer: Short Stories*, ed. Vanajam Ravindran (New Delhi: Katha, Rupa, 1996): 94–134.

26. Selected excerpts from Nandakuman's novel are included in Ruth Vanita and Saleem Kidwai, eds., *Same-Sex Love in India: Readings in Indian Literature* (New York: St. Martin's Press, 2000). I would like to thank Ruth Vanita for generously sharing T. Muraleedharan's translation of Nandakumar's novel with me, prior to publication.

27. See Lalithambika Antherjanam, "Admission of Guilt" ("Kuttassammatham"), in *Cast Me Out if You Will: Stories and Memoir*, ed. Gita Krishnakutty (Calcutta: Stree, 1998), 31–43; hereafter, page numbers will be cited parenthetically in the text.

28. However, critics like K. R. R. Nair have insisted that *My Story* is itself fictional and that the "queer and shocking experiences" and the marital infidelity scripted in *My Story* are no more than "an exciting theme in literature since Aeschylus' *Agamemnon* and Shakespeare's *Winter's Tale*"; Nair, *The Poetry of Kamala Das* (New Delhi: Reliance, 1993), 103.

29. See my "Calling Kamala Das Queer" for a discussion of the feminist postcolonial interpretations of sexuality (produced both in and outside India) in this autobiography.

30. Kamala Das, *My Story* (New Delhi: Sterling Press, 1976), 152; hereafter, page numbers will be cited parenthetically in the text.

31. See Sudhir Kakar, *The Inner World: A Psycho-analytical Study of Childhood and Society in India*, especially: "Ontogeny of homo hierarchicus" (133–39), and "The Psycho-social Matrix of Infancy: Feminine Identity in India" (56–79).

32. See for instance, K. R. R. Nair's use of the phrase "the hermaphroditic instincts of adolescence" to explain female cross-dressing in the passage in "An Introduction" discussed earlier in this essay (17).

33. From "The Conflagration" in Kamala Das, *The Descendants*, 20.

34. See *The Indian Literary Review* 1.

35. Das, "Composition," 46.

9

Homophobic Fiction/
Homoerotic Advertising

The Pleasures and Perils of Twentieth-Century Indianness

Ruth Vanita

In twentieth-century Indian fiction published in India, same-sex desire is almost always imbricated with notions not only of gender but also of "Indianness" and "foreignness." The popular myth that homosexuality was imported to India by invading West Asian Muslims or colonizing Europeans has been stated and restated by both left-wing and right-wing nationalists, from at least the late nineteenth century onward. The Shiv Sena's repetition of this myth to attack Deepa Mehtar's film *Fire* found some credence precisely because the myth took root during the movement for national independence.

Framed by this myth, most twentieth-century texts that represent same-sex desire strive to reinforce an imagined pure Indianness of manhood or womanhood. They generally do so in one of two ways: first, by relegating same-sex desire to the underworld or to same-sex spaces such as college dorms, and, second, by punishing it violently. On the other hand, the few texts that admit, whether cheerfully or anxiously, that Indian manhood and womanhood are necessarily hybrid and thus not purely "Indian," represent homosexuality as present in the everyday world of average Indians and as frequently going unpunished.

The latter kind of text is much more likely to be attacked as obscene. Such texts include Pandey Bechan Sharma's *Chocolate* (1927), a text I examine here; Ismat Chughtai's short story "Lihaf"; the writings of Kamala Das; and Mehta's film *Fire*. Advertisements, on the other hand, because of certain generic differences I examine later, can get away with a much greater degree of celebratory suggestiveness, although when they become more explicit they too may be exposed to attack as obscene.

Boys in the Bazaar, Dykes in the Dorm[1]

Under these constraints, two relatively acceptable sites for the representation of homosexuality emerge in twentieth-century fiction—the underworld for men and premarital college life for women. These sites work on the assumption that no options are available to the unfortunate persons concerned. Examples of men in the underworld include Kamleshwar's depiction in his Hindi novel *Ek Sadak Sattavan Galiyan* (1956) of a trucker and part-time dacoit's relations with his kept boy while the heterosexual involvements of both are thwarted by circumstances, and Vaikom Muhammad Basheer's depiction in his Malayalam novel *Shabdangal* (1947) of a vagrant soldier's unwitting involvement with a transvestite male prostitute from whom he gets venereal disease.[2]

Both male and female writers represent female homosexuality far more frequently and in more detail than male homosexuality.[3] They usually show lesbianism subsisting between students as a premarital phase. The representations vary widely in terms of the degree of homophobia displayed, but the relationships are often depicted as tension-ridden and always culminate in the heterosexual involvement of one or both partners.[4] I have found only two stories by women writers and two by men in which the married protagonist is shown yearning for her lost lesbian romance.[5]

The other way to depict lesbianism and get away with it is to show it as causing unhappiness. When lesbians are depicted as adult women with choices available to them, they often appear frustrated and unloved, doomed to suicide or to loneliness.[6] In more homophobic depictions, they prey on, beat, or even murder one another or else are "cured" of their lesbianism by male intervention. In almost all cases, the terms of denunciation are drawn from Western discourse. Lesbianism is often figured as having a Western source—Bani Ray's Bengali story "Sappho" (1977) signals this in its title; its lesbian protagonist, spurned by the man who induces her to fall in love with him, ends up committing suicide.[7] The language of demonization in this story is similar to that in Shobha De's English novel *Strange Obsession*.[8] In both texts the lesbian is compared to such creatures as lizards, snakes, cockroaches, or spiders swallowing flies. The latest in this genre is the Punjabi story "Aak ke Phool" by feminist writer Ajeet Kaur, in which an older woman preys on a younger woman who in turn cheats on her with a man. The story ends with the older woman mercilessly thrashing the younger one while the other inmates of the working-women's hostel look on.[9] In all of these stories (unlike *Chocolate*, "Lihaf," or *Fire*) lesbianism is violently punished.

I should add here that there is at least one remarkable exception to this rule—Vijay Dan Detha's Rajasthani story "Dohri Joon" (1979). Translated into Hindi and acted as a play in Delhi, it escaped attack.[10] Perhaps this is because the adult lesbian relationship it celebrates occurs in an entirely premodern, rural, Indian setting without any reference to Western sources or settings. The anxieties of Westernization are never evoked either in terminology (while the loving sexual relationship is explicitly described, it is not categorized as "lesbian" or any equivalent) or in allusion.

My examination here of two fictional texts shows how two contrasting approaches to homosexuality lead to one kind of text being attacked and the other applauded. The first, *Chocolate*, depicts homosexuality as pervading the everyday world and often going unpunished. It also shows modern Indianness as a hybrid of elements drawn from various cultures including the Hindu, the Muslim, and the Western. The second, Rajkamal Chaudhuri's novel *Machhli Mari Hui*, violently purges its protagonists of both homosexuality and Westernness.

Everybody Loves Chocolate?

On the title page of *Chocolate*, its author, Pandey Bechan Sharma (1901–1967), better known by his pen name Ugra ("Extreme"), is described as "novelist, dramatist, story-writer, poet, satirist, and journalist."[11] Ugra, who never married, was a well-known nationalist; his writings champion the causes of oppressed women and of lower castes and critique corruption in high places, alcoholism, gambling, adultery, prostitution, and communalism. In 1924 he became associated with the Hindi weekly *Matvala*, which was founded in Calcutta in 1923 under the editorship of the famous poet Suryakant Tripathi "Nirala." *Matvala* was a nationalist paper whose style tended to the satirical.

On May 31, 1924, Ugra published a story entitled "Chocolate" in *Matvala*. This story is about Mr. Dinkar Prasad, who is enamored of a fourteen-year-old boy named Ramesh. The narrator Gopal is informed that Ramesh is Dinkar's "chocolate." Gopal's friend Manohar offers a definition of this term that was to be much quoted in the ensuing controversy: " 'Chocolate' is the name for those innocent, tender and beautiful boys of the country, whom society's demons push into the mouth of ruin to quench their own lusts" (100). The story depicts the relationship and ends with Gopal denouncing Dinkar to Ramesh's father; Dinkar then disappears from the neighborhood.

When the story was published, the *Matvala* office was flooded with readers' letters, both of praise and protest. Ugra was encouraged by this controversy to write four more stories on the theme. At this juncture, the British government imprisoned him for nine months under Section 124-A of the Indian Penal Code for his nationalist writings in the paper *Swadesh*. He recounts that when he was released, his friends advised him not to publish any more such stories as he was being slanderously accused of being homosexual.[12] He proceeded to write three more stories on the subject and in 1927 published all eight as a collection entitled *Chocolate,* with over fifty pages of homophobic introductory materials, including a pseudo-scientific essay by Ugra's close friend Ramnath Lal "Suman," which quoted Havelock Ellis and Sigmund Freud, among others. The book gave rise to a tremendous furor. Lines formed to buy the book at Calcutta bookshops, and it was reprinted in the same year.[13]

Ugra's unprecedented crusade against homosexuality was not appreciated by other nationalists. Hindi litterateur Pandit Banarsidas Chaturvedi, nationalist editor of *Vishal Bharat*, began a movement against what he termed *Ghasleti* literature, of which he dubbed Ugra the foremost exponent. *Ghaslet* literally refers to kerosene oil, widely used as cooking fuel in India, and metaphorically to inflammatory—that is, sensational and obscene—literature. Ugra's opponents argued that such filthy topics as homosexuality were not fit for literary representation.

The controversy spread like wildfire. Almost every Hindi newspaper and magazine entered the fray. Several Hindi literary bodies formally denounced Ugra's writings at their annual meetings, as did many famous writers including the left-leaning Munshi Premchand.[14] Some of Ugra's other writings, such as those on prostitution, were also accused of obscenity; but *Chocolate* was the main target. This was perhaps the first major public debate in the Hindi literary world on homosexuality. It also rapidly became a debate on censorship.

Both Chaturvedi's claim that Ugra had dealt with the subject in a way that made it attractive and Ugra's supporters' counterclaim that his opponents were inspired by envy point to the same phenomenon—the book had attracted a record number of readers. The questions that perhaps cannot be answered definitively are, first, how many of these readers were actuated by the revulsion against homosexuality expressed by both Ugra and his opponents, and how many were merely eager to read fiction about homosexuals? Second, despite the overt homophobia, do elements of representation in these stories lend themselves to positive interpretation? Ugra's opponents thought so. Gay activist Ashok Row Kavi, founder of the gay magazine *Bombay Dost*, informed me that elderly gay men of his acquaintance, who were young when *Chocolate* was published, told him they had received it with delight as a representation of their lives.

Chaturvedi singled out for attack those passages where Ugra allows his homosexual characters a voice that they use not only to defend their practices but also to claim an illustrious ancestry. In the story "Chocolate," Dinkar Prasad quotes the famous Urdu poet Mir Taqi Mir's love poetry but also looks further afield: "[H]e told me, on the basis of an English book, that even Socrates was guilty of this offence. He said that Shakespeare too was the slave of a beautiful friend of his. He also talked of Mr. Oscar Wilde" (101). Mahashay (whose full name is Shri Ramcharan), in the story "Paalat," makes even more daring claims:

> NARRATOR: I think, brother, that just as "Woman is not charmed by woman's beauty" [quote from Tulsidas's medieval epic *Ramcharitmanas*—ed.] neither should man be charmed by man's beauty.
>
> . . . .
>
> MAHASHAY: Search history. Raskhan fell in love with a boy and then became a devotee of Krishna. Surdas was madly in love with Krishna. Tulsi? Have you read the blazon of Rama's beauty in *Vinaya Patrika*? What else is it but the portrait of an extremely beautiful boy?
>
> NARRATOR: Be quiet! You seem like an atheist. To justify boy-love, you even drag in Lord Rama and Shri Krishna. Be thankful you are in your own room. If you present such arguments in an assembly, it will be impossible to protect the hairs on your head. (117)

Banarsidas Chaturvedi wrote, "It is the height of impertinence to discuss such fancies and ideas in the book. Any cultured person who reads the names of Socrates and Shakespeare, Surdas and Tulsidas, Rama and Krishna, in such a context will denounce the author a thousand times."[15] Chaturvedi's anxiety here clearly centers on the question of who owns culture. Almost all of the protagonists in Ugra's stories are highly cultured and educated men; in fact, they are the mirror images of the Hindi litterateurs engaged in the controversy. These men claim Hindi, Urdu, and English literatures as in some sense their own. In the passage quoted above, the homophobic narrator quotes a famous line from Tulsidas's fifteenth-century epic that is, even today, the most popular version of the Rama story in north India. What is unsettling, however, is that Mahashay cites Tulsidas right back, thus confidently claiming a right to interpret a common literary heritage in his own way.

Except for one story set in jail, none of Ugra's protagonists is a member of the underworld. They are respectable members of society; they include teachers, college students, writers, and men-about-town. They carry on their homosexual affairs both in public and in domestic spaces. Most of them are married—thus their desire for men cannot be explained away as due to a lack of options.

More importantly, the protagonists are not represented as isolated. If some of their male friends and acquaintances denounce their desire, several others are sympathetic and view it as a completely natural response to beauty. In each of the eight stories, the narrator is hostile to male-male desire. But when he enters into a debate with the homosexually inclined characters, he never wins on logical grounds. Sometimes, he compromises and advises his determined friend to act discreetly. More often, he summons outraged authority figures to his aid. Though he may succeed in punishing the lover, it is by no means clear that he succeeds in eradicating homosexual activity. Of the eight stories, in two the lover is defamed and disappears; in one he loses his job and is later imprisoned; in one he is driven to suicide by public embarrassment; in one the boy dies (of asthma, supposedly induced by homosexuality) but the lover goes unpunished; and in one he is beaten by the police and frightened into silence.

Of the remaining two stories, one is set in jail where two men fighting over a third are punished but it is clear that homosexuality is uncontainable; and the other, the last story in the collection, is set in a men's college where it is equally clear that the principal's rebuke of the students' desires has no effect whatsoever. That these two settings may be more representative of the wider society than one might think is emphatically stated more than once.

The character Shivmohan, who shamefacedly acknowledges that he shares Mahashay's predilections, remarks, "I think about fifty percent boys in this country and in some regions ninety-nine percent are destroying their characters, virility, and strength in a fearsome manner. But society is silent" (122). The last story, "Chocolate Charcha" ("Discussion of Chocolate"), is framed as a self-reflexive debate among passengers in a train, some of whom read *Matvala* while others loathe it. A defender of the magazine exclaims, "Society does not even hide this weakness. Chocolate is openly discussed in schools, colleges, theater companies and Ramlila groups. Many great poets, writers, and even political leaders are said to be suffering from this sickness" (156).

This view is reinforced by the terms Ugra chooses. Apropos of Indrani Chatterjee's discussion of man-boy relations in the context of slavery (see her essay in this volume), Ugra's framing of the term *launda* ("boy"), a term with a long history, is interesting. Ugra makes it clear that the term is often detached not only from age but also from status. In the story set in prison, two men fight over a twenty-five-year-old man named Sundar ("beautiful") and a prisoner informs the narrator: "*Laundas* here may sometimes be even sixty years old" (92). The stories also represent men engaged in affairs with others of their own age group. While men desire boys in six of the eight stories, some of these boys themselves desire other boys. In "Paalat" a kept boy is caught having sex with another boy among the bushes. "Chocolate Charcha" describes nineteen- and twenty-year-old college students who desire one another. Nor do the stories represent lower class status as always linked to "passivity." In only two of the stories is the desired boy clearly of lower class origins than his lover (in one he is a female impersonator in a Parsi theater company but is also a Gujarati Brahman; in the other, he is the son of a poor man on the lover's estate). In all the other stories, both lovers belong to the same class. One boy is the son of a lawyer; another the son of a deputy collector.

Ugra's term *chocolate,* which he sometimes represents as popular slang (I have not been able to locate any other source for it) but also claims is his own term for what is more generally termed *laundebaazi* ("boy chasing"), refers not to the homosexually inclined men but to their love objects. While wonderfully encapsulating how ineradicably Westernness is part of modern Indian identity, it also works to "normalize" male-male desire.[16] One of the most widely available consumer items, chocolate is so indigenized as to have become a Hindi word but is nevertheless non-Indian in origin. Ugra's choice of it as a symbol for male-male desire cannot but suggest that the desire is as ubiquitous as the delicacy. His narratorial denunciations are not sufficient to dispel the anxiety generated by the implied question: Would eradication of homosexuality in India today be as difficult as eradication of a taste for chocolate among Indians? Or, more insidiously, is the attempt to eradicate homosexuality as absurdly self-defeating and antipleasure as an attempt to eradicate chocolate would be? Many of Ugra's characters defend their desires as demonstrative of a natural human inclination to take pleasure in beauty. Mahashay argues, "Wherever beauty may be found, in a woman or in a man, it will enslave me to love" (117).

Hindus, Muslims, and the Precolonial Past

In Ugra's stories, the view of male-male desire as *any man's* natural but perhaps not always desirable response to beauty coexists with the view of *some men* as more given to this desire than others and of such men as comprising an *us,* a group whose philosophy of life is inflected by their desire. Prasad, in "Hum Fidaye Lucknow," seems to invoke the latter sense of a group when he tells the censorious narrator, "Our goal in life is to enjoy ourselves. Even in hell we will try to enjoy ourselves" (126). While this second view of homosexual desire has displaced the first in much of the West, they arguably coexist in India even today. It is also arguable, contra David Halperin, that the second view coexisted with the first in precolonial India, as Saleem Kidwai suggests in his exploration of networks of homoerotically inclined men in precolonial Indian cities, even in societies that conceived of same-sex desire as a desire anyone might experience.[17]

If the trope of chocolate signals the Western component of modern Indianness, the trope of the *ghazal* signals its Muslim component. Almost all of Ugra's "chocolate lovers" are Hindus but they constantly quote Urdu ghazals and some even compose them. Ghazals are liberally quoted in four of the stories; they also inspire appreciative listeners to respond with Hindi love poetry. Because of its grammatical convention of using the male gender for both the lover and the beloved, the Urdu ghazal lent itself to the expression of same-sex desire, and some of the greatest poets, such as Mir, had composed love poems to men. This convention came under attack in the nineteenth century, first by the British and then by Indian nationalists, including Urdu litterateurs (see Scott Kugle's essay in this volume). The dominant trend, however, was to explain the male gendering of the ghazal as expressive only of spiritual love between man and God.

As Kidwai has demonstrated, so rapid was the heterosexualization of the ghazal in the twentieth century that modern poets like Josh Malihabadi and Firaq Gorakhpuri, well known to be homosexual, went out of their way to gender the beloved female in their poetry.[18] Nevertheless, older Urdu ghazals using the male-male convention continued to be widely popular, both in the new media, such as cinema, radio, television, and audiotapes, and in oral tradition. In Uttar Pradesh, where the Hindi literary establishment was based, most litterateurs were (and are) given to quoting ghazals at the drop of a hat. Thus, Ugra's depiction of his openly homosexual protagonists claiming this high literary tradition—supposedly spiritual in its orientation—as expressive of their own desires generated extreme anxiety among the literati.

The story "Chocolate" opens with an Urdu *shair* (couplet); its first sentence unsettlingly links Urdu love poetry and homosexual love with the word *matvala* "intoxicated man," which is also the title of the magazine in which the story first appeared: "'Why should I not be restless? I have just fallen prey to love / I have suffered a wound in my heart that I had never suffered before.' My friend Babu Dinkar Prasad, B.A., recited this couplet in a low, pathetic tone and lolled to one side on his chair like a *matvala*" (68).

Ugra's representation of his protagonists' hybridity muddies the waters of Indianness. He accurately represents his young, educated men-about-town as a group comprising both Hindus and Muslims who are fluent in Hindi, English, and Urdu. Ugra denounces the Western education system, with its residential schools and universities, as encouraging same-sex desire; one character goes so far as to say that he would rather kill his son than allow him to be educated in this system. However, by the early twentieth century the Western education system was too deeply entrenched in India for middle-class Indians to see its eradication as either possible or desirable.

The denunciations of *Chocolate* display a very similar mix of attitudes. On the one hand, they associate homosexuality with the West: "This is a murderous attack on Indian culture and mores. Decent people should boycott such newspapers just as they do foreign cloth and intoxicating substances."[19] On the other hand, they draw on Western sources to legitimize their homophobia. Thus, *Vishal Bharat* (August 1929) published a translation of professor Gilbert Murray's letter to the editor of the *Nation* (March 23, 1929). This letter, arguing against obscenity in literature, appeared in the course of a six-month-long debate in the *Nation* generated in the aftermath of the 1928 ban on Radclyffe Hall's *The Well of Loneliness*. Such eminent writers as Leonard Woolf, Lytton Strachey, and E. F. Benson ably argued the anticensorship case from a nonhomophobic perspective. In the Indian debate, however, the eminent writers who became identified with an anticensorship position were avowedly as homophobic as their opponents. Although they claimed that their pure Indianness precluded such "Western" vices as homosexuality, their actual hybridity was exemplified by the closeness of the Indian and British literary worlds, enabled the letter from the *Nation* to be translated into Hindi within five months.

In 1944 Ismat Chughtai's story "Lihaf" created a furor and the author was tried for obscenity. Lesbianism in this story is practiced by women within the domestic sphere and they are not punished for it. The husband of one of the women is also depicted as homosexually inclined. Thus, homosexuality is shown as part of the everyday world, practiced by people who have other "options." The Muslim setting might simultaneously generate anxiety for Hindu readers regarding the "Indianness" of the practice and for Muslim readers at having the practice once again identified with them. The domestic world of women depicted in "Lihaf" is the same as that depicted in Urdu *rekhti* poetry of the late eighteenth and early nineteenth centuries. The suppression of rekhti by Urdu litterateurs in the twentieth century was fueled by a similar nationalist panic at the depiction of homosexuality as ensconced within domestic life.[20]

Punishing the Westernized Homosexual

Between the *Chocolate* and "Lihaf" controversies in the first half of the twentieth century and that around *Fire* toward its close, several other fictions about homosexuality appeared in Hindi but did not generate controversy. One of these is Rajkamal Chaudhuri's Hindi novel *Machhli Mari Hui* (*Dead Fish*). First published in 1965, and reissued in 1994, it is typical in its configuration of a nexus between homosexuality and a homogenized West.[21] The blurb on the jacket of the 1994 edition frames it as a text that warns against the dangers of Westernized modernity. In his foreword, entitled "About Dead Fish," the author (who died in 1967 at the age of thirty-eight) lists a large number of Western texts he has read on the subject of homosexuality. He conflates the homophobic ("Female Sex Perversion" by Morris Sidekel) with the homophilic (Ronald Webster Cory's eloquent defense *The Homosexual in America*) and the feminist (Simone de Beauvoir's *Second Sex*), as well as the nonfictional (Alfred Kinsey's *Sexual Behavior in the Human Female*) with the semifictional (Diana Frederick's putative autobiography). Chaudhuri goes on to complain that while male homosexual behavior is criminalized in most "civilized" countries, female homosexual behavior is not, with the result that in cities like Paris, New York, and Tokyo, lesbians meet in clubs and have sex "in different ways and with different instruments" (11). He claims that most Indian women who engage in lesbian acts "do not know what they are doing and why they are doing it—they do it in their sleep, in intoxication, unknowingly" (11).

The novel traces the progress of its protagonist Nirmal Padmavat from the mires of Westernization to an indigenous apotheosis. Nirmal is a Bihari village boy who, after working at a variety of jobs such as waiter and sailor, comes to an appreciation of Marxism while imprisoned by the British for his nationalist activities. He is inscribed simultaneously as heterosexual and "Indian" when he resists the homosexual advances of a Maulana. While working as a waiter in a Muslim hotel in Lahore, he is befriended by the Maulana, a perfumier. When the Maulana takes him to his room, Nirmal draws a knife on him and thereafter men are afraid to take him to their rooms (41).

In the United States Nirmal gets seduced by the rhetoric of individual liberty and returns to Calcutta to found a business empire. The price he pays is that of impotence, a condition the narrator attributes both to his being a machine in the service of capitalism and to his never having known the love of a woman. His mother abandoned him as a child, and Kalyani, the woman he falls in love with in New York, is corrupted by Western ways, given to drinking, smoking, acting in pornographic films, and working as a model and call girl. When she tries to seduce him, he turns impotent; thereafter, whenever he approaches a woman his memory of Kalyani's taunts has the same effect on him. When Nirmal reaches Calcutta, he finds that Kalyani has just died, leaving behind a husband and a daughter, Priya. The husband, Dr. Raghuvansh, had married her out of compassion. He and Nirmal strike up a friendship and they are repeatedly compared to a Greek philosopher and a Roman conqueror, respectively. Nirmal, who is not only impotent but also lame, builds the tallest skyscraper in Calcutta, thirty stories high, and names it Kalyani Mansion; it is black like himself and its compensatory symbolism is pretty obvious.

Eight years later, he marries a divorcée, Shirin Salzberg. Shirin is literally and metaphorically half-Indian, half-Western. Daughter of a Christian father and a Jewish mother, she is turned against men by her mother's complaints of her father's sexual inconsiderateness and further by her mother's death during the birth of her younger sister. As teenagers Shirin and her sister develop a lesbian relationship with one another, and work as nightclub singers. Shirin dresses in Western clothes and sings English songs onstage. Following her first marriage, she lives for a couple of years in Europe, where she learns to drink and gamble. Nirmal remains impotent after marriage and punishes his wife by mauling her and covering her with bruises. She masturbates and turns to lesbianism, which is described as "Self-love! If one does not get the love of the Other, what else can one do?" (108).

Shirin drowns her sorrows in alcohol, in gazing at a lesbian painting in her bedroom, and finally, in an affair with Kalyani's eighteen-year-old daughter Priya. One day Priya remonstrates with Nirmal about his mistreatment of Shirin. At this point, the narrator intervenes with a description of Priya and Shirin's ineffective lovemaking, which is described as that of two fishes swimming in a dark void:

> The fish swim in the dark, and leap up to catch one another. But they have no arms. The fish throb to embrace one another, but they have no feet. . . . One fish says: 'Come closer, drink me with your lips. Put your tongue in my lips. Keep rubbing me with your body. I am dying . . . '
>
> The other fish says, 'I am dying. Break my bones. Bite my lips with your teeth. Kill me—I want to die.'
>
> But it is not easy to die when one wants to. The fish remain alive even while they are dying. Because a man is alive in the hearts of both. Only one man. His name is Nirmal Padmavat. Although he is not near, Nirmal Padmavat stands in Shirin's and Priya's hearts like a black bronze statue, smiling. Two lesbian [the English word *lesbian* is used here] women and in both their hearts, both their minds, every part of their bodies, is a bronze statue. (121–22)

This description is followed immediately and without explanation by a catalog of Western literature about lesbians. It begins with the Marquis de Sade and continues through Honoré de Balzac, Thomas Hardy, and a heavily distorted summary of *The Well of Loneliness*, concluding with a quote from Carol Hales's 1953 novel *Wind Women*. After thus framing both lesbianism and male impotence as being caused by the West, the text proceeds to cure both through indigenous heterosexuality. Priya's remonstrations with Nirmal, whom she terms a "wild beast," recall to him her mother Kalyani's taunts. Nirmal then rapes her repeatedly while forcing her to drink rum. When she emerges from his house late at night, her clothes are in tatters, covered with blood and vomit, and her body is bruised and torn. On Nirmal's orders, a servant drives her home.

When she recovers, her father suggests that she go to meet Nirmal but she refuses. Her father then commits suicide, leaving a letter for Nirmal, in which he tells him that Kalyani always loved Nirmal. He adds: "I too have loved you. . . . When you married Shirin I felt sorry for you. Shirin was a 'homosexual' [in English]. Her first husband Vishwajit Mehta had brought her to me many times. I had no cure so I sent her to other doctors though she didn't want to go. The life she led was dear to her. Girls were dear to her" (134).

The letter goes on to argue that because Shirin could not give her womanhood to Nirmal, he could not become an ordinary man. "There is no happiness greater than that of being an ordinary man, Nirmal. . . . To be out of the ordinary, to be 'abnormal' [in English] is easy. . . . A little intoxication of wealth, somewhat out-of-control sexual desire, a few antisocial and unethical acts make a man 'abnormal.' It is difficult to be ordinary" (135). He adds that Priya, by becoming the prey of Nirmal's beastliness, has made Nirmal a man. He does not regret Nirmal's having repeatedly raped Priya because this has cured not only Nirmal but also Priya, who had become homosexual in Shirin's company: "Only this type of demonic behavior could have made her an ordinary woman again. Now she is not ill. She is healthy and natural" (136).

Priya's father wills all his property to his hospital, leaving his daughter penniless. Nirmal carries the corpse to cremation, and Priya mentally salutes Nirmal. He then loses all his property because he refuses to bribe corrupt income tax authorities. He saves only Kalyani Mansion, which he gives to Priya. Now entirely free of Western capitalism and of impotence, he returns to his wife and has sex with her. Next morning, she wakes up singing a song about a dead fish that comes to life in the monsoon. The stamp of a specifically Indian heterosexuality is placed on this supposedly happy ending: "Shirin has tied her long black tresses into a Manipuri bun. In her hair parting she has made a thick bloodline—*sindoor*. A thick line of *sindoor* shines and Shirin Padmavat's whole face glows. In this glow is modesty and pride! And also compassion!" (149).

In this novel the West generally, and the United States specifically, are the main causes of evil—corrupt sexuality is depicted as a symptom of capitalism and neocolonialism. In the tradition of Nehruvian Soviet-leaning socialist opposition to the West, especially the United States, indigenous Indian business is contrasted with U.S. capitalism. Heterosexuality is identified with India and perverted sexuality with the States. Nirmal's mentor, a traditional Indian businessman named Niyogi, is a self-made man who, from the age of twelve, has supported his widowed mother and siblings. He is one of the few Indian businessmen who has never visited the States and who preaches against U.S. capital in Calcutta's chambers of commerce. He warns that having gotten rid of British colonialism, India will become enslaved to those capitalist countries who buy her economy by giving her technology, education, weapons, consumer goods, and aid. He insists that all the capital and technology invested in India should be of Indian origin.

Nirmal's loss of his potency in the United States through his relations with the Westernized Kalyani signifies the loss of Indian manhood both economically and sexually. In New York, the distraught Kalyani writes out a list of the main features of contemporary U.S. culture and tacks it up on her wall. The list consists of nine items: "1. blue films 2. jazz music and Negro girls 3. Dale Carnegie 4. Tennessee

Williams's plays 5. yellow journalism 6. Marilyn Monroe 7. pubs and dirty coffee houses 8. the fear of communism 9. skyscrapers" (52–53). Nirmal's attempt to regain his manhood by achieving success as a capitalist is symbolized by the skyscraper he builds in Calcutta. This phallic skyscraper is futile because it becomes the site for his wife's lesbian affairs and his own impotence. He truly regains his manhood only when he renounces capitalism and the skyscraper, at the same time regaining his potency and destroying lesbianism.

While Ugra's claim to be "revolutionary" was upheld by only a minority of Hindi litterateurs, with the majority terming his writings about homosexuality obscene, in Rajkamal Chaudhuri's case the situation was reversed. A few considered his writings obscene but most Hindi litterateurs termed them "revolutionary." Where Ugra's stories figure homosexuality as an integral and perhaps ineradicable part of indigenous urban life (with Muslims sited, however uneasily, as indigenous), Chaudhuri's novel figures homosexuality as directly originating in the West, and demonstrates how the Indian city should be purged of it. Another crucial difference is that Ugra's characters are shown as thoroughly enjoying homosexual relations, while Chaudhuri's characters are depicted as agonized rather than pleasured by homosexual sex. Chaudhuri's representation and rhetoric formed a perfect fit with the Hindi literary world's anti-Western nationalism. Commentators characterized his writings as exposés of the emptiness and perversity of upper-middle-class urban Indian life, influenced by Western capitalism.

It is important to point out here that the worlds of English and Hindi in modern India are far from separate. Many readers are bilingual, just as were those litterateurs in the late 1920s who wrote about *Chocolate* in Hindi newspapers and also read Leonard Woolf and Gilbert Murray in the *Nation*. Most Hindi literary critics throughout the twentieth century were bilingual urbanites. For example, Mohanlal Ratnakar, an Ugra expert, taught at a Delhi University college in the 1970s. He supports Ugra for "proving that same-sex eroticism is a terrible sin."[22] Another critic, Madhu Dhar, also urban and bilingual, refers to homosexuality as "unnatural fornication" in his book on Ugra, which is based on his Ph.D. dissertation at Jodhpur University.[23] These late-twentieth-century critics use a term, *samlingi rati*, that now appears in Hindi dictionaries as a translation of "homosexuality but was not in use in the 1920s and '30s when the *Chocolate* controversy occurred. These critics' access to English-Hindi dictionaries that participate in a new discourse of homosexuality does not lead them to take a less homophobic view than Ugra or Chaturvedi did, yet readers like them have not so far objected to most of the English-language advertisements that figure urban Indians as homoerotically inclined. This could be because of different generic expectations.

The Hybrid Indian

The inscription of the West is not as fraught in Indian advertisements as it is in Indian fiction since ads are not didactic in the way that much Indian fiction, with its genesis in the period of national struggle, tends to be. The purpose of an ad is to sell, not to educate, and these ads sell products that are clearly marked as Western or Westernized, that being one of their attractions. Furthermore, an advertisement operates on the premise that for options to be available to the reader is a good thing.

Literature, whether Indian or Western, does not always operate on such a premise:
Ugra's opponents explicitly claimed that the option of reading obscene literature
should not be available to readers.

English-language advertisements in Indian newspapers and magazines in the
1980s and '90s often have a subtext that represents homoeroticism as a seamless
part of urban middle-class life. In these ads homoeroticism is not relegated to the
underworld or to premarital college life; it is integrated with icons of professional
middle-class aspiration. For the bilingual urban middle class, a complete repudi-
ation of the West is neither possible nor desirable. At the same time, a new confident nationalism is evident in the way this class uses English (liberally intermixing
it with Indian-language words), and integrates Western influences into its hybrid
culture. Examples of this hybridization include the way the Indian urban elite comfortably wears Indian as well as Western clothing, and adds Western dishes to its
preponderantly Indian diet or spices up Chinese and Western cuisine to suit its
palate. An even more interesting example of the way Western products get modified

Figure 9.1
Double spread
appeared in
*The Illustrated
Weekly of India*

to suit Indian cultural requirements is that in India both Wimpy's and McDonald's prominently display notices stating that they do not serve either beef or pork. Both have also devised a number of vegetarian meals and snacks, in complete contrast to the fare available in their U.S. outlets.

While differing reader expectations play a role in the figuring of homosexuality in fiction and in advertisements, the different conditions of production are also important. For a fiction writer, writing about homosexuality inevitably triggers anxieties about being read as homosexual oneself. But the copywriter of an advertisement is completely anonymous: since an advertisement is not a signed text, he can afford to be much more playful and daring if the ad can somehow get past the boss and into print.

Modern Indian advertisements strongly suggest that as many options as possible should be available to the individual. This suggestion functions as enabling for the representation of homoeroticism. In my favorite, an early-1980s Calico ad for its Caliber suitings line (see fig. 9.1), the attitude apparently being marketed is

cali—ber°: It's what some men look for in other men and all men look for in suitings.

cali—ber° suitings from calico.

that of the individual male's confidence in his ability to make choices as an autonomous self with a distinctive temperament. However, the visual images of the closet door swinging open and the delicately handsome young man wearing a bow tie, accompanied by the tagline "what some men look for in other men," may suggest to some sections of the readership that one of the possible choices the suiting will aid them to make is very specific. The ad also plays on the word *calibre/caliber* suggesting that not only those who wear the suiting but also perhaps another group of men constitute an elite with a special calibre.

Like lyric poems, ads of this type use suggestion rather than statement to attract the reader. A directly sexual image can often be counterproductive because the reader may remember the image but not connect it with the product. In addition, explicitly sexual images in Indian ads have often been attacked as obscene by women's organizations on both the right and the left. One example is the 1990s Tuffs shoes ad where a nude male model and female model were shown embracing in profile, with a snake wrapped around them. Another example is the 1990s

Figure 9.2
This ad appeared in several magazines and on billboards in the late 1990s.

Chelsea jeans ad in which two women in jeans and leather embrace each other next to their motorbike and the tagline reads "F*** off Leave Us Alone" (see fig. 9.2).[24] Significantly, in both these ads the images are completely Western, not a hybrid Western-Indianness. In the Tuffs ad, nudity removes markers of nationality and culture while the snake evokes Adam and Eve. In the Chelsea jeans ad, nothing in the black-and-white visual suggests Indianness. Explicitness and lack of hybridity both set off the alarm signals.

In contrast, a 1990s ad for Contessa cars (see fig. 9.3) is noteworthy for its seamless integration of a Western icon into a narrative worded in wonderfully Indian English (phrases like "known him all along" and "on our first round of beers"). The domestic scene of the two men chatting outside their homes is noticeably devoid of any markers of heterosexuality—no wives or children appear either in picture or text. One man's attraction to the other finds its consummation in the ambiguous last line: "And he turned out to be just the kind of person I'd built a mental picture of when I first saw him." The cleverness of this line consists in the

CHELSEA

JEANS
THE BOLD NEW STATEMENT

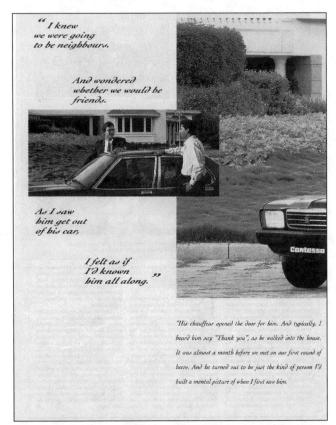

"I knew we were going to be neighbours.

And wondered whether we would be friends.

As I saw him get out of his car,

I felt as if I'd known him all along."

"His chauffeur opened the door for him. And typically, I heard him say "Thank you", as he walked into the house. It was almost a month before we met on our first round of beers. And he turned out to be just the kind of person I'd built a mental picture of when I first saw him.

Figure 9.3
Appeared in
India Today,
May 11, 1995.

phrase "just the kind of person." which for many readers would mean "a nice person" but for some readers might suggest a more specific meaning.

A late-1990s Rivolta underwear ad risks a little more in its wording (see fig. 9.4). Apparently making a comparison only between two types of comfort level—that with the boss and that at the end of a long hot day (the heat level in the office signals the Indianness of the setting)—the text manages to suggest much more:

> A simple gesture (let's face it) could have its share of complex undertones. And so while you continue to wrestle with the eternal "To schmooze/Or not to schmooze with the boss" dilemma, the good news is that progress/change seem to have done their bit on another front: your underwear."

The gender of the boss is revealed only in the last line: "Even if it's the boss himself who happens to be reading this." This line is followed by the slogan "Undress code for men." By connecting attractive underwear not with dressing but with undressing, in a context that never mentions a woman but only mentions a fraught relationship between men, in which one man needs to please the other, the ad places its suggestiveness in a nonheterosexual context.

Several other ads in the 1990s work by eliding the gender of the speaker and/or

Figure 9.4
Appeared
in magazines
in the 1990s.

implied viewer, thus managing to appeal to both heterosexual and homosexual readers. A good example is the Ray-Ban sunglasses ad (see fig. 9.5). At first glance, one might make the heterosexist assumption that the "I" is a woman and the man smiling flirtatiously in the visual is the "him" she sees. But a closer reading shows that clues have been built in to make the ad work almost like a puzzle. The "him" is described as wearing a tie, but the man in the visual is not wearing one. The "him" does not wear a Ray-Ban, which is how the "I" can outdo him. Since the man in the visual is wearing a Ray-Ban, *he* must be the "I"!

A Bombay Dyeing ad for bed sheets shows one woman lying in bed, the sheet pulled up to her underarms, another stepping off the bed with a sheet draped around her unclothed body. Pall Mall, a men's clothing shop based in South Extension, a posh neighborhood in New Delhi, accompanies its visual of two sherry glasses touching one another with the copy: "For Men. Who Charm Other Men. And Their Women" (see fig. 9.6). As is evident from this list, this kind of ad is put out both by Indian business (Bombay Dyeing) and by foreign business based in India.

Figure 9.5
Appeared
in magazines
in the nineties.

Among other homoerotic ads are those of Calvin Klein, and Newport Jeans, showing groups of men, some dressed, some undressed, posing together and smilingly admiring one another (see fig 9.7).

It would be easy but somewhat reductive to argue that the Ugra and Chughtai controversies were fueled by a type of defensive nationalism that is replaced by a new internationalism in postliberalization, independent India. In fact, the arguments used to denounce Ugra's and Chughtai's writings in the 1930s and 40s are almost exactly the same as those used by the Shiv Sena to denounce Deepa Mehta's *Fire* in the late 1990s. However, the Shiv Sena, whose primary base consists of the urban lower middle class, the urban poor, and sections of the peasantry, found its arguments for censorship of *Fire* decisively rejected by the bilingual, educated middle class in the big cities as also, somewhat reluctantly, by the Bharatiya Janata Party government at the center. Thus, it may be arguable that the class base of the kind of defensive nationalism that claims indigenous purity is shifting. Also, the

For Men.
Who Charm Other Men.
And Their Women.

Particularly when such men think of little details. Like wearing cravats for a
Sunday afternoon lunch party. And hanging Donegal Tweeds on their shoulders.

Men who insist on the slice of orange in their chilled glass of Campari.
Men who believe in a complete wardrobe for all occasions.
They are men who shop at Pall Mall.

PALL MALL

The men's shop with a British accent
E-15 South Ex. Market Part II New Delhi

Figure 9.6
Appeared
in magazines
in the 1990s.

attitude displayed in the advertisements analyzed above is not merely or even primarily internationalism. Rather, it is a new type of confident nationalism that aggressively asserts its right to the hybrid pleasures of Indian bed sheets and Contessa cars as also of charming both women and men.

These ads simultaneously refigure Indian manhood and womanhood as not exclusively heterosexual (or homosexual) and not exclusively Indian (or Western). The blurring of sexual categories involves a blurring of national or cultural boundaries, and in both cases the claim to a homogenized and unified purity of identity is given up. These ads, like the ultimate outcome of the *Fire* controversy, suggest that the rapidly growing urban, bilingual Indian middle class, with its many transnational

Figure 9.7
In *The Sunday Review*
of *The Times of India*,
May 25, 1997.

affiliations, has the confidence to partake of such a blurring and enjoys its access to choices, despite temporary outbreaks of moral panic.

It is an interesting paradox that if India's first major encounter with the modern West, via British colonialism, was the primary source of a new kind of homophobia visible in twentieth-century Indian texts, another kind of encounter between independent India and the West may now be fostering challenges to that homophobia both in self-consciously gay-and-lesbian-produced texts, and in more mainstream texts like these advertisements.

Notes

1. I am grateful to Saleem Kidwai for suggesting this heading.
2. This text did excite some controversy, but not the same degree of acrimony as that excited by *Chocolate*. It has been translated into English by V. Abdulla in Vaikom Muhammad Basheer, *Poovan Banana and Other Stories* (Hyderabad: Orient Longman, 1994).
3. This is a reversal of the precolonial pattern in which male homoeroticism was much more frequently represented, as in Urdu poetry. A major cause of the reversal was the anxiety induced by colonial attacks on Indian masculinity. See Ashis Nandy, *The Intimate Enemy* (Delhi: Oxford University Press, 1983).
4. See, for example, Nirmala Deshpande's Marathi story, "Mary Had a Little Lamb," V. T. Nandakumar's Malayalam novel *Rantu Penkuttikal* (*Two Girls*), and Ismat Chughtai's Urdu novel *Tehri Lakeer* (*The Crooked Line*). Extracts from all three appear in English translation in Ruth Vanita and Saleem Kidwai, eds., *Same-Sex Love in India: Readings from Literature and History* (New York: St Martin's Press, 2000), 327–31, 311–17, and 283–86, respectively.
5. These stories are Kamala Das, "The Sandal Trees" (Malayalam), Shobhana Siddique, "Full to the Brim" (Hindi), K. C. Das, "Sarama's Romance" (Oriya), and a recent story by

Sukirat Anand, "The Sexual Exile" (Punjabi). The first has been translated by V. C. Ummer Harris and C. K. Mohamed Ummer in *The Sandal Trees and Other Stories* (Hyderabad: Orient Longman, 1995); the second and third appear in English translation in Vanita and Kidwai, eds., *Same-Sex Love in India*, 304–10 and 298–300.

6. See, for example, Vijay Tendulkar's play *Mitrachi Goshtha* (*Mitra's Story*), extracts of which are translated in Vanita and Kidwai, eds., Same-*Sex Love in India*, 332–35.

7. Bani Ray, "Sappho," English translation in Enakshi Chatterjee, ed., *An Anthology of Modern Bengali Short Stories* (Calcutta: Prayer Books, 1977).

8. Shobha De, *Strange Obsession* (New Delhi: Penguin India, 1992).

9. Ajeet Kaur, "Aak ke Phool," Hindi translation, in *Kaley Kuen* (New Delhi: Kitabghar, 1995), 36–64.

10. For an English translation of Detha's "Dohri Joon," see Vanita and Kidwai, eds., *Same-Sex Love in India*, 318–24.

11. Ugra, *Chocolate* (Calcutta: Tandon Brothers, 1953). All references are to this edition and are hereafter cited parenthetically in the text. Translations from Hindi are mine. Some parts of my analysis appeared in Vanita and Kidwai, eds., *Same-Sex Love in India*, 246–52.

12. Ugra's foreword, "Kaiphiyat," in *Chocolate* (1953), pages *ka* to *ja*.

13. Ratnakar Pandey, *Ugra aur Unka Sahitya* (Varanasi: Nagaripracharini Sabha, Samvat 2026 [1969 C.E.]), 258.

14. Premchand opined that homosexuality should be combated in pamphlets, not in literature, whose ideals should be kept pure; Pandey, *Ugra*, 266–67.

15. Ibid., 261.

16. The term *chocolate* currently has homoerotic resonances in other cultures; cf. the Cuban film *Strawberries and Chocolate* (1993) and the American film *Better than Chocolate* (1999).

17. Vanita and Kidwai, eds., *Same-Sex Love in India*, 119–25.

18. Ibid., 201.

19. Padma Singh Sharma, editorial, *Vishal Bharat* 2, no. 1 (Shravan Samvat 1985), 132.

20. See Carla Petievich's essay in this volume; see also Saleem Kidwai's differing analysis and translations in Vanita and Kidwai, eds., *Same-Sex Love in India*, 191–94 and 220–28.

21. Rajkamal Chaudhuri, *Machli Mari Hui* (Delhi: Rajkamal Prakashan, 1994). This is the edition cited throughout. Translations from Hindi are mine.

22. Mohanlal Ratnakar, *Pandey Bechan Sharma Ugra, Kahanikar, Upanyaskar* (Delhi: Rishabhchand Jain, 1974), 69.

23. Madhu Dhar, *Ugra ka Katha Sahitya* (Delhi: Rajpal and Sons, 1977), 73.

24. See Shohini Ghosh's essay in this volume for an analysis of the moral panic evoked in the middle class in the 1990s by some texts, including these ads.

10

What Mrs. Besahara Saw

Reflections on the Gay Goonda

Lawrence Cohen

Preface: The Wife, Her Husband, Their Television, and a Lumpen Lover

In 1989, the glossy Indian magazine *Society* published a spoof of contemporary advertising slogans. Various lines and jingles designed to promote brand identification were turned on their head for supplemental, usually sexual meaning, with suggestive photographs to match. A television ad exhorting "Trust Your Eyes Only" became bedroom farce. Mrs. Masoom Besahara, literally Mrs. Innocent Without Support, goes into her bedroom carrying the new television set she has chosen, and finds her husband Bijoy (spelled "Bi-Joy") in bed with another man. Embarrassed, Bi-Joy leaps out of bed and pulls on his pants. His wife, in shock, drops the TV.

The old set had jiggled in all the wrong places; the ad copy intimates a threat to the marriage. Husband and wife each seek solace elsewhere. The television embraced by Mrs. Besahara is nondescript; the male lover embraced by her husband is not. He is thin, wiry, and muscled; has a beard, and a string amulet around his neck; and stares nonchalantly, with evident disdain, at the triangular chaos of husband, wife, and television. Signifiably working class, perhaps a servant or hustler, he foreshadows a repeated query in elite women's magazines of the 1990s: What to do with gay husbands who sleep with male servants or tradesmen. The magazine *Savvy*, for example, after a largely supportive 1997 feature on the mother of Mumbai [Bombay] gay activist Ashok Row Kavi, turned, in the next issue, to a more critical cover story with the headline "I found my husband in bed with the tailor!" The theme is common and the problem— women with "gay husbands" in a society where marriages are often arranged and divorce is frowned upon—was clearly a recognizable, for some painful, and for many an eagerly consumable story.

That tailors or domestic servants, like drivers, are the usual third figure in these triangles presents a series of questions not immediately in the foreground of such exposés, more concerned as they are with disastrous husbands and the dishonest in-laws who support them. In the *Society* spoof, the other man, unlike Bijoy, is not threatened by exposure. Tough, insouciant, and sexual with men, his figure draws upon a variety of sources, one of which I will focus on here and which we might provisionally call the gay *goonda*. Goonda, from which stems the English *goon,* is a tough guy, a hired thug or lumpen character. *Gay* here is offered as a provocation, in anticipation of its usage in some of the texts and situations that follow. In the 1990s many activists and health workers in India and Bangladesh came to question the usefulness of *gay* as an identity for most men outside the English-speaking elite; their critique differed from an anticolonial rather than class-focused 1980s concern that *gay* was a Western import and thus culturally inauthentic. The recent emergence of new and contested terms like *kothi* to replace *gay* has drawn on both of these critiques, of inauthenticity and elitism, in service of the imperative of HIV prevention as public health good and lynchpin of transnational nongovernmental organizations governance.[1]

Such "antigay" critique, building as it does on a generation of men with poor or no command of English who have tried but failed to assimilate into the new gay groups, is for many cogent and timely. Yet *gay* floats and persists as a mode of contemporary signification in India and comes to rest far from the globalizing and elite "gay groups" of the AIDS era.[2] The goonda, with his violent logic of class mobility, and the signifiably middle-class Mr. and Mrs. Besahara struggling over their jiggling commodity prostheses, turn out to be recognizable figures in the career of the *gay* I trace here. Locating and analyzing them may help us trace a broader deployment of the sexual that reassembles fragments of kingship to engage the split political subject of modernity. What I mean by this split subject will become clear through a series of interpretive exercises.

These exercises will focus on the goonda, and will return to the Besaharas, their television, and the commodity only in closing.

Figures of Excess

No Limits

Bhaitu, an ad executive and friend in Calcutta, once confided in me his thoughts on gay people. This was in 1985, when Bhaitu was still an unmarried engineering student and I was a medical student who thought of myself as fairly straight. "Gays have no *limits,*" I recall him saying, though to be fair the words he used are dimly remembered fifteen years later. I asked him what he meant, and he surprised me. "I'm single," Bhaitu said. "And it's hard to meet girls in Calcutta the way you do in the States. But I don't go after guys the way gays do. I have self-control."

I asked Bhaitu if according to him all gays were unmarried guys who couldn't meet women. Not at all, he told me, and explained. Some guys do it with everyone—not just one girl, but many—and some take it further. They visit prostitutes, or they have sex with men. The same thing held, he was fairly sure, for some married men—again, it was a matter of self-control. Consonant with Bhaitu's understanding was the idea that almost any man, if he were lacking in a certain kind of will, might go for other guys.

The Politician's Son

Three years later, I was in the hostel room of a friend who studied English literature in Allahabad, a city in Uttar Pradesh in north India. I was now calling myself
gay and pursuing anthropology. The Allahabad friend studied English literature.
We bumped into a young man, barely eighteen and very thin. "He is my room-
mate, but he more or less lives in the next room," this friend said. "The next-door
guy is a big goonda, a thug. The goonda killed someone and is wanted by the police.
But his father is a politician and the son is carrying on as a student leader. He makes
my roommate have sex with him." *Makes* him? "This guy is his junior by several
years, and he's from a small village without money or friends. There's a lot of this
in the hostels, older and goonda-type students who get other guys to do these
things."

The Libertine Poet

The Allahabad University visit was in 1989; four years later, I was beginning a project on AIDS in Varanasi (Banaras), working with MSMs ("men who have sex with
men"), to use the public health language that graced my research proposals then.
I spent a fair amount of time with guys who lived in hostels on the campus of
Banaras Hindu University. Some of them were by common account goonda types,
and a number of the goondas were doing M.A.s in Hindi. Once, I asked two of
these guys if they had read much in Hindi on homosexuality. We had been discussing the Urdu poet Firaq Gorakhpuri, who had taught at Allahabad University
and was well known in Banaras. Firaq was a complex figure of libertinage who, in
these conversations, sometimes called to mind sexual license with women even
while standing as the classic figure of the exultant and unrepentant lover of young
men. He was said to have been Jawaharlal Nehru's teacher when Nehru was a student. Pungent couplets were attributed to the poet, telling of his seduction of the
future prime minister.

The question surprised them—they knew I was writing about homosexuality,
but they hadn't realized I was in search of texts. The conversation turned to girls.
One said, "We know a shopkeeper who can tell you what to read."

A Novel

The shopkeeper recommended a book I have written of elsewhere, Amarkant's 1956
Hindi novel *Sukha Patta*, written in the form of a memoir.[3] Amarkant belonged to
the Hindi and English literary worlds in Allahabad that overlapped with those of
Firaq and of my Allahabad friend's teachers. *Sukha Patta* was reprinted in an inex-
pensive paperback by a major publishing house, Rajkamal Prakashan, and was
widely available. It opens with the adolescent narrator Krishna trying to act tough
to be seen as a real man. It was 1943, Krishna tells the reader, and a time and place
in which you were seen either as beautiful (*sundar*) or as manly, but never as both.
To be respected as a real man, you had to be strong, pick fights, speak local Bhojpuri
and not refined Hindi, and do everything you could to prove you were not a well-
mannered, well-groomed, and well-schooled wimp. On the one side was a form of

self-styling steeped in local language and habit and resistant to being rationalized, nationalized, or modernized; on the other was an alternate form that promised revolutionary change but threatened abjection. Krishna and his friends embraced the local and styled themselves as goondas-in-training. All took on projects of manliness: Krishna skipped school, another friend made his own explosives, and a third tried to seduce every girl and boy.

Carnival

This figure of rough and criminal manliness extending to the seduction of everything, signifying lack of control to my friend Bhaitu but a defense against new and possibly alienating forms of national and modern habit in Amarkant's novel, is in at least one variant of local Banaras slang given a name: *mahaland*, "supercock." During the spring Hindu festival of Holi in many north Indian cities, organized gatherings or publications of local poets overturn everyday convention and poke ribald fun at political and social leaders. This carnival genre is known as *gali*, or "abuse."

Banaras Holi is known to be distinctive, its jokes operating not only within the logic of what is sometimes termed *barhi* "line"—the big line of sex, between men and women—but also the more carnivalesque mode of *chhoti* "line"—the little line between men. A male figure marked as the *janata*, "the people," is penetrated by a familiar set of predators—the police, the politician. Each year the Hindi tabloid press surreptitiously publishes chapbooks with pages of poetic abuses—often attributed to the master libertine, Firaq—along with grainy photos and cartoons. Mahaland appears in cartoons and abuses, a wild phallic hero that mocks political order and everyday pretense and has access to innumerable women. Some cartoons identify him with Firaq.[4]

The Banaras abuses and chapbooks produced each Holi call attention to their own localness. Many of the pseudonymous poets have titles that end with "Banarsi," meaning "resident of Banaras"; their language is exquisitely local, *Banarsi Boli*, the mark, Krishna tells us in *Sukha Patta*, of manly speech. In similar Holi chapbooks produced less regularly in the city of Lucknow (also in Uttar Pradesh but farther to the north and west than Banaras and Allahabad) *barhi* line cartoons and abuses predominate. Politics are less likely to be framed as akin to sex between men, and caricatures of primarily male politicians are grafted onto female bodies. However, many of the *chhoti* line cartoons from the Banaras chapbooks are borrowed and reprinted—the localness of Banaras offers a translocal value, and travels.

Landlords and Pathans

Mahaland is a figure of carnival excess—the logic of the abuse presumes forms of everyday abjection for which excess offers a fantastic reversal. In Banaras in the 1980s and early 1990s, in many of my conversations not only with local goondas but with journalists, academics, and neighbors, a stock figure of excess in its everyday embodiment was the rapacious landowner, particularly across the border in the neighboring state of Bihar, to the east. Lucknow journalists in 1997, describing to me the decline in political civility in the state capital and the ongoing criminalization of everything, referred to the noxious creeping influence of eastern Uttar Pradesh—Banaras,

Allahabad, and environs—and Bihar. One way the limitless desire of the Bihari landowner, the *zamindar*, was marked was in his constitution of the sexual object as anything that moved. Women, young men, and third-gendered *hijras* were all at risk for a hunger framed as sodomitical—*laundebaazi*. History was measured through the corruption of a more courtly sovereignty by such excess.

I had gone to meet the Lucknow journalists to discuss the recent murder of a physical education teacher, Gomes, at the famous English-language school La Martinière. A variety of theories had surfaced to explain the murder: the teacher was a drug dealer, he was a womanizer, he was involved with unsavory elements that were turning the august school into a den of goondas. All of these were summarized in a headline in *The Pioneer*: "Gomes was a gay." Sharma, the journalist who wrote the story, was poking fun at the profusion of rumors, the teacher's being gay was but the latest feeble attempt to write off the crime. But when I spoke with him, he linked the variants together. "It's Pathans," he said, "from the town of Malihabad." Moneylenders and agents, they were taking over the heroin trade in the region and with their new money moving into the city. La Martinière has been affected, like everything else. And the once pastoralist Pathans like boys; rising "goondaism" and homosexuality went hand in hand. Malihabad, Ghazipur, much of Bihar—all these Pathan towns are infamous, and their particular proclivity is spreading as local black money and the drug mafia extend their reach.

As Sharma put it, "And if you think the Gomes case is bad, you should look at the serial killer." Before I could respond to the unexpected comment, Sharma's editor came by and asked what I was doing there. When Sharma explained, the editor—a sociologist by training, from Jawaharlal Nehru University in Delhi—pulled me into his office. "Don't listen to him," he said. "It has nothing to do with Pathans. It's all about land tenure. Look, I'm from Punjab. We don't have that much homosexuality there. Not in West Bengal, either. But in eastern Uttar Pradesh and Bihar, the British land settlement produced relations of extreme bondage and dependency between men, and the result was that this kind of behavior became entrenched as part of local political life." His argument was intriguing, and got me momentarily away from Pathans, staple of the colonial homoerotic. Certainly the forms of landlordism that the myriad variations on the colonial rule of property set in motion throughout India were distinctive. Bihari landowners and others were known to keep *laundas*—young men for sex—and newspapers reported on the occasional young man who resisted.[5] But genealogical studies of labor servitude in Bihar by scholars like Gyan Prakash suggest that neither local cultures of hierarchy and rule nor the British Permanent Settlement are in themselves adequate glosses of the embodied logics of domination, gentleness, and violence.[6] But there was no place within critical journalism for laundebaazi ever being other than predation on the one side, desperation on the other. Moving away from the origins of local laundebaazi to the interpretive frames that give it political force, one confronts the figure of kingship.

The Inverted Crown

In reconfiguring Louis Dumont's famous dictum that "the secret of Hinduism may be found in the dialogue between the renouncer and the man-in-the-world," T. N. Madan suggested a way of thinking about the normative significance of pleasure and excess.[7] Madan argues that the Kashmiri Brahman village householders he interviewed in the 1950s framed their *dharma*, their local moral world, not against some radical and therefore unachievable renunciate ethic but as a space of negotiation and practice *between* renunciation and unregulated pleasure, between *yoga* and *bhoga*. The other pole of daily practice is that of the libertine. Though Madan does not draw out the point, the position of libertinage in many textual examples in his book *Non-Renunciation* is that of a king or landholder.

The analyses of many scholars have led to a conversation around medieval and precolonial kingship in which the king is at the symbolic and transactional center of a moral and territorial universe stabilized through gift-giving raised to the level of an ethic of dissemination.[8] In early and medieval epic and Puranic narrative, subjects often urge their kings not to renounce but to remain vigorous and youthful, maintaining the ideal commonwealth through the mixing of their substance with that of the land and its people. In her study of the "temple prostitute" *devadasis* of Puri, Frederique Appfel-Marglin examines the close relations of auspiciousness that have linked king and courtesan—against the often inauspicious purity of the Brahman or widow. The king's totalizing ability to mix successfully with all is mirrored in his links to figures like devadasis who stand simultaneously at the impure margins and at the auspicious center.

In Uttar Pradesh and Bihar folklore and popular culture, laundas (Young male dancers and prostitutes) and hijras (transgendered prostitute-ascetics) often stand in relation to landlords as Marglin's devadasis do to kings. In the 1989 Bhojpuri film Mai (directed by Rajkumar Sharma), a rapacious landlord forces young men to flee the village in order to escape bonded labor or worse; one—the hero—returns disguised as a launda. The landlord immediately falls for him and brings him into the inner sanctum of his home, promising him marriage with flowery words, as he has promised various women falsely in the past. The disseminating flow of this latter-day king's gift fails, since his ejaculations take instead of giving. But the totality of his desire has brought a hero into his house, allowing for the circulation of power—the king is killed.

Ajay Skaria, in his study of Bhil "tribal" history in western India, suggests compelling links between normative kingship and the wilderness of the margin.[9] The persistent links between landlordism and laundebaazi, like Krishna and his friends' efforts to be socially and sexually aggressive in *Sukha Patta* so as not to become marginalized by a civilized center, recall norms of kingship that may differ from the civilized and centralized body politics of Nehruvian modernity. Thus the pleasure, for the Banaras Hindu University goondas, of a couplet in which Firaq the laundebaaz has sex with the future prime minister Nehru.

The Serial Killer

I went back to Sharma's office. "Serial killer?" I asked him. Three years earlier, he told me, six young men were found strangled in Lucknow, their bodies discovered with pants pulled down and the genitals sometimes mutilated, with apparent signs of anal penetration. The young men's corpses were left in prominent locations, nodes of power and privilege in the capital city: next to the VIP colony where senior bureaucrats lived; outside the state guest house, where senior party men and opposition figures often stayed; by the beautiful gardens where many of the city's well-to-do took their morning constitutionals. The last body was found on the grounds of the state capitol building.

I spent several days in the catacombs of *The Pioneer* and several other local papers hunting down the reports of these 1994 events. As bodies piled up, the primary story shifted from random killings of poor and unknown men to a "gay killer" to the activities of a criminal gang. Then a white Ambassador car was sighted in the proximity of one body, and other accounts of the murder vehicle began to circulate. Cars of this color and make were not only the most common vehicles for hire in Lucknow at that time, they were the VIP cars senior politicians and bureaucrats used for official business. Minor chaos reigned. A driver was arrested and prodded to confess that his boss, a minister, had ordered the rapes and killings. In the papers I read, the politician in question was not named, and the story disappeared rather suddenly, with the case never resolved nor closed.

In the next few years two mystery novels by white North Americans featured the serial killing in Bombay of Indian male prostitutes or hijras.[10] I interviewed one of the authors; he had never heard of the Lucknow killings but wanted to use violence against poor gay men to exemplify how "cheap" life in India could be. The novels were rather close to one another in their details; one author had sued the other, but lost.

The MLA

Few in Lucknow thought of the killings as sustained attacks on "gay men"—the victims were young and poor, doing what either youth or necessity or both demanded. But many in the city were confident they knew who the politician and his supporters were. Several names of state parliamentarians, or MLAs, were brought up, one of which was Reoti Raman Singh. Uttar Pradesh chief minister Mulayam Singh Yadav of the Samajwadi Party had brought his former enemy Reoti over from the rival Janata Dal with the promise of a ministry. Political journalist Seema Mustafa noted, three years later, how Mulayam bided his time in seeking revenge, writing, "Later, he wooed Singh, promising him the moon, so much so that the latter was mesmerised into leaving the Janata Dal and joining the Samajwadi Party. He has not been heard of again. Shortly after he joined his name was dragged into a sodomy-murder scandal that had hit Lucknow at the time and Reoti Raman Singh literally went into political oblivion."[11] The suggestion was that the sodomitical serial killer was created, or at least appropriated, by the chief minister himself. Mustafa has had Janata Dal ties, so her discussion here of Mulayam might be taken with a grain of salt. Whatever did happen, what stuck was that it made sense, to many of the inhabitants of Lucknow I interviewed in 1997, that a political leader would create a state scandal by leaving the penetrated, throttled, and almost castrated bodies of insignificant young men in places of record. I could be writing a mystery.

The Contractor

In Makarand Paranjape's 1995 novel *The Narrator*, a professor of English in Hyderabad named Rahul, bored with his conventional marriage and career, tells of being confronted with his alter ego in the person of one Badri, a wealthy self-made contractor who maims and kills when he deems it necessary, yet plans to write a successful Hindi film screenplay. Recognizing his cultural and class limitations and seeking help in turning his ideas and experience into saleable narrative, Badri seeks out Rahul, authorized master of the language of rule. The professor is both scared and attracted by Badri, who lives in the far more real and palpable "other" India that Rahul has managed to skirt through middle-class discipline. Throughout his life, Rahul has avoided following his passions, allowing a fantasy double named Baddy (short for Libido) to take the risks, kiss the girls, and write the searing texts he defers.

Desire, relegated to Baddy's crass moves with girls, also persists in Rahul's memory as a gentle adolescent longing for a visiting "beautiful English boy, Jerry Collier," a missionary's son. Jerry "looked so much like a girl that everyone was excited having him in our midst." When the young Rahul shyly takes his hand, Jerry tells him that "ever since I've joined this school the boys are always trying to get me into their beds. They hug me, kiss, and try to fondle me." The narrator apologizes, but Jerry continues, "I know all about sex and homosexuality. It's perfectly natural, provided people know what they are about. But I have my limits. I let people hold my hand. Sometimes, I let them kiss me too. But not on the lips. Only on my cheeks."[12] Rahul is allowed the privilege, after which he notes, "I felt I had kissed Cinderella."

In Badri, Baddy's autoerotic presence is materialized. Badri's life is as visceral as Baddy's imaginary one. Difference is not feared and banished nor guiltless pleasure restricted to the girlish condescension of a white boy. As Paranjape writes, "Badri seemed to know that he was different and had reconciled himself to the fact after a lot of pain. And once he had accepted that, he had become a complete person, someone who knew what he wanted, knew how to get it, enjoyed it while he had it, and didn't have regrets afterwards. He could feel pleasure without guilt."[13] Whereas for the professor the difference feared is in one sense the undisciplined future toward which his own pleasure might have led him, and in another the *real* "Indianness" his middle-class morality and desire to fondle whiteness has kept him from, Badri grew up a poor street orphan surrounded by predatory adults. His difference is another matter—Badri the dangerous contractor, we are told, is "gay."

Badri was "made" gay, sexually used for years as a boy by both his uncle and his uncle's daughter, his ugly cousin Meena. In the end, the uncle's rapes were less disturbing than Meena's claims of love, for the former were more honest to the reality of using and being used. Further repetitions in adulthood led him to a vow: "From then on, I knew that I would have no home, no wife, no children, no place to call my own in this world." He would live for pleasure, without expectations, in the crude honesty of subterranean Indian homosexuality—what you see is what you get.

The gay-identified short-story writer, activist, and Pune-based English professor Raj Rao has remarked that *The Narrator* is not "gay" writing, as Paranjape is not able to get *into* the head of a gay man, to write his specificity and difference.[14] Badri is not the first gay character to bear the burden of pure exteriority in standing for the real. Rahul speaks for the self-consciousness of a class that has displaced the violence of its own desires to succeed as renouncers; Badri's asceticism is forced upon him, materialized in the rape, and his rise to mastery has come through *bhoga*, homosexual rape into homosexual pleasure.

For Amarkant's Krishna in *Sukha Patta*, the path of manliness is to resist disciplined and effete cosmopolitanism in favor of a polymorphous and aggressive desire. Yet Krishna yearns for something more, some impossible combination of discipline and force, modernity and masculinity. For a brief moment he finds it in an older boy, Manmohan, who is a goonda and yet does well in school, is aggressive and yet honorable. The year is 1943, and Krishna recognizes the need for heroes. Manmohan, the good goonda, with his perfect marriage of yoga and bhoga, suggests another Raj, a lost kingship. But Manmohan, it turns out, is in love with Krishna, and when he sends the younger boy a love letter Krishna's admiration turns to scorn. To attempt to seduce boys may be part of goonda aggression, but to desire so vulnerably produces incoherence. The promise of the good goonda dissipates as Manmohan is revealed as something not yet gay.

Rahul's moment in history is different. He does not seek heroic kingship and has trusted his future to the cosmopolitan renunciation Krishna disparaged. Yet he feels, like Krishna, that something is missing, something between the violence out there and Baddy in here. The position of the householder is framed not between yoga and bhoga as ascetic civility versus violent passion. Civility is a Cinderella place—someone else's desire begrudgingly accepting your kisses; but you remain a frog. The shared text among everyone else in Rahul's world is not the fairy tale but the sensuous Hindi film, and the ascetic position is that of the viewing subject, Baddy in heat. Badri's screenplay links the violence out there to the shared male subjectivity of the screen, where heroes abound. The gay goonda internalizes the political relation exemplified in carnival—life is about fucking and getting fucked. Able to stand on both sides, simultaneously, of the other India beyond Rahul's imagination, Badri is the master of the real, like Reoti Raman Singh, accused serial sodomitical killer fucked royally by Mulayam Singh Yadav, dispatched into the abjection of the political wilderness only to return, four years later in 1998, once again a rising political star. But Singh, if he is anything besides Mulayam's victim, is a user of young men, neofeudal predator and not much of a hero for those past the ordeal of civility.

In the worlds of eastern Uttar Pradesh and Bihar, much asymmetric sex between men—across generational and gendered lines—is not nasty or brutish for the launda but pleasurable. Paranjape's creation of Badri may misrecognize much, but it does understand that the redemptive position it would convey by "the gay" refuses abjection by the powerful at precisely the site—the *gand*, the asshole—where dominant masculinized narratives of hierarchy locate it. The gay goonda, naming his desire for both sides of the relation of force, redeems the political real for the middle-class narrator.

Epilogue: What Mrs. Besahara Saw

To celebrate the millennium, Mumbai ad magazine *The Brief* chose a "modern" and "fun" topic for its annual contest. Teams were asked to produce an ad for "Bombay's first gay bar."[15] The fantasy bars that emerged bore little resemblance to the varied night spots men had been seeking out for the previous decade. When I interviewed the editor and contest organizer, he said he was trying to find a theme that would not be too political.

In the ten years between *Society*'s parody and *The Brief*'s contest, a number of "lesbian" and "gay"-themed advertisements, music videos, and other public texts have been created (see Ruth Vanita's and Shohini Ghosh's essays in this volume). Unlike the more frequent but regional newspaper reports of the sodomitical violence of politicians and police, these texts are cosmopolitan, apolitical, and fun. In Badri's crossing over to gay and in Bi-Joy's assignation with the goonda, these two orders of gayness intersect.

I have used this essay to explore the first order. I have suggested that the sodomitical and the gay are critical figures of the imagined excess of force and desire outside the ascetic modernity of the middle class. Yet contrary to this excess, these figures hold out a barely imaginable position of some other wildness that can renounce effete renunciation *without* a decline into Mahaland, an ever-expanding celebration of predatory violence.

In closing, I offer a brief account of the second order so as to appreciate the appearance of the goonda in Rahul's study and Bi-Joy's bedroom. One way into *The Brief*'s millennial gay bar is to note the centrality of fashion industry reporting to Indian urban mass media in the 1990s. Fashion design outsourcing, more than the textile and clothing industries that had shifted to smaller cities and production units, was central to urban India's interface with the global economy in the 1990s. With the fashion boom, media descriptions of models, designers, shows, and the salability of these abroad became ubiquitous.

In many discussions of the new urban subjects of fashion, same-sex figuration is notable. Gay designers are depicted as the new Indian *übermenschen*. Refigured male flesh, no longer just poor or Brahmanic, is continually on display. Fluff pieces in the media appear and reappear, querying scholars and others on the new masculinity. On the one side is a new narcissism and an implied retreat from extended family values. On the other is a global competitiveness, if not in the Olympics then in an infrastructurally more achievable masculine performance. If the luminous figure of Fashion India is the international beauty queen, India having garnered many titles in the 1990s, her flame less ignites the fuse of male pulchritude than illuminates the mirrored surfaces of this new masculinity. And this masculinity is frequently framed as somehow "gay," not gay as sexual orientation but gay as trope for the consumption that produces a global style.

Rachel Dwyer has written of the importance of a new urban middle class in any rethinking of Indian public culture.[16] The cosmopolitan order of the gay may figure an emerging class identification in reference to new norms and forms in at least two ways. I have suggested that the appearance of the "gay ad" is predominantly a use of the gay as a figure of global value and of self-refashioning through the brand.[17] But there is a second way; consumption as a threat, a haunting by something else.

The threat is double. Bi-Joy is found out, and his wife is left "without support." As a literalization of the gay order of consumption, the ad pokes fun at the new masculinity, suggesting its inattentiveness to the family. Mrs. Besahara is ultimately not served by her husband's new style. The brand and the gay do not offer *sahara*.

Perhaps this is why *Savvy* was so threatened by the interview with activist Row Kavi's mother—as industry gossip had it—that its editor followed the story in the next issue with that of the gay husband in bed with the tailor. Mrs. Row Kavi had said that her gay son was the only one of her children to take care of her.

But the threat is not only the ambivalence to a new relational order of consumption. The other man in the bed is radically unlike Bi-Joy or his wife. This new order implies that everything his presence represents cannot be contained in the space of middle-class domesticity. The political real, the unknown yet familiar violence pressing on the ramparts of civility, is already close at hand. The global order of fashion is suddenly intimate with the global order of heroin.

Trust your eyes only: domesticity isn't pretty; no more so than politics. Various fragments and memories of sovereignty—Nehruvian civility, family patriarchy, Lucknow courtliness, Hindu kingship—seem increasingly illegible, shot through with wildness. Neither yoga (as in middle-class renunciation) nor bhoga (as in sovereignty's excess, the persistent politics of that other agrarian India that refuses to be marginalized by the cosmopolitan center) seems to offer an imaginable ethics. In the meeting of the two, in the *besahara* bed before it is once again split into laundebaazi use-or-get-used predation, or the abjection and weak will of the married gay, some possibility continually hovers.

Notes

1. See Shivananda Khan, "Males Who Have Sex with Males in South Asia," *Pukaar*, October 2000, 12–13, 22–23.
2. On the globalizing of the gay, see Dennis Altman, "Global Gaze/Global Gays," *GLQ* 3, no. 4 (1997): 417–36. For critical rethinkings of this argument, see Tom Boellstorff, "The Perfect Path," *GLQ* 5, no. 4 (1999): 475–509; and Lisa Rofel, "Qualities of Desire," *GLQ* 5, no. 4 (1999): 451–74.
3. Amarkant, *Sukha Patta* (Delhi: Prakasana Samsthana, 1979).
4. Lawrence Cohen, "Holi in Banaras and the Mahaland of Modernity," *GLQ* 2, no. 4 (1995): 399–424.
5. Kanhaiah Bhelari, "The Male Concubines," *The Week*, July 19, 1998.
6. Gyan Prakash, *Bonded Histories: Genealogies of Labor Servitude in Colonial India* (Cambridge: Cambridge University Press, 1990).
7. T. N. Madan, *Non-Renunciation* (Delhi: Oxford University Press, 1987). Madan's work is part of a larger conversation with Louis Dumont on the figure of renunciation. See also Frederique Apffel-Marglin, *Wives of the God-King* (Delhi: Oxford University Press, 1985); Veena Das, *Structure and Cognition* (Delhi: Oxford University Press, 1977); and J. P. S. Uberoi, *Religion, Civil Society, and the State* (Delhi: Oxford University Press, 1996).
8. Ronald B. Inden, *Marriage and Rank in Bengali Culture* (Berkeley and Los Angeles: University of California Press, 1972); Apffel-Marglin, *Wives of the God-King*; Nicholas B. Dirks, *The Hollow Crown* (Cambridge: Cambridge University Press, 1987); Gloria Goodwin Raheja, "India: Caste, Kingship, and Dominance Reconsidered," *Annual Review of Anthropology* 17 (1988): 497–522.
9. Ajay Skaria, *Hybrid Histories* (Delhi: Oxford University Press, 1999).
10. Paul Mann, *Season of the Monsoon* (Sydney: Pan, 1992); Leslie Forbes, *Bombay Ice* (New York: Farrar, Straus and Giroux, 1998).
11. Seema Mustafa, "Two Yadavs and Misplaced Sense of Importance," *The Asian Age*, February 1, 1997.

12. Makarand Paranjape, *The Narrator: A Novel* (New Delhi: Rupa & Co., 1995), 36–37.

13. Paranjape, *The Narrator*, 120.

14. Raj Rao, "If You're Not a Gay, a Dalit, a Black or a Woman, You're Literally Dead!" Online at http://www.tehelka.com October 18, 2000.

15. "Mumbai notes," *Indian Express*, November 5, 1999.

16. Rachel Dwyer, *All You Want Is Money, All You Need Is Love* (London: Cassell, 2000).

17. See William Mazzarella, "Shoveling Smoke: The Production of Advertising and the Cultural Politics of Globalization in Contemporary India," Ph.D. diss., University of California, Berkeley, 2000.

Part 3

Performative Pleasures in Theater, TV, and Cinema

11

A Different Desire,
a Different Femininity

Theatrical Transvestism in the Parsi, Gujarati,
and Marathi Theaters, 1850–1940

Kathryn Hansen

Female impersonation, the practice of men playing women's roles, has a long history in South Asian theater. In Patanjali's grammatical text the *Mahabhasya* (ca. 150 B.C.E.), a male actor who plays female roles is described as a *bhrukumsa*, one who "flutters his brows."[1] The well-known dramaturgical compendium of ancient India, the *Natyashastra* (second to fourth centuries C.E.) mentions both men assuming the woman's character, an impersonation termed *rupanusarini* ("imitative"), and women taking on the man's role.[2] Today female impersonation continues in regional theatrical arts such as the Kathakali of Kerala, the Ram Lila of Uttar Pradesh, and numerous local and folk forms.[3] As a customary mode of enacting female characters, however, theatrical transvestism has vanished from the urban cultural zone. It surfaces in current film and drama either in the mimetic representation of the *hijra*, the transgendered social actor (for example, the protagonist of Amol Palekar's 1996 film *Dayra* [*The Square Circle*] or the minor character who appears during the riots in Mani Rathnam's 1995 film *Bombay*), or as a self-conscious interrogation of the earlier female impersonator (for example, Anuradha Kapur's 1998 theater piece *Sundari: An Actor Prepares*).

With this disappearance, a cultural space that valorized cross-gender role play and its associated spectatorial pleasures has vanished. Theatrical transvestism not only enabled actors to transform their own gender identities but also sustained and eventually reworked viewing practices predicated on interest in transgender identification and the homoerotic gaze. This article excavates the buried trove of theatrical transvestism that existed in western urban India in the Parsi, Gujarati, and Marathi theaters between approximately 1850 and 1940. Within the public culture of that time, female impersonators like Naslu Sarkari, Jayshankar Sundari, and Bal Gandharva achieved the renown of a Madhuri Dixit or Lata Mangeshkar today. The present essay addresses this phenomenon as the historical resurgence of a long-standing practice in the context of late colonial cultural formations. It explores the ramifications of theatrical cross-dressing for the constitution of gendered subjectivities, posing questions about homoerotic plea-sure and homosexual culture that may be extrapolated to a wider range of spaces and times.

The analysis presented here challenges the time-honored but fundamentally homophobic premise that female impersonators were mere surrogates for missing women. Although women in the nineteenth century were disenfranchised both as social actors and as theatrical performers, my argument is that female impersonators were desired in their own right, as men who embodied the feminine. Contrary to popular notions, they often coexisted with stage actresses and were chosen by their fans in preference to them.

Moreover, these cross-dressed actors, with their huge followings, were vital agents in the redesigning of gender relations and roles. They set new standards for feminine conduct and fashion, transforming the visual construct of womanhood into an image of bourgeois respectability. Simultaneously, female impersonators crafted a new sense of the interior person. They formulated attitudes of modesty and vulnerability that became the hallmark of the new femininity, paving the way for the emergence of the dutiful, demure *bharatiya nari* ("Indian woman") of the nationalist era.

Contours of the Bombay Stage

Soon after 1850, Bombay developed a metropolitan theatrical culture structured by the overlapping practices of the Parsi, Gujarati, and Marathi theaters. Although separated to a certain extent by language, these theaters shared much beyond their orientation toward female impersonation. They participated in a commercial enter-tainment economy based on corporate ownership of theatrical companies, which arose in tandem with the city's rapid population growth and prosperity. Music, dance, and dramatic entertainments once restricted in circulation by aristocratic patronage were transformed into commodities of mass consumption with the rise of a bourgeois class and the institutionalization of public space and leisure time. The appropriation of European stage technologies and new styles of drama deep-ened the divide between the older representational arena of court and countryside and the new public of the metropolis. Impersonations of gender, although contin-uous with earlier practices, entered the modern era and assumed meanings specific to the reconstituted audience.

That this audience was not bounded by the geographical perimeters of Bombay adds to the importance of the phenomenon for the construction of gendered sub-jectivities. Beginning in the 1870s, Parsi theatrical companies routinely traveled as far as Madras and Ceylon, Calcutta and Rangoon, Peshawar and Sindh. In each locale, companies styled after the Parsi companies sprang up, often adding the glam-orous phrase "of Bombay" to their names. Their popularity within the regions extended the Parsi theater's impact far beyond the point of origin. Even within Bombay the Parsi theater was a broadly based institution whose historical identity was never coterminous with the Parsi community.[4] Writers, actors, company man-agers, musicians, and stagehands belonged to a variety of class, caste, and religious backgrounds. Audiences were comprised initially of British officials, the military, and wealthy Parsi merchants, soon joined by the growing class of educated professionals. Textile workers, artisans, and small traders formed a large share by the end of the nineteenth century, accommodated by low ticket prices that ensured a heterogeneous public.

Although much has been made of the derivative, colonial character of the Parsi theater, largely on account of its fascination with the works of William Shakespeare and Victorian stagecraft, the overwhelming majority of the productions were in Gujarati, Urdu, and Hindi. Indic poetry and song genres embedded in Sanskritic and Persian narratives formed the dominant literary substratum. The stage medium was fluid and polyglot; modern forms of the languages had not yet stabilized, and the association of community and region with linguistic identity was yet to become fixed. Bombay's theater houses, although owned mostly by Parsis, were available for use by theater companies regardless of language or community affiliation. Most of these were built on Grant Road, in what was rapidly developing into a red light district, but the prestigious Gaiety and Novelty theaters near the Victoria railway terminus also attracted large audiences. There was much imitation and rivalry within the urban theater economy, allowing popular trends like female impersonation to circulate fluidly.

The rise of these urban theaters can be directly linked to the desires of the urban professional and mercantile classes for "rational amusement" in respectable public spaces. Prince Albert's dictum, "Rational entertainment, in which popular amusement was combined with moral instruction and intellectual culture," was printed in English and Gujarati translation on the title pages of the earliest Gujarati dramas to be published.[5] Authorial prefaces to the plays stressed the efficacy of the drama as an instrument of moral improvement. This principle was reinforced by the coverage of theater shows in print journalism. Newspapers in English and Gujarati carried playbills, synopses, reviews, and letters to the editor on the subject of theater, with the explicit intention of building an audience and nurturing the theater "in its infancy." Theatrical discourse thereby allied itself with the adjacent discourses of bourgeois respectability, civic order, and moral reform, and patronage of theater became a demonstration of public virtue.

Theater pioneers, including playwrights, managers, and company owners, were careful to demarcate their efforts at constructing a new culture of educative leisure in contradistinction to older forms of entertainment. In a Gujarati preface that begins by contrasting *natak*, the Sanskrit term for "drama," with *chetak* ("sorcery, witchcraft") playwright Delta takes pains to discriminate between acceptable and unacceptable styles of performance: "In short, rather than the black stamp of immorality that is slapped on the mind of the viewer by the dance of prostitutes, the shows of Mahlaris, and the Bhavai of the folk-players, the blameless amusement of theater enlarges the mind, gladdens the heart, cools the eyes, and speeds morality."[6] For Delta, immorality resides in the prevalent styles of popular entertainment, the *nautch* ("dance of prostitutes"), the folk drama Bhavai, and the shows of itinerant performers such as Mahlaris. Bhavaiyas and Mahlaris were designated as low caste primarily because of their occupation as hereditary performers, whereas dancing girls were marginalized on account of their violation of normative gender codes. Patronizing the shows of such performers, although widespread among British and Indian elites as well as ordinary people in the eighteenth and early nineteenth centuries, had become at least somewhat stigmatized by 1850. Part of the success of the emergent public theater lay in its ability to offer itself as an alternate site of respectable, "blameless" entertainment, in contrast with these increasingly denigrated artistic traditions.

These older practices nonetheless contributed to the spectatorial economy of the urban theaters and are salient to an understanding of the changes in theatrical trans-vestism that emerge in this period. Actors in Bhavai, a rural folk theater of Rajasthan and Gujarat, came from a hereditary caste called the Targalas (also called Bhojaks or Nayaks). The Targalas traced their descent to Asaita Thakur, the orig-inator of Bhavai, a Brahman who lost his "purity" by dining with a Muslim and an untouchable. This narrative of origins asserts the nonhierarchical, nonsectarian char-acter of the tradition. Bhavaiyas often targeted moneylenders, priests, and other figures of authority, bringing a strong flavor of social critique to their skits. Female roles in Bhavai were played either by boys or by mature males who specialized in female impersonation. Termed *kanchalias*, in reference to the woman's blouse (*kan-chali*) that was worn, these transvestite performers satirized women and male-female relations, while delighting audiences with dances such as the *ras* and *garba*.[7]

Although Bhavai performances were allegedly eschewed for their lewdness, sep-aration from Bhavai must have been largely motivated by the desire to mark one's distinction in terms of caste and class. Moreover, the informality of Bhavai con-trasted unfavorably with the Parsi theater's elaborate proscenium stage. Buttressed by stage technologies that privileged spectacle and realism, dramatic narratives were moving toward tight plots divided into fixed acts and scenes. Grandiose melo-dramas of ancient glory and virtue, replete with luxurious costumes and large painted sets, replaced the rustic satiric thrusts of Bhavai. Nonetheless, continuities with older forms remained, particularly in the performative vocabularies of music, mime, and movement. Late in the nineteenth century, the Targala community con-tributed significantly to the professional urban stage, when talented actors such as Jayshankar Sundari, Amritlal Nayak, and others entered the ranks of female imper-sonators in the Parsi and Gujarati theaters and achieved extraordinary success.

Tamasha, another regional dramatic tradition, had developed in Maharashtra by the late eighteenth century into a multiact folk drama.[8] A Persian word signifying "entertainment" or "show," *Tamasha* incorporated several earlier styles such as Gondhal, Povada, and Turra-Kalagi, while increasingly becoming infused with *lavani* singing and erotic dancing. During the late Peshwa period, female concu-bines and slaves were kept at court to perform sexually explicit lavanis in the royal playhouses.[9] Dancing boys (*nachya poryas*) were also common in Peshwa times, and courtesans are said to have learned their melodies and dance movements from them.[10] The British takeover in 1818 forced Tamasha performers to seek new sources of patronage. Folk theater retreated to rural Maharashtra, where rural land-lords patronized it. Whereas earlier it had attracted Brahman performers like Ram Joshi, it now became the province of the Mahars and Mangs, two low-caste groups. Entering the urban theatrical arena in the nineteenth century, Tamasha still employed "effeminate males" in opposition to the ideal of manhood projected in the "national theater" of Vishnudas Bhave.[11] During the first decades of the twen-tieth century, if not before, Tamasha performances had become regular offerings in Bombay's gentrified theaters.

Dance recitals by women who came to be known as nautch girls formed a customary part of celebrations like birthdays and weddings in Indian aristocratic families. The practice of holding a nautch (from Hindi *nach,* "dance") was adopted by the British in the early nineteenth century both for private enjoyment and to honor a guest. D. E. Wacha writes of Bombay in the 1860s, "Dancing girls, both Hindu and Mahomedan, were invited to enliven every important domestic entertainment of a joyous character." It was a "social duty" for Parsis as well as Hindus and Muslims to host such occasions.[12] Missionary-led aversion to the nautch took root in midcentury and prompted Indian and British elites to look for alternative entertainments. In the columns of newspapers and letters to the editor, the urban theater was often proposed as a respectable substitute. Nonetheless, the taint associated with the female performer on account of her presumed sexuality and low social origins carried over into attitudes toward actresses in the urban theater. The stigma accompanying the presence of actresses, who were viewed as prostitutes, was often cited as the rationale for the policy of certain theatrical companies to hire only men to play female roles. Yet fondness among spectators for erotic genres of song and dance such as *thumri* and *ghazal* dictated that these items be retained within the performative structure of the urban drama. In consequence, female impersonators took on the double burden of enacting noble womanly characters even as they inherited the arts of courtesans.

The theatrical transvestism of urban Bombay, then, in one sense was formed at a point of convergence among older living traditions of erotic performance and gender impersonation. The kanchalia of Bhavai and the nachya porya of Tamasha, both roles that involved male-to-female impersonation, contributed to the reconfiguration of the actor as woman in the new urban theater. Equally, the female lavani performer and the nautch girl served as templates for the reworking of the performer in female guise. While s/he was required, to a great extent, to deliver the same kinds of pleasure as these earlier models, the particular moment at which the female impersonator entered the Parsi theater required further adjustments to the formulation of the gendered performer. Before considering these additional attributes, however, I examine the explanatory apparatus that is so often given for the phenomenon of female impersonation.

Prohibition or Preference?

The most common reason offered for the prevalence of female impersonation in South Asia, as in China and Japan, is that it was a theatrical compulsion imposed by the social taboo against women appearing on stage. By the eighteenth century, the gendered segregation of public and private spheres forced the seclusion of women in the households of socially prominent families. Singing, dancing, and other performance arts were relegated to stigmatized classes of women like the devadasis of south India, the *maharis* of Orissa, the *naikins* of Goa and the western coast, and the *tawaifs* of the north. "Respectable" women were thus at an extreme social disadvantage with respect to the stage, and were not only unwilling to become actresses but ill equipped for its rigors and lacking in skills. To the question why professional performing women were not available to the nineteenth-century public theater, it is claimed that they kept themselves away from the stage because of the excessive degree of publicity, relative to the more private encounter between patron and performer in the setting of the *kotha* or salon. It is also mentioned that while professional women were trained in music and dance, they had little by way of dramatic experience and required extensive coaching.

This simplistic notion of men substituting for absent women must be questioned. Even in the ancient period, actresses (*natabharya* in Patanjali, *nati* in Bharata's *Natyashastra*) existed side by side with female impersonators in theatrical troupes. Syed Jamil Ahmed documents the presence of both male and female performers from the earliest times in Bengal, noting that the gender of the performer was never made to conform to the gender of the character: "both male and female performers have portrayed both male and female characters."[13] In the Tamasha, female performers and men performing women's roles filled complementary functions. It is certainly a fallacy that actresses were unavailable to Parsi theater. Actresses were recruited to the Parsi stage as early as 1874, when actor/ manager Dadi Patel brought back four *begams* from the harem in Hyderabad to play the parts of the fairies in the *Indar Sabha*. Khurshed Baliwala, the popular actor/manager who led the Victoria Theatrical Company on a number of foreign tours, introduced a series of women—Miss Gohar, Miss Malka, Miss Khatun, Miss Fatima—whose courtesan origins were thinly veiled under the anglophilic classifier *Miss*.[14]

The preferences exercised by publics and patrons for female performers, male-to-female impersonators, or both, need to be understood as shifting over time in conjunction with strictures relating to caste, class, gender, and codes of morality. Historical and regional variations in the popularity of female impersonation are not always easy to explain. In Calcutta actresses from the class of rejected and outcast women ("prostitutes") like Binodini Dasi proved their merit to bourgeois audiences and directors early on. With the acceptance of actresses in the public theater, female impersonation in that city ended in the 1870s. To explain this, Rimli Bhattacharya asserts that "change in forms of representation required same-sex impersonation," citing the influential playwright Michael Madhusudan Dutt, who stated that "clean-shaven gentlemen just would not do any more" for his heroines.[15]

Yet in western India, where forms of representation were also changing under conditions in many ways comparable to those in Calcutta, female impersonation entered a cosmopolitan phase and developed into a beloved art that continued through the 1930s. With the arrival of the Anglo-Indian actress Mary Fenton in the 1880s, female performers began to compete successfully in the Parsi theater. Nonetheless, companies like the Natak Uttejak Mandali and the New Alfred employed only female impersonators. The latter banned women from the stage until the death of director Sohrabji Ogra in the 1930s. For these companies and their audiences, performing women were undesirable rather than unavailable.[16]

The ruse of unavailability may have been constructed to deflect attention from the extraordinary popularity of female impersonation. Although correct in acknowledging the widespread exclusion of women from public life, this explanation confuses the agency of company managers and publics with that of performing women. The historical record indicates that rather than filling in for absent women, female impersonators competed against them for female roles within the theatrical troupe.

These roles may have been divided by character type, replacing competition with cooperation in certain cases. In any event, it is clear that companies and publics made choices about whom they wished to see representing women on stage, and they often chose men over women.

Present-day attempts to naturalize theatrical transvestism as a sociological imperative suggest an underlying anxiety of more recent origins regarding cross-dressing and its implications of effeminacy. Even as a relatively compartmentalized theatrical practice, female impersonation appears to threaten the construction of masculinity. Bringing it into the limelight seems to reinvigorate stereotypes of weakness and inferiority among the male population, a bitter legacy of colonial domination. As Mrinalini Sinha, Ashis Nandy, Uma Chakravarti, and others have shown, late-nineteenth-century Indian reformists responded to British disdain for Indian civilization and morality, and the concomitant characterization of Indian men as effeminate, both by recasting womanhood in the image of Vedic purity and by reinventing a belligerent style of masculinity.[17] T. M. Luhrmann similarly documents the process of hypermasculinization among Bombay's Parsi community, who were closely allied with the British in entrepreneurial ventures.[18] The particular kind of masculinity cultivated as a defensive strategy during colonial domination has been revived and restyled by advocates of Hindu nationalism in the postcolonial period. Thus the god Rama, the divine hero whose temple in Ayodhya has become a mobilizing symbol for the right-wing Bharatiya Janata Party, has been widely represented in calendar art and visual imagery as a deity with bulging muscles, a depiction formerly associated only with his monkey attendant, Hanuman.[19]

Femininity Re-Formed

I have elsewhere demonstrated how the theatrical representation of women's roles or parts by men's bodies was crucial to the visual construction of the feminine in this period.[20] In that analysis, the effects of theatrical transvestism are understood to reach beyond the reification of existing gender boundaries, or the transgression of those boundaries for the purpose of generating laughter.[21] In the South Asian context, where women of status had long been secluded within private domestic spaces, masquerades of gender were productive of new ways of imagining and viewing the female form. Through the transvestite performer, the external look of the "woman" was regulated by minute attention to the details of fashion and feminine accoutrements. This reworking of the surface was conjoined to a new focus on the interiority of character.

My emphasis here will be on how the operations of female impersonation within the reforming, educative program of the late-nineteenth-century Parsi theater also complicated the viewing of the male body and the construction of masculine subjectivity. For men as well as women, cross-dressing opened up an arena in which gender could be articulated in complicated ways. I propose that transgender masquerades, in addition to renewing a preexisting culture of homosociality in the context of a reconstituted urban public, introduced new possibilities for homoerotic pleasure and expression. As in the construction of heteronormative roles, these possibilities were predicated on exchanging devalued, "traditional" ways of encoding gender difference, or more accurately gender ambiguity, for esteemed, updated, "modern" ones. These urban theaters moved away from a burlesque, transgressive mode of female embodiment, often associated with folk practice, to a high mimetic style emphasizing naturalism. The display of overt sexuality was replaced by an elaborate code of modesty, propriety, and respectability that identified the "new woman" in heteronormative terms. But equally they positioned the homoerotic gaze toward a refined, transgendered performer who aroused a different kind of desire.

These distinctions emerge within the first two decades of the Parsi theater. The young Parsi men who pioneered the cosmopolitan practice of female impersonation were of high social standing, unlike their forebears in the rural or "folk" theaters, who were traditionally of low rank. When the students of Elphinstone College in Bombay formed a club to rehearse Shakespeare and try out new Gujarati plays, it was probably obvious that some of them would take up women's roles, although it is not known by what criteria they were chosen. The first on record to play female roles was D. N. Parekh, later a medical doctor and lieutenant colonel in the Indian Medical Service. While at Elphinstone College, he played Portia in *The Merchant of Venice* and Mrs. Smart in G. O. Trevelyan's *The Dawk Bungalow*. These performances were held under the patronage of Sir Jamsetji Jeejeebhoy, a leading Parsi businessman and philanthropist, and Jagannath Shankarsheth, a wealthy Hindu banker, both of whom had been active in the public campaign to open the Grant Road Theatre.[22]

Even at a time when theatrical activity was principally conceived as an amateur pastime, anecdotes suggest that a considerable premium was placed on successful female impersonators. Framji Joshi completed his matriculation in 1868, and in the same year played the female lead in a Gujarati version of Robert Bulwer-Lytton's *The Lady of Lyons*, presented by the Gentlemen Amateurs Club. His performance was so impressive that the club's director feared his star performer would be lured away by another company. Indeed, Joshi left the Gentlemen Amateurs and went on to new female roles with the Alfred Company, before he resigned from the stage to become superintendent of the Government Central Press.[23]

The social prominence of the actors, the prestige of their wealthy patrons, and the location of amateur dramatics as a supplement to college life all established the early Parsi theater as a "rational" amusement, in contrast to the older nautch performances sponsored by "feudal" aristocrats. By the end of the 1860s, the fondness for "theatricals" was such that Parsi businessmen were drawn to theater as an investment opportunity. With the establishment of the Victoria Theatrical Company in 1868, Parsi theater entered a period of capitalist reorganization and professionalization. Productions became more lavish, and audience size expanded. A premium was now placed on young men of pleasing figure and superlative voice, who would ensure company profits through their virtuosity in women's roles. The split in the Victoria Theatrical Company in 1873 supplies an example. The former manager, Dadi Patel (1844–1876), took his leading female impersonator with him when he separated to form the Original Victoria Theatrical Company. C. S. Nazir, the new manager of the Victoria, was at a loss and immediately organized a group of recruiters to look for new boys. This was particularly urgent as Nazir wanted to make a strong showing before the princes at Lord Lytton's Imperial Assemblage, the Delhi Darbar of 1877. He could not outdo his rivals and win a sizable audience without top-notch female impersonators.[24]

The Parsi theater invested in the recruitment and training of boys because it needed their labor to ensure its economic viability. An acting career normally began in a period of apprenticeship with schooling in female roles such as that of the *saheli* or *sakhi*, companions of the heroine. This practice continued well into the twentieth century. The actor Fida Husain, who began his apprenticeship in the New Alfred Company around 1918, became famous first for his female roles.[25] Certain actors became known as "all-rounders," performing the hero, heroine, or comedian, as needed. With age and changing physique, others shifted from female to male roles. Khurshed Baliwala (1852–1913), who later managed the Victoria Theatrical Company and became one of the most renowned Parsi theater personalities, played a female role in *Rustam and Sohrab* when he was eighteen.[26] A year later, he appeared as the hero of *Sone ke Mul ki Khurshed,* and from then on, acted primarily male roles.[27]

Other actors specialized as female impersonators. Success in a role led to the public affixing the name of the character to the actor's name or nickname. It is only through this assignment of feminine stage names that the identity of many female impersonators can be determined from the record. Two brothers of the influential Madan clan acquired this popular status. Nasharvanji Framji became famous as Naslu "Tahmina" for his performance as Sohrab's mother in *Rustam and Sohrab*. Naslu's younger brother, Pestanji Framji, was called Pesu "Avan," after the heroine in a Gujarati version of Shakespeare's *Pericles*.[28]

Female impersonators performed various types of stage roles. One was the romantic heroine, beloved of the hero and the embodiment of feminine perfection and modesty. A mellifluous voice became a valuable adjunct to such a role as songs gained ascendancy in the format of the musical drama. When Jehangir Khambata founded the Empress Victoria Theatrical Company in 1877, he took full advantage of the talents of a popular female impersonator known as Naslu Sarkari. Famed for his sweet, "cuckoo" voice (*kokil kanth*), Naslu played the Emerald Fairy to Kavas Khatau's Prince Gulfam in the *Indar Sabha*.[29]

Then there were the female magician roles, like the *jogin* ("female ascetic") in *Harishchandra*.[30] During the Victoria Company's tour to Delhi in 1874, Kavasji Manakji Contractor, a female impersonator affectionately called "Bahuji" ("daughter-in-law," "bride") created a sensation in this role by delivering countless lashes to the tormented dancing figure of Baliwala playing Lotan. This particular gesture was later to become a trademark of the actress Nadia, known as "Hunterwali" ("Lady with the whip"), who appeared in stunt films in the 1930s and '40s. Nadia took on the androgynous aspect of womanhood, an extension of the construct associated with the *virangana* or warrior-queen in Indian myth and popular culture.[31] Such virtuous embodiments of female power were also common on the Parsi stage, as seen in the warlike demeanor of Master Nainuram (see fig. 11.1).

Female impersonation continued on the Parsi stage well into the twentieth century, retaining its popularity with audiences and with company managers. The long lists of men who played women's roles in the history of Parsi theater are remarkable; they seem to form the majority rather than the minority of actors. Unfortunately, these actors have been virtually forgotten. Written documentation of their lives, their habits, even their careers, are extremely limited. No biography or autobiography has emerged to illuminate this important institution.

Figure 11.1
Master Nainuram playing a *viran-gana* (woman warrior) in the Parsi theatre. Early twentieth century. Photograph courtesy of Natya Shodh Sansthan, archival collection, Calcutta, India, 1998.

Records are somewhat more complete in the case of two non-Parsi actors, Jayshankar Sundari (1888–1967) from the Gujarati stage and Bal Gandharva (1889–1975) from the Marathi musical theater. Both excelled in the embodiment of feminine sensibility and decorum, creating prototypes for the ideal Indian woman. Their tremendous success was recognized during their active careers and late in life by the award of Padmabhushan, the government of India's prize for achievement on the national cultural stage. Sundari's Gujarati autobiography, an English biography by B. B. Panchotia, and two English biographies of Bal Gandharva by Dnyaneshwar Nadkarni and Mohan Nadkarni supply a number of incidents that enlarge the picture of female impersonation as it flourished earlier in this century.

Legendary Heroines

Sundari launched his career on the Gujarati stage at the age of twelve, starring in *Saubhagya Sundari*, in the role of the auspicious young wife that gave him his stage name. Before that, he had served an apprenticeship for three years in Calcutta with the Parsi theater company of Dadabhai Thunthi. On a salary of six rupees a month, he performed in the chorus of "girls" every night at the Thanthania Theatre. His first important role was the Emerald Fairy in Amanat's *Indar Sabha*, and he starred in a number of other Urdu-language plays. During his Calcutta training, Sundari perfected the distinctive feminine gait and stage entry that secured his fame as a modest yet alluring heroine.[32]

Returning to Bombay he played Rambha, the milkmaid in the Gujarati drama *Vikram Charitra*. The play was performed every Saturday night between 1902 and 1905—a total of 160 times. Sundari was between thirteen and sixteen years of age. In his most memorable scene, he entered the stage with a pot on his head and offered milk to the hero, singing *Koi dudh lyo dilrangi*. The Vaishnava trope of the youthful lord Krishna with his adoring *gopis* ("cowherd women") associated sexual/mystical enjoyment with the pleasures of oral consumption. As the bestower of "milk" from her "pot," the transvestite heroine maintained a demure, inward-turned posture that legitimized her seductive gesture. Her carefully arranged hair, jewelery, bodice, and sari border worked to produce a sublimation of sexuality, an interiorization of virtue as "moral character." This song became so popular that Bombay textile companies printed it on the milled lengths of cloth that were sold for men's dhotis and women's saris.[33]

Moral purity and its counterpart, forbearance in distress, were invoked by impersonators like Sundari in scenes of pathos and tragedy, as found in the epics based on Hindu mythology and contemporary domestic melodramas. In *Kamalata* (1904), an adaptation of the Shakuntala story, Sundari played his part with such finesse that it moved the entire audience to tears (see fig. 11.2). Similarly, Bal Gandharva was acclaimed for his 1911 performance in Khadilkar's drama *Manapman*, which he refused to cancel even though his eldest child had died on the very day of the drama's debut. The ability to summon up pathos distinguished these impersonators from transvestite entertainers who aimed to titillate or ridicule. The histrionic power of these actors and their capacity to transform themselves into vulnerable, unfortunate females served to expand the emotional field of the male viewer/subject. A desire to explore and experience the interior realms associated with feminine feeling, thereby expanding one's humanity through the test of suffering, seems to have been a large part of the fascination with transgender roles at this time. Sundari as female impersonator crafted a self that found deep sources of satisfaction in its entry into feminine subjectivity. In his autobiography, he describes the first time he dressed himself in a woman's bodice, writing, "I saw a beautiful young girl emerging from myself. Whose shapely, intoxicating limbs oozed youthful exuberance. In whose form is the fragrance of woman's beauty. From whose eyes feminine feelings keep brimming. In whose gait is expressed the mannerism of a Gujarati girl. Who is not a man, but solely a woman—a woman. I saw such a portrait in the mirror. . . . Reflecting the difference the mirror was saying, 'This is not Jaishankar. It is a shy and proud young Gujaratin. That graceful movement, that expressivity, that enchantment.' A sweet shiver ran through my body's limbs. For a moment, I thought that I was not a man—not a man at all."[34] This rare self-reflective glimpse of the process of transformation from man to woman illuminates the possibilities for transgender identification and behavior opened up by the practice of theatrical transvestism.

In the autobiography, Sundari further describes the methods he used to give verisimilitude to his impersonations. He carefully studied the manners of female acquaintances, whom he observed in social situations where his own presence was

Figure 11.2
Jayshankar Sundari as Kamalata,
opposite Shri Bapulal as Minuketu,
in the Gujarati play *Kamalata*,
staged at the Gaiety Theatre,
Bombay in 1904. Reprinted with
permission from B. B. Panchotia,
*Jayashankar Sundari and
Abhinayakala* (Bombay: Bharatiya
Vidya Bhavan, 1987).

unobtrusive. One of the most captivating for him was Gulab, a young girl who was soon to be married. Her shyness coupled with budding excitement and self-consciousness about her body and dress fascinated him. He even asked for the address of her tailor so that he could have the same style of blouses she favored made up.[35] To perfect his understanding of what it meant to be a "complete human being" (*sampurna manav*), he read a number of manuals of womanly conduct, considered "useful for women" (*stri-upyogi*), from which he learned about cooking, embroidery, and how to manage a household.[36]

He reflected on feminine characters like Kumud Sundari and Kusum, whom he encountered in Govardhan Ram's *Sarasvatichandra*, the monumental Gujarati novel in four volumes. In his autobiography we read, "Having found here the woman of Gujarat that I had been researching, I began to sport with the depicted creation. . . . I found a new way to practice [the part]. . . . I would take the novel and read it aloud in front of the mirror and practice the parts while looking into the mirror. In this way, I tried to match my feelings with the feelings in the hearts of the characters."[37] Although narrated as testimonials to his artistic dedication, these accounts point to an engagement with cross-gender identification that goes beyond technique. Whereas it is commonplace to read that both Bal Gandharva's and Sundari's stage movements, attire, and speech became models for women offstage, one suspects that they also were compelling examples of transgender exploration for men. The very earnestness of Sundari's portrayals would recommend such theatrics not only as stimulants of desire but also as templates for incorporation into the affective and somatic domains of the spectator's being.

Bal Gandharva (a.k.a. Narayan Shripad Rajhans) was a contemporary of Sundari's. He was born into a middle-class Maharashtrian family, where he came under the tutelage of male relatives with strong interests in music and drama. In 1905, at the age of sixteen, he joined the Kirloskar Drama Company, replacing Bhaurau Kolhatkar, the first successful female impersonator of the Marathi musical theater, who had just died. His debut was in the title role in *Shakuntala*, on a newly built stage, before the prince of Miraj. The object of adoration and esteem from the start, Bal Gandharva became the pet of the students at Deccan College, where he was frequently invited to sing, and he struck up a special friendship with one of them, Balasaheb Pandit.[38]

In the accounts of Bal Gandharva, the erotic allure of his impersonations is striking. When Bal Gandharva entered the stage as Shakuntala surrounded by her "companions," the college boys used to greet him with "lusty applause," according to one biography. Similarly, actor Londhe recalls "all the sensuousness of female beauty" that Bal Gandharva emitted when he played opposite him, such that a "unique thrill" passed through his veins as he stood close by.[39] One way that Bal Gandharva exploited his seductiveness was by displaying his long hair, which flowed to the waist. In *Manapman* he entered the stage with his hair hanging loosely, indicating that the heroine had not yet had her bath, while in another scene he turned his back to the audience to reveal a long braid.[40] Photographs show him flirtatiously casting sidelong glances at the hero while partially concealing himself behind a fan, or beckoning the hero with a certain bend backward from the waist (see fig. 11.3). These gestures, rather than being read as crude, were understood as modest and charming representations of the educated young women of the day. As a contemporary noted, "The manner in which Balgandharva made himself up and the way he moved on the stage fully evoked the *persona* of the contemporary young woman of the middle or upper middle classes."[41]

The pleasures of homoerotic spectatorship and transgender performance were linked in the urban theater with the satisfactions of social and economic privilege. Both Jayshankar Sundari and Bal Gandharva, rather than bearing any stigma, became national icons. The position of their audiences within the burgeoning consumer economy introduced opportunities for the commodification of their images. Just as textile companies advertised cloth using Sundari's lyrics, Bal Gandharva's photograph appeared on products such as medicinal tonic, soap, toilet powder, and even key chains. A particular kind of cap, the Gandharva *topi*, was widely sold among male admirers, as were the Gandharva turban, coat, and trousers. Bal Gandharva also popularized particular styles of wearing the sari and adornments such as weaving garlands of flowers in the hair. He brought into vogue the bun, introduced the nose pin (*nath*), and promoted the carrying of handkerchiefs. His image radiated such a sense of fashion and prestige that framed photographs of his female roles adorned the drawing rooms of elite homes, appearing on mantels and sideboards throughout Maharashtra. Through the extratheatrical circulation of his image, Bal Gandharva developed a cult following that reinforced his career on stage. His particular transvestite style was completely assimilated within visual culture. To our benefit, more photographs of Bal

Figure 11.3
Bal Gandharva playing opposite actor
Petkar, in the Marathi drama
Sanshaykallol, performed by the
Gandharva Sangit Natak Mandali.
Reproduced with permission of the
National Centre for the Performing
Arts, Mumbai.

Gandharva exist than of any other Indian female impersonator, including both studio portraits and re-creations of staged scenes.

Beyond the visual, moreover, Bal Gandharva made a tremendous impact as a singing actor. Like other female impersonators but probably to a unique degree, his voice communicated the complex yearnings of the heroines he played and added a significant layer of erotic power to his performances. His voice production was not falsetto but midway between today's male and female registers, a kind of androgynous timbre that was fairly typical of both male and female vocalists at that time. His spoken voice is said to have been a stylized version of presumably upper-caste women's speech. Bal Gandharva sang in the classically based *natya sangit* style, and many of his recordings survive in private collections. It is beyond the scope of this essay to treat fully the topics of vocal style, voice production, and their role in the creation of gendered subjectivities. I simply wish to underscore the role of the voice in projecting affect (the power to move the listener), agency (the attribution of volition to a characterization), and authority (the display of musical virtuosity). Outstanding vocal artistry immeasurably enriched the performances of actors like Bal Gandharva, adding as well to the allure of countless lesser-known female impersonators.

Sexuality and Subculture

When consideration of the voice is combined with the more readily accessed external look of the transvestite performer and the gaze that links the hero and male heroine on stage, an enlarged expressive space comes into play. In the variety of responses evoked, between spectators and actors, among actors, and among spectators and even those outside the theater, could such a collective zone of interaction be said to constitute a transgender or homosexual subculture? Jennifer Robertson, in her discussion of the all-male Kabuki and all-female Takarazuka, argues that theatrical transvestism in Japan has long been linked to alternative subcultures. These practices, in her treatment, have both reproduced dominant gender ideology and subverted it. While the *onnagata* in Kabuki, like the female impersonator of western India, constructed the ideal standard of femininity for Japanese women to follow, specific *onnagata* were known to prefer homosexual relations. As early as 1652, boy actors were banned because of their offstage homosexual activity. In the case of the twentieth-century Takarazuka, "The Revue continues both to uphold the dominant ideal of heterosexuality and to inform a lesbian subcultural style."[42]

Significantly, Robertson highlights the importation of European sexological discourse into Japan that began in the early twentieth century. The works of Sigmund Freud, Richard Krafft-Ebing, Edward Carpenter, Havelock Ellis, and Magnus Hirschfeld were translated into Japanese and employed in the identification of "social problems."[43] The naming of homosexual practices, even though it stigmatized them, enabled public debates and rhetorics to develop around theatrical practices involving transvestism. In the South Asian context, such naming and specificity are missing. The wives and mistresses of Jayshankar Sundari and Bal Gandharva are mentioned in the record, as are the special friendships between leading hero and heroine actor pairs: Bal Gandharva's long-lived relationship with Balasaheb Pandit and Jayshankar Sundari's with Bapulal Nayak. But what does this tell us? The celebratory character of the biographical literature makes it nearly impossible to get beyond the public persona. Indeed, so little is known about how the "private" and the "public" subject were constructed in India at this time, especially in terms of an alternate sexuality, that one balks at interpreting the silence of the biographer as innocence, evasion, or erasure.

A few scattered accounts confirm the general impression that, in India as in China and Japan, the theatrical subculture afforded a space for homosexual inclinations and practices. Madhavacharya, the author of a Hindi commentary on the *Kama Sutra*, asserts that theater personnel were known for their proclivity for oral sex with other men. He obliquely recounts a knife fight that once broke out between M.A. and B.A. students "on this account."[44] Theater histories also report that actor/managers had their favorite "boys." Female impersonators were called by female kinship terms as well as by proper and pet female names. In a report of the first performances of the *Indar Sabha* in Lucknow, Nasir describes "thousands of people [who] became captivated and went mad over these beautiful beardless youths." Elaborating, he attributes the production of homosexual lust to the popular performance: "Just as having read Mir Hasan's poetic romance, thousands of women became debauched, similarly from this romance *Indar Sabha*, thousands of men became sodomites and pederasts."[45]

As a project in the recovery of alternative sexual histories, it may be important to claim the urban theatrical environment of western India as a site that enabled transgender or homosexual activity. The evidence I have presented may well be sufficient to prove the case. However, it needs to be added that the theatrical milieu was (and for some, still is) associated with excessive sexuality in general. Actors and actresses, regardless of their sexual orientation, were deemed suspect as moral agents from the days of the *Natyashastra*, and invariably placed in inferior social and caste categories because of their allegedly unrestrained sexual behavior. The transgressive energies that spilled out from the playhouse into the surrounding neighborhoods were controlled and kept at a distance in nineteenth-century Bombay by establishing the red light district on Grant Road, far from the residences of the elite in the Fort district on the southern part of the island. The problem for modern South Asian theater has been primarily that of defusing or denying heteronormative sexuality, in contrast with which concerns about homosexuality fade into insignificance.

Even if it is argued that the simultaneous attraction and aversion that characterizes the societal attitude toward theater does not prevent the theatrical space from being used for diverse ends, the difficulty remains of identifying the boundaries around such a space. Were the transformations of gender effected by the female impersonator part of a fluid system of role play available to certain males (but not to females) in this period? Was the lower-class man excluded when the urban middle-class indulged in play with transgender identity? How did men whose gender and sexual identities were in formation—college students for example—move in and out of this expressive arena? Where did the specificity of homosexual preference fit in?

Even as the ambiguities surrounding gender and its representation opened outward toward the end of the nineteenth century in a public embrace of transvestism, a more rigid system of binary difference was being implanted, in part by the same theatrical culture. The eclipse of theatrical transvestism has been heralded as a triumph for the female performer and therefore for women in general, but it also marked the end of an era of gender ambiguity. A binary sex/gender regime allied to differences of class and caste has displaced the transvestite performer and distanced urban spectators from the circulation of homoerotic imagery. This sea change makes it difficult to recover the nuances of meaning that envelop a bygone practice. For clues to interpretation, we must continue to scour the historical evidence within South Asia as well as bring forward comparative data from other cultures.

Notes

1. V. Raghavan, "Sanskrit Drama in Performance," in *Sanskrit Drama in Performance*, ed. Rachel Van M. Baumer and James R. Brandon (Honolulu: University Press of Hawaii, 1981), 13.
2. *Natyashastra* 35: 31–32, cited in Syed Jamil Ahmed, "Female Performers in the Indigenous Theatre of Bengal," in *Infinite Variety: Women in Society and Literature*, ed. Firdous Azim and Niaz Zaman (Dhaka: University Press Limited, 1994), 265.

3. Jiwan Pani, "The Female Impersonator in Traditional Indian Theatre," *Sangeet Natak* 45 (1977): 37–42.

4. As immigrants to India from Iran after its conquest by Islamic rulers, Parsis preserved their distinct faith of Zoroastrianism while adopting the Gujarati language and other customs of the surrounding society. In the eighteenth century, many migrated from Gujarat to Bombay. Collaboration with European traders and the British East India Company enabled the Parsi mercantile elite to achieve extraordinary financial success. Middle-class Parsis eagerly sought English education in the second half of the nineteenth century, filling a disproportionate number of seats in the recently opened Elphinstone College. It was here that amateur theatricals became fashionable among Parsi students in midcentury.

5. Kaikkhushro Navrojji Kabra, *Jamshed* (Mumbai: Ashkkara Press, 1870) and *Faredun* (Mumbai: Ashkara Press, 1874).

6. Delta, preface to *Romyo ane Julyat*, trans. Samira Sheikh (Mumbai: Fort Printing Press, 1876).

7. Sudha R. Desai, *Bhavai: A Medieval Form of Ancient Indian Dramatic Art* (Ahmedabad: Gujarat University, 1972); Balwant Gargi, *Folk Theater of India* (Seattle: University of Washington Press, 1966), 51–72.

8. Kathryn Hansen, *Grounds for Play: The Nautanki Theatre of North India* (Berkeley and Los Angeles: University of California Press, 1992), 66.

9. Sharmila Rege, "The Hegemonic Appropriation of Sexuality: The Case of the *Lavani* Performers of Maharashtra," in *Social Reform, Sexuality, and the State*, ed. Patricia Uberoi (Delhi: Sage, 1996), 23–38.

10. Gargi, *Folk Theater*, 75.

11. Neera Adarkar, "In Search of Women in History of Marathi Theatre, 1843 to 1933," *Economic and Political Weekly*, October 26, 1991, WS-87.

12. Dinshaw E. Wacha, *Shells from the Sands of Bombay: Being My Recollections and Reminiscences, 1860–1875* (Bombay: Bombay Chronicle Press, 1920), 697–98.

13. Ahmed, "Female Performers," 280.

14. Somnath Gupta, *Parsi Thiyetar: Udbhav aur Vikas. [Parsi Theater: Origin and Development]* (Allahabad: Lokbharati Prakashan, 1981), 109, 210–12.

15. Rimli Bhattacharya, ed. and trans., *Binodini Dasi: My Story and My Life as an Actress* (New Delhi: Kali for Women, 1998), 11.

16. The regional difference between Bombay and Calcutta parallels the variation in responses to female impersonation in Renaissance Europe. England barred actresses and preferred boys; Spain chose theatrical women over the spectacle of transvestite boys. See Stephen Orgel, "Nobody's Perfect: Or Why Did the English Stage Take Boys for Women?" *South Atlantic Quarterly* 88, no. 1 (1989), 7–29.

17. Mrinalini Sinha, *Colonial Masculinity: The "Manly Englishman" and the "Effeminate Bengali" in the Late Nineteenth Century* (Manchester: Manchester University Press, 1995); Ashis Nandy, *The Intimate Enemy: Loss and Recovery of Self under Colonialism* (Delhi: Oxford University Press, 1988); Uma Chakravarti, "Whatever Happened to the Vedic *Dasi*? Orientalism, Nationalism, and a Script for the Past," in *Recasting Women: Essays in Colonial History*, ed. Kumkum Sangari and Sudesh Vaid (New Delhi: Kali for Women, 1989), 27–87.

18. T. M. Luhrmann, *The Good Parsi: The Fate of a Colonial Elite in a Postcolonial Society* (Cambridge: Harvard University Press, 1996).

19. Anuradha Kapur, "Deity to Crusader: The Changing Iconography of Ram," in *Hindus and Others*, ed. Gyanendra Pandey (New Delhi: Viking, 1993). Similar ideas relating to virility, masculinity, and Hindu chauvinism are explored in Anand Patwardhan's powerful documentary film *Father, Son, and Holy War*.

20. Kathryn Hansen, "*Stri Bhumika*: Female Impersonators and Actresses on the Parsi Stage," *Economic and Political Weekly*, August 19, 1998, 2291–2300; Kathryn Hansen, "Making

Women Visible: Gender and Race Cross-Dressing in the Parsi Theatre," *Theatre Journal* 51 (1999): 127–47.

21. These are the outcomes most discussed in the literature on theatrical cross-dressing in the West. See Lesley Ferris, ed., *Crossing the Stage: Controversies on Cross-Dressing* (London: Routledge, 1993); and Laurence Senelick, ed., *Gender in Performance: The Presentation of Difference in the Performing Arts* (Hanover: University Press of New England, 1992).

22. Somnath Gupta, *Parsi Thiyetar*, 133–37; Vidyavati Lakshmanrao Namra, *Hindi Rangmanch aur Pandit Narayanprasad "Betab"* [*The Hindi Stage and Pandit Narayanprasad "Betab"*] (Varanasi: Vishvavidyalaya Prakashan, 1972), 93–95; Kumud A. Mehta, "Bombay's Theatre World 1860–1880," *Journal of the Asiatic Society of Bombay* 43–44 (n.s., 1968), 262–64.

23. Gupta, *Parsi Thiyetar*, 122, 147–48, 174–75.

24. Ibid., 109–10.

25. Namra, *Hindi Rangmanch*, 83; Pratibha Agraval, *Mastar Fida Husain: Parsi Thiyetar men Pachas Varsh* [*Master Fida Husain: Fifty Years in the Parsi Theater*] (Calcutta: Natya Shodh Sansthan, 1986).

26. Namra, *Hindi Rangmanch*, 52; Gupta, *Parsi Thiyetar*, 108.

27. Namra, *Hindi Rangmanch*, 55.

28. Gupta, *Parsi Thiyetar*, 201.

29. S/he was Laila with Khatau as Majnun; Bakavali with Khatau as Tajulmulk; and performed a number of other classic themes opposite Khatau, the actor known as "India's Irving." Ibid., 118–19.

30. The jogin role occurs in *Harishchandra*, according to Gupta, *Parsi Thiyetar*, 111. However, in another place, Gupta refers to this role as occurring in the play *Gopichand* (Gupta, 166).

31. Kathryn Hansen, "The *Virangana* in North Indian Myth, History, and Popular Culture," *Economic and Political Weekly of India,* April 30, 1988, WS-25–WS-33.

32. B. B. Panchotia, *Jayashankar Sundari and Abhinayakala* (Bombay: Bharatiya Vidya Bhavan, 1987), 2–23.

33. Ibid., 42.

34. Jayshankar Sundari, *Thodan Ansu Thodan Ful* [*Some Teardrops, Some Blossoms*], trans. Sunil Sharma and Kathryn Hansen (Ahmedabad: Gandhi Sombarsa, 1976), 73.

35. Ibid., 80–81.

36. Ibid., 114.

37. Ibid., 70.

38. Dnyaneshwar Nadkarni, *Balgandharva and the Marathi Theatre* (Bombay: Roopak Books, 1988), 41.

39. D. Nadkarni, *Balgandharva and the Marathi Theatre*, 106; M. Nadkarni, *Bal Gandharva:The Nonpareil Thespian* (New Delhi: National Book Trust, 1988), 17.

40. D. Nadkarni, *Balgandharva*, 36, 49, 57.

41. Govindrao Tembe, cited in ibid., 34.

42. Jennifer Robertson, *Takarazuka: Sexual Politics and Popular Culture in Modern Japan* (Berkeley and Los Angeles: University of California Press, 1998), 73.

43. Ibid., 20.

44. Vatsyayana, *Kamasutra* vol. 1 ed. Madhavacharya (Bombay: Khemraj Shrikrishna Das Prakashan, 1995), 522. I am indebted to Ruth Vanita for this reference, which appears in her essay, "The Kamasutra in the Twentieth Century," in *Same-Sex Love in India: Readings from Literature and History*, Ruth Vanita and Saleem Kidwai, eds. (New York: St Martin's Press, 2000), 239.

45. Sa'adat Ali Khan Nasir, *Tazkirah Khush Ma'arika-i Ziba* [*An Elegant Encounter: An Anecdotal Literary Biography*] (Lahore: Majlis-i Taraqqi-i adab, 1970), 231. Translated with aid from Carla Petievich.

12

Queer Bonds

Male Friendships in Contemporary Malayalam Cinema

Muraleedharan T.

Queerness as an attitude, a way of responding that is not concerned with or limited by a binary opposition of gender (man versus woman) or sexuality (homo versus hetero), is, in my opinion, very valuable for an appraisal of the libidinal subjectivities that circulate in regions like South Asia, where history provides little evidence of religious or social repression of nonheterosexual aptitudes until the onset of colonial domination. As a reading strategy, queerness is concerned with any expression that can be marked as contra-, non-, or antistraight. Alexander Doty reminds us that the queerness of most mass culture texts is the result of acts of production or reception. He maintains that the queerness some readers or viewers may attribute to mass culture texts is not in any way less real than the straightness others would claim for these same texts. There is queerness *of* and *in* straight cultures.[1] The so-called hegemonic straight culture in India can be seen to have many queer traits, and examination of this "queerness within the straight" can provide us with a better understanding of sexual subjectivities in this region.

The seeming absence of a recognizable gay/lesbian cinema need not undermine the relevance of queer mass culture studies in India. Neither should such studies be limited to the few recent Hindi films with overt "queer" representations.[2] On the contrary, such studies need to venture beyond the overtly articulated, and explore the unnamed expressions of queerness that structure popular culture in this part of the world. Doty has observed that the queerness of mass culture develops in three areas: (1) influences during the production of texts; (2) historically specific cultural readings and uses of texts by self-identified gays, lesbians, bisexuals, and queers; and (3) reception positions that can be considered "queer" regardless of a person's declared sexual and gender allegiances.[3]

As I attempt to read three Malayalam films from a queer perspective, my main motivation is certainly the pleasure I, as a gay man, derived from watching these films. The queerness of my reception is also a conscious choice, a political location I prefer to inhabit, to contest the straight perspectives from which these

films are usually read. I do not consider this reading any less true than other readings these films are likely to engender. Reception studies remains a slippery terrain
as audiences all over the world exist as already fragmented, always already polymorphous. As heterocentric texts may contain queer elements, so also can heterosexual and straight-identified people experience queer moments. Doty argues that
films ostensibly addressed to straight audiences have greater potential for encouraging a wide range of queer responses than films clearly addressed to gay and lesbian audiences.[4]

Queer Dimensions of Star Personae

I have reason to presume that the queerness I read in the films chosen for this study
had some moorings, conscious or unconscious, at the level of production. For
example, the gestures and mannerisms of the central characters in these films are
largely constitutive of the queer dimension I read in them; hence the fact that all
these films have the same actor portraying the central character appears significant.
This actor, Mohanlal, and his rival superstar, Mamooty, at present constitute the
uncrowned royalty of Malayalam cinema.

Mohanlal and Mamooty entered the film industry around the same time.
Mohanlal started as a villain in the film *Manjil Virinja Pookal* (*Flowers That Blossomed
in Winter*, 1980), portraying a sadistic husband who pursues his ex-wife to wreck
her new relationship. After playing negative characters in several films, he started
playing the lead and slowly became a superstar. His major breakthrough came in
a series of dark comedies made by popular director Sathyan Anthikad in the mid-
1980s. In these films he repeatedly portrayed an educated, unemployed youth from
rural Kerala struggling to survive in a hostile urban environment. In most of these
films he was paired with another male actor, Srinivasan, who portrayed another
youth in a similar predicament. Mamooty started by playing the lead in *Mela* (1980)
and achieved star status with the success of *Yavanika* (*Curtain*, 1982), in which he
portrayed a suave police officer investigating a murder case. By the late 1980s both
Mohanlal and Mamooty had attained the superstar status they currently enjoy.

The differences between the characters these two actors generally portray are significant. The star system in Indian cinema tends to make it mandatory for a popular actor to repeat his or her star identity in every film, irrespective of the cultural,
economic, or personal characteristics of the role portrayed. Filmmakers give popular stars considerable freedom to improvise. Such improvisations, when repeated
in film after film, become recognizable and thus constitutive of the star's personality. Audiences expect these gestures or mannerisms to appear in real-life appear-
ances by the star and also in each film as distinguishing features of characters played
by the star. These features thus shape the generic characteristics of films in which
the star appears.

Though both Mamooty and Mohanlal have occasionally portrayed unconven-
tional characters in offbeat films, the broad outlines of their star personalities are
strictly maintained in most of their (mainstream) films. The masculinities represented by these two actors are defined by certain clearly articulated contrasts. The
distinguishing characteristic of Mamooty's star persona is his "family man" image.
He usually portrays the head of a big family, a domineering patriarch who safe-

guards heterosexual, middle-class family morality by disciplining all members with an iron hand. Occasionally the family is replaced by the wider society and he appears as a self-righteous bureaucrat, but the values he represents and protects remain by and large the same. He rarely has a male companion but if there is one, he is generally a subordinate or a younger brother who maintains a respectable distance. The other males in his films are rivals or antagonists who strive and predictably fail to undermine his authority. In contrast, Mohanlal has been regularly playing a loner—someone outside the system. His fights are mostly single-handed, quite often desperate, and at times comic. Yet, as is customary in Indian commercial cinema, he too ends up justifying and supporting the establishment—but not without raising certain disturbing doubts about it.

A distinguishing feature of the star persona of Mohanlal is his "man's man" image. In most of his films he has a male companion who is usually not a biological relative. Another prominent feature of the Mohanlal persona is his naughty, "big child" kind of behavior, which provides the actor ample opportunity to resort to gestures with homoerotic implications.

Thus, in one of his recent films, *Ayal Katha Eezhuthukayanu (That Man Is Writing a Story*, 1998), Mohanlal portrays an anarchic pulp-fiction writer who suddenly turns up at the house of an unmarried male friend. A lengthy song sequence in the film, rampant with a misogynist subtext, shows the two men harassing and ill-treating a haughty female neighbor. As the song concludes we see the men getting into bed and a subsequent top angle shot records them covering themselves completely with a sheet, followed by some clearly suggestive movements underneath the sheet. In an earlier film, *Nanayam (Coin*, 1983), there is a similar song sequence in which both Mohanlal and Mamooty, who play half brothers in the film, keep hugging and kissing each other and at the same time harass and tease a band of girls. In *No. 20 Madras Mail* (1990), Mohanlal plays a wayward and debauched youngster who accidentally encounters a popular male film star (played by Mamooty) on a train journey. After befriending the film star, the Mohanlal character pretends to whisper something in the star's ear. Then he suddenly, and unexpectedly, kisses the actor on the cheek, causing him to blush. In another film, *Dhanam (Wealth*, 1991), Mohanlal makes use of every opportunity, during a couple of song sequences, to hug his male companion, played by the actor Murali.

Such identical gestures that pop up in most of his films give the impression that a queer subtext is more than coincidental in Mohanlal films. These may be dismissed by some as comic interludes or seen as disciplined by the heterosexist conclusions of the films. But the question I would like to raise is whether such conclusions—that is, the eventual union of the male hero with a woman—necessarily undermine the queerness of such films. Alexander Doty argues, "The day someone can establish without a doubt that images and other representations of men and women getting married, with their children, or even having sex, undeniably depict 'straightness,' is the day someone can say no lesbian or gay has ever been married, had children from heterosexual intercourse, or had sex with someone of the other gender for any reason."[5] This comment is particularly relevant in the Indian context as most of even self-identified gay men and lesbians here are or have at some time been heterosexually married.

A detailed discussion of Mohanlal's star identity is beyond the scope of this paper.

I confine this discussion to a brief examination of three of his recent films—
Manichithrathazhu (*The Quaint Lock*, 1994),[6] *Thacholi Verghese Chekavar* (*The Warrior
Verghese from the Thacholi Family*, 1996),[7] and *Aram Thampuran* (*The Sixth Feudal
Lord*, 1998).[8] The protagonists in these films represent three important facets of
the Mohanlal star persona. He plays an educated young man with a penchant for
comedy in *Manichithrathazhu*, and in *Thacholi Verghese Chekavar* he is a simpleton
forced into unwilling battles by society. In *Aram Thampuran* he is a tough guy with
a grim past, seeking vengeance. Yet all three, otherwise very different, characters
share a strong friendship with another male. While examining these friendships I
also investigate the maleness represented by the Mohanlal character in these films,
in terms of gendered desire and its disruptions.

All three films draw significantly from the contemporary rearticulation of
Hindutva, which unproblematically designates the upper-caste Hindu in terms of
a Vedic Brahmanical tradition even when he is from a marginal and culturally complicated location like Kerala. This is a prominent trend in contemporary Malayalam
cinema in general and Mohanlal films in particular. Yet I do not intend to discuss
it in this paper, except in tangential terms, as it has already merited substantial
critical attention.[9]

Desire and the Single Man

In these three films Mohanlal portrays a single unattached man, without a wife or
even a girlfriend. At the outset he is located outside normative heterosexual bonding. He is initially defined by a male bond, a close friendship with another man
who either desires or is desired by him. All three films subsequently explore the
taming of this man within the heterosexual matrix.

Dr. Sunny, the psychiatrist in *Manichithrathazhu*, makes his initial appearance
in the film as the best friend of Nakulan, whose wife Ganga requires psychiatric
help. Verghese, the protagonist in *Thacholi Verghese Chekavar*, is also defined in terms
of his close friendship with Shyam, his young male protégé. Jagan, the protagonist
in *Aram Thampuran*, is introduced as the best friend and muscleman of
Nandakumar, a wealthy businessman. Dr. Sunny is an eccentric globe-trotter who,
in the episode that introduces him, provides a detailed description of his journeys
during the previous few months, which include brief stays in several all-male spaces.
He recounts his travels from the United States to Bangalore and then to Sabarimalai
in Kerala, focus of an all-male pilgrimage, and mentions having stayed with various male friends. Verghese is a martial arts expert who is frequently seen in the all-
male space of a traditional gym, the *kalari*. Besides, he is indifferent to his mother's
constant appeal to get married. Jagan, a muscleman hired by business magnates,
is a loner without a family who constantly inhabits sites frequented by the city
mafia that are marked as "masculine." The introductory episode presents him sharing a drink with a male rickshaw puller on the roadside. In a subsequent telephone
conversation with his patron Nandakumar, he describes his activities during the
previous few days, all of which are connected with male friends.

Apart from being confined to "masculine" locations and male bonds, these men
are also presented as indifferent or even hostile to women. Verghese violently rejects
the advances of an attractive young girl, Annie, who relentlessly pursues him

through the first half of the film. Later, when he kidnaps the heroine, Maya, mistaking her for Shyam's truant girlfriend, he repeatedly makes it clear that he has absolutely no personal interest in her. It is his emotional commitment to Shyam that persuades him to be rude and violent to Maya. Dr. Sunny's initial reaction to the women he meets in Nakulan's house is marked by humorous sarcasm. He playfully harasses most of the women there till he embarks on the serious mission of curing Ganga, Nakulan's wife, of her mental illness. Jagan is not enthusiastic when his patron Nandakumar offers him a "few expensive blankets" (slang for expensive female sex workers) in return for his services. After relocating to the village, Jagan initially reacts with sarcasm to the heroine Unnimaya's confident defiance. Later when his female friend, a city girl named Nayantara, proposes to him, Jagan rejects her without hesitation.

It is also interesting to examine the contradictions between visual and oral narratives in the film. Jagan describes Nayantara as a good friend but the sequences in which they appear together present him as stiff and uneasy in her company. While Nayantara's words and body language clearly denote her warmth toward Jagan, his response is cold and remote—preoccupied as he is with several other issues that constitute the main concern of the narrative. Yet Jagan is the only character among these three who shows any heterosexual inclinations. A subsequent song sequence in the film suggests an earlier heterosexual affair he had—perhaps a brief relationship with a northern Indian girl that ended tragically.

The weariness or hostility that these men exhibit toward women directly contrasts with the warmth, affection, and commitment they show toward male friends. The Mohanlal character in all the films discussed here is either desiring or desired by a male friend. Verghese, the martial arts expert, is clearly depicted as desiring his young male disciple and friend, Shyam, and the entire film is about his struggle to win him back after a brief estrangement. When Annie's desperate attempts to seduce Verghese fail, she taunts Verghese by telling him that when she last met Shyam he looked "so cute and sexy." Instead of being worried about the possible alienation of Annie's affections, Verghese's anxieties about Shyam are heightened, since Shyam has been avoiding him for the past few days.

Dr. Sunny and Jagan do not express such overt desire for their male friends. Yet these friendships are the most important commitments in their lives. Though he is a busy psychiatrist, Dr. Sunny puts off all other engagements to be with his friend in his hour of need. Jagan's commitment to business magnate Nandakumar is similar; he violently assaults and almost kills a rival businessman for his friend's sake and later refuses to accept the monetary reward offered by Nandakumar.

Negotiating the Physical

Male bonding has been a prominent trope in mainstream cinema all over the world ever since the film industry was established. Patterns of male bonding and structures of same-sex friendships have changed over time. Commercial concerns make it mandatory for mainstream cinema to engage in a dialectic with changing attitudes and realignments of desire in hegemonic social discourses. Thus, the solidarity of two white males that appeared in early Hollywood Westerns is replaced in more recent films by an interracial friendship between white and black men. The function of the female vis-à-vis male bonding has also been changing. Conventionally, it was the destiny of one of the two men to die so as to facilitate his friend's union with the woman. But in some recent films it is the woman who dies while the male buddies survive the final catastrophe (for example, in *The Deep Blue Sea,* 1999). In this context I am interested in the evolving structure of male bonds in Malayalam cinema, particularly its negotiations with the physical.

Most striking in these male solidarities is the recognition and definition of the male body's organic existence as both desiring and desired. For example, Jagan's stiff response to Nayantara stands in contrast to his response to similar overtures from Nandakumar. In an earlier scene we see a jubilant Nandakumar celebrating the achievement of a sought-after business deal that Jagan had earned for him. Nanadakumar expresses his joy by repeatedly uttering phrases like "ever since I got you," and "since you became mine," while holding Jagan by his shoulders and caressing his hair. He also offers him a few curious rewards; prominent among these is a joint trip to Europe. Throughout the scene, Jagan is more composed than Nandakumar, yet warm and willing. The scene ends with Nanadakumar declaring that they are going to forget everything that night and "sleep together." Thus, Jagan is more desired by than desiring Nandakumar.

The queer implications in this sequence are underscored by the fact that Nandakumar is presented in the film as having little emotional interest in women. Three young male friends accompany him when he visits Jagan in the village. These men go around teasing the village women, including the heroine Unnimaya. Yet Nandakumar shows no interest in such matters; he is more intent on spending time with Jagan. Though he defends his friends when Jagan criticizes them he is as averse to their activities as is Jagan. A psychoanalytic reading of these sequences might suggest that Nandakumar's association with these men could be a ploy to spite Jagan, who is now otherwise preoccupied; it could also be read as his desperate attempt to fill the gap in his life left by Jagan's migration to the village where he is engaged in a heterosexual romance with Unnimaya. The final reconciliation of Nandakumar and Jagan is also laden with muted queer dynamics. Having fulfilled his mission of saving the villagers, Jagan prepares to leave, taking with him Unnimaya and her father. But he is promptly stopped by the villagers, who now consider him their savior and feudal lord (*Thampuran*). Nandakumar now realizes that Jagan is no longer his. He bids an emotional farewell to his friend after conferring on him the ownership of the palatial house. His parting words may reflect the pain of a lost love: "I shall come back to spend a few days here whenever I feel like seeing you."

Yet the queer elements in this film are not confined to Nandakumar and Jagan's friendship. They surface in the scene where Jagan confronts the two musclemen sent by Kolapully Thampuran, the villain. This is a clichéd episode that would conventionally call for a fistfight. Surprisingly, Jagan does not attempt anything of the sort. Instead, he approaches one of the thugs, looks intently into his eyes, and makes a sudden move to grab his groin. As the antagonist blushes and buckles down, the watching villagers roar with laughter. In the process the muscleman is thoroughly emasculated. The gesture is repeated by Jagan later, now in a more humorous vein, with another muscleman attached to the villain.

The queer bond between Nakulan and Dr. Sunny in *Manichitrathazhu* is also subtly stated. It surfaces mainly when Sunny explains his plans to Nakulan. This scene is set in the early morning when Nakulan is still in bed. Dr. Sunny enters the room, gets on the bed, and starts explaining how he plans to deal with the problems of Ganga's mental disturbance and the apparent haunting of the ancestral house. He jokingly declares that since he is now in charge, he has the freedom to do whatever he wishes—"even to lie with Nakulan's wife on the same bed." While these words assign a sensual dimension to the act of "lying together on the same bed," the shot records not a man and woman in bed, but two men—thereby suggesting both the sensual potential of the male bond as well as the contrasting "innocence" of Sunny's proposed presence in bed with Nakulan's wife. The signification is further tilted toward the former by an unexpected gesture from Sunny—he grabs a pillow and places it between his thighs before proceeding with the discussion.

Dr. Sunny's queerness is more clearly depicted when he meets another young man, Ajayan, who is Nakulan's cousin, and who also lives in the ancestral home with his mother and sister. On his first night in the haunted house, Sunny is awakened by the sound of a dancer's ankle bells. He starts searching for its source. Suddenly a brass vessel with a spout, called a *kindi* in Malayalam, is thrown at him. Searching for the thrower of the missile, he comes across Ajayan, who had woken up to relieve himself. A suspicious Sunny follows Ajayan and watches him pissing, causing the young man to blush. As Ajayan finishes the task, Sunny whispers meaningfully, "I saw!" The young man is baffled and Sunny explains: "I saw—the *kindi*." Here he is playing on the word *kindi*, colloquially used to refer to the penis, since the spout of the vessel resembles a penis. During the rest of the sequence Sunny keeps repeating this line to the obvious embarrassment of the young man. Similar patterns of playful sexual harassment frequently appear in heterosexual contexts in Indian cinema, but what makes this sequence striking is its deployment in a same-sex context.

The two men meet again in the bathing enclosure at the pond the next day. Initially Ajayan is uneasy in Sunny's presence, especially after the previous night's happenings. He is also worried about his elder sister Indu because many suspect her of responsibility for the strange happenings in the haunted house. After some initial hostilities, the young man begins to weep and this becomes instrumental in initiating a friendship between the two men. In this sequence, Ajayan wears only a bath towel around his waist while Sunny is in a sleeveless T-shirt and shorts. Sunny assures Ajayan that Indu will not be harmed, and proceeds to dry the young man's hair with a towel as a token of his affection. The physical intimacy of the two male bodies becomes a striking visual statement, with Ajayan's bulging crotch clearly visible. Sunny's as well as the viewers' gaze is directed toward his bare torso, repeatedly framed in middle shots. The sequence acquires further significance because in Kerala the bathing enclosures near ponds are traditionally associated with clandestine romantic encounters, mostly heterosexual.[10]

Compared to these two films, the representation of same-sex physicality in *Thacholi Verghese Chekavar* is more straightforward. The film presents Verghese as singularly concerned with and devoted to young Shyam. The pattern of their friendship fits a popular gay stereotype: Verghese is the dominant, protective, older man and Shyam the dependent, less powerful one. Their intimacy is celebrated in a song sequence where they assume several postures usually assumed by heterosexual lovers in mainstream cinema. The sequence is presented in the form of a reverie—after their friendship has temporarily broken up, Verghese nostalgically recalls his happy days with Shyam. The shots record several instances of physical intimacy between the two men—Verghese teasing Shyam, Shyam trying to tickle Verghese, both of them hugging each other, and both of them mock fighting to rest their heads on the lap of Shyam's mother. Meanwhile the voice-over song demonstrates Verghese's longing for Shyam, whom he addresses by various terms of endearment such as "my little icon of flowers."

The crisis that sets the narrative in motion is Shyam's unexpected disappearance from Verghese's life. This strain in the male bond is caused by Shyam's growing friendship with another male, the villain Rajan Gurukkal, who consequently becomes Verghese's arch rival. Verghese's mission in the film, which he states more than once, is to win back Shyam "at any cost." The main purpose of the action sequence that constitutes the film's climax is to prove Shyam's innocence and release him from Rajan's dominance.

The film ends with Verghese and Maya deciding to get married. But even this seemingly heterosexist ending does not dampen the queer warmth that pervades this text. Maya and Verghese drift out of a church in which the priest is performing a marriage rite. Outside the church, Shyam joins them and the last shot of the film has the trio posing together. This shot records a beaming Verghese with his protective hands on the shoulders of his two consorts—Maya on one side and Shyam on the other—implying the birth of a curious alternative family. An unexpected gesture further tilts this triangle toward a queer matrix—while Maya stands gazing at the camera, Shyam tenderly buries his face in Verghese's shoulder. Thus, the final image the film leaves in the viewer's mind is that of Verghese (the dominant man) with one hand officially on the shoulder of a woman (Maya) while his other hand hugs a dependent man (Shyam), who clings to him.

The heterosexual resolutions of the other two films have a similar structure. Sunny's decision to marry Indu, Ajayan's sister and Nakulan's cousin, comes as a surprise toward the end of *Manichitrathazhu*, since there is no prior indication of emotional or physical attraction between them. The film's early episodes present Indu as silently in love with Nakulan. The complete absence of any intimacy between Sunny and Indu is in direct contrast to the clearly recorded emotional and physical intimacy and companionship between Sunny and Ajayan. Hence, the surprising final twist—Sunny's unexpected proposal and Indu's silent acceptance—acquires other connotations, especially since Indu is Ajayan's sister. Forming a socially acceptable relationship with the elder sister would enable Sunny to retain his contact with her family in general and her younger brother in particular—especially since his only other link with the family, Nakulan, is set to leave for Calcutta. Yet the final sequence of the film presents Sunny leaving the village with Nakulan and his wife, Ganga, creating a triangle similar to the one seen at the end of *Thacholi Verghese Chekavar*. This gives the impression that the promised marriage is a ploy to camouflage a queer resolution. It also indicates that Sunny's marriage with Indu might only mark his shift from one queer triangle to another, both premised on a prominently stated male bond.

Aram Thampuran ends with Jagan's decision to marry Unnimaya. Once again, there are no prior visuals that hint of his desire for the girl. The only romantic song sequence that features them together is presented as Unnimaya's daydream, which represents her desire, not his. According to Jagan, his decision to marry her is prompted by his patriarchal instinct to protect a helpless girl. The only girl with whom Jagan seems to have some emotional intimacy is Nayantara, whom he refuses to marry. Is this because of a fear that she might come in the way of his emotional link with Nandakumar? The final parting of the male pair underscores the possibility of a continuing sentimental bond—they bid farewell, promising to rush to each other whenever they feel like seeing each other. In other words, the male bond is not broken, but temporarily suspended.

Thus, it can be said that all three Mohanlal films recurrently negotiate male-male desire, imagined in both physical and emotional terms. The ideal "masculine" identity is defined alternatively as desiring and desired by another male. This desire is sharply contrasted with the male's near-total indifference to a physically alluring female. The final happy resolutions of these films are anchored on a muted promise of the continuation of the male bond.

The Goddess in the Attic

Women play an important part in these films, and each film presents two contrasting female characters. One is a city girl who briefly visits the village to woo a man and thus explicitly declare her desire; this desiring woman is either rejected or reformed and sent back to the city. This is what Verghese does to the lusty Annie, whom he was supposed to marry. Jagan does almost the same, perhaps more politely, to Nayantara. Though the pattern is different, Ganga in *Manichitrathazhu* is also such a woman; Sunny discovers that her boredom with wifehood and repressed desire for the neighborhood male poet have caused her to become mentally disturbed and to identify with the legendary concubine Nagavally, who was murdered by one of Nakulan's ancestors and now haunts the ancestral house.

All these women are clearly projected as "phallic" women who could emasculate if not annihilate the male. Annie is frequently seen wielding a phallic camera with a protruding zoom lens, with which she attempts to capture the yogic postures of Verghese, at the same time trying to arrest him with her castrating gaze. Nayantara's phallic associations are less pronounced, yet she too has a camera—a camcorder. She generally appears in leather jeans and has a body language indicative of power and freedom. Her flirtatious, almost lesbian, overtures toward Unnimaya also imply a subtle "phallic" power. Yet the most powerful of the three women is Ganga of *Manichitrathazhu*, who, in her hallucinations, metamorphoses into the bloodthirsty Nagavally and attempts to murder her husband, Nakulan.

These phallic and sometimes murderous women who declare their desires have no obvious impact on the Mohanlal hero. His relative lack of desire for women immunizes him and enables him to discipline and cure them. He almost assaults Annie and politely rebuffs Nayantara. As for the powerful Ganga-Nagavally, he uses his modern psychiatric techniques in conjunction with the skills of a Brahman priest to exorcise her. Thus, tradition, imagined in Vedic Brahmanical terms, and modernity, represented by Dr. Sunny's training in Western medicine, join hands to discipline the desiring woman into a faithful, monogamous housewife. Toward the end of *Manichitrathazhu* we see an obviously exhausted Ganga, "cured" of her desire

and eager to go back to the city where she can once more live as Nakulan's faithful wife. She even identifies herself as "Ganga Nakulan."

Yet the taming of the desiring woman also brings the Mohanlal hero in contact
with another femme fatale—one who is virginal, and whose desires are muted and
consequently deemed more dangerous. The concept of such a wrathful virgin "goddess in the attic" is integral to feudal upper-caste mythologies in Kerala.
Traditionally, wealthy rural households used to have a shrine for this goddess in the
attic, and sometimes in the cellar as well, where she was regularly worshiped. It
was believed that if the worship was irregular, her wrath would unleash misfortunes that could lead to the ruin of the household. Difficult to please and notori-
ously quick-tempered, these goddesses were imagined as simultaneously virginal
and maternal. The archetype of such a goddess recurs both in *Aram Thampuran* and
Manichitrathazhu.

The legendary Nagavally in *Manichitrathazhu* has some features of the wrathful
female deity in the attic. Yet throughout the first half of the film, it is the mysterious and virginal Indu who assumes a similar function. She is considered responsible for the signs of haunting that mysteriously reappear in the house and is looked
upon with fear by the other members of the family. Her unrequited desire for
Nakulan is considered responsible for this state of affairs. Her "muted desire" is
projected as more dangerous than Ganga's expressed desire.

In *Aram Thampuran*, there are several references to the presiding female deity of
the village whose annual festival has not been conducted for several years. Her wrath
is believed to be causing misfortunes in the village. The narrative then cleverly
identifies the village girl Unnimaya, abandoned and lonely, with this goddess.
When Jagan meets her for the first time in the temple, she is in red, with her hair
let down—appearing like a human incarnation of the goddess. Hence Jagan's
attempt to appease the goddess and rid the villagers of her wrath is simultaneous
with his decision to marry and protect Unnimaya. As the new feudal lord, he must
undertake such protective gestures.

Thacholi Verghese Chekavar does not present any such ominous figures. Maya is certainly not a mysterious figure: she is an orphan, and it is her helpless condition that
triggers off all the crises in the narrative. Eventually she decides to stay with Verghese
because she feels safe in his presence. Thus, though not projected as a goddess, she
has a function similar to that of Maya and Indu in the other two films.

Conclusion: Marriage and Same-Sex Bonds Coexist

In conclusion it can be said that all three films construct ideal companionship as
existing only between men. Male bonds are defined through a remarkably overt
physicality, often contrasted with a near absence of male desire for women. These
films define women as a social responsibility that intervenes and disrupts male
bonds. Desire for women, if openly expressed, is censored and rejected; if muted,
on the other hand, it is imagined as threatening and mysteriously dangerous.
Defusing this threat through marriage is defined as a male responsibility.

A strikingly similar concept of marriage emerges in all three films. For men it
is a responsibility but for women a privilege. The male bond can continue even

after a marriage predicated on social responsibility, for emotional companionship and physical desire still circulate primarily between men.

Commercial cinema is a social institution that strives to provide visual pleasure. These reimaginings of gendered subjectivities also constitute the technologies of pleasure deployed by these films. Both *Manichitrathazhu* and *Aram Thampuran* achieved phenomenal commercial success and were among the biggest hits in the recent history of Malayalam cinema, while *Thacholi Verghese Chekavar* was a middling commercial success. Admittedly patriarchal, and even misogynist, these films nonetheless demonstrate that gendered subjectivities and desire in contemporary India overflow conventional heterosexist frameworks of reading.

Notes

1. Alexander Doty, *Making Things Perfectly Queer: Interpreting Mass Culture* (Minneapolis: University of Minnesota Press, 1993), xi.
2. Deepa Mehta's *Fire* (1996); Amol Palekar's *Dayra* (1996), about a cross-dressing man; and Kalpana Lajmi's *Darmiyan* (1997) and Pooja Bhat's *Tamanna* (1996), both about eunuchs, are some of the prominent films in this category.
3. Doty, *Making Things Queer*, xi.
4. Ibid., 8.
5. Ibid., xii.
6. The central character is an artistic girl, Ganga, married to a businessman Nakulan, and living in Calcutta. They visit Nakulan's ancestral mansion in a Kerala village. The mansion is rumored to be haunted by the ghost of Nagavally, a dancer who was the concubine of one of Nakulan's ancestors. When Nagavally fell in love with another dancer, Ramanathan, the patriarch had her killed. When her ghost started haunting the mansion, an exorcist was hired who imprisoned her in the attic, which has been locked ever since. Ganga discovers that a young poet whose work she adores lives next door. Fascinated by the myth of Nagavally, she forges a key and opens the locked attic. Soon, signs of haunting reappear in the household. Dr. Sunny discovers that Ganga is bored with Nakulan. Her desire for the neighborhood poet (which her civilized self refuses to accept) inspires her to unconsciously identify with Nagavally. By strangely re-creating a situation in which Nagavally gets an opportunity to murder her enemy, Dr. Sunny restores Ganga's sanity.
7. In a remote Kerala village, Verghese trains youngsters in Kalaripayattu, a traditional martial art. His rival, Rajan Gurukkal, also a martial arts expert, has a more fashionable gym in Madras. The narrative is set in motion by a murder in which Verghese's disciple Shyam gets entangled. Rajan convinces Shyam that the only way to escape incarceration is by murdering Maya, a girl who is the only eyewitness to the murder. Shyam lies to Verghese that he is in love with Maya, who deserted him. Verghese kidnaps Maya and brings her to Shyam. After a series of misunderstandings, Verghese learns that the murder was actually committed by Rajan. In a mundane climax, Verghese bashes up the villain and hands him to the police.
8. As the reward for a difficult business deal that Jagannathan earns for his patron Nandakumar, he asks for an old mansion in a remote village in Kerala. The only inmates of the derelict mansion are a young girl, Unnimaya, and her foster father. She is the illegitimate daughter of the last member of an erstwhile royal family. The sad state of the palace is due to the wrath of a patriarch from a rival royal family, Kolapully Thampuran, who is hated by all the villagers. Jagan takes over the protection of mansion, village, and Unnimaya. He decides to revive the annual festival of the village temple, which the villain had stopped. There follow several intrigues until it is revealed that Jagan was the

only son of the temple priest, who had committed suicide when wrongly accused of theft. After a spectacular climax the villains are punished and the festival celebrated. At the villagers' request, Jagan decides to stay on as their new lord, with Unnimaya as his wife. Nandakumar bestows the mansion on them as a wedding present and leaves for Bangalore.

9. Gopinathan R., "Return of the Popular," *Deep Focus* 8, nos. 1–2 (1988): 11–15.

10. This is structurally different from the association of male homoeroticism with bathing in open air that recurs in British fiction and painting of the late nineteenth and early twentieth centuries. The bathing enclosures of rural ponds in Kerala are well-covered public spaces that provide substantial privacy for clandestine erotic encounters.

13

"I Sleep behind You"

Male Homosociality and Homoeroticism
in Indian Parallel Cinema

Thomas Waugh

Over the last couple of generations Indian cinemas, like the cinemas of the West, have engaged with modernity through acting out the so-called crisis of masculinity, but have done so in their own distinct ways. Commercial popular cinema has done so through the volcanic fulgurations of the erotic marketplace, through *danses macabres* with censors, fightmasters, blackmarketeers, and schizophrenic star personae, through cataclysmic gender disruptions no sooner registered than disavowed by hyperbolic restabilizations. Increasingly, in recent years, as I have observed elsewhere,[1] Bollywood has escalated this crisis through probings of marginal and subversive sexualities, probings both tentative and kamikaze, of which gay villains and sidekicks as well as *hijras* coming brashly out of the Bollywood closet are the most conspicuous instances.

The so-called parallel or art cinema has participated no less profoundly in the crisis of masculinity, but in more restrained and distinctly different ways. Over the last generation, this peripatetic "international" cinema has almost entirely repressed or at best camouflaged discourses of eroticism in general and homoeroticism in particular. Whether this chastity is due to the parallel cinema's overwhelming dogma of middle-class social realism or because of the centrality of the state as both artistic patron and censor hardly matters. The recent *Fire* outbreak (Deepa Mehta, 1997) and the selective circulation of other diasporic queer texts, from *My Beautiful Laundrette* (Stephen Frears and Hanif Kureishi, 1986) to *Kama Sutra* (Mira Nair, 1997) and *Bombay Boys* (Kaizad Gustad, 1998), as well as recent queer inroads in indigenously produced work by Rajkumar Sharma (*Mai*, 1989), Amol Palekar (*Dayra* [*The Square Circle*], 1996), Kalpana Lajmi (*Darmiyan* [*In Between*], 1997), Sumitra Bhave (*Zindagi Zindabad* [*Long Live Life!*], with Sunil Sukhthankar, 1998), and Pankaj Butalia (*Kaarvan*, [*Shadows in the Dark*], 1999) demonstrate how hard it will be for the parallel cinema to maintain its virginity, the tightening political atmosphere notwithstanding.

The parallel cinema's historic avoidance pattern with regard to *explicit* same-sex discourses and identities does not mean that same-sex relations have not been one of its central preoccupations. On the contrary: as in the popular cinema, the mythologies of homosociality constitute one of its fundamental cores. These homosocial mythologies offer a safe and unique conduit for same-sex desire in this parallel cinema and thus their apparently innocent surfaces are continually disturbed by symptoms of trouble beneath. This chapter looks not at the recent queer inroads mentioned above, but at four films by and about men, films not especially blatant in their queer affirmations (nor for that matter wholly typical, admittedly, of the diverse corpus of Indian art cinema since 1977[2]), but four films especially and symptomatically fraught with trouble all the same within the male homosocial generic momentum of the 1970s, '80s, and '90s. Of these four films, two are historical costume melodramas that depict dominance-submission relations among men within and across colonial boundaries of race, class, and culture: *The Chess Players* (Satyajit Ray, 1977) and *Massey Sahib* (Pradeep Krishen, 1985). The othere two are postcolonial black comedies that use male homosocial institutions, a college and the Indian Civil Service, respectively, as the setting for eruptions and containments in the sex gender system[3]: *Holi* (Ketan Mehta, 1984), a parablelike revolt in a men's college that culminates in the lynching of a "third sex" scapegoat, and *English August* (Dev Benegal, 1996), in which Agastya, a cosmopolitan intellectual on duty at a remote posting in Andhra Pradesh called Madna, discovers his alienation from the great unwashed hinterland. Interestingly, all four films are adapted from prestigious sources in other media, namely theater and literature—a factor that may add to their anomalous status but no doubt to their cultural resonance as well.[4]

I will situate all four films, which chronologically span twenty years (more than thirty if one remembers the Mahesh Elkunchwar late-sixties Marathi stage play that is the source of *Holi*), as crystallizations of the homosocial turbulence of the parallel cinema in general, of the way same-sex desire has been constructed *textually* within these films' masculinist ideological apparatus. I am also looking for symptomatic *subtextual* signs of homoerotic stress and of emerging queer imaginaries. I will principally employ textual analysis in this endeavor, without downloading significant quantities of "theory" onto these films.

To set the stage, I look at a fifth film, *Bomgay*, one of the very rare Indian parallel films that might be called "queer" in the Euro-American sense. This film, an eleven-minute short made in 1996, is in fact so parallel that director Riyad Wadia apparently declined to submit it to the censors—wisely, one might add—and has screened it abroad only in queer festivals and special screenings, and for invited audiences at home. According to an interview and quasireview in *Bombay Dost*, *Bomgay* is self-styled as "India's First Gay Film. . . . the 'first' indigenously produced 'gay' film from India. . . . [a work] bringing the subject of homosexuality out in the open [and emboldening] the emerging gay culture in India. . . . the first film the gay community can call their own."[5]

Bomgay is a collection of cinematic adaptations and embellishments of six short poems by Pune-based English-language poet and playwright R. Raj Rao—all vignettes, variously heavy and light, about Mumbai same-sex subcultural life. Wadia's extravagant and unnuanced promotional claims to a certain model of same-sex identification are echoed by *Bomgay*'s expository captions that fill up the space between the six nuanced and rather cryptic film poems. The captions pad the film both literally and symbolically with statistics about 50 million men who have sex with men and 12.5 million exclusively homosexual men in India—about one percent of the population—and other statements of dubious facticity about Indian gay men as sociopsychic personae and as an identifiable demographic constituency in the Western "ethnic" sense. Though the film has hardly had its share of favorable reviews, it has clear value not only as a cinematic "first" but also as an entry point to a much larger discussion of Indian parallel cinema.

This model of same-sex identification, which I have called elsewhere middle-class metropolitan movements and identities or MMMIs (after Lawrence Cohen[6]), is especially illuminated by the shortest of the film poems, which gives its title to the collection. The film and poem succinctly present a gay male New Yorker as a "sex tourist" whom the narrator, "the postcolonial pimp," has introduced to three sites of homoerotic expression in the Mumbai urban landscape, the network of Western-style gay clubs and discos, the underground ghetto of men's public toilets, and finally the steeple of the Apsara Theatre, a secular pop architectural statement of the phallic core of certain Shaivite corners of Hindu spirituality and culture. According to the poet, gay male foreign sex tourists love the tour but prefer the architectural tower most of all, apparently fetishizing the camp exoticity of this unexpected *lingam*, or phallus. This short film is told primarily through scenes of the American perusing snapshot stills of the tour, himself posing with his pimp and others, snapshots being the natural medium for the touristic experience. Why does the narrator characterize himself with such relish as a postcolonial pimp? Perhaps for having commodified and betrayed these sexual mysteries for the outsider. But one senses that he is perhaps not as anxious for the foreign pounds and dollars as he says, but rather invokes them to mask his own shamed engagement in all three sites, in *domestic* cross-class sex tourism, with equal parts of obsession and ambivalence. In fact like the sex tourist, the narrator and entire film/poem seem to be negotiating various models of same-sex desire on a culturally specific continuum between homosociality and homoeroticism, confronting indigenous sex-gender discourses with those comfortably recognizable as transculturally queer.

I thus see *Bomgay* in an unwitting dialogue with the foregoing tradition of crisis-fraught homosocial art cinema, inadvertently recapitulating those earlier films' negotiations, both textual and subtextual, among models of desire. I would like now to explore three iconographical clusters taken from *Bomgay*—the family, the body, and violence—and examine how they extend the four parallel features' earlier and more oblique rehearsal of them.

The Family

The poet characterizes his sex-tourist clients as "family members," a wry parodic pointer to both bodily appendages and queer kinship. But he is pointing also to the overwhelmingly normative institution of Indian social life, the family idealized and enshrined in Bollywood but routinely held up for dissection in feminist parallel cinema and in much of the parallel cinema of male crisis. For one thing, *Bomgay*, and in particular the first subfilm, "Opinions," make the clash explicit between the MMMI model of the postcolonial bachelor and the traditional family as unit of reproduction, inheritance, curry preparation, and funeral rites. In

"Opinions," the narrator knows that Shantabai, his female domestic employee, does not understand bachelorhood and presumably does not even see him cruising the bare-chested hunk who passes them in the corridor. The narrator, played by Rao himself, is seen buying onions, but Shantabai worries that they are not ending up in vegetable curries, knowing full well that culinary activity is a marker of "normal" familial organization. But the adapted family of queer friendship circles also defines itself in terms of culinary activity, having friends over for a dinner: significantly the meal in "Friends," the sixth subfilm, is cosmopolitan spaghetti, not curry—a sign of imported identities? Furthermore, there is no domestic servant visible in this chic bachelor flat, and their obvious socioeconomic privilege is both taken for granted and understated. In the other domestic arrangement depicted in *Bomgay*, in "Enema," the male-male conjugal unit is depicted, in fact side by side in the monogamous bed. Yet culinary issues are present even here, for the character's gastrointestinal problems are brought on by eating "junk food" outside of the domestic zone. Fortunately they can be remedied by the elixir of anal penetration, which stimulates the excretory function as well as solidifying the conjugal unit. Thus the traditional family is problematized by its absence, or is redefined, both by sexuality and by food and the other materials of domesticity.

In the four feature films I am analyzing, the family is also problematized but not defined by anything so wholesome as shared food. In the homosocial world of these films—and indeed in large swaths of parallel cinema over the years—there is very little of Bollywood's hollowly sanctimonious cult of familitude. Indeed, in this world of unfulfilled and betrayed marriages, and heterosexual initiations characterized by alienation, violence, and deception, the family is a glaringly evident structuring absence. *English August*'s outsider hero, Agastya, is an outsider as much to the family network he experiences peripherally in his world, as to his homosocial world of Indian Civil Service cuckolds, bachelors, abandoned husbands, and closeted gay romantic drunks. Likewise, the *Holi* boys, Massey, and the chess players are all situated in relation to problematical, stressful, or threatened heterosexual courtships and families and all much prefer the sociality of the all-male world, or, as Massey's colonial boss's wife Ruby scornfully puts it, "playing boy scout" (see fig. 13.1). Massey's pathetic attempt at heterosexual family foundation, from courtship to ceremony to reproduction, would delight Judith Butler[7]—it is so much an imitation, a parodic performance of his boss Charles Adams's marriage ideal, which itself, we see behind the scenes, also turns out to be a mess hardly worthy of such rote repetition. The two parallel marriages in *Massey Sahib*, like those in *The Chess Players* and others in this corpus, are triangular homosocial arrangements in which the husband's male comrade is the third term. As for *English August*'s Agastya, this poor bachelor is so badgered by Madna-ites' queries about his marital status and his wife that he invents fantastic stories about her, including her recent bout with breast cancer, to liven up their lives with a dose of conjugal melodrama. The structure of this world is not the hysterical hetero versus homo binary that Eve Kosofsky Sedgwick has so convincingly established as the base of modern Euro-American sex-gender systems,[8] but a positional relationship with the family, kinship, and reproduction, an insider-outsider binary of familied versus nonfamilied that has little to do with sex.

Figure 13.1
"Playing boy scout" in
Massey Sahib: homo-
social, corporal intimacy
between colonial boss
and babu.

The Body

Bomgay is naturally full of male bodies, almost all young, firm, and eroticized, appearing to the film/poem narrators and protagonists as either fantasy or real-life corporalities, especially in the poem segments entitled "Opinions," "Underground," "Enema," and "Bomgay." Wadia's hunky cast are strictly Mumbai male model material, unrecognizable in relation to the population of India's other cinematic or social realms, even Bollywood's, with their sculpted hairless bodies, gym-pumped pectorals and buttocks from heaven, clean-shaven classically north Indian faces, and perfect haircuts—not to mention an ambiguous sexual orientation that is prudently disavowed in the credits. The hunks have a privileged role, especially in the fantasy "Lefty" segment, where the brazenness of male nudity and simulated male-male sex are unprecedented in Indian (nondiasporic) cinema. The original poem is about marginality, a first-person fantasy of a left-handed writer feeling stared at in a university library, which then suddenly shifts to a meditation about "family" and "your lover" and the paradoxical social justice of public space where, thanks in part to mirrors, fully democratic sexual staring back is permitted. Wadia transforms the rather nuanced and discreet poem into the protagonist's graphic fantasy of being anally ravished by suddenly nude fellow library users, replicated in the library mirrors. Most recognizable to parallel cinephiles is the actor Rahul Bose, who plays the left-handed fantasizer. Bose also plays the aimless civil service hero in *English August* and the gay character in *Bombay Boys*, and has thus acquired a queer iconicity.[9] Bose is very cosmopolitan looking, with his stylish short haircut but with a smaller body and larger personality than the MMMIs—nowhere more fetching than in his *English August* jogging outfit. There is certainly no resemblance to the realist star stable that has maintained the parallel cinema elsewhere, full of "character" rather than beauty, gangling like Naseeruddin Shah or pockmarked like Om

Puri (who, interestingly, play the small parts of the sympathetic hostel warden and manipulative principal, respectively, in *Holi*), always looking but seldom to be looked at. There is no resemblance either to the traditionally epicene "pretty boy" leading men of Bollywood—little resemblance even to the pumped-up Sanjay Dutt types who made inroads after Amitabh Bachchan parachuted his Westernized macho body onto the scene in the 1970s.

The explicit theme of masturbation is virgin territory for Indian cinema (except for Anand Patwardhan's communalist documentary subjects in *Ram Ke Naam* [*In the Name of God*, 1992] who boast of jerking off to Bollywood rape scenes!). Thus it was easy for Bose's persona to become the epitomous Hindu wanker. It is unclear whether Agastya's efforts to swear off the continual furtive movement beneath the sheets ("I don't want to waste my sperm on Madna" [the sweltering Andhra town to which he has been exiled]) stem from a nineteenth-century Judeo-Christian ethic of seminal productivity or a Hindu ethic of karmic sperm recycling—perhaps both. His efforts include the decidedly Western activity of nocturnal jogging rather than Eastern meditation at dawn, but significantly the former simply attracts the quasi-sexual attention of marauding teasers. Masturbation is mostly a comic motif in this and the rare other homosocial films where it is referred to; we are not spared the predictable spilt milk metaphor, and *English August*'s clever publicity slogan joined in the fun ("In a strange place, you have to hold your own"). But it is deadly serious behind the jokes, the symptomatic sign of existential crisis for Agastya and his generation, gender, and class; one critic reproached the character for narcissism.[10] Loving the self has vague but unavoidable associations with same-sex desire in both *English August*, where it is shown, and in *Holi*, where it is acknowledged only verbally as an obsessive activity of the frustrated college boys in the cramped intimacy of their collective space and of the cinema hall.

This homoerotic association is heightened in *English August* by the hyperbolic erotic inscription of Agastya's fetching body. The character is transgressively heterosexual in Upamanyu Chatterji's novel of the same name (1988), but here in this visual medium Agastya is habitually posed beguilingly and delectably nude (not frontal of course; after all, the film sought a censor certificate and the national award for English-language cinema, and got both!). But this uninhibited look at the actor's body is camouflaged by director Benegal's retention of the original novel's minor gay character as a disavowal mechanism. Treated with the usual symptomatic comedic levity, together with a tinge of pathos, and with none of the visual eroticism present everywhere else, harmonium-player Shankar is a mournful and drunken neighbor in the Indian Civil Service bachelor compound. His unintentional double entendres in faulty English are a source of great sexual wit (for example, "I sleep behind you") and his tentative hand on Agastya's thigh is quickly noted and as quickly disengaged (see fig. 13.2). Suitably inoculated by the fag jokes, the spectator can then relish the spectacle of Bose's corporal display without anxiety or guilt.

If Agastya and his younger middle-class peers in *Holi* are associated with semen, their lower-class *desi* homologues are associated with another bodily material—namely, excrement. For, to reverse Yeats's aphorism, excrement, too, is pitched in the place of love's mansion. One of Rao's favorite themes, excremental eros is elaborated most fully in "Underground," where sexual fantasies, memories, and expe-

Figure 13.2

riences are scented with the abjection of the underground toilet network. It is also associated with the voyeurism of the commuter rail passenger who is on the pruri- ent lookout for male squatters as he enters Mumbai along the tracks through the slums, a "ripe harvest" with "power of ammunition." Elsewhere in *Bomgay*, excre- tion symbolizes release from the constipation of urban life, a release triggered, as already mentioned, by receptive anal intercourse, and thus acquiring a particular association with pleasure, desire, and sexual exchange, associated this time, how- ever, with the sanitized glamour of a European-style toilet, not the train tracks.

In *English August*, too, excrement is a continuous motif, from a sacrilegious visual gag about a Gandhi statue with his walking staff stuck up his ass to jokes about in-the-street urination. Such a blatant scatological texture has never been seen in any other Indian film. The topper is a climactic image of an anonymous pile of human turds deposited nightly on a bridgepost, seeming to stand in its indeci- pherability for the absurdity and savage physicality of the outpost, Madna, where the hero has been sent to encounter the "other" and himself. *Holi* has a less impor- tant but quite visible excretory interest as well. The communal bathroom is a cen- tral location where rear views of voiders and shakers recur, and the boisterous dialogue is fraught with scatological vulgarity, all especially daring for a 1986 film. No doubt the scatological thrust of this and the other films (the urbane Ray is the exception here), the fascination with the bowels, effectively connotes the abject material substratum of the male body in crisis, the lower end of a continuum of intensely physical and homosocial activities that the male bodies engage in, includ- ing nude bathing, smoking ganja, jogging, and masturbation, and in *Holi*, eating, drinking, fighting, singing, and debauchery. Though Agastya and the *Holi* boys all pass through their perfunctory opposite-sex moments and articulations, by and large their physical and sexual habitus is homosocial, a universe of intense physi- cal intimacy whose flirtation with homoerotic sensuousness belies the disavowals that are also in play.

In the two colonial costume films, the articulation of the male body is less earthy. In *The Chess Players*, Ray clothes his three principal Indian protagonists—the musical poet-king who is ousted by the British, and the two aristocrats who play chess while the British take over their kingdom and adulterers infiltrate their bedrooms— in the epicene corporality and brocaded robes of their class and period (the king also gets makeup and perfume), and in so doing provokes no little debate over this implied interface of masculinity, history, and nationality.[11] (Whether the adulterer and the British soldiers are implied objects of desire in this narrative world is another question that had apparently not dawned on Ray, or even the critics who debated the film.) Ashis Nandy has quite correctly observed that conflicts over gender roles are played out within the male camps of both colonizers and colonized, but these conflicts are enacted not only in the script he quotes lavishly, but also in the gestural and corporal languages of the body—in the dances of the deposed king as well as the courtly and graceful languorousness of the chess players (in contradiction to the stiff formality of the conquerors). The bottom line is that the elegant chess players, too, would far rather be with each other in this world of corporal elegance and sensual fellowship than with their wives, their political constituency, or anyone else. In general, however, Ray is too much a poet of middle-class repression to be an interpreter of male corporality—(though his homosocially triangular narratives inspired by Rabindranath Tagore (*Charulata* [1964] and *Home and the World* [1984]) see men's bodies vividly through the eyes of their wavering female heroines, and the palpably physical gang of male vacationers in *Days and Nights in the Forest* (1969) is no doubt the exception that proves the rule. Ray has never shown the slightest interest in homoeroticism, though a stiff homosocial intimacy is part of his everyday vocabulary.

A less restrained case in point is *Massey Sahib*, where the male body performs a very carnal cinematic schizophrenia of masculinity. Before the British male administrators whom he imitates and idolizes in a kind of erotic mimicry, Massey is a slapstick object of ridicule. There is one point where, having been humiliated in his heterosexual aspirations, his nakedness itself is the object of that shame. When he is within his own culture's homosocial environment, his small taut body tells another story, acquiring leadership, strength, confidence, charisma, and its own sensual grace. Two scenes each associate this transformed body with music and performance; one is with his comrades around a campfire, and one is at the jungle construction site. In both cases his singing and exhortation, bare chested and gleaming with sweat, pulsing with motion and rhythm—with prize-winning actor Raghuvir Yadav at his most intense—belie the clumsy asexual colonial babu. (Significantly, this is the only one of the five films under discussion that specularize the physicality of manual work: an odd index of the art cinema's moorings in the middle-class intelligentsia?) But Massey's physical pleasure and grace immediately repressed in his obsessive attachment to the British men he adores, and repudiated entirely in the literal imprisonment of the final scene, as we shall see.

Interestingly, no hijras or third sexers had intruded on the parallel cinema until the 1990s, when there appeared the exceptional and well-received films by the directors listed at the outset of this chapter. For the most part these films have attracted academics and restricted TV or art house audiences abroad. Significantly, *Darmiyan* is by a woman director/writer, Kalpana Lajmi, and transpires within a historical female homosocial universe rather than its hegemonic male counterpart. When what Lawrence Cohen refers to as "intergendered, auspicious and playful thirdness" first surfaced more than a decade earlier in *Holi*[12] it was far from a reclamation of the alterior body, irrecuperably articulated with all the playfulness of a lynch mob, imposed rather than embodied. Here the "third" body, taunted with "hijra" and "prostitute," branded with marks of repulsion, scorned, assaulted, prodded, denuded, doused, daubed, and bedecked, is flaunted as the abject alien element— devoid even of Massey's dignity as victim (fig. 13.3). This body is purged and ritually expelled from the choreography of "normalized" male bodies that drew praise as Mehta's brilliant long take mise-en-scène. If the male body is a battleground over power and desire, in the parallel cinema until recently sex gender deviants were too frightening to be engaged even as combatants.

Violence/Submission

In discussing bodies, we have repeatedly and unavoidably veered toward the theme of violence, for where there is homosociality violence predictably erupts. *Bomgay*'s "Underground" shows with great graphic efficacy the unresisted and bloody bludgeoning of the middle-class cruiser by the sexy young goonda he has made eye con-

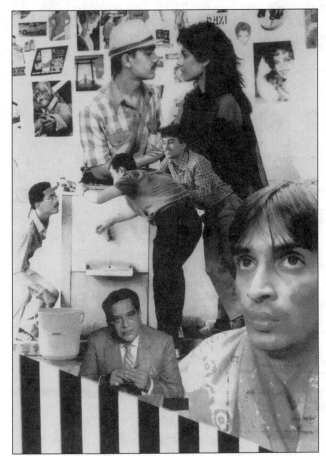

Figure 13.3
Holi video jacket shows queer scapegoat Anand (foregrounded), humiliated with sari and lipstick and framed by normative configurations of heterosexuality and homosociality.

tact with, propositioned, and groped at the underground station urinals—a moment chillingly dramatized through Wadia's use of stills. This device may reflect Wadia's budget rather than his discretion, as do, no doubt, the ritualized colonial violence of territorial invasion and capital punishment in *The Chess Players* and *Massey Sahib*, respectively, which are largely offscreen. However, the graphic climax of *Holi* overcompensates in its explicitness and ranks surely as one of the most horrifying in a national cinema already littered with subaltern corpses—it culminates in the graphic sight of the dead queer hanging from his fan. The escalating tension within the young men's dormitory is connected throughout to vague student discontent, the amorphous class resentment of middle-class youth, and in general a high testosterone level, so much so that the fisticuffs, masturbation, heterosexual transgressions, and verbal aggression do not seem to dissipate it. The scapegoat is Anand, an obsequious and less macho dorm-mate who is said to provide sexual services to his bully roommate and others, and submits to their blackmail for tea, sunglasses, and money. Anand's homosexuality is thus made all but explicit, with even the school principal alluding threateningly and evasively to the kind of relationships he has with certain kinds of friends.

The film's actual avoidance of names for these relationships extends to discourses around the film as well. The three indigenous commentaries on the film that I have tracked down all mysteriously avoid the narrative's sexual politics and its queer-bashing, scapegoating thrust, as does even an interview with director Ketan Mehta (a respected auteur with radical and feminist political credentials). This avoidance is orchestrated by the narrative. Anand's principal offense is at the outset construed by his classmates as his privileged family ties to the college administration. Toward the climax of the film, Anand succumbs to the administration's pressure and threats and informs on those of his classmates who were involved in an ineffectual student revolt, but he omits from the hit list his roommate/lover. The latter repays the favor by inciting the others to the mob frenzy at the film's climax. Blackmail is not only an element of the plot but also the essence of the film's moral manipulation of the spectator—the queer sacrificial victim is shown to be a whining, sycophantic, and spoiled loser who surely deserves what he gets.

A critic in the diasporic *Trikone* aptly summarizes the film's climax, noting, "the students burst into an orgy of violence. This sequence, filmed with multiple cameras and imaginatively edited, produces an effect so graphic and humiliating that I couldn't watch it a second time. The students swear at Anand, kick and beat him, dunk his head in a sewer, smear red lipstick on his lips, strip him down to his black nylon underwear, drape a purple sari around him, and make him dance a *mujra*. Finally, they shave his head as he sobs silently."[13] But even this critic cannot bear to detail the final revelation of Anand's suicide, where the victim seems to have submitted to his humiliation as silently as Wadia's toilet cruiser. Thereupon his mournful hallmates file out to face the legal consequences with a dignity they have not previously shown, as if this catharsis at the expense of the queer scapegoat has awakened them to the tragic realities of adult citizenship in an unjust society. The various dynamics in play—coming of age at the expense of the other, the sexual metaphorization of politics—are all familiar formulae in homosocial cinemas in Euro-American cultures, but it is perhaps the innocence of this rendition, the discursive and moral vacuum around it, that marks *Holi* in its specific cultural context. *Trikone* correctly identified homophobia as the motor of the film, but no one else noticed.

The other three films similarly conclude on a moment of violence and submission, albeit offscreen, displaced, or aestheticized. It is displaced in the case of *English August*, where Agastya seems to be punished for a sudden surge of conscience with regard to his *adivasi* (tribal) clients. A ritual castration is administered, but not to him; rather, in oblique and surrogate fashion his ICS buddy Mandi's arms are cut off in punishment for his interference with a woman from a remote community. It is significant that this sudden and unexpected intrusion of violence—offscreen—is in response to sexual transgression, rather than motivated by the politics of class and economics, whose invisible Naxalite arbiters hover in the background of the film. The shock triggers Agastya's abandonment of Madna, his resignation, and introduces a note of moral ambiguity at the end of a film that has lured us into an easy mix of irreverent laughter and complicit desire.

In the two colonial films, the acts of violence and submission are highly ritualized through politicomilitary, judicial, and religious codes. There is an uncanny cinematic common ground between the moments when the androgynous Nawab Wajid Ali histrionically surrenders his crown to the British general in *The Chess Players* and when the death row prisoner Massey ecstatically fantasizes his English idol's penetration of his mouth with his gun, followed by his mercy-killing as the pair recite the Lord's Prayer in *Massey Sahib*. Both not only construct colonialism as a sexual metaphor but also ritualistically eroticize the colonized's submission to violence and power.[14] Sexual metaphorization has never been far from the public discourse around colonialism since its historical origins, but these two scenes are especially volatile in terms of both their disturbing cinematic effect and their suggestion of consensuality in relations between colonizer and colonized. The combination of the deposed king's androgyny and the aura of masochistic desire around his act of submission, in a context where the melodramatic moral requirement of riposte, vengeance, or redress is absent, anticipates the generically similar dénouements of this paper's four other texts. Unlike in the Bollywood realm of the action hero, violence in this cinematic world of troubled homosociality is suffered, indulged, and absorbed by the sex-gender outsider, never initiated or repaid. If one accepts the common assumption of a dialogue between the parallel cinema and Bollywood, can one see this submissiveness on the part of these parallel outsiders as being ultimately avenged by the delectably marauding gay villains of popular cinema of the 1990s?

Conclusion

One might have expected from the growing visibility of MMMIs, especially in Mumbai and the other large urban areas, and from the circulation of postcolonial, transcultural "queer" identities and theories in the globalized marketplace of sexual media, commodities, and desires, that they would have made more inroads into the parallel cinemas rooted in the Indian metropoles. *Bomgay* does show such inroads, but the film's solitariness is a reminder of how little penetration has actually occurred (though activity on the low-budget video documentary scene has stepped up at the turn of the millennium).[15] I have tried to show how *Bomgay*, instead of grafting onto Indian soil a transplanted Western queer cinema (which is far from monolithic in any case), recapitulates, despite its anomalous status, several of the problematics and preoccupations of earlier homosocial cinemas. I am not arguing that *Bomgay* is involved in a developmental teleology with the earlier parallel features, and that Indian incarnations of Todd Haynes and Derek Jarman are about to appear on the horizon. Instead, the crisis of masculinity performed and confronted by *The Chess Players, Holi, Massey Sahib,* and *English August* within the iconographic sets of family, the male body, and violence is reenacted within the discursive overlay of Western-style sexual identity in Wadia's *Bomgay.*

And what is that crisis? A multiple one, with the male cinematic and social subject facing modernization and encircled on all sides by challenges to gender hegemony and cultural and economic well-being, and within an increasingly insistent and commoditized sexual universe. Among other things, it is a crisis of discovery, perhaps, the discovery that the hegemonic homosocial universe of Indian culture and society, as interpreted by the male directors of an androcentric art cinema, contains disruptive corners where homosocial desire melds with the homoerotic and cannot be closed off. In enacting this crisis and making this discovery, in foreshadowing this queer cinematic imaginary, or rather these imaginary cinematic queernesses, the Indian parallel cinema has not articulated the adamant binaries of homo versus hetero that have been intrinsic to Western culture, *Bomgay* notwithstanding. Rather, it has articulated same-sex desire through narrative hierarchies inherited and continually extrapolated from colonialism's binary of colonizer and colonized so vividly sketched by Satyajit Ray and Pradeep Krishen; through the contemporary relations around the familied, the nonfamilied, and the neofamilied; around the idealizations and abjectnesses of the male body; around violence, submission, and scapegoating. Sex tourism, postcolonial pimpery, MMMI spaghetti dinners, and toilet encounters are terms in a much larger sphere in which male bodies and desires are constructed and performed. You can no longer simply disregard your own look in the mirror, rebuff the hand on your thigh, or ignore the specter sleeping behind you.

Notes

My appreciation to Ruth Vanita for her invitation to contribute to this volume and her helpful feedback, and to many friends and colleagues for feedback, hospitality, and help navigating this corpus, including Dipti Gupti, Saleem Kidwai, Madhava Prasad, Ashish Rajadhyaksha, R. Raj Rao, Krishna Sarbadhikary, Niranjana Tejaswini, Riyad Wadia; and to Concordia University for funding my Indian research over the years.

1. Thomas Waugh, "Queer Bollywood, or 'I'm the Player, You're the Naive One': Patterns of Sexual Subversion in Recent Indian Popular Cinema," in *Popular Film and Cultural Studies*, ed. Amy Villarejo and Matthew Tinkcom (New York: Routledge, 2001).

2. Is the end of the Emergency (1977) a suitable point for periodizing contemporary parallel cinema?

3. I borrow this concept from Gayle Rubin, developed in such articles as "Thinking Sex: Notes for a Radical Theory of the Politics of Sexuality," in *Pleasure and Danger: Exploring Female Sexuality*, ed. Carole S. Vance (New York: Routledge and Kegan Paul, 1984).

4. *Bomgay* (dir. Riyad Wadia, based on poems by R. Raj Rao, 1996, in English, 11 min.); *English August* (dir. Dev Benegal, based on the novel by Upamanyu Chatterjee, in English, Telegu, and Bengali, 1996, 115 min., available commercially on video in India and the West); *Holi* ([*Festival of Fire*] dir. Ketan Mehta, cowritten by Mahesh Elkunchwar, based on his play, in Hindi, 1984, 120 min., available commercially on video in India). The plot details of these three films are evident in the text of my paper; outlines of the other two follow, since they may not be as easily available. In *Massey Sahib* (dir. Pradeep Krishen, based on Joyce Cary's novel *Mister Johnson*, in Hindi, 1986, 118 min.), civil servant Francis Massey (Raghuvir Yadav) works at the office of the deputy commissioner, and obsessively cultivates his attachment to British culture, religion, and administrators, especially his new boss, Charles Adams. Both men marry and continue to bond over the task of empire building, but Massey's excessive devotion gets him in trouble, first for tampering with the books, and finally for murder. Sentenced to hang, Massey wrongly believes that Charles will save him, and finally fantasizes that Charles will take his life in an ultimate act of comradeship. Available on video from the National Film Development Corporation, Mumbai. In *Shatranj Ke Khilari* ([*The Chess Players*], Satyajit Ray, based on the story by Munshi Premchand, in Urdu, 1977, 133 min.), the year is 1856; the British develop their designs on the kingdom of Avadh (Lucknow), ruled by Nawab Wajid Ali. Two of his courtiers, the urbane Mirza Sajjad Ali and Mir Roshan Ali, spend their days playing chess, despite the impending political crisis and the complaints and adulteries of their wives. General Outram presents an ultimatum to the king, who promptly surrenders the crown with great ceremony. The chess players leave town to continue their match in the country, as the files of redcoats march past on their way to Lucknow. Since his death, Ray's films have become increasingly available commercially on video, in both India and the West.

5. Nitin Karani, "India's First Gay Film," *Bombay Dost* 5, nos. 2–3 (n.d. ca. 1997): 18.

6. Lawrence Cohen, "The Pleasures of Castration: The Postoperative Status of Hijras, Jankhas, and Academics," in *Sexual Nature Sexual Culture*, ed. Paul Abramson and Steven Pinkerton (Chicago: University of Chicago Press, 1995), 276–403.

7. See Judith Butler, *Gender Trouble: Feminism and the Subversion of Identity* (New York: Routledge, 1990).

8. See Eve Kosofsky Sedgwick, *Epistemology of the Closet* (Berkeley and Los Angeles: University of California Press, 1990).

9. In a more recent appearance in Govind Nihalani's socially conscious foray into Bollywood, *Takshak* (2000), Bose's gay iconicity is exploited in a role as an especially perverse and sadistic villain who is even seen working out at the gym!

10. Sudhir Mahadevan, "*English August*: The Uses of Holding Your Own," *Deep Focus* 7, nos. 3–4 (1997–98): 75–82.

11. Ashis Nandy defends Ray against 1970s nationalist attacks on his "orientalist" depiction of Wajid Ali; see "An Intelligent Critic's Guide to Indian Cinema—II," *Deep Focus* 1, no. 2 (1988): 53–60, developing ideas from his own 1981 review of the film, and his *The Intimate Enemy: Loss and Recovery of Self under Colonialism* (Delhi: Oxford University Press, 1983). Some years later, in the same periodical, Vinay Lal offered a more detailed assessment of the issues at stake, making more use of cinematic terms of reference and contemporary sex/gender theory: "Sexuality in *The Chess Players*," *Deep Focus* (1996): 48–58. Lawrence Cohen joined the fray in passing in "Castration," scolding Nandy for the way his abstractions of masculinity bypass the political materiality of "thirdness" and its very real stakes for real bodies.

12. Cohen, "Castration," 298.

13. Ashok Jethanandani, "Festival of Fire: Homosexuals as Scapegoats of a Frustrated Society," *Trikone* 2, no. 4 (1987): 1, 5.

14. Whether or not colonialism itself serves as a metaphor for the submission of Indian middle classes and intellectuals to a corrupt and authoritarian state is of course another question. It must not be forgotten that *The Chess Players* was gestated during the Emergency, when Aesopian language was de rigeur for any filmmaker not already in bed with Sanjay Gandhi.

15. For example, the video documentary on the Mumbai "gay community," *Pink Moon* (Prabal Baruah, English, 1999), shown at the Mumbai International Film Festival 2000, was pitifully inept in its futile attempt to move beyond its outsider status vis-à-vis the distrustful outsider milieu that is its subject, substituting stiff interviews with "experts" for encounters with enfranchised social agents. Other recent parallel videos of note are Nishit Saran's *Summer in My Veins* (in English, 1999), a first-person cinéma vérité documentary diary of coming out, Western-style; Naveen Kishore's *Performing the Goddess* (in Bengali, 1999), an interview portrait of a traditional male-to-female transgender thespian that raises questions of indigenous same-sex models; and Balan's *Male Flower* (in Malayalam, 1995), another transgender portrait, this time female-to-male and set in Kerala.

14

Queer Pleasures for Queer People

Film, Television, and Queer Sexuality in India

Shohini Ghosh

In the feature film *Hera Pheri* (*The Con Job*, 2000), Raju (Akshay Kumar), an underpaid worker in a small laundry, dreams of a lavish and exotic lifestyle. The dream, articulated through a song, shows him driving expensive cars, cavorting with women, and visiting exotic locales. In this transnational landscape he spots a row of bikini-clad women lying on the beach and sunning their backs. An excited Raju leaps into the air, lands next to them, and propositions them through song. As the women respond by turning their faces toward him, they turn out to be bikini-clad men in blond wigs! A surprised and amused Raju jumps into the sea, and beckons them to follow. As he runs on, the men also jump into the sea and chase him. This brief but determined queer disruption is emblematic of queer emergence in the transnationalized mediascape of popular culture in the last decade.[1]

Popular Cinema and Same-Sex Love

Popular films enjoy an iconic status among gay and lesbian subcultures in India even though explicit references to homosexuality have been largely absent from mainstream commercial films.[2] A spectator's engagement with any cultural text is complex and is negotiated variously through a multiplicity of identities. It has often been suggested that queer people have a special relationship with cinema. Queer film scholarship on Hollywood cinema has pointed out that a particular stance or gesture of certain actresses like Marlene Dietrich or cross-dressing by Greta Garbo often has greater resonance for queerly predisposed viewers than do explicit gay or lesbian characters. In an overwhelmingly heterosexual popular culture, reading "against the grain" becomes a significant imperative.[3]

However, it is important to avoid crude essentialism in such a formulation. It has been somewhat unproblematically claimed, for instance, that "lesbian-feminist readers resist 'heterotexts' by privately rewriting and thus appropriating them as lesbian texts."[4] The totalizing claim that a lesbian can "cut a hole" through the narrative labyrinth and "follow her own path" flattens the complicated process of negotiating texts and creates a monolithic queer spectator. Sexual difference is only one among many identities that constitute the spectator. Furthermore, socially imposed identities may not determine personal identifications and political allegiances. This is not to suggest that constitutive identities are irrelevant, but that there may not be a direct correspondence between social identity and identification. Without being essentialist, therefore, it is possible to examine how queerness may complicate the gaze.

I suggest that one reason Bombay cinema has had a special attraction for queer subcultures is its privileging of romantic love as the most important of all emotions. This passionate engagement with love has been articulated not so much through plot as through song and dance sequences. Explicit depictions of homosexual love have been absent from popular cinema except in minor subplots or comic relief. But Bombay cinema has a continuous tradition of framing narratives with the love of two friends. These buddy films can be read as evocative of homoerotic love, suggested through overlapping boundaries between love and friendship.

In *Namak Haram* (*The Traitor*, 1973) a passionate and homoerotic story about two male friends, one protagonist declares, "Without friendship there is no love. Without love there is no friendship." In a popular song from another buddy melodrama, *Dosti* (*Friendship*, 1964), love and friendship figure as inseparable: "If friendship is the brother, the sister is love." Most importantly, since Bombay cinema rarely represents romance in a sexually explicit way, the cinematic tropes deployed to represent love are similar, even identical, to those depicting friendship. *Dosti* is the story of love between two poor and physically disabled young men who live together and struggle to survive in the city. This story of passionate friendship is narrated through established tropes of romance, separation, and eventual reconciliation extrapolated directly from the conventions of heterosexual love in popular cinema. *Dosti* can be read as addressing the issue of homosexuality through the deployment of disability as an allegory of difference.[5]

Like *Namak Haram*, *Anand* (*Joy*, 1970) places two men in the diagetic space conventionally occupied by heterosexual couples. Both films were directed by Hrishikesh Mukherjee and feature 1970s superstar Rajesh Khanna in an intense, passionate, and exclusive relationship with emerging superstar Amitabh Bachchan. In both films, Khanna plays the role of the hyperemotional, feminized man while Bachchan plays the intense, brooding lover consumed simultaneously by love for the other man and rage at finally losing him. In these parables of love and eventual loss, the feminized man dies in the arms of his distraught partner. The passion that marks the emotional trajectory of heterosexual love stories is revisited with perhaps greater intensity. In both films, the men have heterosexual love interests either in the past or in the present but minimal space is provided for elaboration on these interests.

Heterosexual involvement notwithstanding, men choose other men as their most important partners in films like *Sholay* (*Embers*, 1975), *Anurodh* (*Request*, 1977), *Yaraana* (*Friendship*, 1981), *Naam* (*Name*, 1986) and *Main Khilari, Tu Anari* (*I Am the Expert and You the Amateur*, 1994). *Sholay*, starring a large number of male and female stars, was the most successful film in Indian cinema up to the late 1980s.

In this action romance, intense love and loyalty bond the two central male protagonists. The shy, brooding Jai (Amitabh Bachchan) is silently attracted to a widow
in the village (Jaya Bhaduri), while the more ebullient Veeru (Dharmendra) falls
for Basanti (Hema Malini), a garrulous woman from the same village. One day a
drunken Veeru forces a reluctant Jai to go and arrange his wedding with Basanti.
In a hugely popular comic sequence, Jai jeopardizes Veeru's wedding while negotiating the match with Basanti's elderly *Mausi* ("maternal aunt"):

MAUSI: What kind of family does he come from? I need to find out. What kind of
    man is he? And what does he earn?

JAI: As far as income is concerned . . . well, once he has a family he will start
    earning.

MAUSI: You mean he has no income?

JAI: When did I say that, Mausi? Now look . . . no one can win every day, you
    see . . . so sometimes he loses.

MAUSI: Loses?

JAI: Gambling is like that. What can I say?

MAUSI: Is he a gambler?

JAI: No, no, Mausi . . . what are you saying? He is a straightforward, honest
    man. But when one drinks, one does lose one's sense of good and bad.

MAUSI: He's a gambler, he's an alcoholic yet you continue to say he's a nice man.

JAI: You don't know Veeru. He's a simple and honest man. Just let him marry
    Basanti and you will see, once he is married he will stop visiting the cour-
    tesan.

MAUSI: That's all that was left. So he visits a courtesan as well?

JAI: So what's wrong with that? Even kings and emperors used to visit courte-
    sans.

MAUSI: I see! Now will you tell me what lineage your meritorious friend
    descends from?

JAI: As soon as we get to know, we will let you know, Mausi. (*Pause*). Should I
    consider the proposal accepted?

Understandably, Mausi sends Jai away. This sequence is commonly read as a clever
maneuver by which Jai tries to prevent Veeru from marrying too hastily. However,
it can also be read as Jai jealously guarding his relationship with Veeru from any
permanent heterosexual intrusion.

The tradition of same-sex love and bonding among men continues today. Films
like *Naam* and *Chal Mere Bhai* (*Come on, Brother*, 2000), starring Sanjay Dutt and
Salman Khan, walked the tightrope between sibling affection and sexual love.
Today, the implicit homoeroticism of these films is evident not just to queer subcultures but even to sections of the mainstream press. Reviewing the film, Maithili
Rao writes that it is about "two brothers who not only get up to the usual brotherly high jinks but hug and kiss and dance and sleep together . . . [the film] will
be grist to the academic mill churning out readings of the homoerotic subtext of
mainstream Hindi films." [6]

In popular cinema, love between women has not enjoyed the same narrative centrality as love between men. Female bonding, while appearing around the margins, has almost always lacked the vitality of male bonding. Female homoeroticism appeared fleetingly in films like *Razia Sultan* (*Queen Razia*, 1983), *Mere Mehboob* (*My Beloved*, 1963), *Humjoli* (*Beloved Friend*, 1970), and *Yeh Aag Kab Bujhegi* (*When Will This Fire Be Quenched?*, 1991), and self-consciously in Shyam Benegal's *Mandi* (*Brothel*, 1983). The most obvious reason for this absence is the male-centeredness of popular cinema's narratives. Barring genres that privilege the female protagonist, such as the courtesan genre, women never enjoyed the same central significance that male protagonists did. The 1990s finally heralded the shifts and ruptures whereby narrative spaces conventionally held by men began to be occupied by women.

A significant development of the 1990s mediascape was the arrival of both real and representational women. There was a marked increase in women's participation in the newly emerging media industries. Both film and television saw a proliferation of women as central protagonists. Kalpana Lajmi's *Rudaali* (*The Mourner*, 1992), based on a story by Mahashweta Devi, was the first equivalent to the male buddy film. Two of Bombay's top actresses, Dimple Kapadia and Rakhee, occupy the diagetic space of leading protagonists. The film, however, displaced the homoeroticism implicit in the original story by disclosing the two women to be mother and daughter.

The 1990s also saw the emergence of India's first female superstar, Madhuri Dixit, who starred in several films like *Ansoo Baney Angarey* (*Tears Turn to Fire*, 1993), *Anjam* (*Consequence*, 1994), and *Mrityudand* (*Death Penalty*, 1997), where she occupies the diagetic space reserved for the male hero.[7] The Bombay film industry's first significant transgender film, *Tamanna* (*Desire*, 1997), was scripted by a woman, Tanuja Chandra, who subsequently directed two major woman-centered films, *Dushman* (*Enemy*, 1998) and *Sangharsh* (*Struggle*, 1999). Actress Pooja Bhatt produced all three films. *Tamanna*'s central character is a *hijra* (eunuch) played by Paresh Rawal.[8] The controversial dance from the film *Khalnayak* (*Villain*, 1993), which started a cycle of anxieties around sex and sexuality, was choreographed by a woman, Saroj Khan, the leading choreographer of the 1990s. The dancer-choreographer combination of Saroj Khan and Madhuri Dixit sparked off a series of panic attacks around an excess of "vulgarity and obscenity." I have argued elsewhere that the moral panics of the 1990s indicted the emerging sexually assertive female body.[9]

In a break with cinematic convention, female protagonists in the 1990s began to reconcile in their characters the personae of both heroine and vamp. In pre-1990s cinema, the Westernized vamp (immortalized by stars like Helen, Bindu, Shashikala, and Aruna Irani) stood in opposition to the chaste and virtuous heroine. The smoking, drinking, and seducing vamp embodied sexual agency while the heroine subordinated her sexual desires to romantic love, duty, and honor. Yet the spaces of the vamp and heroine were never hermetically sealed. The heroine often took on the persona of the vamp but always for a noble purpose, not for pleasure. In *Inteqam* (*Revenge*, 1969) the seemingly inebriated heroine (Sadhana) performs a seductive dance as part of a vendetta plot. In *Ziddi* (*The Headstrong One*, 1964) the heroine (Asha Parekh) discovers she is the daughter of a criminal and then performs a vampish dance to dissuade her lover from marrying her. This trope of pretense and masquerade continues in the 1990s but with critical ruptures. The female protagonist now expresses sexual desire both inside and outside the masquerade, and even without the compulsions of romantic love. In the 1990s, moral panic was frequently ignited by such sequences.

The Obsession with Obscenity

Two moments of homoerotically inflected visual pleasure embodying transgressive desire occur around the songs "Choli ke Peechey Kya Hai" ("What Is behind the Blouse?") from the film *Khalnayak* (*The Villain*, 1993) and "Didi Tera Devar Divana" ("Elder Sister, Your Husband's Younger Brother Is Crazy") from the film *Hum Apke Hain Kaun* (*Who Am I of Yours?*, 1994).

"Choli ke Peechey Kya Hai" sparked off a raging controversy over whether or not the song was vulgar and obscene. The Hindu Right's attack on the song was led by the Shiv Sena in Bombay and the Akhil Bharatiya Vidyarthi Parishad, the student wing of the Bharatiya Janata Party, in Delhi. A Delhi-based organization filed a petition in court asking that the song be deleted from the film and its sale on audiocassettes be banned. The petition alleged that the song was "vulgar, against public morality and decency." When the trial court dismissed the case, the petitioners appealed to the High Court, claiming that the trial court's decision would be an incentive to increased vulgarity in films, which in turn would lead to increased sexual harassment. After watching the film, the High Court dismissed the petition in a fourteen-page order on the grounds that (a) film viewing is voluntary, involving no coercion; (b) it is "sheer imagination" to claim that songs lead to harassment; and (c) the alleged vulgarity is acceptable in keeping with the "latest developments" in the film world.

None of the protesters mentioned that the film actually features two versions of the song. The second version is a parody sung by men, which culminates in the female protagonist being assaulted by the male protagonist. It is interesting that despite their anxiety around "increased sexual harassment," the protesters did not demand a ban on the version that actually depicted violence against women but on the one that represented women's sexual agency.

Song and dance sequences are integral to the formal aesthetics of much of popular cinema. As powerful vehicles of emotions and aspirations, songs and dances often play out Mikhail Bakhtin's notion of the carnivalesque.[10] For Bakhtin, the carnival is an expression of people's "second life" that shatters, symbolically at least, "all oppressive hierarchies." The transporting into art of "the spirit of popular festivities" allows people "a brief entry into a symbolic sphere of utopian freedom." It is "a joyful affirmation of change, a dress rehearsal for utopia" that allows those on the margins to move to the center of the narrative.[11] For this reason, song and dance sequences allow female protagonists a centrality that film narratives usually deny them. Masquerade or the device of performance-within-performance allows female protagonists to escape narrative constraints and indulge in excess, badness, abandon, and revelry.

"Choli ke Peechey" represents both a continuation of the transgressive conventions of the masquerade and a departure from them. The song is performed by two women (Ila Aruna and Neena Gupta) who masquerade as courtesans in order to nab an escaped convict. Of the two female studio singers who recorded the song, one has a conventionally high female voice and the other a deep, husky voice. In an inversion of the conventional heterosexual duet, sung by male and female singers, the two women engage in erotic banter. One asks, "What is behind the blouse?" and the other replies, "My heart is behind my blouse / This heart I will give to my lover." The song self-reflexively alludes to the notion of masquerade, using the motifs of covering and uncovering. It is also replete with direct and indirect references to the female body. It is as though the women use their own bodies to disguise their desires. One entreats, "Tell us. What should the boy be like? / What should the girl be like?" to which the other replies, "The girl should be like me. The boy should be like you. / That's when love will begin to be fun." Despite the silent presence of the male spectators in the visual sequence, the homoerotic possibilities of the mise-en-scène are not displaced for the queerly predisposed reader. Although the playful homoeroticism of the song did not figure in the public debate, I suggest that it contributed to the discomfort some listeners experienced.

Film songs acquire an independent life in Indian society because they are often released on audiocassette before the film's release, and song sequences are shown on television on their own. Long after a film is forgotten, one or more of its songs may continue to be very popular, regularly played on radio and TV. Many people know scores of songs by heart and they are sung as entertainment at weddings and other festivities. The proliferation of music channels and music-based shows on television have provided the narratives of song and dance sequences even greater autonomy.

Despite the controversy, "Choli ke Peechey" was the most popular song of the year and won all the major music awards. While it became the target of vituperative attacks, it also inspired several more sexually charged songs, like "Choli ke Neechey Tabahi" ("There Is Destruction under My Blouse") from *Khalnayika* (*The She-Villain*, 1993), "Sexy, Sexy, Sexy, Mujhe Log Boley" ("People Say I Am Sexy, Sexy, Sexy") from *Khuddar* (*The Self-Respecting One*, 1993), "Meri Pant Bhi Sexy" ("My Pants Are Sexy") from *Dulara* (*The Loved One*, 1993), "Sarkayleo Khatiya Jada Lage" ("Bring Your Bed Closer, I am Cold") from *Raja Babu* (*His Lordship*, 1993). The Central Board of Film Certification (CBFC) came down heavily on the word *sexy*, and in the *Khuddar* song and others, the word *sexy* was changed to *baby*. The censored version was shown on state-owned TV channels while satellite channels continued to show the "sexy" version. The most stringent public indictment was reserved for the "Sarkayleo Khatia" song. Performed by Govinda and Karishma Kapoor, this song and dance dispensed with all romantic conventions to explicitly simulate the act of heterosexual copulation.

Some of these songs became targets for moral panic and others fell through the cracks. Thus, while protests around speech and representation extended the limits of intolerance, the speech or representation itself extended the limits of tolerance, even resistance.

The most popular song to emerge after "Choli ke Peechey" was "Didi Tera Devar Divana" from the 1994 blockbuster *Hum Apke Hain Kaun?* (*HAHK*). Replete with iconography popularized by the Hindu Right, *HAHK* evokes a conservative and renascent Hindu ambience. It tells the story of love between Nisha (Madhuri Dixit) and her sister Puja's husband's younger brother, Prem (Salman Khan). When Puja dies in an accident, leaving behind a small child, her natal and marital families decide to marry Nisha to Puja's widower Rajesh (Monish Behl). Nisha and Prem decide to sacrifice their love at the altar of family duty. All ends well because Rajesh realizes that Prem and Nisha are in love. But the happy ending occurs only after it is established that the virtuous individual will not marry against the family's wishes.

While pre-1990s films frequently valorized rebel lovers who resisted family opposition to either live or die together, 1990s family films tend to show duty and family honor triumphing over love. Released at the peak of moral panic around "obscenity and vulgarity," HAHK was applauded as clean and wholesome entertainment. Although some reviewers initially dismissed it as nothing but a long wedding video, the film, described by its director Sooraj Barjatya as "a tribute to the Indian joint family," proved hugely successful. Best described as a family carnival, HAHK presents a dream family that negotiates its way through numerous social and religious rituals with few crises and fewer conflicts. In the fragmented and dystopian early 1990s, following the national crisis precipitated by the demolition of the Babri Masjid, HAHK proffered the utopic dream of a happy and supportive community.[12] In an interview a year later, filmmaker Saeed Mirza remarked that after the violent fallout of the demolition, HAHK was the first healing touch.

The film attempts to resurrect a vamp of sorts in the character of Mamiji (Bindu). Mamiji ("maternal uncle's wife") becomes the prime vehicle for the film's conservative attitude toward women. Unlike the self-effacing Puja, Mamiji is selfish, materialistic, and vain. Her mirror and beauty aids function as signifiers of her narcissistic self-absorption. Beauty, the film seems to suggest, is natural for Puja and Nisha but artificially constructed for Mamiji. Her niece Rita (Sahila Chaddha) is better liked by the family but does not measure up to the film's notion of ideal womanhood. She dares to be in love with Prem although she is not good enough for him. This is quickly established when she prepares a dessert for him using salt instead of sugar. A sneering Prem tells her she is not cut out for the job. As he turns away, she asks, "If I cannot make [dessert] for you, who will?" In reply, as it were, the scene cuts to a shot of Nisha. Later, we discover that among the qualities that endear Nisha to Prem's family is her ability to make just the dessert he likes. At the end of the film, Rita marries one of the film's minor comic characters, an old-fashioned Sanskrit scholar working on a study of Shakuntala.[13] His obsession with Rita and his fantasies of her as Shakuntala provide comic relief. Although Rita disdains him throughout the film she accepts him at the end.

Ironically, even a conservative text like HAHK is not inured to ruptures. As Ashis Nandy points out, "like all politics, the politics of popular cinema too . . . has to be all things to all people, by restoring balances and reconciling opposites, often within the same film."[14] The song "Didi, Tera Devar" offers a reconciliatory moment when the good woman momentarily becomes a "bad" woman and the "bad" woman's "badness" is celebrated. As the second line of the song's refrain declares, "Hai Ram, kudiyon ka hai zamana" ("Oh God, this era belongs to girls!").

The song occurs during an elaborate ritual celebrating the pregnancy of Nisha's sister, Puja. In a large room filled with brightly dressed women, with Puja and others as spectators, Nisha sings the song and in her dance mime switches between playing herself and playing Puja. Men are scrupulously kept out of this all-woman celebration but Prem spies on it through a window. He is scandalized when the short-haired Rita appears, wearing clothes identical to his. Through the song, Nisha makes fun of Prem, Puja's husband's younger brother. She says he is so busy flirting with women that he never gets anything right; for example, when Puja asks to eat something sour, he gives her something sweet, and so on. Throughout the song, Nisha and Rita interact erotically while masquerading as Puja and her brother-in-law Prem. Pretending to be a doctor, Rita presses a stethoscope to Nisha's bosom. She then takes out a syringe, frightening the women with its size. Finally she jumps onto a bed with the phallic syringe, and both she and Nisha disappear beneath the bed sheets. There is a top angle shot of the other women watching Nisha and Rita as they cavort while completely covered by the sheets. A spectator pulls off the sheet, doctor Rita runs off, and in an exaggerated mime Nisha complains about "his" misconduct.

The song is transgressive at several levels. At one level, it allows for sexually suggestive banter between Nisha and Prem as she flirts with his surrogate while he plays the voyeur. At another level, it suggests an erotic relationship between Prem and Puja. Indian literature and cinema have a long tradition of playing with the erotic charge between a woman and her husband's younger brother, as well as that between a man and his wife's younger sister. Hence, the audience could easily pick up this dimension.[15] The tongue-in-cheek lament that Prem always runs the wrong errand implies that he does not get the "right" message.

At the most explicit level, the song depicts erotic play between two women. Since Prem has rejected Rita, what better revenge than to romance the beautiful Nisha? Hindi cinema has frequently made space for lesbian eroticism in situations of masquerade and theater. In *Mere Mehboob* (*My Lover*, 1963) a romantic interaction is briefly developed between two women, one of whom pretends to be a surrogate male. There are similar situations in *Yeh Aag Kab Bujhegi* (*When Will This Fire Be Quenched*, 1991) and *Kamasutra* (1997). Soon after *HAHK*, Deepa Mehta used the same trope in *Fire* to explicitly sexualize a relationship between two women. In *HAHK*, the cross-dressed Rita flirts with Nisha until the real brother-in-law Prem joins the dance to restore heteronormativity. However, those who enter queer spaces seldom escape unscathed. The song's finale represents yet another moment of queer rupture, with Prem appearing in drag, complete with lingerie, full makeup, and "pregnant" belly.

"Didi, Tera Devar" was the most popular song of 1994 and topped the charts for nearly a year. Yet it neither provoked anxiety nor elicited discussion. There could be several reasons for this. *HAHK* was advertised and received as a "family film." Family films are defined as those the whole family can watch together, so they are supposed to be free of violence and sexual content. When sung without the visuals, this song, unlike "Choli ke Peechey," sounds like affectionate banter between a married woman and her brother-in-law and is consequently devoid of homoeroticism. It is also important that in the popular television programs that show songs on their own, the visual sequence that accompanied this song, and therefore had wider out-of-context exposure in middle-class homes, was a censored version that carefully excluded the cross-dressed Rita. In order to see the uncensored version, viewers would have to watch the film in a movie theater and therefore in its larger familial context, which might defuse its homoerotic content. On the other hand, when "Choli ke Peechey" is shown out of context on television, its homoerotic content is foregrounded. This might have been largely responsible for the controversy it aroused.

Multiple Registers of the Mediascape

The early 1990s witnessed three major developments that had far-reaching implications for the country and also for media and communications.[16] In 1991 the government confronted a severe economic crisis in the country by initiating a widespread restructuring of the economy with globalization as its main imperative. This was accompanied by an "open-sky" policy that initiated and accelerated the proliferation of satellite television.[17] These two developments ran parallel to what is perhaps the darkest phenomenon of contemporary times—the rise of the Hindu Right, led by its political front the Bharatiya Janata Party (BJP).[18] On December 6, 1992, supporters and allies of the Hindu Right demolished the Babri Masjid, an ancient mosque, thereby dealing a critical blow to India's claims to democracy and secularism. The rise of the Hindu Right was concurrent with the disintegration of the congress and the growth of regional parties that came to power in some states. In 1998, the BJP, with the help of coalition partners, formed the national government.

The inception and proliferation of satellite television and cable networks dismantled the state's monopoly over television and provided South Asian urban audiences with a wide variety of Indian and international programming. The contemporaneous spread of other communication technologies, with computer interfaces, national and international phone lines, e-mail, and fax becoming available in small commercial centers on almost every corner in the cities and towns, radically transformed the practices of the urban middle class. These technological innovations changed the nature of contemporary spectatorship by allowing for a multiplicity of images and channels, panoramic screens, multiplexes, interactivity, and virtuality. This seemed frighteningly uncontrollable in contrast to the earlier predictable flow of images from state-controlled media.

The anxieties caused by the larger cultural transition were expressed primarily in debates about the media. Due to its visibility, geographical spread, and psychological presence in homes, television (and thereby popular culture) loomed large in the urban mind as an ominous and unmanageable force.[19] Satellite TV was blamed for causing deviant acts and for corroding Indian "culture and tradition." The increased availability of film images in urban middle-class homes was largely responsible for the anxiety. The 1990s witnessed spiraling moral panic around speech and representations alleged to be vulgar and obscene. In my essay "The Troubled Existence of Sex and Sexuality" I argued that the debate on censorship is actually a debate about sex and sexuality that has revolved primarily, if not exclusively, around sexual speech to the exclusion of hate speech, even though the 1990s saw the rise of the Hindu Right and the circulation of hate speech against Muslims and Christians who are minorites in India.[20] However, attempts to censor sexual speech also paradoxically resulted in issues around homosexuality gaining greater visibility. Homophobic speech, intended to counter queer speech and representation, inadvertently resulted in circulating it.

Examples are the controversies around the Chelsea Jeans advertisement and the Nikki Tonite television show in 1995. The Chelsea Jeans company shot into notoriety when they started an ad campaign with the copy "F*** off! Leave Us Alone." The photograph that appeared above the copy showed two women in leather and jeans standing in close proximity to one another. (Ruth Vanita's chapter in this volume shows this ad; see 9, fig. 9.2, page 140) Earlier, the same copy had appeared with two men in similar proximity. Soon after its appearance in popular magazines, the ad featuring the women had to be withdrawn under pressure from the Ad Standards Council and the Advertising Agencies Association of India. The president of the latter organization condemned the "obscene advertisement" without seeing it and blamed publications that carried it.[21] In the same month a controversy broke out over a Star TV talk show called *Nikki Tonite* that featured gay rights activist Ashok Row Kavi. During the interview, Kavi described Mahatma Gandhi as a "bastard *bania* [a reference to his caste]." A huge public uproar followed, including protests by outraged parliamentarians and Gandhi's own family. Confronted with allegations of arrogance and cultural imperialism, Star TV issued a public apology and scrapped the talk show. It is possible that part of the anxiety generated by the show had to do with Kavi's homosexuality even though it was never explicitly mentioned except indirectly by a schoolteacher who later wanted to know why Star TV had interviewed "that funny guy anyway." Writer Shobha De was the only one to draw attention, in one of her newspaper columns, to the underlying homophobia and sexism in this "get the gay, get the gal" situation.[22] The withdrawal of *Nikki Tonite* notwithstanding, television continued to create spaces for diverse articulations around sexualities. Queerness was also emerging in the larger public culture, in popular magazines, theater, dance, and other cultural forms.[23]

Female Bonding Queers the Television Landscape

In the 1990s, television challenged heteronormativity by creating space for queer representations. Queer issues were addressed directly in newscasts, talk shows, and interviews. Queer spaces also appeared in television serials. Teleserials (like soap operas) narrate stories set in domestic spaces that are generally conflicted, if not entirely dystopian. By representing the family and home as fraught with marital discord, domestic violence, sibling rivalry, property disputes, and oppressive familial hierarchies, television ruptures the utopic imaginary of "Indian family values." This move runs counter to the trend of the family film inaugurated in the 1990s by *HAHK* and continued by films like *Dilwale Dulhaniya Le Jayenge* (*The One with a Heart Will Take the Bride*, 1995), *Hum Dil De Chuke Sanam* (*I Have Already Given My Heart, My Love*, 1999), and *Hum Saath Saath Hain* (*We Are All Together*, 1999). These "family films" evoke nostalgia for the Indian joint family whose members live in utopic harmony, and were the most successful Indian films of the 1990s.

Television's challenge to family values and sexual normativity includes the representation of characters who, while not explicitly identified as gay or lesbian, rupture heterosexist assumptions. Television serials and sitcoms recoded spaces that were hitherto distinctly masculine or feminine. For instance, one of the five protagonists of the hugely popular Zee TV serial *Hum Panch* (*Five of Us*) is the masculinized Kajal, who always wears men's clothing. A tough with contacts in the local underworld, she is called Kajalbhai by her four sisters and the rest of the neighborhood.[24] Kajal disdains all feminine preoccupations, including marriage, and dreams of running a mafia empire. In one fantasy episode Kajalbhai's father dreams of celebrating his fiftieth wedding anniversary with his five daughters. Kajalbhai is the only daughter who is single; she is a powerful underworld don. In another episode, an excessively feminine male dance instructor falls in love with Kajalbhai. The narrative builds a deliberate and playful ambiguity about whether the dance instructor falls in love with Kajal because he mistakes her for a man or because he feels attracted to a masculine woman.

Just as women on television move out of spaces and practices designated feminine, male protagonists also resist conventional masculine expectations. Dilruba in the sitcom *Shriman Shrimati* (*Mr. and Mrs.*) is the excessively feminine househusband of a famous actress. Despite his marriage and attempts to flirt with the woman next door, Dilruba carries all the subcultural markers of an effeminate gay man.

Through its promotionals and music videos, television also dismantles the male-female bipolarity of performative space. A notable example is the performance and persona of popular singer Phalguni Pathak. She has a voice that is conventionally feminine in the female studio singer tradition dominated by Lata Mangeshkar, but her clothes and persona disrupt notions of conventional femininity. Her music videos often have a heterosexual narrative but these are ruptured by homoerotic suggestiveness. In one video, Pathak calls a woman up on stage and dances with her, thereby inverting a common heterosexual performance tradition. In the music video of her song "Meri Chunar Udd Udd Jaye" ("My Scarf Flies, Flies Away," 2000), Pathak cleverly inserts herself into the diagetic space of the heterosexual hero.

In the 1990s, television also foregrounds a theme that was underrepresented in pre-1990s films and television—female friendship and female bonding. Serials like *Adhikar* (*Rights*), *Mujhe Chand Chahiye* (*I Want the Moon*), *Kabhi Kabhi* (*Once in a While*), and *Hasratein* (*Desires*) depicted female friendships of varying intensity. In *Mujhe Chand Chahiye*, a young girl falls in love with a woman teacher.[25] One of the longest running and most critically acclaimed serials, *Adhikar*, revolves around the relationship between a Muslim woman, Shama, and a Hindu woman, Amita. Their male partners notwithstanding, the relationship between the two women remains the most privileged. In one episode, a crisis is precipitated when Amita's boyfriend, Narendra, jealously accuses her of loving Shama more than she loves him. In another episode, an anguished Amita tells her father that she and Shama are one and inseparable. The women are not oblivious to their mutual attraction, as is evident from a sequence in the twenty-third episode. This sequence is located in Shama's marital home after Amita has provided eloquent testimony in a rape trial. Amita and Shama are seated on the bed looking deep into one another's eyes. Amita raises her mouth and blows a kiss toward Shama, who laughs:

SHAMA: You are unmatched. Only you could have said what you did in that crowded courtroom. When I look at you, I wonder—what am I? I am probably beautiful, my complexion is fair—what else do I have? But look at you—I so feel like kissing you.

AMITA: Don't! You'll spoil me. Narendra has already kissed me.

SHAMA: What? You shameless woman . . .

AMITA: Why shameless? If he doesn't kiss me on such an occasion . . .

SHAMA: What nonsense you can speak . . .

AMITA: Even when I speak nonsense, I speak the truth. Really—if I were a man, I swear, I would have married you.

SHAMA [*laughing*]: Earlier, I only suspected it but now it's confirmed.

AMITA: What?

SHAMA: That you are not a woman. There is nothing womanlike in you. There is a man inside you.

AMITA [*delighted*]: Wah! How well you have spoken. That's precisely the point, my friend. You have described me absolutely right. Now, what prize should I give you? Should I kiss you?

[*Leans over and kisses her on her lips*]

AMITA: I've kissed you.

SHAMA [*delighted and laughing*]: You've polluted me.

AMITA: Pollution is part of our religion—not yours. You people drink from the same cup.

SHAMA: I don't want to drink from everyone's cup.

AMITA: Not everyone—just two! [*Holds up two fingers.*]

Shama [*amused*]: Two?

AMITA: Yes. First it was only me. [Your husband] arrived much later.

Shama [*amused, looks toward the door of the room to see if anyone has heard*]: Idiot! You don't care about your reputation. At least care about mine. [*She gets up and shuts the door, returns and sits in front of Amita*]. What would have happened if someone had heard?

Blouse and Brother-in-Law Go up in Flames

The "coming out" of women in film and TV narrative spaces reached its climax with the release of Deepa Mehta's *Fire* (1998), a film about two sisters-in-law falling in love in a middle-class urban joint family. The public debate around the film marks a significant moment in the history of sexual politics in India. In "Choli ke Peechey" and "Didi, Tera Devar" homoeroticism is subtextual; in *Fire* it is explicit. Through print and electronic reproduction, *Fire* enabled an unprecedented circulation of speech and representation around queerness. The film's publicity posters showed the two women occupying the same diagetic space as that occupied by heterosexual lovers in cinematic convention.

As I have argued elsewhere, *Fire* is important because it is the first Indian film to bring women in love out of the margins into the mainstream and provide a body to the shadowlike subliminal lesbian of film narrative in India.[26] *Fire* makes visible the "invisible" lesbian by representing her on screen, but also facilitates the reclamation of other texts by validating an interpretive strategy that makes lesbianism visible. Gayatri Gopinath has noted how the film produces a "complicated relay between female homosociality and female homoerotic practices."[27] For instance, she describes the sequence in which Sita massages Radha's feet at a family picnic as "transforming a daily female homosocial activity into an intensely homoerotic one." Similarly, Sita oiling Radha's hair becomes charged with erotic energy in view of their sexual involvement.

By explicitly crossing the line between homosociality and homosexuality, *Fire* allows a new interpretive strategy to come into play. The homosocial domestic and other activities that Radha and Sita engage in are the same activities we have seen

Indian women perform before, both in earlier cinematic representations and in real life. By framing these activities in social, romantic, erotic, and, finally, explicitly sexual frameworks, the film inscribes these images with an ambiguity that dislocates any deterministic reading of them as heterosexual. Thus, an interpretive strategy that was hitherto deployed in Indian gay/lesbian subcultures has now imploded into Indian public culture.

A joke making the rounds in Delhi's feminist circles is that *Fire* has "outed" all lesbians by making it impossible to camouflage the homoerotic as the homosocial. There is both anxiety and affection in the circulation of this joke. Women's rights activist Madhu Kishwar, who characterizes *Fire* as a "mean spirited caricature of middle class family life among urban Hindus," writes that by "pushing Radha and Sita into the lesbian mould . . . Mehta has done a disservice to the cause of women."[28] She further argues, "There is a danger that many of those exposed to this controversy will learn to view all such signs of affection through the prism of homosexuality. As a consequence many women may feel inhibited in expressing physical fondness for other women for fear of being branded as lesbians." Such deeply homophobic perspectives have been contested by other Indian feminists. When a feminist scholar in one seminar remarked that *Fire* had "vulgarized" interpretations of women's physical relationships by leading people to conclude that such contacts were necessarily sexual, another feminist scholar pointed out that the "vulgarity" perhaps lay in concluding that all such contact was necessarily *non*sexual.

Conclusion

The arrival of this homoerotic and ambivalent discourse has reopened older texts for newer readings. Interestingly, two of the most popular films of the 1990s, *Dil To Pagal Hai* (*The Heart Is Crazy*, 1999) and *Kuch Kuch Hota Hai* (*A Little Something Happens*, 1998), explore the overlap of friendship and eroticism. The title song of *Dil To Pagal Hai* uses the visual conventions of the romantic duet in a situation wherein the couples depicted are not romantically involved, even though two of the four individuals are interested in the possibility. In *Kuch Kuch Hota Hai*, a young girl facilitates a romantic reunion between her father (Shah Rukh Khan) and his female friend from college, Anjali (Kajol). She does so after reading a letter that her mother had written to her before dying. The letter reads, "Your father always said love is friendship. I could become his friend but never his best friend. I could never take Anjali's place in his life and heart."

In conclusion, I would like to revisit the sequence from *Hera Pheri* in which Raju (Akshay Kumar) encounters the bikini-clad men in blond wigs. Audiences today may not feel compelled to believe that Raju (Akshay Kumar) was disappointed to discover that the bikini-clad women on the beach were men, especially since he remains without any heterosexual love interest throughout the film, despite the heteronormative fantasy song sequences that feature him. Since his role in the homoerotic buddy film *Mein Khilari Tu Anari*, actor Akshay Kumar has become an Indian gay male icon, so this reading of the beach scene is a very likely subcultural reading. But today it may no longer be just a subcultural reading. In other words, the answer to *Choli ke Peechey Kya Hai?* has become complicated indeed.

Notes

I am grateful to Roopa Dhawan for helpful suggestions and to Shikha Jhingan for drawing my attention to several instances of homoeroticism on television. Ruth Vanita has been the inspiration for this chapter and has provided excellent feedback on the various drafts. To her I dedicate this paper.

1. I will use the term *queer* instead of *gay/lesbian* except when specifically referring to same-sex relationships.

2. I use the term *popular cinema* to refer only to Hindi films produced in Bombay and not to films produced in south India.

3. "Misreading" has been an important strategy for queer pleasure. The documentary *The Celluloid Closet* (1995), based on Vito Russo's book and directed by Robert Epstein and Jeffrey Freidman, is an important text for cultural theorists, as it focuses on the unmistakable mark of homosexuality in films that may or may not have been queer identified.

4. Bonnie Zimmerman, "Perverse Reading," in *Sexual Practice and Textual Theory*, ed. Susan J. Wolfe and Julia Penelope (Cambridge: Blackwell, 1993), 135–49.

5. For an analysis of *Dosti* and *Tamanna* along these lines, see Ruth Vanita, "*Dosti* to *Tamanna*: Love between Men in Hindi Cinema," in *Everyday Life in South Asia*, ed. Sarah Lamb and Diane Mines (New York: St Martin's Press, 2001).

6. Maithili Rao, "*Chal Mere Bhai*: Brotherly Boredom," *Zee Premiere*, June 2000, 118–19.

7. Shohini Ghosh, "The Cult of Madhuri," *Gentleman*, October 1998, 26–28, and "The Importance of Being Madhuri," *Zee Premiere*, December 2000, 164–69. Dixit is considered India's first female superstar because she was the highest paid actress in Bombay, delivering a superhit every year between 1988 and 1994. Dixit was the first and only heroine whose name presold films in different distribution territories. In posters, billboards, and publicity material, Dixit demanded the same prominence as the hero. In many film posters she even predominated. Throughout the 1990s, film and trade magazines referred to her as the first female superstar and the biggest star after Amitabh Bachchan.

8. In the same year, 1997, were released Amol Palekar's *Daayra* (*The Square Hole*) and Kalpana Lajmi's *Darmiyan* (*In Between*). Both films were frontal engagements with issues of transgender, transsexuality, and intersexuality. In *Daayra*, the protagonist is a cross-dressed dancer, while *Darmiyan* depicted the relationship of an aging actress with her *hijra* (eunuch) son.

9. Shohini Ghosh, "The Troubled Existence of Sex and Sexuality: Feminists Engage with Censorship," in *Image Journeys: Audio-Visual Media and Cultural Change in India*, ed. Christiane Brosius and Melissa Butcher (New Delhi: Sage, 1999).

10. Mikhail Bakhtin, *Rabelais and His World*, trans. Helene Islowsky (Bloomington: Indiana University Press, 1984).

11. Robert Stam, "Of Cannibals and Carnivals," in *Subversive Pleasures: Bakhtin, Cultural Criticism, and Film,* ed. Robert Stam (Baltimore: Johns Hopkins University Press, 1989). This is not to suggest that song and dance sequences are necessarily subversive. On the contrary, these sequences are often deployed to privilege dominant discourses.

12. On December 6, 1992, activists of the Hindu Right destroyed a medieval mosque called the Babri Masjid in Ayodhya, Uttar Pradesh. This culmination of a protracted dispute was the Hindu Right's method of demonstrating its supposed strength and superiority to Indian Muslims. The trouble began decades earlier, when the Hindu Right claimed that the Babri Mosque, built by emperor Babar, stood on the site of a temple he had destroyed that marked the birthplace of the Hindu God Rama. The demolition of the Babri Masjid led to riots in several parts of India.

13. Shakuntala is a character in the ancient Sanskrit epic *Mahabharata* about whom Sanskrit poet Kalidasa wrote a play in the fourth century B.C.E. For more information see Romila Thapar's *Sakuntala: Texts, Readings, Histories* (New Delhi: Kali For Women, 1999).

14. Ashis Nandy, "The Politics of Triviality," *Times of India*, February 11, 1995.

15. In my essay titled "Hum Apke Hain Koun?! Pluralizing Pleasures of Viewership," *Social Scientist* (New Delhi), March–April 2000, I suggest that the primary emotional thread running through the film is the erotic attraction between Prem and Puja.

16. This paper traces the cartography of the 1990s mediascape primarily through urban clusters in India . Satellite TV is largely an urban middle-class phenomenon. Urban India has 14.98 million cable homes as opposed to 4.7 million in rural areas (Source: Indian Readership Survey cited in Brosius and Butcher, *Image Journeys*, 308–9).

17. For a detailed discussion see Nikhil Sinha, "Doordarshan, Public Service, and the Impact of Globalization," in *Broadcasting Reform in India*, ed. M. E. Price and S. G. Verhulst (Delhi: Oxford University Press, 1998). Sinha points out that throughout the 1970s and 1980s India was in the vanguard of the call for a "new world information and communication order." Anxieties around cultural imperialism and the domination of Western news organizations resulted in a closed broadcasting system, which was consonant with India's closed economic system.

18. Hindu nationalists in Indian politics are led by their political front, the Bharatiya Janata Party, and draw their ideological impetus from the parent organization Rashtriya Swayam Sewak Sangh. More aggressive and militant factions include the Bajrang Dal, the Vishwa Hindu Parishad, and the Shiv Sena.

19. Ashis Nandy, *The Secret Politics of Our Desires: Innocence, Culpability, and Indian Popular Cinema,* (New Delhi: Oxford University Press, 1998).

20. In *Image Journey*, ed. Brosius and Butcher.

21. Ruchira Singh, "Homosexuality and the Bold Art of Selling Jeans," *Asian Age*, May 26, 1995.

22. Shobha De, "What Has Nikki Done That Others Have Not Done in the Past?" *Times of India*, May 12, 1995, 3.

23. Urban English-language theater in India has a tradition of representing queerness onstage, which dates back to at least the late 1970s. In the 1990s there was a greater proliferation of such plays, including those of gay dramatist Mahesh Dattani; Rustom Bharucha's Hindi adaptation of Manuel Puig's *The Kiss of the Spiderwoman* (1993) and Barry John's *Varun* (1993). In 1994–95 Shantanu Nagpal produced the play *O Bulky Stomach.* "The Friends of Siddhartha Gautam" started holding an annual festival of queer films in Delhi, commemorating the 1993 death of gay activist Siddhartha Gautam. In 1998 Nishit Saran's *Summer in My Veins*, an autobiographical video documentary on coming out to his mother, was widely screened and discussed.

24. The suffix *bhai* literally means "brother," but also refers to members of the underworld.

25. *Mujhe Chand Chahiye* is based on a Hindi novel by Surinder Verma (Delhi: Radhakrishna Prakashan, 1993). I am grateful to Shikha Jhingan for drawing my attention to this serial.

26. Shohini Ghosh, "From the Frying Pan to the Fire," *Studies in Humanities and Social Sciences* (Indian Institute of Advanced Studies, Shimla) 5, no. 2 (1998): 143–49.

27. Gayatri Gopinath, "Nostalgia, Desire, Diaspora: South Asian Sexualities in Motion," *Positions: East Asia Cultures Critique* 5, n. 2 (1997): 467–87.

28. Madhu Kishwar, "Naïve Outpourings of a Self-Hating Indian," *Manushi* 19 (1989): 3–14.

15

On Fire

Sexuality and Its Incitements

Geeta Patel

Act 1: Scene 1

April 7, 1998: The film *Fire* is screened at a small women's college on the eastern seaboard of the United States. Filmmaker Deepa Mehta attends the screening.

The show is packed. The South Asian gossip circuit has done its work; grandmothers, parents, babies pile into the theater: for once the fire regulations have been slightly abrogated. The film ends, the filmmaker moves to the podium. A young South Asian woman, who heads the college's South Asian student association, stands up. Men, she says, are unsatisfactorily depicted; the film violates Indian manhood. The filmmaker judiciously points out her subtle evocations of men in pain. The conversation veers to other topics.

Act 1: Scene 2

May 1998: The semester has come to a close at this women's college. E-mails are flying around the local circuit. The donors, whose money was used to screen *Fire* as well as other films by women filmmakers such as Trinh. T. Minh-Ha, Chantal Ackerman, and the Soong sisters, have asked to see the films. The daughter of the donor family calls a male administrator who oversees funding bequests. She is extremely upset about *Fire*. She says her money has gone to fund porn, the film is offensive, and students on a women's campus should not be exposed to it. Her mother is perturbed and if her late father knew that his money was being used thus he would withdraw funds from the institution. The administrator asks the associate director of the museum to be more careful about the content of programs funded with this money. The museum director asks him to tell the family that funders cannot control art and that academic professionals have the right to decide what they teach, view, and show. But the family is adamant.

Act 1: Scene 3

I talk to students about the controversy. The students are mainly white, with a sprinkling of Latinas. They are unaware of the brouhaha at the museum. When I tell them about it, they say that the head of the Indian students' association, who is a nonresident Indian woman, dislikes the representations of Indian men in the film. It seems to me that the silence that follows my attempts to continue this discussion signals a retreat—the voice of the designated "other" has spoken her will, through a speaking of her injury. As Lauren Berlant points out in her recent work, the other's injured self will win out because the discourse of personal injury seems impassable.[1] The discussion is forestalled by the violations of community constructed as a violation of an "ethnic" person by "bad" representations—not of her own body, but of the bodies of the male gender that shares community rights. Bad representations of Indian men hurt Indian women in the diaspora. Another sentence slips into the silence—isn't Deepa Mehta Canadian, not really Indian? Suddenly we are haunted by a struggle among women in the diaspora over how the behavior of Indian men (in India) ought to look. This is a curious upturning of the formula coined by feminists to expose the allegiances of colonial administrators when they endorsed policies that ostensibly protected Indian women, "white men saving brown (Indian) women from brown men."[2] The formula's reiteration for the diasporic text of *Fire* is "brown women must protect brown men (and themselves) from white men and women."

At other public forums where *Fire* provokes South Asian U.S. diasporic audiences, it is clear that their anxieties about masculinities are based on the assumption that the only bodies possible for raced beings in the United States are wounded bodies, bodies whose rights have been abrogated by being produced as failed or excessive. Under these circumstances playing up failure returns raced bodies to the circuit of failure. What cannot be completely spoken here is that this virile heteromasculinity is fully implicated in a right-wing production of proper masculine citizenship in South Asia. Forms of this South Asian, explicitly upper-middle-class masculinity, and the women whose instrumentality make it possible, are sold on Internet websites in the diaspora under the guise of "just culture" to garner financial support for right-wing constituencies in India that will come to be deployed against *Fire* shortly after it opens in India.[3]

Act 2: Scenes 1, 2, 3, 4, and So On . . .

November 13, 1998: India's Censor Board of Film Certification, headed by former film star Asha Parekh, releases *Fire* uncut, stating that it is an important movie for Indian women. It asks for only one change—that the name Sita be changed to Nita. The shift in names articulates an awareness of modern evocations of Indian womanhood that signify through the mythic character Sita.

Fire opens in forty-two theaters throughout India.[4] In a November 6 article in the *Times of India* the film's distributor described its subject matter as masturbation and lesbian interaction. He is cautious about its prospects for popularity since it has no songs. It shows to packed houses, 80 to 90 percent full. Several theaters have women-only shows.

November 20, 1998: Meenakshi Shinde, reviewing *Fire* in the *Times of India* says the film is about Indian gender politics and traditional values.[5] She believes that labeling it a lesbian film does it a disservice, because it is more than that. It questions traditional values, accepts pluralistic sexual choices, and expresses love with a dignity and compassion rarely seen in Indian cinema. Shinde thinks that Mehta's lesbians, two middle-class housewives who walk out of the domestic scene, are not "real" lesbians like those generated by Suniti Namjoshi and Pratibha Parmar. They are generated by the nonresident Mehta's longing for women's liberation on home ground. Unlike the Indian student in the United States, Shinde feels that the men in the film are sympathetic characters, in pain and constrained by tradition, as are the women.

November 28, 1998: The Bharatiya Janata Party (BJP), which, in coalition with several regional parties, is in power in Delhi, loses elections in several key states. Their losses in Maharashtra, Delhi, and Rajasthan are predicted in the polls. The Congress Party sweeps the elections in Rajasthan. It gets 197 seats, and the ruling Bharatiya Janata Party manages to grab only 33.[6] The price of onions has brought the house down.[7] Women, assiduously wooed but never adequately represented, have voted the BJP out.[8] The nuclear tests, conducted in Pokhran in Rajasthan, which prime minister Atal Behari Vajpayee hoped would consolidate power for his party, have not succeeded in helping them win the local elections. The BJP is faced with the possibility of a no-confidence motion at the center.[9]

December 3, 1998: Home minister L. K. Advani assures the upper house of the parliament, Rajya Sabha, that arrangements have been made to protect a Muslim shrine in Karnataka that has recently turned controversial. Extreme right-wing organizations, the Vishwa Hindu Parishad and the Bajrang Dal, announce that they will lead suicide squads to liberate the shrine. Groups of Hindu worshippers, given special dispensation by the Karnataka High Court, arrive for three days to observe Guru Dattatreya Jayanti. Muslims visit the shrine to commemorate the burial of Peer Baba Budhan. When Advani discusses the shrine, his statements appear to give Hindus and Muslims equal access to the shrine's past and the property that forms its domain. Muslim congressmen point out that the shrine is Muslim, and Hindus are only "given permission" to come and pray. The parliament in Delhi is worried about a repeat of the Babri Masjid events that culminated in its demolition by right-wingers on December 6, 1992.[10]

Property grounds these calls for "communalized" access to particular spaces. The Hindu right wing challenges the rights of the Muslims, who have religious use of particular pieces of property, mandated by a particular rendition of the historical record. The right-wing challenge to the record attempts to put right what they see as use in seizure and a failure to read the historical through the mythic. Nationalism is contested in the process. With this particular Hindu challenge comes a branded body. To order up nostalgic, desiring affiliation to a plot of land, "Hinduness" must be produced as violated by the historical violences attributed to Islam.[11] Hinduness must also be deployed as the proper national religion of the country, for which support must be garnered through state institutions.

December 3, 1998: Newspapers report that two hundred Shiv Sainiks, men and women, storm into two theaters, the New Empire and Cinemax, in Mumbai (Bombay), break the glass on the display windows, damage a ticket counter, and burn posters of *Fire*. In the photographs, women of the Mahila Agadhi, the women's wing of the far-right organization Shiv Sena) are seen brandishing sticks in front of the theater. They allege that the film is "against Indian tradition." A portion of the burden for defending "Indian tradition" is given to women. Filmmakers, writers, and artists protest the violent shutting down of the film.

December 3, 1998: Twenty-nine people are arrested in Mumbai (three municipal corporators, and three Shiv Sena chiefs) in connection with the vandalized film houses. Cinema managers shut down showings of *Fire* in Mumbai. Many cinemagoers complain of being prevented from seeing the film. Meena Kulkarni, of the Shiv Sena women's wing, argues, "If women's physical needs get fulfilled through lesbian acts, the institution of marriage will collapse, reproduction of human beings will stop." *Outlook* sardonically responds, "Not a supreme tragedy . . . in a nation of 950 million."[12]

While the film is showing in Delhi theaters, about forty Shiv Sena members attack; at the Regal cinema they smash windows, tear posters, and attempt to storm the manager's office. The noon show resumes after they leave but the management cancels the last three shows. "This means that a mob can enter any house and do whatever they feel like," the beleaguered manager comments. Jai Bhagwan Goyal, head of the Shiv Sena's Delhi unit, threatens more attacks. Opposition members of parliament's upper house, the Rajya Sabha, lodge complaints against the Sena's attempts to shut the film down. One of them, senior journalist Kuldip Nayyar, is upset that the Maharashtra chief minister and the Shiv Sena chief Bal Thackeray are supporting the arson, and asks for government intervention against them. Nayyar, heckled throughout by BJP supporters, draws attention to the discrepancy that the film showed uninterrupted for about two weeks before it was attacked. Another journalist member, Pritish Nandy, links assassins and lesbians when he refers to the Maharashtra government's earlier ban on the play *Me Nathuram Godse Boltoy* (*I, Nathuram Godse, Speak*) which explored the psyche of Mahatma Gandhi's assassin. Nandy argues that by banning such perspectives, the government makes heroes of their protagonists. He suggests that the women's wings of various parties should take the matter up and leave the government to more important national business. Bharati Ray is the only member who connects the shrine at Karnataka with *Fire*, since positions on both are mediated by the demands of fascism. As the Campaign for Lesbian Rights will later point out (in an August 1999 report), the "private," religion and sexuality, must be kept outside the provenance of the state; in my view, this makes this realm subject to violence that the state supports by not intervening.[13]

December 4, 1998: Ayodhya is tense on the eve of the anniversary of the Babri Masjid demolition. The administration is sealing off routes into town. The Vishwa Hindu Parishad and Bajrang Dal are gearing up to celebrate December 6, as Shaurya Divas (Valor Day). Muslim families, for perhaps the first time, are refusing to leave town this week, but will keep their shutters down and wear black badges, symbolic of protest. Uttar Pradesh education minister says his ministry has asked all schools to recite the Vande Mataram (Prayer to the Motherland as embodied goddess, which Muslims consider idolatrous) and the Saraswati Vandana (prayer to the Hindu goddess of learning, Saraswati). Whether this will actually occur is a matter of some dispute since the Uttar Pradesh chief minister informed the prime minister the previous week that the recitations would not be compulsory.

The opposition in the Lok Sabha (the lower house of parliament, at the center) is upset at the BJP government's failure to protect minorities. Christians plan a nationwide protest against increasing violence.[14]

December 5, 1998: Six people, including well-respected senior film star Dilip Kumar (a Muslim with a Hindu screen name), bring a writ to the Supreme Court. The writ calls for the right to show *Fire* and asks for protection of screenings of the film under articles 14, 19, 21, and 25 of the Indian Constitution.[15] These articles promise the right to equality, life and liberty, freedom of speech and expression, freedom of conscience and free expression of religious practice and belief, and the right to hold peaceful meetings.

December 6, 1998: Southern states Kerala and Karnataka are torn by violence as two thousand protesters are arrested on the sixth anniversary of the Babri Masjid demolition. Five hundred are incarcerated in Ayodhya. Demonstrations are held in Delhi to condemn the demolition of the mosque.[16]

December 7, 1998: About twelve members of the Shiv Sena try to stop viewers from entering the Chaplin Auditorium in Calcutta, where *Fire* is showing. Viewers charge out of the hall and disperse demonstrators; the protest turns into a name-calling match.

December 7, 1998, to February 18, 1999: The Campaign for Lesbian Rights (CALERI), a coalition of various groups, is formed in Delhi. Lesbian organization Stree Sangam in Mumbai, SALGA in New York, and CALERI in Delhi take to the streets in various cities in India and the diaspora in support of the film, garnering support from a range of organizations, and individuals.[17] Demonstrators (including thirty-two civil liberties and women's organizations, lesbians, and artists) hold a candlelight vigil in front of the Regal cinema in Delhi on December 7.

December 14, 1998: Shiv Sena men strip to their underwear and cavort in front of actor Dilip Kumar's house. They accuse him of encouraging the exhibition of perverse acts and say he should not be offended when they too behave, as is their right, in an obscene manner. Dilip Kumar asks the Supreme Court for protection for himself, Javed Akhtar (husband of Shabana Azmi, who plays Radha in *Fire*), and Deepa Mehta.

December 16, 1998: The Supreme Court issues notices to the Maharashtra and Union governments and the Shiv Sena that a police investigation will be conducted into the violent protests against *Fire*. The court "will examine the larger question— whether a grievance can be settled by resorting to violence." The court gives the police four weeks, and asks for adequate protection for the petitioners. Proceedings in both houses of parliament in Delhi are dominated by the *Fire* debate.[18]

December 18, 1998: Cinemax will resume showing the movie. The police commissioner says "arrangements" have been made to ensure its unhampered viewing, but a hundred young BJP members in Kanpur, including Satish Misra and Ahmad Ali Khan, circle the Sundar Theater and tear down posters. They have filed a petition in the district court against the film.[19]

The end of December, 1998: Shiv Sainiks in Tamil Nadu and Varanasi protest the film.

January 10, 1999: The Bajrang Dal announces that it will file a court petition against both *Fire* and an anthology by Pakistani women, *So That You Can Know Me*. They allege that both hurt the sentiments of Hindus.

February 12, 1999: The Censor Board rereleases *Fire*, again without a cut.

February 24: Uday Dhurat, producer of the play on Gandhi's assassin, Nathuram Godse (*Me Nathuram Godse Boltoy*), urges the Maharashtra government to lift the ban on his play. His insistence on a reassessment is based on the fact that *Fire* has been cleared of wrongdoing.

February 25: *Fire* opens again.

February 26: Both English and Hindi versions of the film reopen in Delhi. There seems to be a failure of consensus between the various right-wing factions on the question of *Fire*. Extreme right-wingers attack Prime Minister Vajpayee, and Shiv Sena chief Thackeray says that BJP minister Sushma Swaraj might have been responsible for helping *Fire* along since she is a good friend of Shabana Azmi's.[20]

Made by a diasporic intellectual, *Fire* resonates simultaneously with Indianness in the diaspora and in India. The film does its work through nostalgic evocations around cultural nationalism, and around national, bounded, citizenship produced in a call for culture versus art enunciated through religion/tradition.[21] In thinking about *Fire* as a node of incitement, I turned to other such nodes, around which protests by the right wing, traveling across the borders of India, transacted sites of queerness.

The first two diasporic events occurred almost contiguously. One was an episode of the TV show *Xena, Warrior Princess* called "The Way," which featured Hindu gods Krishna and Hanuman, and goddess Kali. Krishna helped save Xena's friend Gabrielle. Although the Xena-Gabrielle friendship is never depicted or named as explicitly lesbian in the show, and both women have heterosexual involvements from time to time, Hindu protesters possibly in the United States argued that this "makes it appear that Krishna and Vedic religion approves of and gives its blessing to homosexual relationships."[22] The episode aired for the first time on April 2, 1999, but the right wing got involved on a global scale in October 1999. The second incident occurred in Australia, where protesters claimed that homosexual activists attacked Hindus by displaying mock Vishnus and statues of Ganesh during a gay and lesbian "Sleaze Ball" on October 2, 1999.[23] Both episodes are important in that they display the deployment of Hindutva (nationalized Hinduism as concerned by the Hindu Right), through different organizational voices on the Internet, to generate opinion and in the process produce public spheres. The third protest was against the cover of *Genre* magazine, which had a picture of Krishna played by a young actor who is known as an occasional drag queen.[24] I will not discuss this here, because the protests have stayed within California.[25]

In the case of *Xena*, the World Vaishnava Association (WVA), a handmaiden of the Hare Krishna movement, collated letters, news stories, and reader responses in a time line that anyone could access on the World Wide Web. In the case of the ball, an umbrella organization with the unexplained acronym AARV, whose aim was to educate "the public with information you normally wouldn't find in the mainstream media about religious vilification,"[26] was formed through a coalition that included the Vishwa Hindu Parishad America, the World Vaishnava Association, Stop Promoting Homosexuality, the Hindu Student Council, EarthSave, and American Hindus against Defamation. The AARV, like the WVA, produced a time line in which a reader could access all web links.

In both cases, the alternative public spheres presented the appearance of a free and open discussion, but then posed the incidents they discussed as anti-Hindu, antifamily, even antihumanity. The reach of the message was clearly global. The continual temporality produced by the time lines, spatialized to cover a range of sources from different national papers and transnational organizations, expanded the reach of the protests. The links that each time line permitted, each opening up to highlights, required the reader to travel time and traverse the web illusion of extended, mapped spaces.[27]

Both episodes spoke to the denigration of Hindu religious beliefs through representation of icons used to promote homosexuality, which therefore returned the representation of Hindus to "second-class" and "lower-class" citizens of the world.[28] Both, and more explicitly that of *Xena*, also spoke to the truth of religion as a uniform, unified truth where fiction had no place.[29] The AARV concerned itself with the "well-being" of religions, and produced this well-being through the possibilities of the wounded, offended body of religion. Religious fullness, wholeness, and health came into their own through the wounds inflicted on the body of Hinduism by its imbrication with nonheterosexual sexualities.

So what was the complete body of religion offered on the web to readers who could access it through a computer? The Vaishnava Network proposes an explicitly religious one. The Hindunet, however, couches religion as a cultural public sphere, set apart from both economics and politics.[30] Though its webpage is liberally littered with the term *Hindu*, which is the qualifier preceding *universe, kids, youth, women, books, links,* and *web*, it also promises much more: "a survey, events, resource center, culture, authors, courses, activism, noble causes, Support-a-child"; some of these links are specifically organized by region and city.

Hindunet is appropriately consistent on the questions of women and sexuality. On the women's page the married woman is depicted as rounded, round-eyed, covered head to foot in a sari, holding a baby, and standing beside her husband, a young girl between them. The radical assumption here is that the girl is the oldest child, followed perhaps by a young boy.[31] This picture is centered between the four directions, each depicted by a square. North and south contain spirituality and family, east and west biographies that range from sages to scientists. Below this are two more squares: "Issues and Politics" and "Workplace." Between these two is an older woman, clothed in a white sari and speaking through a microphone, one fist up in the air. Information on religion is given in two ways, through "original sources" and through the *Amar Chitra Katha*, a comic-book version of epic and religious stories.

On the pages dedicated to both men and women, most of the postings are by men, who seem to be the assumed audience and speakers. Pages that promise neutral access to the day's news quickly lead one into scenes of violence and violation. The pages are sprinkled with accounts of terrorism, relations between India and Pakistan, Hindu/Muslim and Hindu/Christian relationships in India, and a history of India that begins with the Aryan invasion theory, and ends with the Islamic invasion of India and the effect of Islamic rule (never represented as a theory that could be disputed). India under Islamic rule begins with the Ramjanamabhoomi temple, travels through the destruction of Hindu temples, and almost comes to a close with the Hindu Holocaust Museum. Here tradition is constructed through modernity, through mandating desire around the lost, around use in seizure, around sentimental affiliation to land and place. Proper religion becomes national religion, here articulated specifically as discussions conducted freely in the diaspora and on the net. The site for economics is empty; it has no postings. So the question of capital is deliberately occluded, inserted without question into the simple spaces of religion/culture and public discussion.

I suggest, using the dense time line above, that the discussions on *Fire* must be considered in relation to other kinds of debates that seem to be different but, in fact, cohere around certain nodes. One is the question of religion, and the ways in which religion gets settled into certain notions of property—religion as property, and religion sedimented into certain sites that become the proper property of groups of citizens. The other is the question of cultural capital, what constitutes capital that ought to travel, and traverse national borders, and what constitutes the proper allocation of capital in relation to nationhood, nationality, and locality. The third is the way that voting banks come to define what forms political opinion. Publics are formed in relation to property and capital, simultaneously religious, political, and cultural.

The circulations, repressions, and incitements of *Fire* were profoundly and simultaneously national and transnational. The film reads very differently in the United States and in South Asia. In the United States, a viewer unfamiliar with South Asia or a South Asian viewer unfamiliar with Indian-language literature and cinema needs to have the film "unpacked." Its registers have to be translated to enable them to see its alignments and gestures. In South Asia, the film can be read immediately, and what may be subtly subdued for diasporic audiences becomes needlessly excessive. Here the film overstates its critiques of tradition and Hinduism through the disruption of a middle-class urban household. The plot can be understood as one safely ensconced in a Bollywood lineage—the trials and tribulations of difficult love. The plot of love against the grain within a joint family is a genre with a long history, beginning in the nineteenth century (think Rabindranath Tagore). In that genre, heteropatriarchy of a sort (usually anticolonial nationalist) is the ground for the disruptions provoked by desire and the resolutions offered for those provocations. Rarely does the triangle go awry, lodging desire in places of sexed sameness.

Deepa Mehta, presenting her film in the United States, was repeatedly asked again and again to account for her representations of masculinity. The nonresident Indian student at the women's college was no exception—she spoke for the violations that circulate in the diaspora. In South Asia, neither men nor women seem to have obsessed about masculinity. Instead, the three nodes of incitement, each produced through the other, were Indianness, women and sexuality, and the freedom of expression in the public sphere. Who has the right to speak for and about tradition, to control its production? Who has the right to speak for and of women? And who has the right to control discourse in the public sphere?

Both supporters and detractors of *Fire* assumed that women were the film's ideal target audience. Its supporters said that all women needed to see the film; they claimed that women turned out in droves to see it and that some women saw it more than once. The film was said to provide choices for *all* women.

Some of the film's detractors invoked motherhood; they claimed that *some* innocent women who had never been exposed to such perversion would be swayed by the film to leave their failing marriages and their children. They would learn the "message" (from the West) that they did not have to stay in miserable marriages.[32] "Dilip Kumar," said Bal Thackeray, "seems to have spread like an epidemic guidelines to unhappy wives not to depend on their husbands."[33] The sanctity of marriage was at stake and a Muslim man was responsible for the infection. Though lesbians were rarely named, they were the specter in these right-wing speakings. Discussions of tradition occasionally incorporated lesbians only to expel them into the West. In one newspaper report of the Delhi candlelight vigil, the CALERI banner with the slogan "We are Indians. Lesbianism is our heritage" was described thus: "A banner screamed." The verb *screamed* indicates how those who break the social contract of silence are heard.[34]

In India, in the debates over *Fire*, the public sphere was formed through bringing together nationalisms and Indian citizenship. The fiduciary rights that accrued to cultural nationalisms were at stake here, and the debate centered around what forms these nationalisms might take and which citizens would have access to controlling them. The debate resolved itself in appeals to the Constitution. The writ in the Supreme Court sought to uphold all citizens' democratic rights to free viewing and showing. It demanded an open public sphere, open for discussion, open to multiple representations that could be articulated and watched in safety. The film was sent back to the Board of Censors under Article 6 of the Constitution, which permits the government to evoke emergency powers against threats to public order. Shabana Azmi, writing in the *Times of India* on December 17, 1998, critiqued Bal Thackeray for intimating that Dilip Kumar, a Muslim, could not be a real Indian.[35]

One moment seems worth noting because though it appeared incidental to the general discussion on *Fire* it is relevant to the debates on culture traveling across borders. Pramod Mahajan, Maharashtra minister for information and broadcasting), said that the right to information should be guarded as a basic right of the people and that his ministry would endeavor to ensure that information would be free from control. However, he added that as far as Indian films were concerned, since many of them were being seen by Indians abroad, steps should be taken to ensure that the country's culture was projected correctly.[36]

In the disputes conducted around *Xena, Warrior Princess* and the "Sleaze Ball," the publics produced outside the borders of the nation-state argued for a different assembly of nationality and citizenship from those that speak from within India. Nationality traverses borders, finding its definition through religion as culture, and carries with it the same registers that religious/cultural nationality has when it is defined within India. But citizenship breaks away from the territory of the Indian nation-state to be articulated as either global, or as a kind of belonging vested in another, "Western" nation, such as the United States, Australia, New Zealand, or Great Britain. This despite, or perhaps because of, the ways that groups whose range of operation is supposed to be India, like the right-wing organization Vishwa Hindu Parishad, cross borders to ensure that proper attitudes to Hinduism prevail and that only appropriate kinds of Hinduism travel as culture outside Indian borders. Cultural capital is invested in religion, and its control is mandated through the body whose investments have failed. Political capital or economic capital is never explicitly marked or marketed. Its returns appear only in sidelines—as investments in bodies thought to have lost class, or in histories that propose Hinduism as a religion under siege by the political mandates thought to reside in Muslim communities.

Whether viewed in Indian diasporic communities, at a women's college in the United States, or in urban sites in India, *Fire* seems to have demanded that its detractors and supporters consider sex in relation to political economies. This becomes clearer when *Fire* is considered in relation to representations of religion/sexuality, like *Xena* and the ball, that occur in the diaspora. It is clear that the force of the debates, discussions, evocations of sex framed by capital, differentials in value, tradition, nation, diaspora, and the censorship of speech constituted as "excitable" engenders bodies sometimes abstract, sometimes unfortunately solid—body violated, male or female religious body sullied, women's bodies that need protection, body that must have access to liberal rights of choice, of freedom. It is also clear that bringing *Fire* to the fore to site these discussions aligns them in unexpected ways. It transmutes the body of person into forms of the body politic. And here, the formal representatives of politicized bodies negotiate traversals—sometimes deliberately, sometimes askance.

The ethics offered by the continuing disputations around *Fire* need to be contextualized by a rigorous demand neither to keep the constitutional body politic as nation in place, nor to keep the body as body violated (and therefore squelching discussion) in place. These ethics also need to be attended to in their particularities, so that, at the very least, communalism becomes an axis for an analysis of same-sex sexuality, and so that the kinds of gestures, modulations, differences that transmute bodies away from abstraction are taken into account in matters of policy (that themselves attend to such located transmutations).

Notes

1. Lauren Berlant, *The Queen of America Goes to Washington: Essays on Sex and Citizenship* (Durham: Duke University Press, 1997).

2. Lata Mani, *Contentious Traditions: The Debate on Sati in Colonial India* (Berkeley and Los Angeles: University of California Press, 1998).

3. "The Hindu Universe: Hindu Resource Center, http://www.hindunet.org/home.shtml. Vijay Prasad, "Of Authentic Cultural Lives," and "Of Yankee Hindutva," in *The Karma of Brown Folk* (Minneapolis: University of Minnesota Press, 2000).

4. "Film *Fire* Opens," The *Times of India* (*TOI*) November 13, 1998.

5. "That Burning Feeling," *TOI*, November 20, 1998.

6. K. T. R. Menon, "Winter Woes Await Government as Parliament Reopens," *TOI*, November 30, 1998.

7. "Vegetable Stew," *Outlook*, November 9, 1998.

8. Zoya Hasan, "When BJP Discovered Eve," and "The Female Principle, '98," in *Outlook*, January 19, 1998.

9. "Winter Woes," *TOI*, November 30, 1998.

10. N. Chandra Mohan, "Sangh Parivar Twists Government's Arm on Insurance Bill," *TOI*, December 3, 1998.

11. "Human Rights Violations against Hindu Minorities in Various Countries," http://www.hindunet.org/human_rights focuses on genocide against Hindus by Muslims in Kashmir, Pakistan, Bangladesh, and Fiji. Another webpage sponsored by the Hindu Students Council concentrates on terrorism, including violence by Muslims against Hindus in India. Its address is telling: http://www.hindunet.org/india_terrorism. The link that leads to these from the Hindunet website, which opens with Seva Programs and Support a Child, thus resorting to common global save-the-world sentiment that is comfortingly neutrally charitable, is titled "Social and Contemporary Issues." The list of its links, like its page, seems innocuous. But once one enters any of its domains, one encounters the burning issues of the day, which, in addition to the sites tallied above, include a "Hindu Genocide Museum."

12. Sunil Mehra, Saira Menezes, "What's Burning," *Outlook*, December 14, 1998.

13. Taken from *Lesbian Emergence*, the record and analyses offered by the Campaign for Lesbian Rights, August 1999, New Delhi.

14. "Keshubhai's Remarks Upset Christians," *TOI*, December 4, 1998.

15. "Fire Referred to Censor Board," *TOI*, December 5, 1998.

16. "Masjid Demolition Anniversary," *The Tribune*, December 6, 1998.

17. Mona Bachmann's essay in this volume covers the various resistances, so I do not consider them here. See *Lesbian Emergence*; Nija Asmi and Bina, "Fire, Sparks, and Smouldering Ashes," *Scripts* 1, nos. 2–3 (1999): 17–21; Mukund Padmanabhan, "Freedom and Hurt Sentiment," *TOI*, December 29, 1998; Surabhi Kukke, Svati Shah, and Javed Syed, "The 'Fire' Controversy," *SALGA Newsletter*, http://www.salganyc.org/newspage11.htm.

18. "Sena M. P. Withdraws Remarks against Dilip Kumar," *TOI*, December 16, 1998.

19. "Hearing in *Fire* Case Deferred," *TOI*, December 18, 1998.

20. *TOI*, January 2, 1999; also January 5, 1999, and January 8, 1999.

21. Shohini Ghosh, "From the Frying Pan to the Fire," *Communalism Combat*, January 1999, 16–19; Ratna Kapur, "Is *Fire* about Free Speech? Sex? Or Culture?" *Communalism Combat*, January 1999, 19.

22. www.anotheruniverse.com/tv/xena/thewayprotest.html.

23. http://aarv.net.

24. www.hvk.org/right/htm, www.ncmonline.com/in-depth/2000-04-28/krishna.hmtl; www.indiainnewyork.com/iny042882000/Chronicle/Lord.*html*; www.indiaabroadonline.com/PublicAccess/ia-05052000/*Spirituality/Some.html*; www.rediff.com/us/2000/may/10us4.htm.

25. Phone interview with Lisa Tsering, September 28, 2000. Tsering is the news writer who wrote the initial, syndicated story, in *India-West* on April 27, 2000, and also covered the story of the *Xena* episode.
26. http://aarv.net/about.html.
27. Amit S. Rai, "India On-Line: Electronic Bulletin Boards and the Construction of a Diasporic Hindu Identity," *Diaspora* 4, no. 1(1995): 31–57; Jürgen Habermas, *The Inclusion of the Other: Studies in Political Theory* (Cambridge: MIT Press, 1999).
28. http://aarv.net/article1html; http://aarv.net/asianage.html.
29. http://www.warriorprincess.com/wayprotest.html. The attacks against *Xena* evoked counter-responses by *Xena*-lovers, whose slogan was "Censorship is not the way." Like the right wing, which offered preformatted letters one could send in via the Net to a range of addresses, *Xena* supporters offered the option of an online petition that could be forwarded to the show's producers to help them garner information to keep the episode intact and rebroadcast it.
30. See Bruce Robbins, *Feeling Global: Internationalism in Distress* (New York: New York University Press, 1999); "The Globalization Issue," *Social Text* 60 (1999); and *The Politics of Culture in the Shadow of Capital*, ed. Lisa Lowe and David Lloyd (Durham: Duke University Press, 1997).
31. Families that constitute themselves in hegemonic Hindu terms (having to do with a kind of Hinduism produced from the nineteenth century onward, in the wake of primogeniture and rural property inheritance bills) tended to promote the idea that the ideal eldest child would be a male.
32. There has been a spate of articles (and studies) on the shifting grounds for personhood as South Asia encounters the phenomena associated with globalization, such as the burgeoning of adolescent sexuality; sex education in schools; the variations in "tribal" sexual practices; the breakdown of extended families in urban areas (without an adequate analysis of the return of children to parents in cities where it is often too expensive for married children to support their own households); new desires for commodities, leisure, and entertainment; and body technologies like working out and dieting that can produce the dressed female body that can win international beauty competitions.
33. Rasheeda Bhagat, "Big Brother Thackeray," *Business Line,* December 17, 1998.
34. "The Wrong End of the Telescope," *TOI*, December 6, 1998.
35. Shabana Azmi, "Freedom under Fire: Smokescreen for a Hidden Agenda," *TOI*, December 17, 1998.
36. *"Fire* Not Banned, Says Mahajan," *TOI*, December 8, 1998.

16

After the Fire

Monica Bachmann

In Deepa Mehta's 1998 film *Fire*, the two protagonists discuss the problem of communicating information about their relationship. After Radha's husband walks in on the women while they are being physically intimate, she tells Sita, "I only wish he hadn't found out by accident; I wanted to *tell* him." Sita replies, "What would you have said? 'Goodbye, Ashok, I am leaving you for Sita. I love her but not like a sister-in-law'? Now listen, Radha, there's no word in our language for what we are, how we feel for each other." Radha agrees: "Perhaps you're right. Seeing is less complicated."

This exchange highlights the representational difficulties pertaining not only to the family relations within the film, but also to the film itself, as it circulates in India and elsewhere. As the first widely distributed unambiguous representation of lesbian love in India, *Fire* evoked strong responses from a range of competing and overlapping interests: nationalist, feminist, homophobic, communal, and progay forces have put forward widely varying interpretations of the film's meanings and effects. Radha asserts that seeing is less complicated than telling; however, the firestorm of public discourse raised in response to this film demonstrates that when it comes to the vexed intersection of sexuality and culture, there is nothing simple about either seeing or telling.

While in the West *Fire* is seen primarily as a lesbian movie, in India and among the Indian diaspora the film takes on more complex meanings, participating in related but distinct debates about representations of Hinduism, the influence of the West, standards of obscenity, and the role of women in the family and in society. Critics who want to discuss in the Indian media the politics of lesbianism and its representation must first establish female homosexual relations as a topic separable from these other concerns. But these critics, homophobic and otherwise, inevitably return to the connections between lesbianism and other issues, demonstrating that no single aspect of the film can be entirely separated from the work as a whole, indeed from the larger political and economic relations in which it circulates.

Geeta Patel's essay in this volume recounts in detail the right-wing attack on *Fire* in India; my essay focuses on Indian left-wing, liberal, and feminist debates sparked by the Shiv Sena's attacks on the film. Many writers on all sides assert that the controversy about the film constitutes India's first major public discussion of lesbianism. Like a pyrophyte tree, whose seeds only germinate after exposure to the extreme heat of a forest fire, discourse about female same-sex desire has proliferated following the release of the film.

Some commentators believe that this representation of lesbianism and the ensuing discussion present a danger to society, a corrupting force that will undermine the social order they cherish. Others value the film for precisely the same reason, the open representation of a female homosexual relationship as loving and positive. A number of writers who themselves identify as gay or lesbian testify to the liberating effect of finally seeing this issue brought into the light of day. As S. L., a member of the Campaign for Lesbian Rights, notes, "By the morning of December 8 it had all happened. . . . The word 'lesbian' was on the front pages of every newspaper I picked up in Delhi. LESBIAN. It looked odd and out-of-place."[1] It looked out of place because of what S. L. and other Campaign for Lesbian Rights (CALERI) members refer to as "a conspiracy of silence," the intense social pressure forcing people involved in homosexuality to hide those relations. S. L. describes this conspiracy, and the toll it takes on its victims: "Don't let your family know who you are and how you live, nor many of your friends, certainly not co-workers, not your boss, as also neighbours, not to mention (neither last nor least) your landlords . . . never, never speak about who you are and how you live. Silence. That will protect you."[2] The CALERI report repeatedly expresses the importance of speaking out, breaking the enforced silence about lesbian lives.

In an early response to the film, media studies scholar Shohini Ghosh also discusses the importance of seeing female desire, particularly female same-sex desire, on the screen. Citing Terry Castle's discussion of the apparitional lesbian in numerous Western literary and cinematic works,[3] Ghosh asserts, "Female bonding, whether homosocial or homo-erotic, have been largely absent from the Indian film screen. They have existed either as suggestions or in fleeting moments only to disappear into the margins. *Fire* is the first film to bring women in love out of the margins into the mainstream and provide a body to the shadow-like subliminal lesbian of film narrative in India."[4]

In spite of her criticisms of the film's artistic merit, Ghosh argues that *Fire* is important because it represents female sexual agency and female homosexuality in an unambiguous way. "[T]hose in the audience waiting to see women in love," she writes, "need no longer read against the grain."[5] In an article in the *Economic and Political Weekly*, feminist legal scholar Ratna Kapur echoes this sentiment: "After years we actually have the representation of female sexual pleasure on screen—in this instance lesbian rather than heterosexual pleasure."[6]

These writers figure silence as an obstacle to social change, and assert the role of speech in the process of securing the rights of a group whose oppression has been rendered invisible. This rhetoric, long familiar from the three decades of the West's gay rights movement, also mirrors at least one strand of the Indian women's movement, which has stressed the need for women to begin to speak out about violence and dangers confronted within the family and the workplace. For example, in 1984

Manushi cofounder and editor Madhu Kishwar wrote, "One special feature of women's oppression is the way they have been trained to consider many crucial areas of their oppression and exploitation unmentionable. . . . Unless the censorship imposed on women by their family, community and society at large, and internalized by women in all areas of life, is made a political issue, women's voices are not likely to be heard in social and political life."[7] These comments are particularly interesting in light of Kishwar's recent assertion that silence rather than speech is the best strategy for people involved in homosexual relationships.

In a lengthy, scathing commentary on *Fire* in *Manushi*, Kishwar claims that homosexuals face no persecution in India. She cites two examples of public figures suspected of being or known to be gay, and insists that these figures are publicly respected, and never attacked for their sexuality. Claiming that India presents an open climate for people inclined toward same-sex desire, Kishwar nevertheless herself reveals the workings of homophobia, as she holds out the promise of limited acceptance and tolerance of homosexuality only in the absence of its open expression or representation. "India," she writes, "despite more than two centuries of western influence and indoctrination, has still not become homophobic. While there is pressure on all to get married, this has not resulted in the extinction of sexual engagement with persons of the same gender. A space for bisexuality usually remains."[8] It is surely disingenuous to assume that because homosexual or bisexual behavior is not entirely "extinct" in India, no oppression exists. As *Manushi* has reported many times in other contexts, the pressure to marry is often overwhelming, involving the most extreme coercion through violence and economic necessity. The effects of this enforced heterosexuality on homosexually inclined people is by now well documented.[9] The "space" supposedly available for bisexuality is the space of hiding and dissembling, of risking life, limb, and position.[10]

Lesbians versus Women?

Kishwar sees the open expression of female homoeroticism as a threat to Indian women's ability freely to express physical affection. She cites practices of massage, hugging, and oiling one another's hair as evidence that female-female intimacy is totally accepted among Indians. This tolerance, however, stops short of accepting a lesbian sexual relationship, which might include all the intensity, sexual intimacy, and commitment associated with passionate heterosexual marriage and lover relationships. Kishwar writes that "in most Indian families, even when sexual overtones develop in the relationship of two women situated as are Radha and Sita, no one generally gets upset about it provided people don't go around flaunting their sexual engagement with each other."[11] Purposefully ambiguous, the term *overtones* implies that the relationship might be somewhat erotic, but is not fully sexual. This formulation then denies space to women who do choose to make their relationships with each other overtly sexual. The choice of the loaded word *flaunting* here also betrays the writer's bias: heterosexual relationships that trumpet themselves from the rooftops, as in marriage, are not "flaunting," but homosexual ones that emerge from hiding are.

"By crudely pushing the Radha-Sita relationship into the lesbian mould," Kishwar writes, "Ms Mehta has done a big disservice to the cause of women."[12]

Women here stands in for heterosexual women; apparently lesbians are something other than women. Using a convoluted form of illogic, Kishwar argues that the increasing visibility of lesbian relations will make "women" self-conscious about expressing affection toward other women for fear that they may be seen as lesbians. Of course this point contradicts her earlier assertion that Indian society is not homophobic; if gay people and same-sex erotic relationships were fully accepted, then nonlesbian women would not worry about the possibility of being seen as lesbian. The very real dangers inherent in being seen (correctly or incorrectly) as lesbian stem not from the supposed indiscretions of lesbians themselves but from a heterosexist and male supremacist society. Entirely missing in Kishwar's analysis is precisely what the ending of Mehta's film shows: the possibility of women not just enjoying acceptable affection within the joint household, not stealing intimate moments together, but rather choosing to make their relationship primary, choosing a life together apart from the demands of compulsory heterosexual marriage. Also missing is what many heterosexual people take for granted: the ability to be open with the world about intimate relationships.[13]

Kishwar's stance, though not unique, represents just one possible feminist response to the increasing visibility of lesbians. Writing in the *Economic and Political Weekly*, Carol Upadhya points out that the lesbian relationship in *Fire* functions as a model of resistance to male control of female sexuality, a model that is open to all women, homosexual or heterosexual.[14] Upadhya sees the film as a challenge to the version of traditional Indian values advocated by the Shiv Sena, the construction of the Indian family as dominated by men's power, men's desires. She writes, "The justification for [Shiv Sena's] action—that the film is against 'Indian tradition' because it depicts a lesbian relationship—demonstrates that Indian 'culture' for the Sangh parivar is defined essentially in terms of male control over female sexuality."[15] She writes that *Fire* portrays two women who resist and reject men's power, and argues that the depiction of Radha and Sita's desire for each other makes more space for all women to challenge oppressive family and social relations. Situating Mehta's depiction of a lesbian relationship within a larger critique of male control of women's sexuality, Upadhya sees the film as a feminist, not just a lesbian, project.

No Homophobia in India?

Many *Manushi* readers wrote in response to Kishwar's article, and in the next three issues she published a selection of these letters. Some agreed with her assessment of the film, while others took issue with her stance on the status of gay people in Indian society. For example, Bisakha Sen objected to the editor's assertion that "lesbianism was quite accepted in India." She suggests that the India in which she grew up must have been a different country from the one described in Kishwar's article. In her middle-class family, she writes, "Homosexuality was taboo, period! While nobody thumped religious texts, homosexuality was considered ridiculous, weird, sick and perverted. If anyone in my generation in the family had come out as a gay, the family's reactions would have made southern Baptists in the USA proud."[16]

Shreya Kishore also contests the picture of a tolerant Indian society, writing, "Ms. Kishwar personally knows gay men and women who have not lost their jobs but she must know that homosexuality is a criminal offence in India, you cannot admit being a homosexual and keep a job. She must also know the trauma, the lies, the deceit that go into ensuring that the job is not lost. Her interaction is too wide for her not to know of men and women, particularly women, driven to desperation, to neurosis, to suicide, and of women abused emotionally and physically because of their sexual preferences."[17]

In a moving testimony, Kishore argues that the kind of hole-and-corner sexual opportunities that Kishwar says should satisfy gay people are not enough: "[the editor suggests that] since such opportunities are available and no one complains if one is quick, clever and discreet, why the fuss? I resent this construction. I find it insulting. It is not just about sex in an alley. It is also not only about sleeping with a same sex partner. It's about waking up together, about having a life together and not having to lie about it."[18] In a second letter, Kishore reasserts that gay people in India are not free to disclose their identities and relationships. "Incidentally," she writes, "as you know people who admit to being gay/lesbian— keep their government jobs—have no trouble on that account and live like any- one else—could you please let me know who they might be?"[19] Of course these names are not forthcoming from the editor. Kishore goes on, "I am a moderately paid management professional but wouldn't mind working as a clerk in any gov- ernment office which allows me to write 'Ms. Lesbian partner' in the appropriate column for Provident Fund nomination."[20] Again, Kishore here asserts the need for gay people to be able to openly declare not only their identity and desire but also their kinship relationships, on par with those of heterosexual people.

Kishwar's response to Kishore illustrates some of the ways in which this issue is bound up with India's colonial past and with questions of "Indian tradition," a phrase used to justify conflicting positions in the debate. Kishwar acknowledges that "homosexuality is listed as an offence in the Indian Penal Code enacted by the British in 1860."[21] But she claims that the presence of this law does not indicate discrimination or oppression in Indian society; some Indians, she writes, respond to homosexuality with abhorrence. "But that is not the standard response of Indian society because our tradition . . . does not treat it either as a moral or a criminal offence. Homophobia is a legacy of our colonial past, not our traditional past."[22] To a woman in present-day India who is held prisoner by her family seeking to keep her from joining her female lover, to a gay man fired from his job, it hardly mat- ters in which past we might locate the origins of homophobia. Despite the British origins of the antisodomy law and the Victorian source of at least some of India's homophobia, those laws and attitudes are today being enforced in independent India. Double-think allows Kishwar to assert both that homophobia does not exist in India, and that it does exist but originates with the British, and is therefore not "really" Indian.

Homophobia/Homosexuality: Indian Tradition/Western Import?

Just as Kishwar asserts that homophobia is an undesirable Western import, many right-wing critics of the film *Fire* argue that homosexuality itself is the Western import. This was Shiv Sena chief Bal Thackery's main argument against *Fire*: "Is it fair to show such things which are not part of Indian culture? It can corrupt tender minds. It is a sort of a social AIDS."[23] Where Kishwar implies that Victorian homophobia corrupted the minds of previously tolerant Indians, Thackery sees innocent Indians being corrupted by imported representations of never-heard-of-before homosexuality. Continuing the disease metaphor, he asks, "Has lesbianism spread like an epidemic . . . that it should be portrayed as a guideline to unhappy wives not to depend on their husbands and is this the meaning and message that should be given to spoil younger generations and those who have no idea about it?"[24] Muktar Abbas Naqvi, the Union minister of state for information and broadcasting, expressed a similar view when he sent the film back to the censor board following the Shiv Sena attacks. He asserted that "the protests showed that whatever was being depicted in the film was not 'Indian culture,'"[25] and claimed that "lesbianism is a pseudo-feminist trend borrowed from the West and is no part of Indian womanhood."[26]

While Kishwar and others assert that homophobia is an import from abroad, and Thackeray and the Shiv Sena label homosexuality an invading virus, some defenders of the film's representation of lesbianism have also taken up the flag of "tradition," asserting that female homoeroticism is indeed a part of traditional Indian culture. In one of the clearest expressions of this idea, some lesbians demonstrating against the Shiv Sena protests and the withdrawal of the film displayed a banner reading "lesbianism is our Indian heritage." Another banner at the Regal Theater protest read, "Indian and lesbian."[27] A Delhi University lecturer told a heckler who objected to the linking of lesbianism and Indian tradition, "Go and ask your nanis and dadis [maternal and paternal grandmothers] and they will tell you lesbianism is not new to our culture. The massagewalis know it's there and folk songs tell you its [sic] there."[28] Similarly, gay activist Ashok Row Kavi referred to the presence of lesbianism in India's past, saying that "this entire jingbang should get its head checked first. What's wrong in two women having sex? If they think it doesn't happen in the Indian society they should see the sculptures of Khajuraho or Konark."[29] Journalist Bachi Karkaria also cited early representations of same-sex desire: "When you are heir to the breathtakingly permissive Kama Sutra, why confine yourself to the missionary position on sexuality? . . . Homosexuality didn't need a visa to enter India, it was already here."[30] The Hindu right may claim a special relationship to India's past, but that same past is also claimed by lesbian-identified women and their supporters.

Landmark or Landmine?

The evidence is strong that female homoeroticism has been present on the subcontinent for a very long time. However, until recently, textual representations of such relations have been somewhat rare.[31] While all commentators agreed that *Fire* sparked perhaps the first widespread public discussion of lesbianism, not all liberal or left-wing writers agreed on the value of this debate. Some, who found the film's cinematic quality unremarkable, thought its primary value lay precisely in the debate surrounding the film. Thus, Rima Banerji asserts, "*Fire*'s most compelling point is the manner in which it has become a truly public text, the subject of controversy in the media and among viewers. . . . The fact that it has elicited such strong reactions from critics and spectators is perhaps its most notable redeeming quality. . . . For those of us who are lesbians, the film is a milestone because it has pushed the politics of same-sex love into the limelight with an unprecedented amount of publicity and hype."[32]

One person's milestone is another's lavender herring. Several commentators thought the debate was a waste of time and energy that could have been better spent on other more significant issues. Mary John and Tejaswini Niranjana set up an opposition between sexuality and what they posit as the more important concerns of a class- and caste-conscious feminism: "*Fire* represents patriarchy as being founded on the denial of female sexuality. A whole range of oppressive structures targeting myriad aspects of women's lives become obscured in this narrowing of critical range, this compulsion to name a root cause of women's subordination."[33] In a critical move that says more about their own ideas concerning the role of art in movements for social change than about the particular weaknesses of the film, the writers look for and fail to find a political manifesto in a text that operates within the generic conventions of romantic narrative.

C. M. Naim also takes the film to task for not doing that which it never sets out to do. He constructs an unnecessary opposition between *Fire* and its supporters on the one hand, and feminists concerned with more "important" issues on the other. Having critiqued the film for what he sees as its collusion with stereotypes of lesbianism and of Muslims, Naim concludes, "More importantly, something else got excluded in all the noisy defence of the film as a bold statement on lesbianism, namely the all too pervasive violence against women in India."[34] He writes that during the week that the national press was preoccupied with the uproar about *Fire*, only one paper reported what Naim sees as "the news that truly represented the anti-women agenda of the Hindutva brigade."[35] The BJP government in Uttar Pradesh dismantled the State Women's Commission, and the rate of crimes against women was reported to have increased sharply. Naim presents these crimes—dowry deaths, rapes, abductions—as the real problems of Indian women, failing to make the connection between the ways in which, under a system of compulsory heterosexuality, these issues also affect lesbian women, and the ways in which closing down women's erotic, kinship, and affectional choices affects all women.

There is surprising agreement here between commentators who otherwise take rather different positions on women's issues. Kishwar, in her six-page response to critics, takes a position not far from Niranjana's, John's, or Naim's. Stating that lesbianism belongs to the realm of "domestic and emotional melodramas and marital or sexual relations,"[36] she contrasts these supposedly unimportant topics with serious political matters "that are important to both women and men such as India's farm policy, economic reforms, ethnic conflicts, sanitation, health and education."[37] This strategy of trivializing the life-and-death concerns of sexual minorities occurs too in the rhetoric of antifeminists, both in India and in the West, who would confine concerns about sexuality and intimate relationships to the realm of the personal, not the political. Analysis has shown that separating these two spheres is impossible, linked as they are by kinship and economic structures that encompass both the most intimate and the most public relations.

Shohini Ghosh, while also expressing criticisms of the film, takes seriously the implications of its groundbreaking lesbian representation and the conventions and limitations of its scope as "a love story that challenges many assumptions."[38] Rather than setting up lesbianism and feminism as opposed to each other, Ghosh makes a connection between the film's depiction of sexuality and its construction of gender. "It will remain a pioneering film," she writes, "in that it casts gender as a construction involving factors far more complex, fluid and abstract than biology would have us believe. Thereby it counters simple biological definitions of male and female that are frequently used to justify homophobia."[39] This analysis links lesbianism and feminism through the concept of gender construction. The visible representation of female same-sex desire, Ghosh argues, unsettles definitions of gender that keep women, quite literally, in their place within the heterosexual home.

Whose Right to Speak?

Among the forces demonstrating against the Shiv Sena attacks, participants disagreed about the focus and significance of the protests. Some protestors wanted to focus on the issue of censorship and free speech, playing down the actual lesbian content of the film, and the homophobia inherent in the right-wing attacks. An activist from the women's group Jagori stated, "Lesbianism is incidental. What we are fighting for is the right to express ourselves."[40] In the CALERI report, S. L. discusses the conflict between those who wanted to stress democratic rights and freedom of speech in general and those who wished to bring forward the specific issue of lesbian rights as she notes, "Interestingly, some of the individuals and groups who had joined in to protest the attack on 'freedom of speech and expression' and 'democratic rights' were upset and vitriolic about the same freedoms being extended to a minority in a peaceful and democratic public protest. We were severely criticised both before and after: why did we have to be visible, how did we dare to use the word 'lesbian'?"[41]

S. L. points out the contradiction inherent in some free-speech protestors' requests that lesbians censor themselves: "there was a presumption that if we talked about freedoms and rights, then lesbians would join in without ever questioning the utter irony of it: where are the freedoms and rights to speech and expression for sexual minorities?"[42] According to the CALERI report, filmmakers involved in the protests were also interested only in the anticensorship issue, not in the specific issue of securing human rights for lesbians. The report also refers to an unnamed "women's group" that circulated a signature campaign letter demanding that the film be reopened in Delhi theaters, while omitting any mention of sexuality. On the other hand, as Ratna Kapur points out, some of the lesbians who protested the canceling of the film's screenings have not consistently supported free expression in the context of other bans or restrictions: "Feminists, and I would add, lesbians have often served as barricades against free speech rather than as its active promoters."[43]

The storm of commentary and countercommentary about *Fire* proves wrong Sita's statement, "there's no word in our language for what we are, how we feel for each other." The many conflicting voices tell us that while there may be no adequate *single* word, there is certainly no shortage of words deployed to explain *what we are,* to interpret and reinterpret the fiery images on contemporary India's cultural screen. Participants disagree, often violently, about the content and meaning of "Indian tradition." The complexity of that tradition can best be seen precisely in the imbrication of many discourses in this historically specific battle over representation and reality.

Notes

1. Campaign for Lesbian Rights, *Silence! The Emergency Is On: Lesbian Emergence* (New Delhi: Usha Printers, 1999), 17.
2. Ibid., 18.
3. Terry Castle, *The Apparitional Lesbian: Female Homosexuality and Modern Culture* (New York: Columbia University Press, 1993).
4. Shohini Ghosh, "From the Frying Pan to the Fire," *Communalism Combat*, January 1999, 19.
5. Ibid.
6. Ratna Kapur, "Cultural Politics of Fire," *Economic and Political Weekly*, May 22, 1999, 1297.
7. Madhu Kishwar, "Some Aspects of Bondage: The Denial of Fundamental Rights to Women," in *In Search of Answers: Indian Women's Voices from Manushi*, ed. Madhu Kishwar and Ruth Vanita (London: Zed Books, 1984), 239.
8. Madhu Kishwar, "Naive Outpourings of a Self-Hating Indian: Deepa Mehta's *Fire*," *Manushi* 109 (March–April 1999): 6.
9. For compelling accounts of problems faced by lesbians who are forced to marry men, see the recent collection *Facing the Mirror: Lesbian Writing from India*, ed. Ashwini Sukthankar (New Delhi: Penguin, 1999). Many young people involved in homosexual relationships (and especially women), commit or attempt suicide. See *Humjinsi: A Resource Book on Lesbian, Gay, and Bisexual Rights in India*, ed. Bina Fernandez (Mumbai: India Centre for Human Rights and Law, 1999).
10. Homosexuality is still a crime under Section 377 of the Indian Penal Code. The extent to which this law, which in its explanatory text specifies that penetration must be involved, can be applied to women is unclear; however, it is often used by police and families to threaten and intimidate lesbians. See Suparna Bhaskaran's essay in this volume.
11. Kishwar, "Naive Outpourings," 11.
12. Ibid.
13. Of course, not all heterosexual relationships find social acceptance; extramarital and commercial heterosexual relations also cannot be openly expressed; premarital relations are usually frowned upon. But marriage does sanction, institutionalize, and celebrate intimate connections between partners of different genders.
14. Carol Upadhya, "Set This House on Fire," *Economic and Political Weekly*, December 12, 1998, 3176–77.
15. Ibid., 3177.
16. Bisakha Sen, "Family Talk," *Manushi* 112 (May–June 1999): 5.
17. Shreya Kishore, "Homosexuality in India," *Manushi* 112 (May–June 1999): 4.
18. Kishore's account of her personal negotiation of the social forces mandating silence is telling: "I am a lesbian woman and I call myself a lesbian even though I neither have a relationship with a woman nor do I seek to have one. I could not reconcile to having such a relationship and having to lie about it, lies necessary to negotiate the tolerance Ms Kishwar talks about.
19. Shreya Kishore, "Letter to Editor," *Manushi* 112 (September–October 1999): 42.

20. Ibid.
21. Madhu Kishwar, "Response to Letters," *Manushi* 112 (May–June 1999): 8.
22. Ibid., 9.
23. Barry Bearak, "A Lesbian Idyll, and the Movie Theaters Surrender," *New York Times*, December 24, 1998, C2.
24. Ghosh, "From the Frying Pan to the Fire," 16.
25. Ibid.
26. Campaign for Lesbian Rights, *Silence!* 16.
27. *Times of India*, December 8, 1998, 3.
28. "Fighting for 'Fire' with Fire." *Times of India*, December 8, 1998, 1.
29. "Sena Attacks Theatres to Douse Fire," Indian Express News Service, December 2, 1998.
30. Campaign for Lesbian Rights, *Silence!*, 16.
31. For a sample of such textual representations, see Ruth Vanita and Saleem Kidwai, eds., *Same-Sex Love in India: Readings from Literature and History* (New York: St. Martin's Press, 2000).
32. Rima Banerji, "Still on Fire," *Manushi* 113 (July–August 1999): 18, 19.
33. Mary E. John and Tejaswini Niranjana, "Mirror Politics: 'Fire,' Hindutva, and Indian Culture," *Economic and Political Weekly*, March 6–13, 1999, 581.
34. C. M. Naim, "A Dissent on 'Fire,'" *The Toronto Review* 18, no. 1 (1999): 18. First published in slightly different form in *Economic and Political Weekly*, April 17–24, 1999, 955–57.
35. Ibid., 18.
36. Kishwar, "Response to Letters," 6.
37. Ibid., 6.
38. Ghosh, "From the Frying Pan to the Fire," 17.
39. Ibid., 19.
40. The Campaign for Lesbian Rights, *Silence!*, 13.
41. Ibid., 19.
42. Ibid.
43. Kapur, "Cultural Politics," 1299.

Notes on Contributors

Suparna Bhaskaran is assistant professor of women's studies, Antioch College.

Scott Kugle is assistant professor in the Department of Religion, Swarthmore College.

Carla Petievich is associate professor of history at Montclair State University, and author of *Assembly of Rivals: Delhi, Lucknow, and the Urdu Ghazal* (1992) and *The Expanding Landscape: South Asians and the Diaspora* (1999).

Indrani Chatterjee is a visiting scholar in the Department of History, Brown University, and author of *Gender, Law, and Slavery in Colonial India* (1999).

Michael J. Sweet is a clinical assistant professor in the Department of Psychiatry, University of Wisconsin at Madison.

Leela Gandhi is a senior lecturer in the School of English, La Trobe University, Victoria, Australia, author of *Postcolonial Theory: A Critical Introduction* (1998), and coauthor of *England through Colonial Eyes in Twentieth-Century Fiction* (2001).

Anannya Dasgupta is a graduate student in the Department of English, Rutgers University.

Rosemary Marangoly George is an associate professor in the Literature Department, University of California at San Diego, and author of *The Politics of Home: Postcolonial Relocations and Twentieth Century Fiction* (1999).

Ruth Vanita is an associate professor in liberal studies and women's studies, University of Montana, author of *Sappho and the Virgin Mary: Same-Sex Love and the English Literary Imagination* (1996), and coeditor of *Same-Sex Love in India: Readings from Literature and History* (2000).

Lawrence Cohen is an associate professor in the Department of Anthropology, University of California at Berkeley, and author of *No Aging in India: Alzheimer's, the Bad Family, and Other Modern Things* (1998).

Kathryn Hansen is the director of the Center for Asian Studies, University of Texas at Austin, and author of *Grounds for Play: The Nautanki Theatre of North India* (1992).

Muraleedharan T. is a lecturer in the Department of English, St. Aloysius' College, Trichur, Kerala.

Thomas Waugh is a professor of film studies in the School of Cinema, Concordia University, Canada, author of *"Show Us Life": Towards a History and Aesthetics of the Committed Documentary* (1984) and *Hard to Imagine: Gay Male Eroticism in Photography and Film from Their Beginnings to Stonewall* (1996).

Shohini Ghosh is a reader for video and TV production at the Mass Communication Research Centre, Jamia Millia Islamia University, New Delhi.

Geeta Patel is an associate professor in the departments of Women's Studies and Anthropology, Wellesley College, and author of *Miraji: Poetry, Gender, Self, and Colonialism* (forthcoming).

Monica Bachmann is a doctoral candidate in the Joint Program in English and Women's Studies, University of Michigan at Ann Arbor.

Index